LIBERALISM, CONSTITUTIONALISM, AND DEMOCRACY

Liberalism, Constitutionalism, and Democracy

RUSSELL HARDIN

OXFORD
UNIVERSITY PRESS

OXFORD

UNIVERSITY PRESS

Great Clarendon Street, Oxford OX2 6DP

Oxford University Press is a department of the University of Oxford.
It furthers the University's objective of excellence in research, scholarship,
and education by publishing worldwide in

Oxford New York

Athens Auckland Bangkok Bogotá Buenos Aires Calcutta
Cape Town Chennai Dar es Salaam Delhi Florence Hong Kong Istanbul
Karachi Kuala Lumpur Madrid Melbourne Mexico City Mumbai
Nairobi Paris São Paulo Singapore Taipei Tokyo Toronto Warsaw

and associated companies in Berlin Ibadan

Oxford is a registered trade mark of Oxford University Press
in the UK and in certain other countries

Published in the United States
by Oxford University Press Inc., New York

British Library Cataloguing in Publication Data

Data available

Library of Congress Cataloging in Publication Data
Hardin, Russell, 1940–
Liberalism, constitutionalism, and democracy/Russell Hardin.
Includes bibliographical references.
1. Democracy. 2. Liberalism.
3. Constitutional history—United States.
I. Title
JC423.H345 1999 320.51—dc21 99–36964
ISBN 0–19–829084–5

1 3 5 7 9 10 8 6 4 2

Typeset by Hope Services (Abingdon) Ltd.
Printed in Great Britain
on acid-free paper by
Biddles Ltd.,
Guildford & King's Lynn

For Robert K. Merton
wonderful friend and colleague

Preface

Perhaps an editor might begin a reformation in some such way as this. Divide his paper into 4 chapters, heading the 1st, Truths. 2nd, Probabilities. 3rd, Possibilities. 4th, Lies. The first chapter would be very short, as it would contain [only such things] as the editor would be willing to risk his own reputation for their truth. The 2nd would contain what, from a mature consideration of all circumstances, his judgment should conclude to be probably true. This, however, should rather contain too little than too much. The 3rd & 4th should be professedly for those readers who would rather have lies for their money than the blank paper they would occupy.

Thomas Jefferson, letter of 14 June 1807 to John Norvell

I would like to think that some of what follows in this book fits in Jefferson's first chapter under Truths and that most of it at least fits in his second chapter under Probabilities. No doubt, some readers will think far too much of it fits in the third chapter under Possibilities, and maybe some detractors will even place much of it in the fourth chapter under Lies, although they might be gracious enough to entitle that chapter Errors. Jefferson omitted what must be a very big chapter for many works, perhaps especially in political theory: Meaningless Claims. The physicist Wolfgang Pauli retorted to a proposed explanation of some phenomenon in physics that, 'It's not even wrong'. One quails at the thought of how much of political theorizing a Pauli would find to be not even wrong. Perhaps that should be the title of Jefferson's fifth chapter: Claims That Are Not Even Wrong. I would therefore be pleased, although perhaps also a bit humbled, to discover that some parts of my claims here are at least wrong.

The central argument of this book is that liberalism, constitutionalism, and democracy, as well as, specifically, liberal constitutional democracy all work, *when they do*, because they serve the mutual advantage of the politically effective groups in the society by coordinating those groups on a political and, perhaps, economic order. In some societies they do not and perhaps cannot be expected to work in this sense. A subsidiary but perhaps equally important claim is that constitutional political institutions and democratic procedures generally require not so much active support as merely acquiescence in order to survive and work.

These are explanatory theses, not normative claims. But they have relevance for normative claims if one takes seriously some relative of Kant's dictum that ought implies can. If we are to insist that some form of government is normatively right for a particular society, we must be able to say that it would or could work for that society. Of course, it does not follow that mere workability makes some form of government right. Stalin's, Mao's, and many lesser, dreadful regimes have worked for a generation at least.

It is commonly argued that what makes democracy right is that it works by consent. If so, it is such a distressingly minimal form of consent—acquiescence—as to be normatively disqualified. No major theorist has argued that mere acquiescence makes government right. In its emptiest form, mere acquiescence was the stance of most of the Czech people to Nazi rule of their society. If we rule out mere acquiescence as adequate for consent, it seems likely that no credible argument can be adduced to defend liberal constitutional democracy in any detail on grounds of consent. In some isolated, small, economically backward community, there might be a government based on communally held values or religious views that could be defended on consent grounds, but no liberal state can be. Hence, concern for workability, which should be central to any moral assessment of principles of social and political order, undercuts the entire consent school of political theory.

Mere acquiescence might be sufficient for fairness or welfarist justifications of a political order to some extent, although such theories have not been sufficiently articulated as to yield clear judgements of whole political orders. This is not to say they are less well articulated than consent theories, but consent theories have a sufficiently simple criterion that they seem to appeal without much articulation of any details.

Surprisingly often, in discussing the issues of this book with colleagues at various institutions, I am told that what I discuss is not what liberalism, a constitution, or democracy is. One of two things typically underlies these objections. For some, the point of their objection is that many real-world cases of, especially, constitutionalism do not involve mutual advantage. This is true, of course, and in fact the vast majority of all constitutions ever adopted seem likely not to have been mutually advantageous to the politically important groups in their societies. But I do not make the matter of whether a constitution, democracy, or liberalism serves mutual advantage a part of the definition of these concepts themselves. Rather, I only argue *causally* that if they are to work, liberalism, constitutionalism, and democracy typically must serve the advantage of these groups. They are therefore sociologically—that is, causally and not either definitionally or normatively—mutual-advantage theories. The vast majority of constitutions, lacking this power to coordinate relevant groups, have failed fairly quickly either by being ignored or by being replaced. Democracy has also often lacked this power and has sometimes therefore led to disaster, as in Burundi in 1993, or has been irrelevant, as in depressingly many 'democratic' societies in which a party rules by monopoly power rather than by citizens' election of it over alternatives. Liberalism, of course, has not even got off the ground in most societies historically or in very many societies still today, where it is often taken to be the enemy of some powerful group, as of course it often is.

For others the point of the objections is a sense that there is a correct meaning, almost a Platonic meaning of each of the terms, and I miss that meaning. In general, I do not think such objections compelling. Any social idea of long standing has meant and will continue to mean many things. (For some of the meaningful variations on the idea of liberalism, see the Appendix.) Those who attempt clean, simple definitions of such ideas in social theory sometimes make them particularly useful in the explanation of some range of phenomena, but sometimes they merely travesty the ideas. For an example of travesty, in the original *Encyclopaedia of the Social Sciences* in 1933, Hermann Heller virtually defines *constitutionalism* as government entirely by the legislature: 'Thus in the constitutional state the legislative and governmental agencies enjoy a virtual monopoly of political power to the exclusion of the administrative and the judicial'.[1] On this odd view, there may be no constitutional state currently in existence.

---

[1] Hermann Heller, 'Power, Political', in Edwin R. A. Seligman and Alvin Johnson, eds., *Encyclopaedia of the Social Sciences* (New York: Macmillan, 1933), xii. 300–5, at p. 301.

Heller's was a bad definitional enterprise. Definitions are typically the culmination of explanatory theory in the natural sciences, not the beginning of it. I think they must generally also be the culmination of explanatory theory in the social sciences and even of normative political theory. They are not pristine ideas that just pop into heads automatically in a state of dismal ignorance of any of their instances. We do not really understand such notions as liberalism, constitutionalism, and democracy until we have studied many cases of what we might finally count as instances of them. For example, democracy has evolved in complexity as society has. There is still a seeming core of meaning in the term as it shifts from small societies in which virtually every qualified citizen could participate in direct votes on policy to societies so large that not even our elected representatives can meaningfully be said to have a substantial causal role in making most policy. At least part of that core of meaning is that losers leave or stay out of office and winners enter or stay in office, as John Adams left office, perhaps grudgingly but still resolutely in 1801 (see Chapter 3).

Many of the discussions here are the culmination of many years of argument, but it would be out of place here to argue many of these at the length that they might seem to deserve individually. For anyone who might wish to follow up on any of these arguments, I refer to more extensive, sometimes somewhat different, presentations elsewhere. I apologize for the consequent frequency of citations to my previous work.

Acknowledgements

For extensive written comments on much or all of the manuscript I thank Brian Barry, Randall Calvert, James Johnson, Annabelle Lever, Margaret Levi, and Mark Roelofs. Many of their comments forced substantial rewriting. For written and oral comments on particular parts of it, I thank Jim Alt, David Austin-Smith, Robert Barros, Bob Bates, Sam Beer, Paul Bullen, Karen Cook, Ingrid Creppell, Roberto d'Alimonte, Donatella della Porta, Ronald Dworkin, Chris Eisgruber, Stephen Elkin, Jon Elster, Jim Fearon, Richard Fenno, John Ferejohn, Paul Gomberg, Bernard Grofman, Edwin T. Haefele, Chong-do Hah, Anna Harvey, Don Herzog, Robert Keohane, Roderick T. Long, Steve Macedo, Bernard Manin, Melanie Manion, Jane Mansbridge, Harvey Mansfield, Jr., Larry Mead, Manus Midlarsky, Leonardo Morlino, John Mueller, Jack Nagel, Thomas Nagel, Yaw Nyarko, Mancur Olson, Jr., Kenneth Oye, Ayse D. Özkan, Pasquale Pasquino, Ellen Paul, Adam Przeworski, Jonathan Riley, Larry Sager, Julio Saguir, Elizabeth Scott, Ian Shapiro, Ken Shepsle, Fritz Stern, Susan Stokes, Elaine Swift, David Weimer, Donald Wittman, and Leonard Wontchekon. Many others have commented in the context of seminars and conferences. Many of these people might wish to protest that they do nothing more than acquiesce in or not mutiny over the publication of the arguments as they stand.

The two chapters on democracy were subjected to intense discussion in the Dworkin–Nagel colloquium on Law and Philosophy at the New York University School of Law (October 1996). I thank the participants in that session and, especially, Ronald Dworkin and Thomas Nagel for their extensive comments in one of the weekly, gruelling, seven-hour marathons for which they have justly become famous. The general arguments of the book were presented at a joint session of the Harvard University Political Theory and Political Economy seminars (December 1995), at a seminar at All Souls

College, Oxford (January 1996), as the Cutler Lectures at the University of Rochester (February 1996), as a Harvard University Ford Lecture (February 1998), and in seminars at the Universidad Torcuato di Tella, Buenos Aires (June 1998). I thank the participants in these events and especially Randall Calvert, G. A. Cohen, James Johnson, Julio Saguir, and Ken Shepsle for their comments and hospitality.

Part of Chapter 2 is drawn from 'Liberalism: Political and Economic', *Social Philosophy and Policy*, 10 (June 1993): 121–44. I thank the editor and publisher for permission to reprint some of that material here. That paper benefited from discussions at Bowling Green State University, where it was presented at the conference, 'Liberalism and the Economic Order', April 1992.

Part of Chapter 3 is based on 'Why a Constitution?' in Bernard Grofman and Donald Wittman (eds.), *The Federalist Papers and the New Institutionalism* (New York: Agathon Press, 1989: 100–20). That paper was the seed for this book. I thank the editors and the publisher for permission to reprint part of that material here. The first version of that paper was prepared for presentation at a conference on 'Constitutive Reason and Political Form' of the Committee on the Foundations of Democratic Government at the University of Pennsylvania (January 1987). For comments on that paper, I am grateful to participants in the Penn conference. The substantially different chapter has benefited from discussions at the Chicago–New York colloquium on constitutionalism (February 1996). I thank the participants in that colloquium and in the Colloquium on Constitutionalism at the New York University School of Law, in which Chris Eisgruber presented a better summary of the arguments than I could have done (February 1996), and in seminars at the Department of Political Science, University of Florence (May 1996), the University of North Carolina School of Law (September 1997), the University of Virginia School of Law (September 1998), and the George Mason University School of Law (November 1998), for discussions of the chapter.

Parts of Chapter 4 were originally written for a conference at Northwestern University on institutions (July 1995). I thank the organizers and the participants for their hospitality and comments.

Much of Chapter 5 is based on an unpublished paper of the same title that was written for presentation in a series on 1989 at Lawrence College, 29 April 1992. I thank Chong-do Hah and his colleagues at

Lawrence for their wonderful hospitality and for engaging discussion. The section on egalitarianism was written for the late William E. Griffith and presented in a colloquium, 'Political Change in the Gorbachev Era', in Griffith's honour on his retirement, at MIT (April 1990), and at a round table at the American Philosophical Association Pacific Division meeting, San Francisco (March 1991). I am grateful to participants in these two sessions for comments. A version of this earlier paper was published as 'Efficiency vs. Equality and the Demise of Socialism', *Canadian Journal of Philosophy*, 22 (June 1992: 149–61). I thank the *Canadian Journal* and its editors for permission to reprint some of that material here. I also thank participants in a seminar at the Department of Political Science at Syracuse University for their comments (October 1995).

Chapter 6 is based on the paper, 'Constitutional Economic Transition', in John Ferejohn, Jack Rakove, and Jonathan Riley (eds.), *Constitutional Culture and Democratic Rule*, forthcoming (presented at the conferences 'Constitutions and Constitutionalism', at the Murphy Institute, Tulane University, New Orleans, February 1994 and March 1995). For their comments, I thank the participants at the Murphy Institute conferences, members of the Austrian Economics Seminar, New York University, the Harvard–MIT workshop in international relations (December 1994), and a conference on Democracy and Economic Performance at Harvard (February 1998).

Chapter 7 is based on the paper, 'Democracy on the Margin', in Albert Breton, Gianluigi Galeotti, Pierre Salmon, and Ronald Wintrobe (eds.), *Understanding Democracy: Economic and Political Perspectives* (Cambridge: Cambridge University Press, 1977: 249–66). I thank the editors and the publisher for permission to reprint most of that material here. That paper was originally written while I was a visiting scholar at the CREA of the École Polytechnique, Paris (July 1994). I thank Pasquale Pasquino for organizing that visit and for arranging a seminar at CREA on the ideas of the paper, which was written for presentation to the Villa Colombella Group meeting, Dijon, France, September 1994. The paper benefited from discussions at that meeting, at CREA, and in the seminar series on Emerging Trends in Political Science, Department of Political Science, Rutgers University (September 1994).

Work on this project has been supported by the National

Endowment for the Humanities, whose grant to Stephen Holmes and me funded a University of Chicago project on constitutionalism (1989–92), the Andrew W. Mellon Foundation, the Russell Sage Foundation, the Center for Institutional Reform and the Informal Sector of the University of Maryland, the University of Chicago, and New York University. I thank Paul Bullen for energetic and creative research assistance on much of the book.

Contents

1

Mutual Advantage

Sometimes the interests of society may require a rule of justice
in a particular case; but may not determine any particular rule,
among several, which are all equally beneficial.

David Hume,
An Enquiry Concerning the Principles of Morals[1]

Three Mutual-Advantage Theories

Theories of liberalism, constitutionalism, and democracy are
mutual-advantage theories. Liberalism is about arranging institutions to allow all of us to prosper in our own individual ways.
Indeed, political liberalism was partly invented in response to religious claims that some ways of believing should be suppressed. And
economic liberalism grew and was eventually more or less institutionalized in government policy because it caused all to prosper
through the prosperity of each. Constitutionalism works when and
only when it serves to coordinate a population on some matters, such
as order, commerce, and national defence, that are more important
than the issues on which they might differ. Similarly, democracy
works only when there are no deeply divisive issues that override the
value of order and other very generally advantageous values. The
pre-eminent theorists of mutual advantage are Thomas Hobbes,
David Hume, and Adam Smith, although there are many strands of
mutual-advantage arguments in virtually all of political theory and
in the predominant school of economic theory of the past several

---

[1] David Hume, *An Enquiry Concerning the Principles of Morals*, in Hume,
Enquiries concerning Human Understanding and concerning the Principles of Morals,
ed. L. A. Selby-Bigge and P. H. Nidditch (Oxford: Oxford University Press, 1975; 1st
pub. 1751), sect. 3, part 2, p. 195.

centuries in Scotland and England, Western Europe, North America, and, recently, most of the world.

Briefly consider Hobbes's position. Mutual advantage is merely what one could call a causal generalization of self-interest in the following sense.[2] The best way to secure our personal interest in survival and economic prosperity is to secure the general mutual interest in these things through establishing or maintaining general order. That is Hobbes's move and it is a seemingly magic move, but it works as nearly as any fundamentally important move in all of political philosophy can be said to work.

One might argue, as many Hobbes scholars do, that Hobbes had a moral theory of some kind that led him to his conclusions, as might be suggested by his discussion of his 'lawes of nature'.[3] These are laws, such as abiding by contract, to govern successful association, laws which must be made positive to work at all.[4] As laws of nature, they are of course prior to positive law, but that is because they are *sociological laws about what would work to our interest*,[5] not because they are in some other sense moral. It is their workability and service to our interests that makes them an appealing basis for positive law.[6]

---

[2] Mutual advantage can also be a conceptual generalization of self-interest, as it is in Pareto's world, as discussed below, but it may be illegitimate to read this vision back into Hobbes. See further, Russell Hardin, 'Magic on the Frontier: The Norm of Efficiency', *University of Pennsylvania Law Review*, 144 (May 1996): 1987–2020.

[3] Thomas Hobbes, *Leviathan* (London: Penguin, 1968, ed. C. B. Macpherson; originally published, London: Andrew Cooke, 1651), chs. 14 and 15.

[4] Hobbes (*Leviathan*, 215) insists that if they are not positively backed by the power of a state—that is, only where there is security—then no one is obliged to follow them.

[5] Hobbes, *Leviathan*, 216–17.

[6] Hence, Hobbes's discussion of his 'lawes' is not contrary to his mutual-advantage vision. Quite apart from the textual warrant for seeing Hobbes's morality as limited to self-interest and its causal generalization, he is a much more useful theorist if he does not burden his argument with a lot of moral clutter, including ad hoc norms and moral principles. His early readers saw no moral principles in his arguments. Even someone, at least a political philosopher, who disagrees with my account of him should nevertheless be interested in the theory I attribute to him, because it is a wonderfully spare baseline theory. If it can plausibly work, no rich morality is necessary for the partial success of government. In any case, it is odd to say Hobbes meant X and only X. He wrote many things in *Leviathan*, not all of them consistent. Moreover, he tried to argue in familiar ways in order to reach a relatively wide audience, using appeals to the model of physics, the Bible, and reason. What I wish to claim is that he made a clear, coherent set of arguments about collective action and sovereignty that make sense. He made these claims in a small number of pages (chs. 13–15) that are arguably the greatest short disquisition in the history of political philosophy.

One might frame a mutual-advantage political theory as a normative theory of the way government should work. However, I wish to treat liberalism, constitutionalism, and democracy as sociological—that is, explanatory—theories and to focus on their actual workability, although I will briefly address the normative status of these theories in the Afterword. One of the reasons they might work is that they have normative appeal, and therefore a normative claim from mutual advantage might play a role even in the explanation of their workability. Workability, however, is far less demanding in its requirement of mutual advantage than is normative theory. Liberalism or constitutionalism or democracy might serve the mutual advantage of only a part of a polity and might therefore be quite workable and enduring. For example, as argued in Chapter 3, the US Constitution served plantation and urban commercial interests well, and that was enough for that constitution to work in the sense of ordering the society and polity of the United States in its first generation or so. It would be much harder to say that a form of government serves the mutual advantage of only part of a polity and is nevertheless normatively justified because of its serving mutual advantage.[7] That constitution, again, left a substantial part of the population bound in slavery. Although some southern ideologues argued that this served the advantage of the slaves, not many other people would find that a credible factual or moral claim.

The reason a claim of only partial mutual advantage is adequate for workability is briefly this. Coordinating a substantial part of a populace on some institution, practice, or norm is commonly sufficient to make it the interest of virtually all to go along with that institution, practice, or norm. When enough of us drive to the right, the rest of us will have an interest in driving to the right also, no matter what preferences we might have in the abstract. A constitution and its government do not require universal *support*, they require only virtually universal *acquiescence*. If enough do acquiesce, others may be coerced and the government will prevail.[8] Sociologically, a mutual advantage theory is therefore *de facto* a coordination theory. The

---

[7] I discuss the inherent difficulty in normative mutual-advantage theory in Russell Hardin, 'Political Obligation', in Alan Hamlin and Philip Pettit, eds., *The Good Polity* (Oxford: Basil Blackwell, 1989), 103–19.

[8] H. L. A. Hart, *The Concept of Law* (Oxford: Oxford University Press, 1961), 88. Also see Russell Hardin, 'Sanction and Obligation', *The Monist*, 68 (July 1985): 403–18.

government that coordinates interests is more likely to sustain support than the government that evokes moral commitments.[9]

The clearest, most urgent claim for the mutual advantage of orderly government is in Hobbes's *Leviathan*, written during the disorder and violence of the struggle between Royalists and Puritans in seventeenth-century England. Hobbes went so far as to claim that order was more important than getting religion right—although he thought that what was necessary for salvation was relatively minimal and would be possible under virtually any Christian church. Perhaps the greatest claims for the mutual advantage of a constitution are those made at the constitutional convention in Philadelphia in 1787 and in the *Federalist Papers* that supported ratification of the constitution drafted at that convention. But similar claims, often theoretically better grounded, have been made in remarkably many nations at the end of the twentieth century. The greatest claims for the mutual advantage of democracy may be the diffuse set of claims in Alexis de Tocqueville's *Democracy in America*, although Tocqueville often supposed that democracy caused certain aspects of American society in the 1830s that may more plausibly be seen as results of its commercialism.[10]

The striking thing about a mutual advantage argument in politics is that it implies there is no argument between the relevant parties. Hobbes supposed it clearly serves our mutual advantage to have even the most draconian government rather than to live in anarchy or civil war. He could therefore suppose we must assent to such a government. That is, the matters on which we could mutually gain so outweigh those on which we might conflict that, in order to coordinate on the former, we should happily dispense with politics over the latter, especially if, as Hobbes thought, politics over reform might tumble us back into destructive anarchy. This sounds like a crude thesis but, with better parlour-room manners in their discourse and a generous addition in their arguments, it is a thesis shared by the

[9] Similarly, norms that are backed by coordination interests are more effective than those that are backed merely by normative commitments. The argument is simple, but not brief. In essence, it is that a group with a coordination norm will spontaneously enforce it against violators because it is in their interest, or at least not counter to their interest, to do so. See Russell Hardin, *One for All: The Logic of Group Conflict* (Princeton: Princeton University Press, 1995), chs. 4 and 5.

[10] Alexis de Tocqueville, *Democracy in America*, 2 vols. (New York: Knopf, 1945; 1st pub. 1835 and 1840). For Tocqueville, democracy is a complex matter. It includes the tendency towards greater social equality that he thought characterized the United States as well as specifically political participation.

Federalist Papers, Tocqueville, and such contemporary democratic theorists as Robert Dahl. The generous addition is that, if a society can coordinate on basic political and economic order, then it can risk politics at the margin over lesser issues or, in Dahl's word, the chaff.[11] Where there is broad consensus on order, we do not need Hobbes's autocrat to rule us. With that addition and one qualification, or emphasis, Hobbes's thesis is also the thesis of this book. The qualification, addressed especially in Chapter 7, is that in some societies there is little hope of coordination on mutual advantage— conflict is too divisive and beyond compromise.

Perhaps one should state as another qualification that the claim of mutual advantage need not apply to everyone or to every significant group in a society for liberalism, constitutionalism, and democracy to work reasonably well. Some politically ineffective groups can be overrun and ignored by the political order, as the communitarian Anti-Federalists were in the American case, and as women, slaves, and those with little or no role in the economy have been through most of history. In advanced liberal democracies in our time, the groups whose mutual advantage *must* be served are the large middle class and the wealthy—especially, among the latter, the entrepreneurially wealthy.

From the beginning, although it had collective implications, liberalism, both political and economic, was an individualist philosophy. Although it took a Benthamite detour into interpersonally additive welfare theory through much of the nineteenth century, early liberal philosophy seems in many ways to be a precursor of the Paretian movement in economic value theory. Vilfredo Pareto asserted that there can be no meaningful interpersonal comparisons of welfare and that, therefore, we cannot found public policy in claims for increasing the sum of welfare. We can make only the limited moral claim, when it is true in a particular case, that at least some are better off and none are worse off from a particular policy move and that, therefore, the move is an improvement over the status quo. Such a move is now called a Pareto improvement. Pareto improvements serve mutual advantage. Broadly speaking, political and economic liberalisms in

<hr>

[11] Alexander Hamilton, John Jay, and James Madison, *The Federalist Papers* (New York: New Amercian Library, 1961); 1st pub. as eighty-five letters in newspapers in 1787–8. Robert A. Dahl, *A Preface to Democratic Theory* (Chicago: University of Chicago Press, 1956), 132–3. The full passage is quoted in Chapter 7 below, in the opening section, 'Divided Society'.

the Anglo-Saxon tradition share the same welfarist value theory and they share Pareto's scepticism about going beyond individualist justification of social arrangements.

If the only changes that could ever take place must be Pareto improvements, the status quo might block most of the economic, technological, and social changes of history. In this respect, the Pareto criterion and the criterion of pure mutual advantage would be generally disastrous. These criteria are sometimes applied politically to government actions to say that some policy would harm some group while helping another. In the economy they are applied almost only to spontaneous actions by dyads, as in a contract, although your contractual deal with someone may have massive negative effects on me.[12] In essence, the central demand on a Paretian liberal government is that it protect individuals and dyads in making self-improving moves.

The central idea in liberalism historically is that individuals should be left to make their own choices.[13] A liberal government allows individuals to make their own choices of religious preference, social relations, and economic commitments, both as producers and as consumers. With a slight, arguably correcting, twist on Tocqueville, liberals hold that it is not what is done *by* a liberal government but what is done *under* such a government by private agency that is the beauty and the good of liberalism.[14]

In our time, at least in North America and much of Europe, the term liberalism has come to be associated with a programme of things government is to do or ought to do for particular groups. We may call this contemporary notion of liberalism *welfare liberalism* to avoid confusion with the liberalism on which virtually all—conservative and liberal alike—concur in contemporary society. Concern

---

[12] Vilfredo Pareto, *Manual of Political Economy*, trans. Ann S. Schwier (New York: Augustus M. Kelley, 1971; 1st pub. 1927), 192. There is a bit of slippery reasoning in many Pareto criticisms of government action. Exchanges between individuals commonly violate the Pareto criteria if we take effects on not only the exchangers but also on everyone else who might be affected into our account. My great success in business may bankrupt you even though all of my dealings may be Pareto efficient in improving the lot of myself and each of my partners in the deals. See further discussion, Chapter 2, section on 'Causal and Conceptual Links'.

[13] John Dewey asserts that the use of the term liberalism in our sense dates from the first decade of the nineteenth century (Dewey, *Liberalism and Social Action*, in *The Later Works of Dewey, 1925–1953*, xi (Carbondale, Ill.: Southern Illinois University Press, 1987; 1st pub. 1935), 1–65, at p. 6).

[14] Tocqueville, *Democracy in America*, i. 252. See further discussion in Chapter 2, section on 'Collective Resolution'.

with welfare liberalism, as a so-called liberalism rather than charity, dates from Bismarck or earlier in Europe and from the 1930s or earlier in the United States.

Government sponsored welfarism is a good on which most might agree more than contemporary political debate makes clear, because virtually all groups in liberal democratic societies support some welfare programmes. Despite sometime claims to the contrary, disagreement is not about social welfarism in principle but about who should benefit from government intervention on behalf of some at apparent cost to others.[15] Some of the disagreement is sociological or causal—a particular welfare programme that some support as generally good for the society may be thought by others to cause more harm than good.[16] Some of the disagreement is moral—people who behave in certain ways do or do not deserve help. And some, perhaps most, is merely solipsistically political—my welfare should be guaranteed by the government, yours should not.

But welfare liberalism and welfare politics are not the subject of this book. Apart from, perhaps, general education and social security, welfare programmes are not a matter of mutual advantage for the politically significant groups in society. Nor is broader social welfarism related to the workability of the constitution or the government. Liberal governments do not commonly fall because of the opposition of the poor. The frequent claim that it serves the interest of the middle class to rescue the poor or the interest of the wealthy northern nations to rescue the impoverished southern nations is false. Sweden is not threatened by Kenya and it is not from mistaken assessment of national interests that the United States government spends less than 1 per cent of its budget on foreign aid (a third of which goes to Egypt and Israel, much of it for military support).[17] Most of the middle class in the United States are only slightly more threatened by the urban poor than Swedes are by Kenyans. Welfare liberalism has a different strategic structure from those of political

---

[15] As is clearly evident and as is proclaimed by the articulate conservative, George F. Will, *Statecraft as Soulcraft* (New York: Simon and Schuster, 1983), 23, 126–32.

[16] Hume argued that the effort to achieve an egalitarian distribution would be generally destructive and would reduce welfare all around while resulting in tyranny (Hume, *Enquiry*, sect. 3, part 2, pp. 193–4). See also, Bertrand de Jouvenel, *The Ethics of Redistribution* (Cambridge: Cambridge University Press, 1952; reprinted by Liberty Press, 1990).

[17] This constitutes 0.15 per cent of the national income (*New York Times*, 30 April 1995: 4.4). Denmark, Norway, and Sweden spend about 1 per cent of their national incomes.

and economic liberalisms, which are mutually advantageous to their supporters. I will generally use the term liberalism to mean only political and economic liberalism unless the term is otherwise qualified (although I briefly survey other liberalisms in the Appendix).

Neither economic nor political liberalism has any hope if it is not backed by a government that can enforce its minimal requirements of order and protection of individuals. It also has little hope if government is not successfully limited, so that it cannot override the liberal protections. Hobbes's concern was with protection of individuals from other individuals. It is a later concern of liberals that the state which ostensibly protects us against each other might itself harm us and pervasively intrude into our lives with greater force than other individuals could do. Hence, the need for constitutionalism to limit government. For some writers, this is the distinctive core of liberalism. Finally, it seems to be a logical or pragmatic inference from liberalism and its need of government that the individuals to be protected should themselves have a role in determining what their political institutions do. Hence, political liberalism seems inexorably to lead to both constitutionalism and democracy.

This is not the claim, often debated, that political and economic liberalisms are inherently causally related, so that, supposedly, we can have political liberalism only if we have economic liberalism. What seems minimally true is that political and economic liberalisms are mutually reinforcing, if only to the extent that the more power government has to intervene in one, the more it also has to intervene in the other. Constraining government is part of the route to both liberalisms. This limited relationship is enough to suggest to some that the achievement of relatively equal economic results, as a route to greater political equality, is not worth the infringements of political liberty that it would enable (even if it did not logically entail such infringements). In the end, economic egalitarianism under state control might produce greater political equality while reducing liberty across the society.

In either case, economic egalitarianism and political liberalism may face a grim trade-off in practice. Egalitarianism is not a matter of mutual advantage even in the limited sociological sense of serving the advantage of the politically effective groups in society. Therefore it does not have the strategic structure of the two liberalisms or of constitutionalism and democracy. A programme of egalitarian redistribution inherently involves substantial conflict of interest and it is implausible to suppose it could ever be made to be self-enforcing. It would require a forceful government to maintain it.

Social Order

There are three grand theories—or schools of theory—on social order. First, there are conflict theories, as represented by Thrasymachus (in Plato's *Republic*), Karl Marx, and Ralf Dahrendorf. Thomas Hobbes is also commonly considered a conflict theorist, but I think this is wrong, as I will note below. Secondly, there are shared-value or shared-norm theories, as represented by John Locke, Emile Durkheim, Ibn Khaldun, and Talcott Parsons.[18] Religious visions of social order are commonly shared-value theories. And, thirdly, there are exchange theories, which are relatively more recent than the other two schools, with Bernard Mandeville and Adam Smith as perhaps the first major figures, and, in our time, George Homans and many social-choice theorists and economists.[19]

Most contemporary shared-value theorists are followers of Durkheim and Parsons. These followers are mostly sociologists and anthropologists—there are virtually no economists and there are now few political scientists in the Durkheim–Parsons camp. There was a grand Parsonian movement in political science from the 1950s up until some time in the 1970s. The most notable example of this movement was the civic culture of Gabriel Almond and Sidney Verba and others.[20] Although there is not much of a grand-synthesis

[18] On conflict and shared-value theories, see Talcott Parsons, *The Structure of Social Action* (New York: Free Press, 1968; 1st pub. 1937), 89–94; and Ralf Dahrendorf, 'In Praise of Thrasymachus', in Dahrendorf, *Essays in the Theory of Society* (Stanford: Stanford University Press, 1968), 129–50. Also see Dennis Wrong, *The Problem of Order: What Unites and Divides Society* (New York: Free Press, 1994); Emile Durkheim, *The Division of Labor in Society* (New York: Macmillan, 1933; 1st pub. 1893), 226–9 and *passim* (Durkheim speaks of the 'common conscience').
[19] There are also, more recently, structural theories, as represented by Marx and articulated by many structuralist sociologists in our time. Much of structuralist theory has been about the breakdown of social order in revolution and is not a grand theory of social order. Structuralist theory might be right as a descriptive theory about social contexts that determine interests. But this school still needs an explanation of why and when particular individuals do the things that the structure suggests are in their collective interest.
[20] Gabriel Almond and Sidney Verba, *The Civic Culture: Political Attitudes and Democracy in Five Nations* (Princeton: Princeton University Press, 1963).

view of norms that remains in political science or even in much of sociology, there are still ad hoc norm theories. For example, political scientists often explain what voting occurs as public spirited, altruistic, or duty-driven. And there is today a rising chorus of political scientists who take a more-or-less ad hoc stand on the importance of a value consensus, as represented by those concerned with the supposed declines in trust, family values, and community.

Contractarians in social theory are typically shared-value theorists. This may sound odd, because contracts typically govern exchanges. But social contract theory requires a motivation for fulfilling one's side of a contractual arrangement and, as argued in Chapter 3, a social contract is not analogous to a legal contract in this respect. Because there is no enforcer of it, a social contract is commonly seen to require a normative commitment—essentially the same normative commitment from everyone. For example, in Thomas Scanlon's view the motivation to keep to a social contract is the desire to achieve reasonable agreement on cooperative arrangements.[21] Contracts for ordinary exchanges are backed by various incentives to perform, especially by the threat of legal enforcement, by the interest the parties have in maintaining the relationship for future exchanges or in maintaining their reputations. The normative character of social contract theory is, oddly, sometimes read backwards into contract in the law, where it did not have a central role historically.[22]

For conflict theorists, coercion is the central way to achieve social order. Of course, coercion is important and may even be a *sine qua non* for order in complex societies, just because there will be some who would take advantage of the reasonable, relatively cooperative behaviour of others. Those people might ruin society for everyone, as Hobbes supposes the few rotten types would wreck the possibility of normal relations even among those whose natural proclivities would be to be cooperative, as he argues for the state of nature. But

---

[21] Thomas M. Scanlon, 'Contractualism and Utilitarianism', in Amartya Sen and Bernard Williams, eds., *Utilitarianism and Beyond* (Cambridge: Cambridge University Press, 1982), 103–28, at p. 115 n. See also, Brian Barry, *Justice as Impartiality* (Oxford: Oxford University Press, 1995), and Russell Hardin, 'Reasonable Agreement: Political Not Normative', in Paul J. Kelly, ed., *Impartiality, Neutrality and Justice: Re-reading Brian Barry's Justice as Impartiality* (Edinburgh: Edinburgh University Press, 1998), 137–53.

[22] See e.g. Charles Fried, *Contract As Promise* (Cambridge, Mass.: Harvard University Press, 1981).

coercion is only one *sine qua non* for social order. Two others are exchange and coordination. All are needed because the strategic structures of our potential interactions are quite varied, and we need devices for handling all of these reasonably well if we are to have desirable order. In a subsistence agricultural society, coercion might be very nearly the only point of government. But in a complex society, coercion seems to be a minor element in the actual lives of most people, although the threat of it might stand behind more of our actions than we are wont to admit. In such a society, exchange and coordination loom very large, radically larger than in the subsistence economy.

The three grand schools—conflict, shared values, and exchange—are right about particular aspects of social order. But they miss the central mode of social order in a complex modern society, which is coordination. We don't necessarily share values but we can coordinate to allow each of us to pursue our own values without destructive interaction or exchange. To grossly simplify much of the problem of social order in a complex society, consider the relatively trivial problem of maintaining order in traffic on roads. There are two main coordinations at stake. The first is the obvious one of merely getting all drivers to drive on the same side of the road—either all on the left or all on the right—in order to prevent constant accidents and difficult problems of negotiating who gets to go first. The second is the problem of controlling the flow of traffic at intersections, for which traffic signals and signs are used when the traffic is heavy enough. Two striking things about the collection of drivers are that *they are not genuinely in conflict with each other* and that *they do not typically have to share any values* in order for these coordinations to work well. I have my purposes, you have yours, and we want merely to avoid getting in each other's way.

As are conflict theories, coordination is an interest theory. Hobbes is perhaps the first major coordination theorist.[23] But David Hume, Adam Smith, and C. E. Lindblom see much of the social order as a matter of coordinating the disparate interests of many people.[24] A

[23] Not all Hobbes scholars would agree with this assessment. For an argument for understanding him as a coordination theorist, see Russell Hardin, 'Hobbesian Political Order', *Political Theory*, 19 (May 1991): 156–80.

[24] David Hume, *A Treatise of Human Nature*, ed. L. A. Selby-Bigge and P. H. Nidditch (Oxford: Oxford University Press, 1978, 2nd edn.; 1st pub. 1739–40), 504–13; Adam Smith, *An Inquiry into the Nature and Causes of the Wealth of Nations*, ed. R. H. Campbell, A. S. Skinner, and W. B. Todd (Oxford: Oxford

shared-value theory could be essentially a coordination theory if the values motivate coordinated actions. But coordination does not require broadly shared values. And shared-value theories typically make the adherence to relevant values a matter of overriding one's interests and, when put into political power, overriding the interests of many citizens. For example, I help to defend my community despite the risks that such effort entails, I submerge my identity in the collective identity (whatever that could possibly mean), or I vote despite the burden to me of doing so and despite the virtual irrelevance of the effect of my vote on my interests. But against the strenuous and implausible view of the Durkheimians and Parsonians, a collection of quite diverse pluralists can coordinate on an order for the society in which they seek their diverse values.

Despite their obvious importance, we should not suppose that exchange relations are the whole of sociology.[25] Exchange relations might be most of economics, or at least of classical economics, but they are arguably less important for political sociology than coordination interactions are. And, in a sense, the residual Parsonians are right to claim that conflict relations are not the whole of political order. They are right, again, because the core or modal character of social order is coordination. I will not make an abstract argument for the power of a coordination theory of social order, but the chapters that follow present such a theory of political order.[26] The general argument here is that liberalism, constitutionalism, and democracy are sociologically coordination theories when they work to establish and maintain social order.

Coordination

While, at a common-sense level, the problem of coordination is typically not difficult to grasp, its general significance and its compelling

University Press, 1976; 1st pub. 1776; reprinted by Liberty Press, 1979); C. E. Lindblom, *Politics and Markets: The World's Political–Economic Systems* (New York: Basic Books).

[25] This is, in essence, the message of Arthur L. Stinchcombe, 'Is the Prisoner's Dilemma All of Sociology?' *Inquiry*, 23 (1980): 187–92.

[26] I argue for such theory in many other contexts as well in relevant parts of Russell Hardin, *Collective Action* (Baltimore: Johns Hopkins University Press for Resources for the Future, 1982), *Morality within the Limits of Reason* (Chicago: University of Chicago Press, 1988), and *One for All*.

nature have not been central understandings in the social sciences or in political philosophy. Hobbes had a nascent coordination theory in his vision of our coordinating on a single sovereign.[27] Had he been slightly more supple in his views, he might have recognized that the dreadful problem of civil war in his England was a matter of *multiple coordinations*. There was no war of all against all but only war between alternative factions for rule, each of which was well enough coordinated to wreak havoc on the other and on non-participant bystanders. Hume made the outstanding philosophical contribution to its understanding, but his insights were largely ignored for two centuries or more after he wrote and they are still commonly misread.[28] Thomas Schelling gave the first insightful game-theoretic account of coordination problems and their strategic and incentive structures.[29] But their pervasive importance in social life is still not a standard part of social scientific and philosophical understanding.

In social life, coordination occurs in two very different forms: spontaneously and institutionally. We can coordinate and we can be coordinated. In Philadelphia a small number of people coordinated spontaneously to create the framework to coordinate the whole nation institutionally. Once they had drafted their constitution, its adoption was beneficial to enough of the politically significant groups in the thirteen states that, for them, it was mutually advantageous. Therefore, they were able to *coordinate spontaneously* on that constitution to subject themselves to being *coordinated institutionally* by it thereafter. This difference defines the focus of the two separate sets of chapters (2 to 4 and 5 to 7) on liberalism, constitutionalism, and democracy.

A very simple instance of a coordination problem is our desire to meet for lunch next week. With adequate communication, we can typically handle this problem very easily. A more important but still simple problem is our desire to drive safely on roads on which there are many other drivers going in opposite directions. At some point during the nineteenth century, wagon drivers became spontaneously coordinated on driving right in some communities and left in others. Eventually, these conventions were made legally binding. But the

[27] Hardin, 'Hobbesian Political Order'.
[28] Hume's arguments may have been overlooked because they are chiefly in a series of long footnotes in Hume, *A Treatise of Human Nature*, 504–13.
[29] Thomas C. Schelling, *The Strategy of Conflict* (Cambridge, Mass.: Harvard University Press, 1960), 54–8.

remarkable thing about their early development is that they worked without the enforcement of any authority. All they required was the self-interested concern of drivers to do well as they went on their way. Once enough people coordinated on the same convention, the convention was self-enforcing.

In much more complicated and rich ways, some constitutions and government regimes are virtually self-enforcing because they too coordinate the bulk of a populace on their own interest in going their own ways. One of the striking features of such coordinations is that they often could go in many different ways. The municipal law, to which Hume refers in the epigraph at the beginning of this chapter, has the purpose of maintaining order and successful social interaction in hundreds of cities, but it varies enormously in its detailed content from city to city. And, as Hume notes, there is often no compelling a priori reason for the laws to go one way rather than another. Any way that would work to coordinate the citizenry is good for our purposes. There is typically no a priori reason for choosing one way of doing things over some other way or even many other ways.

In the driving example, virtually everyone who drives faces essentially the same potential benefit from coordinating in either way—that is why it is such a compelling example of real world coordinations. In most social contexts, not everyone may face exactly the same benefits from any given coordination. Even in the driving example, there might be thrill-seekers who enjoy running the risk of passing in the other lane while cresting a hill or rounding a curve. If a social institution is to work relatively well, it must be designed for the citizen with modal incentives to coordinate. And it will likely require backup institutions to enforce its coordination.

For the slaves under the coordination of the US Constitution, those backup institutions were sometimes draconian. During the later Jim Crow era in the South, the enforcement of racist norms was partially handled by law and its officials and partly by the spontaneous enforcement by individuals against other individuals. The latter worked so well among whites that the many whites who were not racist were unaware that there were so many others of like mind.[30] A delegation of Episcopal priests to Jackson, Mississippi, in 1961, were visited by a white, middle-aged couple who wanted to thank them for what they were doing on behalf of integration. The priests were

[30] See John Howard Griffin, *Black Like Me* (New York: New American Library, 1976; 1st pub. 1961), p. 153. See further discussion in the Appendix below.

amazed and asked how many of their peers felt the same way. 'We have no idea', the couple said. 'No one ever dares to talk.'[31] The many whose interests racism supposedly served were able to force everyone to submit to their views in a coordination that clearly was dismal for many. More generally, exclusionary norms can be powerful coordinators of some group to the great detriment of many of those outside the group.[32]

Perhaps the most impressive thing about it is that *successful coordination gives an oddly different answer than what is expected to the traditional question: who will keep us in order?* From at least Plato and Aristotle forward, it is commonly supposed that the answer will have to be some particular authority. Without someone to regulate our interactions, they will go wrong. We all know better than this in many contexts in which we have rich and rewarding relations with people without any apparent oversight from some powerful authority. James Wilson, one of the Philadelphia conventioneers, posed the traditional question very differently. He asked, 'are men capable of governing *themselves*? . . . and are they disposed to *obey themselves*?'[33] His framing of the question forces a particular answer to the question of who will keep us in order: *we* will keep ourselves in order. We will keep ourselves in order because it will be in everyone's interest to follow the coordination we have settled on. We may have settled on it by deliberate choice, as when you and I schedule a place and time for our lunch, or we may do it spontaneously, as evidently happened with the original driving convention in many communities. Or the coordination regime may just happen to be in place for us already and we therefore simply go along with it, which is the fate of everyone born into an ongoing constitutional order.

A coordination regime is commonly strong just because it is extremely difficult to re-coordinate large numbers on doing things some other way. It took the massive politics of 1787–8, with several years of desultory preparation, to devise the constitutional order of the United States. It took the destructions of a badly lost war to enable coordination of a small group to bring a different government to power in Russia in 1917. Even for so simple a coordination as the

---

[31] Cornelius Hastie, Letter to the Editor, *New Yorker* (9 November 1998), 10.

[32] Hardin, *One for All*, ch. 4.

[33] James Wilson, 'Lectures on Law', in *The Works of James Wilson*, ed. Robert Green McCloskey, 2 vols. (Cambridge, Mass.: Harvard University Press, 1967; essay first published in 1791); excerpted in Philip B. Kurland and Ralph Lerner, eds., *The Founders' Constitution*, 5 vols. (Chicago: University of Chicago Press, 1987) i. 73.

driving convention, it took massive organization and huge expenditures for Sweden to change its convention from driving left to driving right in 1967.[34] In the first and last of these cases, the new coordinations served mutual advantage sufficiently well that there was no major opposition to letting them stand. Most importantly, there was virtually no one who could see it as individually beneficial to go against the new coordination. While this is trivially true for the driving convention, it is also true for the constitutional regime in the United States, as it is in many other nations under remarkably varied structures of government. Once a coordination is well in place and people are following it, *the cost of re-coordinating is the chief obstacle to moving to any supposedly superior order.* This cost can block re-coordination even if it would be in virtually everyone's interest to be in a new order.

Many institutions can be made to work well because they can be backed by superior authority with real force. Hence, if we have a competent government in place, we can enforce laws against those few who would violate them. But the overriding problem for the government itself is how it can maintain itself in power. In grotesque cases such as the years of dictatorship in Haiti, Uganda, Cambodia, and other places, the government survives as a parasitic force, and to do so it typically has to wreak enough violence on the populace as to prevent revolutionary coordination against it.

In the cases of relatively benign governments, it is often supposed that there must be some moral grounding for both the benignity of the government and the obedience of the populace. While there may be a lot of moral behavior and intention throughout most societies, it would be remarkable if that were the reason for the success of orderly government from ancient times to the present. Rather, the chief reason for obedience is the self-enforcing character of governments that serve enough interests well enough to make it the interest of most people to acquiesce and maybe even support their governments. Acquiescence makes sense for me because I can live reasonably well by concentrating on my own life within the order sustained by my government even though I might think a quite different government would be much better for me. If I could help to change the government relatively easily, without having that purpose consume my life, I might no longer acquiesce, but I cannot and few people

---

[34] Russell Hardin, *Morality within the Limits of Reason*, 51–3.

ever could. Similarly, within a government itself, the chief source of reasonable behaviour is the fact that it is in most agents' interest to do their jobs reasonably well, as discussed below (see section on 'The Governors').

In the central arguments of this book, it is coordination that makes things work. Liberalism, constitutionalism, and democracy work for us because we are coordinated enough on various matters. In many aspects of life, coordination makes things work, but badly. For example, perverse, destructive norms of exclusion are grounded in coordination.[35] They are self-enforcing because it is in the interest of various people to do what makes them work. Even brutal, illiberal governments can coordinate enough people to keep themselves in power. Therefore, it should not be taken as an assumption that coordination is good. Indeed, in the issues of this book, the coordinations that are important often leave out important but politically ineffective groups. Women and slaves were given neither voice nor hearing in the US Constitution, and yet the coordination that it stimulated was adequate to control their fates along with the fates of those who more clearly benefited from it.

Given the Paretian presumption of much of liberal theory, we might think to judge outcomes normatively by whether they are conducive to the mutual advantage of all concerned. Generally, we cannot expect to find an outcome that genuinely meets the Pareto condition except with respect to some particular, reasonably well-defined status quo, such as the woeful conditions of grinding civil war or, in Hobbes's vision, a state of nature in which all are murderously suspicious of each other. The Pareto condition requires that at least some be better off and none worse off in the new outcome than in the status quo. The states of affairs in the United States in 1787 and in the Eastern nations in 1989 cannot count as such grim situations that all would genuinely benefit from just *any* regime of order. There were clear losers in 1787–8, most notably the communitarian Anti-Federalists, who were the leading opponents of the ratification of the constitution. There are also sure to be clear losers in the East, especially among those who were well-placed in the former economies, those over 50, and many others (see Chapter 5). The new constitutional orders in these cases were not Paretian moves to make everyone better off or at least not worse off. Hence, these changes

---

[35] Hardin, *One for All*, ch. 4.

cannot be judged morally good according to the simple Paretian standard.

One further normative point: to say that people act from interest is often taken to imply that they are more crass than we know they are. But to say someone acts from interest does not mean that they require money or other standard rewards to get them to behave well. And it does not mean that, in the pursuit of interest, they typically harm others. *In coordination contexts we act from interest and serve the mutual benefit.* And surely there is nothing crass in my following my interest by choosing to drive right when in North America and left when in the United Kingdom. It would be not merely crass but murderous and stupid for me to do otherwise. With a correct understanding of the incentive structures of workable government, we can readily see that citizens commonly follow their interests in acting in ways that are mutually advantageous to themselves and many, perhaps virtually all, others. And we can readily judge that, when they do so, they act morally as well.

Finally, although this is not the place to develop an extensive argument, if we want a general theory of social order, that theory must largely be a compound coordination theory. Stability follows from multiple institutions that must all fit together to some large extent and many of which would have to concur for a big, deliberate change in social relations. In an even moderately diverse society, stability also depends on separate coordinations of various groups, coordinations that keep them out of each other's way, just as the driving convention keeps those who are northbound out of the way of those who are southbound. It is a common thesis that we need various groups and their political participation to sustain political order.[36] It might be even more important that our group involvements keep us out of politics to a large extent, because in politics we will conflict.

Political Obligation

There is an extensive, often dreary literature on political obligation. Much of it turns on definitional quibbles. For example, it is often argued that, by definition, one can be obligated only to do what one

---

[36] See several contributions to Susan J. Pharr and Robert D. Putnam, eds., 'What's Troubling the Trilateral Democracies', book manuscript, Harvard University, 1998.

has somehow agreed to do or otherwise voluntarily assumed as an obligation. One of the ostensible appeals of contractarian arguments that somehow we have consented to our government is that they imply we are therefore obligated to obey it. Locke supposed we are obligated to the degree that our government does what we consented—actually or tacitly—for it to do. But when it goes beyond that we may be justified to rebel.

From the definitional move that one can be obligated only to do what one has agreed to do, some then argue that we are obligated to some extent and others argue that we are not obligated at all since most of us evidently did not consent. Rawls argues that only those who have accepted public office are obligated because only they have clearly consented.[37] Others suppose, more or less with Locke, that various kinds of action are tantamount to acceptance of an obligation. For example, accepting some public benefit, such as the use of roads, is *de facto* consent to the government that has provided the benefit and is therefore obligating.

If contractarian claims of consent are generally hollow, then contractarian claims of obligation are also hollow. But one might assert obligation from other principles. For example, earlier theorists who supposed that monarchs had their mandate from god could simply require obedience as what god commands. In deontological and utilitarian moral theories, one can typically be obligated to do what is right irrespective of any prior consent. In utilitarianism, what is right is what conduces to a better state of affairs or to greater welfare. Hence, one might often have a utilitarian obligation of beneficence.

Hobbes's theory of government required no normative principle of obligation, because all that his sovereign required was acquiescence and because, in the extreme instance in which my sovereign wishes to destroy me, Hobbes held that it would be rational for me to fight for my existence. As noted in Chapter 4, Hobbes claimed that our obligation of obedience to the sovereign derives not from our assent, which we can easily enough revoke, but from our fear of punishment if we do not obey.[38] This claim is contrary to a fairly standard moralized account of Hobbes's intent as, indeed, to present a theory of moral obligation to the sovereign, a moral obligation that follows merely from contracting, although this interpretation makes

[37] John Rawls, *A Theory of Justice* (Cambridge, Mass.: Harvard University Press, 1971), 113–14.
[38] Hobbes, *Leviathan*, ch. 14, p. 65 in original edition, emphasis added.

nonsense of his defence of the obligation to obey a sovereign who
gains power by conquest. Let me therefore spell it out a bit further.

The most plausible reading of Hobbes's 'obligation' is as a rational
or interest term, not a moral term. For him to say we are obligated is
to mean we are obliged by our own interest. This is, for example, the
clear meaning of the term when he said we are obligated to submit to
laws of physics: 'There is no kicking against the pricks'.[39] Hobbes
occasionally interchanged the terms 'obligated' and 'obliged', as in
the passage that ends with this homily. John Austin followed this
usage. He held that 'The greater the eventual evil, and the greater the
chance of incurring it . . ., the greater is the strength of the *obligation*'
to obey it.[40] This might seem less surprising in the light of the traditional view, held by Locke (and common in the era of Hobbes) and
even some of my colleagues today, that only someone who believes
in a god can be trusted to be moral because only those who have the
threat of punishment—in an afterlife, perhaps—from an all-knowing
judge to motivate them will act morally against their own interest.
Those who hold this view might be distressed to know how
Hobbesian they are. Indeed, it is Hobbes's view for the state of
nature that no contract is binding.[41]

H. L. A. Hart objected to this usage. He held that to say I am
obliged to do something means that it would be substantially against
my interest not to do it. To say I am *obligated* to do it means that it
would be morally wrong for me not to do it.[42] On this distinction,
Hobbes's theory is about being obliged to obey and even support a
going government, not about being obligated to obey it. His theory
of government is a theory of workability. There are normative
reasons for wanting government—we'll all be better off with a stable
government—but government works through obliging us, not
through obligating us morally.

A welfarist might construct a normative theory of obligation as a
natural adjunct of the two-stage theory of government articulated in

[39] Thomas Hobbes, *De Cive*, ed. Howard Warrender (Oxford: Oxford University
Press, 1983), 15.7, p. 187; 1st pub. in Latin 1642; in English 1651. The pricks are the
spikes that deter horses in harness to a wagon from kicking up violently, because if
they do, they injure themselves. Horses are therefore obligated in Hobbes's sense not
to kick while in harness.

[40] Austin, John, *The Province of Jurisprudence Determined* (New York: Noonday,
1954; 1st pub. 1832), 16, my emphasis.

[41] Hobbes, *Leviathan*, ch. 14, p. 68 in original edition. For what we normally call
contract, he spoke of covenant.

[42] Hart, *The Concept of Law*, 80–1.

Chapter 3 if that government is justified on welfarist grounds, as Hobbes's sovereign was. That is to say, we would want the government for our own interest and therefore we would be obligated to abide by its second-stage actions, at least in so far as these followed reasonably clearly from the welfarist mandate of the government. But we might also assert, with Hobbes, merely a sociological or self-interest theory of positive obligation. This would be a relatively limited principle of obligation, although not an empty principle. One who refused to abide by government rules could initially be asked, Would you rather there be no government? Often, however, this question would require unpacking and, once unpacked, it would lose its force. In general, this would happen when one could answer either: no, I would not rather there be no government, but I would rather there be a different kind of government even considering the costs of a transition; or, no, but this rule of the government does not follow from our need for a government of this kind. These would be responses in keeping with the mutual advantage grounding of government. Of course, a claim for obligation from the mutual advantage we derive from government has all of the problems that the claim of mutual advantage has.[43]

In answering the question above, a more difficult possibility is that one could answer: no, I would not rather there be no government, but I would rather there merely be a different kind of government. I might fully recognize that the costs of transition to the other kind of government would negate any gain to me of moving to it. But I might still assert that, given my preference for the other kind of government, I owe the one I actually have no obedience or cooperation, that I should act as I please to my greatest advantage. Of course, if I am the only one to take this position, the government should be able to handle my dissent well enough. But virtually everyone could make a similar claim and if all actively dissented, our government would plausibly fail and all would suffer. That fact would not be an argument to me that I should be more cooperative, because my cooperation or dissent would make no difference in the government's success or failure. The argument from mutual advantage simply would not carry any moral force against such a position at large because it could carry no effective causal force against it.

[43] See further, Russell Hardin, 'Political Obligation', in Alan Hamlin and Philip Pettit, eds., *The Good Polity* (Oxford: Basil Blackwell, 1989), 103–19.

The fundamental problem with a mutual-advantage justification of political order is division of society into groups with strongly conflicting interests or programmes, such as economic interests or ethnic or religious programmes. Even an instance of ethnic conflict, such as those of Bosnia, Rwanda, Burundi, and many other societies recently torn by violence, has the character at least in large part of an economic conflict. As in John C. Calhoun's observation in the epigraph to Chapter 7, division into groups each of which might contest for political power means that each of them can benefit economically from gaining control of the government. Calhoun held that this is a general problem that afflicts any system of popular government. But the problem is grievously exacerbated if control of the government is arguably the most valuable resource in the society. Many of the most violent contemporary ethnic conflicts have this character.[44]

Hence, in some deeply divided societies there may actually be consensus on the view of the Federalists that, in the American states, the public good is best promoted by individuals seeking their own good.[45] Hence, one might expect them to be able to coordinate on order. Unfortunately, however, they may be mobilized by groups to seize the individual welfares and may therefore fail to coordinate. These societies, such as Burundi, Rwanda, Somalia, and arguably the former Yugoslavia are perhaps cases for the value of imposing order through an all-powerful sovereign. Yugoslavia once had almost such a sovereign in Marshall Tito, on whom almost everyone could coordinate. But Tito created a federal system of republics with quasi-ethnic boundaries in which political careers were tied to the republics and therefore open to the possibility of manipulation of ethnic loyalties. The second-generation leaders who followed Tito have been lethal in their ethnic politics. Burundi and Rwanda also once had an all-powerful sovereign. But Belgium failed to create native governments before abandoning the nations to chaos.

Some religious conflicts might not have quite the character of Calhoun's comment because the religious regime that wins might actually suppress economic opportunities in general, as the Ayatollahs in Iran and the Taliban in Afghanistan have done. But many fanatical religious groups do share with ethnic groups in impoverished societies such as Somalia, Rwanda, and Burundi the

---

[44] See further, Russell Hardin, *One for All*, 179–80.
[45] Thomas Jefferson and George Washington are both quoted to this effect in Chapter 5, 'Concluding Remarks'.

sense that control of the government is, for their purposes, the most valuable resource in their societies.

Unintended Consequences

Spontaneous coordination underlies another phenomenon that is fundamentally important in social interaction but that is not well grasped in many accounts of institutions. It is the problem of unintended consequences, first identified by the Scottish Enlightenment philosopher Adam Ferguson, who spoke of 'establishments, which are indeed the result of human action, but not the execution of any human design'.[46] You go about what you are doing, I go about my life, and so on, with the result that we have before us some patterned behaviour, either in the larger spontaneous society or in a well-defined institution, that no one of us ever intended.

Sometimes what we unintentionally bring about is good as in the original driving conventions, sometimes not as in many destructive norms, such as norms of racism that arguably make even the racists worse off. One might characterize many of the problems of externalities of great interest in economic analyses as unintended consequences. Among such problems is the externality of pollution that follows unintentionally from various benign intentional actions as driving cars, heating buildings, and so forth. But Ferguson was interested in *behavioural consequences*, as represented in norms or institutions, and the term 'unintended consequences' is now a term of art for just such consequences.

The unintended consequences that interested Ferguson are of interest because the actions that produce them must, by inference, be self-enforcing, because we spontaneously coordinate ourselves to act in ways that produce those consequences. In the end, the constitution or government that coordinates us does so partly through design and partly through unintentional developments or growths. When unintended consequences take us away from the seeming design of some institution, the reason may simply be that the design is not self-enforcing and therefore is not stable. The institution therefore is easily changeable until it reaches a structure or pattern that is

---

[46] Adam Ferguson, *An Essay on the History of Civil Society* (New Brunswick, NJ: Transaction, 1980; 1st edn. 1767), 122.

self-enforcing. It would then be sensible to say that, in a compelling sense, the institution was originally misdesigned, because it was evidently not fitted to people's actual incentives. But it does not follow, of course, that whatever unintended consequence we fall into is good just because we are coordinated on it. We might design an institution for some purpose and then see it produce not merely unintended but unwonted consequences. For example, mercantilist organization of the economy in England had the perverse effect of damping economic productivity.

Much of what happens under a constitution is reasonably characterized as unintended consequences in Ferguson's sense. The constitution of 1787–8 could not conceivably have laid out how the government was to work in much detail. But even where it did, very often what happened sounds quite different from what might have been intended. Originalist interpretations of the constitution—insisting that the laws today must be what the original founders intended them to be—are often a violation of the dictum that ought implies can. The laws are often not what might arguably have been intended because what was intended would not work to motivate and coordinate citizens and officials. Idealists may blanch at the fact, but the world is not tractable to all their ideals and will not support them.

James Madison feared that clearly stated constitutional provisions to protect individual rights would eventually come to have peculiarly narrowed meanings that would make it worse to state them in the constitution than to leave them for conventional enforcement.[47] He feared perverse unintended consequences. The extraordinary distortions of the second-amendment right to keep and bear arms is a case in point. Were he to survey American government today, he might be appalled to find it larded through with unintended consequences. Or, he might share Jefferson's view that 'the earth [and government] belongs in usufruct to the living',[48] and conclude that his constitution had done its job by getting the nation under way to take care of itself in the longer run.

[47] Jack N. Rakove, 'Parchment Barriers and the Politics of Rights', in Michael J. Lacey and Knud Haakonssen, eds., *A Culture of Rights: The Bill of Rights in Philosophy, Politics, and Law, 1791 and 1991* (Cambridge: Cambridge University Press, 1991), 98–143, at p. 103.

[48] Thomas Jefferson, Letter to James Madison of 6 September 1789, in Kurland and Lerner, *Founders' Constitution*, i. 68–70, at p. 68.

The Governors

The discussion of coordination and of unintended consequences suggests an important issue in the account of constitutional government that I will not address in subsequent chapters but that should at least be mentioned lest misunderstandings arise. The discussion above addressed the question how we, the citizens, will be motivated to go along with a constitution, a norm, or our government. There is a related question, which is raised insistently throughout the history of debate on government. Who will govern the governors? The answer has the same strategic form as our answer to the question above of who will govern the citizens.[49]

The problem of self-interested officials was generally a concern of Adam Smith. The problem of a self-interested tyrant was a concern of the *Federalist Papers* and of Montesquieu. Geoffrey Brennan and James Buchanan say that under a despotic government of one person who is given the power to decide on distributional issues, that person is essentially given ownership over all that is to be distributed.[50] The actual problem we face is how to make many, indeed today, millions of officials act in *our* interest. We seemingly resolve the problem through the force of norms for substantially disinterested behaviour. However, to a large extent, the relevant norms can be established and enforced by coordination on a convention, so that we can see the norms as essentially self-interested or at least as congruent with self-interest.

People do not have to be thoroughly public-spirited to be good public servants while in government positions. After all, some of my best friends are good public servants. They can be basically self-interested, that is, interested in income and career. Both bureaucratic and judicial systems generally include many checks on behaviour,

[49] Although the argument here is specific to government agents, it is applicable to organizational contexts of any kind. I discuss the general problem of getting people in any kind of organization to act on behalf of the organization in 'Institutional Commitment: Values or Incentives?' in Avner Ben Ner and Louis Putterman, eds., *Economics, Values, and Organization* (Cambridge: Cambridge University Press, 1998), 419–33, esp. 424–6. I focus on reasons an individual citizen might have to expect government agents to perform more or less as their roles suggest they should in 'Trust in Government', in Valerie Braithwaite and Margaret Levi, eds., *Trust and Governance* (New York: Russell Sage Foundation, 1998), 9–27, esp. 19–22.

[50] Geoffrey Brennan and James M. Buchanan, *The Reason of Rules: Constitutional Political Economy* (Cambridge: Cambridge University Press, 1985), 115, 48.

checks that make it easy for some to advance their careers or to block the careers of others by calling the others' actions properly to account.[51] One of the most important incentives for sustaining the norms is that others cannot generally see benefits in ignoring or cooperating with dereliction by their colleagues and superiors.

Getting such a system established and working well may take several generations of office holders. But once it is in place, it can run reasonably well on the self-interest of its office holders as its primary support. Such a conventional norm system may not work equally well at all levels or in all circumstances. But its force can be seen in recent decades in the forced removal from office of legislators, high-ranking bureaucrats, presidential advisers, a president, and a vice-president in the United States, and of ministers and other high-ranking officials in Japan and several European nations, most notably Italy in recent years.

Although its rationale in part is similar, this is not the system of checks and balances envisioned by Montesquieu. It is a finer grained application of Madison's injunction: 'Ambition must be made to counter ambition' (*Federalist*, 51). In some ways it has more in common with competition among producers in a market than between departments of a government. To be sure, I block your action because I think it is wrong. But I do so with substantial support that makes my action costless or even beneficial to me. Similarly, I do my job well because others will generally support and reward me for working well. Moreover, it would be difficult to disrupt this system to anyone's benefit, including that of a national president or prime minister.

This is not to say that such a system can never be abused for essentially self-interested purposes. In addition, it can be abused in a way that is peculiar evidence of how well the relevant norms can be conventionally created and enforced. It can be subject to what the French call *déformation professionnelle*—the tendency to support one's organization's supposed interests to the detriment of larger public purposes. The organized military is notoriously prone to such deformation, as in the Dreyfus affair. But other bureaucracies, such as regulatory and welfare-delivery agencies, are often accused of such deformation. The oddity of this behaviour is that the enlarge-

---

[51] This is not typically a matter of what is now called whistle-blowing. The latter is an instance of calling an entire agency's systematic actions or policy to account, and there are typically no rewards of promotion or better career prospects for doing this.

ment of an agency's mission is often essentially a collective benefit to its staff and therefore must suffer from the logic of collective action.[52] We individually have better career and income prospects from the protection or expansion of our agency's mission. But, by the logic of collective action, I cannot be motivated by self-interest to take any risk to contribute to the general expansion in return for my paltry share of the benefits of the bit of expansion that results from my contribution. My incentive to contribute comes rather from the specific support I personally receive from colleagues in the agency, perhaps especially from superiors, who are all driven by our agency-specific conventional norm.

In general, then, the answer to who gets government agents to do their jobs properly is the same in form as the answer to why we the citizens typically acquiesce in the government's policies. We all control each other. The most important controllers for government officials may, however, typically be other officials rather than citizens, arguably even for elected officials much of the time.[53] Hence, our governmental order is self-enforcing. It, too, can function well enough on its own with the stuff of ordinary people. We do not need the luck of finding a race of Plato's philosopher kings to keep our government in order.

The Argument of the Book

Political liberalism, constitutionalism, and democracy go together causally, although not conceptually. Where they have succeeded to any great extent they have also often been associated with economic liberalism as well, but this may have been a spurious correlation that results from the political difficulty of contriving a government capable of centralized control of the economy that is not simultaneously able (and likely) to control the polity, although Sweden, India, and many other nations have managed to do this to some extent. Power to control the economy to reorganize agriculture and to produce

[52] Some aspects of an agency's mission might be a burden that its agents would sooner load onto another agency or simply avoid altogether. For example, US military leaders reputedly argue against engagements that their forces might not be able to handle successfully.

[53] Russell Hardin, 'Democratic Epistemology and Accountability', *Social Policy and Philosophy* 17 (forthcoming).

steel too readily becomes power to control artistic tastes and much else.

If coordination on a central programme is possible, there is much less need to have an external force to control the government to make it comply with the constitutional order. Hence, constitutional government is feasibly workable. It can fail, however, if the central coordination requires great power that can be used for purposes other than managing the programme on which we have coordinated. In that case, the constitutional order can fail utterly. This was the Soviet problem, although there was probably never any risk of genuinely constitutional government in the Soviet Union until economic malaise set in. Constitutional government can also fail, of course, under the sway of a dictatorial leader such as Hitler, from a military coup, or from other disasters.

We may see most sharply how compelling the regime of coordination is in certain conflicted cases in which some group is a relative loser. With the adoption of the Constitution, the Anti-Federalists lost out on their central hope for government at the level of the community. They did not then mutiny or leave the nation. They simply made the best of life in a world they could not control but that was better for them than alternatives. The concern of blacks in American politics is not merely a matter of political consensus on equality but also necessarily a matter of pervasive social norms of racism. Kwame Ture and others might assert very forcefully that blacks should reject the system in which they are treated unequally, but few blacks accept that charge. Why? As with the Anti-Federalists: because it is not in their interest or even the interest of their children. These and other relative losers live with an uneasy acquiescence in the messy order we have because, as Hobbes argued more generally, the alternative to acquiescence is worse for all, even for those who suffer from the wrong form of government or from the perverse social norm.

Democracy works only where there is mutual advantage in coordinating on order and any other extremely important background concerns. In the United States throughout most of its constitutional history, the most important other background concerns have been the success of commerce, John Locke's concern with keeping religious conflict out of politics, a host of civil liberties, and, of course, national defence. Oddly, this suggests that government where democracy can work is in important respects easier than government where it cannot, although the image we often have of democracy is of its fractiousness. Where coordination on general background issues is possible, government faces less demands than it otherwise would. As Mill wrote in 1840, America had few outstanding public men for the enviable reason that 'America needs very little government'.[54] Arthur Balfour said of the English that 'we are so fundamentally at one that we can safely afford to bicker'.[55]

The American constitutional experience will be discussed in two different contexts: the static politics of the design and adoption of the constitution (in Chapter 3), and the dynamic politics of its application and workability over time (in Chapter 6). Coordination is the success story in both contexts, although in the design and adoption of the Constitution there was no little contrivance to defeat one large group in the society: the communitarian Anti-Federalists. The successful coordination in the initial constitutional period was that between urban commercial interests and agrarian plantation interests, both of whom needed open, national markets. They wrote a constitution to create a government around this point of coordination. The coordination that made the drafting and ratification of the US Constitution possible was that of the commercial interests of two of the three major groups in contest at the time: plantation agrarians, such as the Virginia constitutionalists, and urban commercial and financial interests, as represented by John Adams, Alexander Hamilton, and James Wilson. Both these groups needed open, national markets. In ratification votes in most of the northern states, representatives of the cities voted for the constitution against rural representatives. In two of the leading cities, New York and Providence, secession from their states was threatened; in their two states ratification carried the states' conventions by narrow margins. The two cities were, of course, Federalist in their views; the hinterlands were Anti-Federalist. To the taunt of no union without New York State, Hamilton retorted that there would be no New York State without union because New York City would secede from the state (as is discussed in Chapter 3).

The government of that constitution, after the trauma of the Civil War, eventually survived to continue the coordination around

[54] John Stuart Mill, 'De Tocqueville on Democracy in America, II, in Mill, *Essays on Politics and Society*, ed. J. M. Robson, *Collected Works of John Stuart Mill*, xviii (Toronto: University of Toronto Press, 1977), 153–204, at p. 175.

[55] Quoted in Samuel H. Beer, 'Constitutionalism, Medieval and Modern', paper presented at a conference on constitutionalism at the Murphy Institute, Tulane University, 18–20 February 1994, p. 9.

commercial interests even after the plantation agrarians had passed from the scene. Commercial interests—including the interests of much of the working class, all of the entrepreneurial, financial, and merchant classes, and the very few residual large farmers—are still the dominant interest in American society. In a Gallup poll in 1994, 78 per cent of respondents agreed with the view that 'The strength of this country today is mostly based on the success of American business'.[56] The same is true in every advanced commercial society, potentially including many of the newly liberalizing nations of the East.

The predominance of commercial interests is so sweeping in established commercial societies that these societies are firmly coordinated on most of what matters so that politics can mainly deal with the chaff at the margins. The coordination is so thorough that democracy is a sideshow, and typically not a very entertaining one. The harshest political moments in the United States come when some group tries to trump the underlying coordination: religious fundamentalists who wish to impose a moral or religious order, rabid nationalists who wish to define some as not Americans or who wish to engage in glorious military conquest, perhaps populist farmers and miners around the turn of the century, and, with less voice, socialists have threatened the order. Only committed slave-owners and their opponents have ever broken the order.

It may be a distressing conclusion, but nevertheless a plausible one, that it is a sign of something quite agreeable that American politics is run by mediocrities.[57] It does not provoke anyone to be a Madison or a Jefferson at their best. Mill wrote in 1840 that the openness of society and politics to improvement in the face of the commercial mass could be sustained only through counterweight workings of 'an agricultural class, a leisured class, and a learned class'.[58] One can only hope he was wrong, as, no doubt, most defenders of the commercial class will insist he was. Since he wrote, the agricultural class has virtually disappeared and arguably much of what remains of it is now merely a branch of the commercial class. Much of the leisured class Mill so valued has become the vacuous

[56] Seymour Martin Lipset, 'Malaise and Resiliency in America', *Journal of Democracy* (July 1995) 6: 4–18, at p. 17.
[57] This is Tocqueville's opinion. See Tocqueville, *Democracy in America*, i. 200, 239–40.
[58] Mill, 'De Tocqueville on Democracy in America, II', 198.

buffoons of the British tabloid press. The burden Mill would now have to place on the learned class is likely too much for it to bear.

The Normative Status of Sociological Mutual Advantage

Actual moves for liberalization prompt the question: what is the normative status of liberalism, constitutionalism, and democracy? They may work well sociologically even in the face of unequal coordination, as discussed in Chapter 7. How then do we justify them? We clearly cannot justify them merely on the Paretian claim that they make everyone better off unless we can say better off compared to some alternative. And when we try to do that, we are likely to find that not all are literally better off, that, indeed, some are worse off.

Hobbes tricked up a solution to this problem with two comparisons. The first was a comparison of an extant government to a gruesome state of nature. That comparison would plausibly make Stalin's regime a Pareto-preferred state. The second was a comparison of an extant regime to any alternative that we could get to through revolution. Given the costs of revolution that Hobbes inferred from the seventeenth-century English experience, most of us could not say we would be better off going through revolution even for a substantial improvement in our form of government. *Leviathan* was published in 1651 after three decades that have been described as 'economically among the most terrible in English history', and 'the 1640s were much the worst decade of the period'.[59] It was not unreasonable to attribute the ills to the drawn-out, violent, often seemingly random revolution.

Even with these comparisons, Hobbes clearly saw the difficulty in his mutual-advantage argument. There was no way to serve the mutual advantage of all in his England. In particular, in his time he thought there were two groups that were outside the pale of his account. Glory seekers actually preferred the turmoil, in which they could enjoy the dashing life of cavalier heroes. And religious fanatics were willing to destroy order if necessary to achieve their religious visions on earth. In our time, there are still religious fanatics who

---

[59] Christopher Hill, *The World Turned Upside Down: Radical Ideas during the English Revolution* (Harmondsworth, Middlesex: Penguin, 1975; 1st pub. 1972), 21, 107.

might be willing to risk all on behalf of their visions. And there are others who are pathologically willing to inflict massive harms to achieve modest goals and there are occasional sociopaths. It would be implausible to suppose they could all see some regime as mutually beneficial. Hobbes's solution of the problems of glory seekers and religious fanatics was to suppress, outlaw, or kill them—hardly a mutual-advantage resolution.

Hobbes's second comparison has been belied by too many experiences for us to believe it compelling in general. One could cite the US case, although it was not much of a revolution. Far more compelling are the astonishing recent cases in Eastern Europe and the late Soviet Union. These were revolutions of massive consequence at extremely low cost. Indeed, huge numbers of people in at least Czechoslovakia and East Germany must have got only great pleasure from the revolutions themselves, which may have been among the greatest and most enjoyable experiences in all history, experiences that would dwarf the sense of liberation that Lisa Peattie reports in Venezuela in the 1960s (see the epigraph to Chapter 5). In these cases, the price of revolution was not a cost; it was an additional, glorious benefit beyond the value of being in the new state.

One quip says that the revolution in Poland took ten years, that in East Germany took ten months, that in Czechoslovakia took ten days, and that in Romania took ten hours, with all of these revolutions culminating in 1989. There is a bit of stretching of the facts in this catalogue, but the general twist is right. Once the message got through that tipping from autocracy to something like democracy was possible, the tipping accelerated through these nations. The year 1989 is now etched in the minds of political scientists as a miracle beyond any expectation, so easily was its supposedly impossible result accomplished. Indeed, at least in economic policy, the tipping has continued in a sense into much of the quasi-socialist and statist Third World, for example, into India and some Latin American nations.

Hobbes went even further in his assessment of the costs of revolution. He supposed that even to seek substantial reform was to run great risk of civil war, so that merely seeking reform was not even in anyone's interest—indeed, politics altogether was not in anyone's interest. Perhaps he would have accepted the possibility that coordination could bring almost everyone to acquiescence with many possible governments even with open politics. In any case, this part of Hobbes's argument is essentially a sociological claim that must appear to most contemporary observers to be false in actual fact in many contexts, including in most nations of the advanced societies and perhaps in almost all nations today.

Hence, the short answer to Hobbes's trick must surely be that there is no ground for claiming that any extant government genuinely serves the mutual advantage of all citizens with respect to certain possible alternatives. The supposition on which Rawls's theory of justice is based is that we could organize society to change the degree to which the worst-off class is worst off. He might be wrong about that, but he is not so casually wrong as Hobbes's trick presumes. One might nevertheless give a welfarist justification of the reign of liberalism, constitutionalism, and democracy. But it would require some comparisons across persons if there can be no genuine claim of full mutual advantage.

There are two leading classes of mutual-advantage theory: contractarian and ordinal utilitarian. The fairness theory of Rawls also has a strong element of justification from mutual advantage. Contractarian theories require some version of consent. There is no credible account of any version of consent; that is to say, there is no plausible claim that all individuals in an actual society would agree to any particular general order of the society unless we reduce the claim of consent to virtual nonsense. Ordinal utilitarian theories are essentially ill-defined except for cases in which we move from one state to another that is Pareto superior to the original state. Even then, they are not fully compelling because there might be another state that would also be Pareto superior to the original state, and our ordinal utilitarianism might not be able to choose the one over the other Pareto superior state.

Rawlsian fairness seemingly salvages the claims of mutual advantage by giving us a rule for the selection of one from among many Pareto-optimal arrangements. (Again, an arrangement is Pareto optimal if there is no other arrangement to which we could move without making someone worse off.) Rawls's rule is that we select the arrangement that makes the worst-off class best off. We compare all possible arrangements of society and we first select that one or that set whose worst-off class is best off; then, if there is more than one such arrangement, we select from them that one or that set whose second worst-off class is best off; and so on until we have a single fairest mutual-advantage arrangement. If we define n classes, we might find at the end of n serial selections that there are still many arrangements that are all equally approved by the complete fairness plus mutual-advantage rule.

The horrendous problem for a Pareto choice is the multiplicity of arrangements that would be optimal. Rawls restricts the application of the Pareto rule and then uses his fairness consideration to narrow the choice to a single arrangement or at least a smaller set of arrangements. The horrendous problem for Rawls's device is, of course, to define classes. Anyone who thinks about that problem for very long might sooner be burdened with the usual Paretian indeterminacy.

A Summary of the Chapters

Chapters 2–4 take up liberalism, constitutionalism, and democracy in order. The burden of these chapters is to show that these are mutual-advantage theories that are workable when the society can be coordinated on them. The following three chapters take up dynamic issues in the workability of these, with special focus on the contemporary problems of newly liberalizing nations and (in Chapter 7) of societies in which there is little prospect of liberalism, constitutionalism, or democracy.

Chapter 2: Liberalism: Political and Economic

In its early days, the English tradition of welfarist liberalism addressed economic concerns of property and exchange at the individual and dyadic levels and political concerns of religious toleration at the collective or group level. Later additions include collective concerns in economic liberalism as in workers' unions and in the provision of collective goods; and individual liberties in political liberalism. While Locke and presumably Hobbes thought economic and political liberties were separable, they have been connected causally in many contexts and they seem connected conceptually through a common welfarist value theory.

(There is an enormous literature on other liberalisms, including liberty from social conventions, from private business institutions, and from poverty. And there are many claims for group liberties. Some of these lack the self-enforcing structure of coordination and none of them has played a role as grand as that of political and economic liberalism in the creation of prosperous liberal democracies. Some of these liberalisms are discussed in the Appendix.)

Chapter 3: Constitutionalism: Contract or Coordination?

A constitution coordinates a populace on a set of institutions that enable them jointly to be better off than they would be without coordination. It is commonly supposed that the establishment of government and, by implication, agreement on a constitution is the equivalent of a contract between the members of a society. Contracts generally regulate exchange relations, which have a specific strategic structure. The interaction that is resolved by coordination on a constitution cannot reasonably be thought to have this structure. Moreover, even a formal constitution, such as that written in 1787 for the United States, has more in common with a convention or certain kinds of norm than with a contract for two reasons: it involves very little actual agreement but only acquiescence; and it is self-enforcing in large part once it is established. It is maintained by the difficulty of re-coordination on any alternative. Hence it is not an analogue of a contract and the view that government is the product of a so-called social contract is misguided.

Chapter 4: Democracy: Agreement or Acquiescence?

The Federalist Caesar, writing in support of ratification of the US Constitution in 1787, asserted openly that, for government to succeed, it was not necessary for the populace to agree with what it did. Rather, they must generally only not mutiny against it. With such public statements, one might suppose Caesar was really an Anti-Federalist writing slyly to undercut support for the constitution. But his view was publicly echoed by Madison and other Federalists, who seemed to think this an argument genuinely in favour of the constitution that was before the people. In essence, the people were told that, once they elected representatives, their government would be able to work without their further agreement. Independently of whether the argument should have persuaded citizens to favour ratification, it was a correct strategic account of the workings of successful government.

Against the normative claims of many advocates of participatory democracy, participation at any significant level is not plausible for most citizens in a large polity, not even in one so small as the original thirteen states, whose population was about three million, roughly that of Chicago or Los Angeles today.

Chapter 5: Liberalization and Its Discontents

Since 1989 many nations of Eastern Europe and many now independent republics of the former Soviet Union have been liberalizing both their politics and their economies. Many other nations are liberalizing the one or the other. For example, for the first time in their collective history, all five nations of Central America have democratic regimes when a decade earlier only Costa Rica had democracy.[60]

The collapse of socialist economies in Eastern Europe, the former Soviet Union, and China is taken by many as evidence that egalitarian economic policies are hopelessly in conflict with productivity. Western economists generally suppose that greater productivity requires economic incentives that lead to great inequality. Even if this is false, it seems likely to be true that egalitarianism in one society cannot survive competition with inegalitarian reward structures in others. Egalitarianism is not self-enforcing if there is freedom of movement while greater rewards tend to go to the more productive. It may also be true that an ideology of egalitarianism cannot prosper without real-world examples or hopes.

Chapter 6: Constitutional Economic Transition

The main difficulty a constitutional regime faces once it has been successfully put in place is to manage the society through social change, especially economic change. Because theory about economic change has historically been poor and is still poor today, it follows that successful management of economic change cannot depend on getting the right economic theory into the constitution. If the American and a few other experiences are indicative of current and future prospects of successful constitutionalism, one must conclude that the best constitutional arrangement for handling economic transitions is to leave the economy relatively free of government management. As with the problem of egalitarianism, attempting to run against economic developments by reinforcing economic relations as

[60] Terry Lynn Karl, 'The Hybrid Regimes of Central America', *Journal of Democracy* (July 1995) 6: 72–86.

of some date is likely to leave a nation at an economic disadvantage in comparison to other nations in which the economy is less encumbered. A government that attempts to run the economy is therefore likely to be tarnished with economic failure. In the end, it was impending economic failure that broke the Soviet regime rather than seven decades of sometimes brutally illiberal social control.

Chapter 7: Democracy on the Margin

There are harsh limits on the possibilities of democracy. In general, democracy works only on the margins of great issues. Indeed, it is inherently a device for regulating marginal political conflicts. The few big issues it can handle are those on which there is broad consensus (such as the consensuses in the United Kingdom, and the United States on fighting World War II). Most forms of government could handle such issues more or less as well. For conflictive issues democracy can work only against a background of rough coordination on order. It will fail if conflict is so intense that one or more parties would sooner risk disorder than lose its issue, as did Royalists and Puritans in seventeenth-century England, the southern and northern states in the 1860s, Serbians and Croatians in the 1990s, and many other groups—or at least as did their leaders. Without that essentially prior coordination, democracy is trammelled or irrelevant. Democracy is in Hobbes's family of mutual-advantage devices and, if it does not serve the advantage of relevant interests in a society, it will be broken.

Afterword: Whether Agreed To Or Not

We first must know what can be done before we can conclude what ought to be done. In political discourse and in political philosophy, remarkably often the only issue is what we ought to do. Much of what writers conclude we ought to do cannot be done or cannot be expected to be done. If some societies attempted to do what they ostensibly ought to do, they could only cause harm. For example, much of the writing on democracy assumes that nations should be democratic. Yet, when Burundi attempted democratic government in 1993, the result was a blood bath beyond the capacity of anyone to control.

An extant government that serves mutual advantage merits our coordination on it to the extent that it serves our interests better than moving to an alternative would, counting both the advantages of being under the other government and the costs of making the transition to it. Even then, mutual advantage cannot be a general moral defence of any actual government of a nation that is at all pluralist in its groups' values. Other strong claims for the normative value of democracy are not compelling—except, perhaps, contingent causal claims that democracy achieves some good better than other forms of government could do.

The Central Controversies

Let me summarize the most important and, also, most controversial arguments of this work. My argument is, again, about *sociological mutual advantage* and is not a normative claim that liberalism, constitutionalism, or democracy genuinely serves the full mutual advantage (that is, the advantage of everyone). A constitution that works fits the interests of those who are politically efficacious. This need not even be a majority, as it was not for the initial US Constitution or for the South African Constitution during the era of white hegemony.

'Reasonable-agreement' or contractualist scholars, such as Thomas Scanlon and Brian Barry, want to claim the universal appeal of their conclusions, universal at least among reasonable people.[61] I think no conclusions in this realm have universal appeal (that is why the contractualist position, which is normative, is hollow). I am concerned with what works, not with 'what ought to be' in some fairly abstract sense. The position of many academics is not pragmatic in the sense of telling us what to do. Rather, its role is in saying how we ought to think about these issues. My vision is strictly pragmatic or positive. It is not about how discussion ought to proceed in the ether of academic life but about what can be made to work on the ground.

There are two theses in *Liberalism, Constitutionalism, and Democracy* that are likely to be controversial. The first of these is the

[61] Thomas Scanlon, 'Contractualism and Utilitarianism', in Amartya Sen and Bernard Williams, eds., *Utilitarianism and Beyond* (Cambridge: Cambridge University Press, 1982), Brian Barry, *Justice As Impartiality* (Oxford: Oxford University Press, 1995), esp. ch. 7. But see Hardin, 'Reasonable Agreement', 137–53. Also see further discussion in Chapter 4, section on 'Contractarianism'.

thesis that each of liberalism, constitutionalism, and democracy is a coordination theory, which runs against what is far and away the most widely held position, which is some variant of contractarianism, as in the contemporary reasonable-agreement school or in the Lockean, Kantian, or Rawlsian traditions. More traditional contractarians focus on the bargains that have to be negotiated and whose resolutions are backed normatively by the agreement reached on them in the constitutional contract. Reasonable-agreement theorists are concerned rather to determine what position reasonable persons must either accept (Barry's view) or must at least not reject (Scanlon's view). On constitutionalism, contractarian positions are virtually the only ones going, despite the obvious irrelevance of standard variants of contractarianism to any actual experience with constitutionalism. There cannot have been many intellectual schools on such an important topic that have been pursued in the face of such glaring irrelevance.

The second controversial thesis is the interpretation of the US Constitution as motivated centrally by the concern with commerce. Gordon Wood and many other historians read the debates very differently. Perhaps the two most common theses are (1) that the central issue in Philadelphia was the worry that democracy and the mob would attack property in the new society and (2) that the real conflict was, as the bulk of the debate suggests, between small and large states. I think the central concerns that made coordination on the constitution and the kind of national government it established possible were with order and commerce—it was to this extent a Hobbesian constitution. Everything else in Philadelphia was incidental or even a sideshow. That sideshow was enabled by the fact that there was successful coordination on the issues that mattered most.

The supposition that the gravity of the issues in Philadelphia is reflected simply in the time spent in debating them is extraordinarily misguided. A couple planning marriage might spend hours debating the details of the wedding but might be long past the need to spend any time at all debating whether they really should be getting married. It would therefore be perverse to say that the latter was a minor issue in comparison to the more extensively debated details of the wedding. The several dozen men who met in Philadelphia were in rough agreement on a form of economic union and order. That is the only reason the convention happened. Debates over some other issues were settled by compromise that could be enforced by the general kind of government that almost everyone at the convention coordinated on (in keeping with the sociological thesis of mutual advantage, only the politically effective groups needed to be coordinated). One could therefore accurately call the Philadelphia document the commercial constitution.

2

Liberalism: Political and Economic

In framing a government which is to be administered by men over men, the great difficulty lies in this: you must first enable the government to control the governed; and in the next place oblige it to control itself.

James Madison, *Federalist*, 51

The natural effort of every individual to better his own condition, when suffered to exert itself with freedom and security, is so powerful a principle, that it is alone, and without any assistance, not only capable of carrying on the society to wealth and prosperity, but of surmounting a hundred impertinent obstructions with which the folly of human laws too often incumbers its operations; though the effect of these obstructions is always more or less either to encroach upon freedom, or to diminish its security.

Adam Smith, *The Wealth of Nations*[1]

Two Liberalisms

Despite the singular term liberalism, there are two relatively distinct historical branches and a collection of variously titled modern branches (some of these latter are discussed in the Appendix). The historically articulated branches are political and economic liberalisms. One can paint the history of these two in broad strokes that miss detail but that capture the spirit of the development. Political liberalism began in the seventeenth century with the effort to establish a secular state in which some religious differences would

[1] Adam Smith, *An Inquiry into the Nature and Causes of the Wealth of Nations*, ed. R. H. Campbell, A. S. Skinner, and W. B. Todd (Oxford: Oxford University Press, 1976; 1st pub. 1776; reprinted by Liberty Press, 1979), book 4, ch. 5, p. 540.

be tolerated. It arose to counter universalistic religious views whose proponents were so ardent as to wish to impose those views by force. In the face of such commitments, diverse religions must conflict, perhaps fatally. In a sense, then, political liberalism was an invention to resolve a then current, awful problem. Its proponents were articulate and finally persuasive.

There have been many comparable social inventions, many of which have failed, as communism, egalitarianism, and perhaps socialism have all failed to date, although it is often the fate of failed political theories to be resuscitated by later generations. The extraordinary thing about political liberalism is that it seems to have succeeded in its authors' initial hope for it. It may have helped end the turmoil occasioned by religious differences and it may even have enabled the decline of disruptive religious fervour. Political liberalism has since expanded in various ways under other influences and, if it were not for Islamic fundamentalism with its seemingly coercive theocratic programme and the issue of abortion with its religious debate on the nature of the zygote and fetus, we might no longer today associate religious conflict with the core of liberalism in its actual practice.[2]

In contrast to political liberalism, economic liberalism more or less grew, mostly out of conspicuous view. It was analysed and understood retrospectively rather than prospectively. It came into being without a party or an intellectual agenda. By the time Bernard Mandeville, Adam Smith, and others came to analyse it, they were analysing characteristics of their own society, some of which had been developing over many centuries. In so far as the early economic liberals had programmes, these were for reforms of political practice to end elements of state-sponsored monopoly and protection, to create, as Thomas Carlyle quipped, anarchy with a constable.[3] But perhaps the large bulk of daily economic activity was already market-driven by the time these authors wrote. Indeed, part of Mandeville's purpose was to give a moral (welfarist) justification for the supposedly immoral greed which drives markets to greater production. As he put it, public virtue comes from private vice.[4]

---

[2] Religious belief as a marker of community, as in Northern Ireland and India, may still wreak havoc.

[3] Contemporary Russians know that it takes more. In particular, it takes a working law of contracts to enable future oriented action.

[4] Bernard Mandeville, *The Fable of the Bees: Private Vices, Publick Benefits*, ed. F. B. Kaye (Oxford: Oxford University Press, 1924; 1st pub. 1714; reprinted by Liberty Press, 1988).

There is a substantial literature that attempts to tie these two liberal traditions together, either conceptually, logically, or causally.
For example, a common claim is that both liberalisms are fundamentally emancipatory. I will discuss some of these claims below. But I
think that the two have not been convincingly shown to be closely
tied historically in any of these ways. Indeed, I think that the most
compelling view is that the core concern of political liberalism is the
individual, while the dominant concern in the main, long tradition of
economic liberalism that passes through Smith is focused on the general prosperity of the society, not on individual advantage.

Causally, the two liberalisms may often be opportunistically
linked, as when a state powerful enough to override one of them is
therefore also powerful enough to override the other, as was the
practice throughout the formerly Communist world. But a state
could evidently choose, as the Asian Tigers and now China, have
done, to suppress political liberty while supporting a substantial
degree of economic liberty. Or it could, as India under Nehru and
his progeny did for more than forty years (disastrously for the mass
of the Indian people), control the economy fairly rigidly while per-
mitting broad political liberty.

In an era of great prosperity, however, the two liberalisms may
finally begin to be tied inextricably together through their value theories. These value theories have been relatively separable for many or
even most people when economic demands have been far from satisfied, as in Thomas Hobbes's remark that first we must eat and then
we turn to politics.[5] As material wants are very well provided for,
people may be increasingly willing to forego some individual material benefits for other concerns. But historically, the only way the two
liberalisms appear clearly to be related is that they both sociologically serve mutual advantage in many, but perhaps not all, societies
in which they have prevailed.

Why is there such a difference in the intellectual bases of the
two liberalisms? The most transparent reason is that the two liberalisms were addressed to logically different problems. In its early
days, political liberalism, which addressed the freedom of the individual, could be accomplished only collectively so that its resolution was essentially a collective issue. It required a substantial shift
in social views and in political organization. Economic liberalism,

[5] Thomas Hobbes, *De Cive*, ed. Howard Warrender (Oxford: Clarendon Press,
1983; 1st pub. 1651), II. 5. 5.

which addressed the welfare of the larger society, could be accomplished through piecemeal, typically small-number interactions that matter directly only piecemeal to a few in each case rather than collectively to all or very many at once. Liberal economic practices could arise spontaneously in some contexts and slowly spread to others.

It might at first sound odd that the problem of individual autonomy could only be resolved collectively, while the problem of collective welfare could be resolved to a substantial extent piecemeal by individuals. But those are the compelling logics of the two liberalisms as they worked their separate transformations on English society. That is why economic liberalism had a slow and relatively quiet history before its power was recognized and finally touted, whereas the arrival or creation of political liberalism was a noisier and more dramatic event that perhaps needed touting to get it on the agenda. Because either of them could be wrecked by the state, they both finally depend on state permission; and either one might sometimes need active state action on its behalf. But in many nations in many periods, they are self-reinforcing once they are in place because they both serve the mutual advantage of almost everyone, which is to say that almost no one stands to benefit from ending them.

We may eventually choose to have an overarching regime of economic regulation—as in contract law—that is itself a collective resolution. Indeed, as Hobbes saw the problem, social order is collectively achieved, and therefore we are able to have stable property relations. Although he did not make the argument, we may reasonably suppose he held that either we resolve the problems of property and exchange the same way for all or we do not resolve them. I cannot alone achieve order in the midst of chaos for all others.

But for Hobbes, order was so paramount and so much at risk that he thought we must have absolute authority in a single sovereign power to keep us in line. Hobbes may have been right in thinking that the problem of weak sovereignty is political activity, which might lead to chaos. But Hobbes went further, concluding that we must even submit to our sovereign's choice of religious practices, because religious differences cause strife that is grossly disorderly. John Locke supposed we might simply set religious political impulses aside and let our state regulate only such things as property relations. People might disagree as they will on religion, but they

could be prohibited from taking action against one another in fur-
therance of their beliefs.[6]

The Grounds of Liberalism

Liberalism has come to us bifurcated in another way. It has both welfarist and deontological variants. In the welfarist variant, a liberal
principle is judged good for what good it does us. In the deontological variant, the principle may be judged good in its own right, perhaps from intuition, perhaps by deduction from some other
principle such as autonomy. As may already be evident, I will generally be concerned with the welfarist tradition, which I think has been
the central driving force politically. Moreover, it is only in the welfarist tradition that one might hope to see a coherent joining of political and economic liberalisms.

In the deontological variant we are given a list of the things that are
right for us to do or that no one may be morally permitted to block
us from doing. The deontological tradition has manifold conflicting
visions within it. Although some of these visions are claimed to
descend from transcendental deduction, many, perhaps all, turn on
bald intuitions that are not widely accepted. For example, the deontological libertarians just happen to know somehow that we have
certain property and other political and economic rights, no matter
that no one may ever positively have had such rights under an actual
constitutional regime. Unfortunately deontological libertarians do
not agree with each other as to what those rights are. More generally,
no deontological position has been developed as extensively as the
welfarist position and none has benefited from a comparably rich
history of criticism and debate. And none is backed by any substantial part of the polity of an advanced democratic society, as welfarism
generally is. Political deontology is almost entirely an academic
sideshow, as is suggested by its frequent cleverness. It is too clever by
half to be a theory for the real world.

The historical anthropologist Leslie White asserts that 'the economic systems of civil society are impersonal, nonhuman, and

[6] Locke worried about Catholics on the ground that they held allegiance to an
alternative political authority in Rome, but not on the ground of their specific religious beliefs otherwise.

nonethical, which, in terms of *human* relationships and values, means impersonal, inhumane, and unethical'.[7] This is a commonplace but shallow misunderstanding. On Hobbes's view, White is obviously wrong. The values of survival and prosperity are clearly human and worthy. Maintaining, even with the threat of limited coercion, an economic and enforcement system to provide these things is therefore good. White goes on to lament pirates and cheats who abuse their fellows for their own benefit. This is a lament about humanity, unethical humanity perhaps, but humanity to the core. The market may enable us to do more lying and cheating than we could in a woefully primitive state, in which there might be much less to lie or cheat about, but it also enables us to serve our interests through production and thereby to benefit others.[8] The market and the political regime that focuses entirely on it may scant other moral concerns, such as fairness and political liberties, but they can still do one big, good thing very well.

In a related complaint, Daniel Bell says that society rests on moral justification of authority and that consumption cannot provide such a justification.[9] Again, Hobbes's vision is compellingly contrary. Surely it is commonly good that we be able to satisfy our urges for consumption, including consumption of education, music, culture, and so forth, as well as consumption of material goods. A supremely successful system of production might provide us with opportunity for satisfying many desires for consumptions that Bell and others think not in our interests or not for the good of our characters. But such consumptions will happen to some extent even in a more primitive economy. The difference between the very primitive economy or anarchy as Hobbes supposed it must be and a very productive economy surely is predominantly good even on Bell's view. But if it is good, then the justification of authority that makes the system work is simply that it is good. Hence, consumption can give a moral grounding for political authority that is used to enhance opportunities for economic exchange and production.

It follows that the early economic and political liberalisms were moral positions. They addressed problems of welfare. The actual

<hr />

[7] Leslie A. White, *The Evolution of Culture: The Development of Civilization to the Fall of Rome* (New York: McGraw-Hill, 1959), 346.

[8] It would be anachronistic to call their view Benthamite, but Mandeville and Smith clearly valued economic liberty for its general effects on all.

[9] Daniel Bell, *The Cultural Contradictions of Capitalism* (London: Heinemann, 1976), 77.

content of the resolution of the political problem matters, whereas the choice of resolutions of the economic problem could vary over many possibilities, all roughly as good as far as economic liberalism is concerned. Hence, our choice is merely a matter of coordination on one of the acceptable forms. This is Hobbes's argument for government. Recall that the central problems he was concerned to resolve were survival and the economic problem. In his simple vision, government is strictly external to the economy. It facilitates and enables us to engage in economic activities.

The Welfarist Core

To use modern terminology that was not his, Hobbes's defence of maintaining order is essentially utilitarian, not deontological. Government has no value in its own right; it is merely a means to the end of human welfare. It is therefore subordinate to economics. In his welfarism, Hobbes is consistent with most of the Anglo-Saxon liberal tradition. The concern of the Levellers with political equality, Locke's theory of property, and some of Mill's justifications of political liberties were not apparently welfarist.[10] But the general tendency to a utilitarian reading of the law[11] over the nineteenth and twentieth centuries seems to have been preceded and accompanied by welfarist readings of the purpose of constitutional law. Perhaps merely as a result of the intellectual tastes of the era, therefore, the welfarist view of liberty is much more richly developed than any other.[12]

Another part of the Anglo-Saxon tradition is a commitment to pragmatic scepticism, as in Hobbes's supposition that we cannot really know enough to choose one particular form of government over another as being more in our interest. Pragmatic scepticism also

[10] Not surprisingly, in their egalitarianism the Levellers appealed both to welfarist considerations—society will be better off—and to deontological considerations that sound like natural rights, even, in Jefferson's term, unalienable rights. See Edmund S. Morgan, *Inventing the People: The Rise of Popular Sovereignty in England and America* (New York: Norton, 1988), 70–1; Gerard Winstanley, *The Law of Freedom in a Platform or, True Magistracy Restored*, ed. Robert W. Kenny (New York: Shocken, 1941; 1st pub. 1652).

[11] H. L. A. Hart, 'Between Utility and Rights', in Hart, *Essays in Jurisprudence and Philosophy* (Oxford: Oxford University Press, 1983; essay first published 1979), 198–222, at p. 198.

[12] See further, Russell Hardin, 'The Morality of Law and Economics', *Law and Philosophy*, 11 (Nov. 1992): 331–84, esp. 380–4.

plays a more clearly fundamental role in welfarist liberalism. We may simply concede many value commitments to other people: if you like chocolate then chocolate is good for you, at least in so far as it contributes to your pleasure. There may be other considerations that trump this one in a particular instance, but your liking of chocolate makes your consumption of it prima-facie good.

For some apparent value commitments, however, we cannot so readily concede. Some values, such as religious values, depend on beliefs about what is true. If I believe god's will is that people X should be destroyed, then I may also believe it is good for people X to be destroyed. If you question my prior belief about what god wills, however, you automatically question the inference I have drawn about the goodness of an action or policy. If we note that there are dozens of religions with contrary visions of what is good or right, and if we can find no way to establish the truth of one of these, we have reason, with Locke, simply to be sceptical. This is a central move in Locke's argument on religious toleration.[13] We should not impose religious views on others when we have such strong, in-principle grounds for scepticism about the correlation of religious truth with political leadership.

Mill's relatively libertarian views have a similar grounding in scepticism. I cannot know that your tastes and preferences are in truth inferior to mine. There may be some objective truths about welfare, such as that smoking or drinking wine laced with lead is dangerous to your health, and that you most likely value your health. But your preference for reading great literary classics and mine for attending the latest junk movie, while potentially subject to revision after debate and a bit of testing, just are our preferences. A welfarist thinks making people better off is good. Since individuals are the subject of welfarist concern, the welfarist must concede that the individual must have substantial say about what is her good. Hence, the welfarist Mill makes a Hobbesian argument for the defence of political liberties. To do so coherently, one need only reject Hobbes's dismal sociology.

Both liberalisms were *de facto* directed at welfare in large part. Economic liberalism, with its defence in Hobbesian theory and in increasingly utilitarian thinking from Mandeville to Hume and Smith, is conspicuously welfarist. Political liberalism, with its avoid-

---

[13] John Locke, *A Letter concerning Toleration* (Indianapolis: Bobbs-Merrill, 1950; 1st pub. 1689).

ance of especially destructive religious conflicts, enables individuals to seek their own values. But material welfare is not all that matters even to a welfarist. Welfarists may benefit and think others also benefit from political criticism, cultural developments, and general freedom from being monitored and controlled by someone else. Hobbes was evidently motivated by such values in his own life. Locke came closer to expressing concern for such values.

Perhaps at low levels of economic development, these values are essentially not coupled, either causally or conceptually. Without the wherewithal to secure life and well-being, few people will be greatly concerned with civil liberties that they have neither the time nor the resources to take up. But at some point, these values seem to involve both economic and political liberties. If they do, then an economic liberal must finally also be a political liberal. Why might Hobbes not have been? Perhaps only for the sociological reason that he thought political liberties must threaten economic prospects by leading to civil war. But perhaps he also lacked the more extensive value theory that puts economic and civil liberty benefits into a joint account of welfare—this move comes later in the hands of the utilitarian economists of the nineteenth century. Or perhaps both he and Locke looked upon a society much less wealthy than modern industrial capitalism and naturally therefore weighed material considerations relatively more heavily than we might.

Deontological Additions

Hobbes's theory requires only one general normative notion: some variant of welfarism that we may call Hobbesian efficiency.[14] In his *Second Treatise of Government*, Locke introduced one and plausibly two normative notions that are not welfarist. First, he presented a deontological-rights theory of appropriation under certain

[14] For further discussion of Hobbesian efficiency and its normative limits, see Hardin, 'Magic on the Frontier: The Norm of Efficiency', *University of Pennsylvania Law Review*, 144 (May 1996): 1987–2020. It is Pareto efficient to make a change that makes some better off and none worse off. Hobbesian efficiency is an early grasp of the core concern in Paretian efficiency in contexts of choosing between government and anarchy (which, in Hobbes's view, entails chaos and grievous losses to all). It yields a resolution only because Hobbes supposes we know too little to distinguish between the benefits we would receive from one form of government (e.g. monarchy) and those from another form (e.g. oligarchy). Hence, epistemological constraints play as strong a role for Hobbes as they do for Locke in his arguments for religious toleration.

conditions (conditions that may generally not be relevant for any
society that might take an interest in Locke's theory), so that his
nascent economic liberalism is, unlike Hobbes's, not strictly welfarist. Secondly, Locke was a nascent democrat, and his commitment
to limited democratic principles may well have been an immediate
deontological concern. It is plausible, however, to read his theory of
government as welfarist. In bringing the focus of political liberty
back to the individual, Mill also often seems to have had a deontological commitment to 'one very simple principle' of liberty.[15]

In much of current discussion, political liberalism is seen as a matter of neutrality with respect to life values or plans of life. The notion
of a plan of life must seem preposterous to many people who wonder how they got where they are while wondering where they will go
from there. According to a quip, life is what happens to us while we
are making other plans—and it is often much saner than the plans.
But if we can escape the florid rhetoric of the life-plans crowd from
Mill onwards,[16] most of us may grant that we are moderately to
strongly committed to various values. Is the point of liberal protection to let us foster and fulfil those values? This might be a reasonable inference even from Hobbes if we have rejected his dismal
political sociology. But clearly, liberalism was not driven by neutrality in earlier times. In particular, it was deployed, as by Locke, to
support the suppression of some manifestations of religious belief.
Standard Anglo-Saxon scepticism about others' minds and their
pleasures might lead us for epistemological reasons to plump for letting them decide their own good, as Mill does. Some of the present
commitment to neutrality, however, seems deontological rather than
merely welfarist. It is morally grounded with Locke's theory of the
appropriation of property. I have the value, and by god therefore it's
my right to have it or it's right that I have it.

In contemporary writings, political and economic liberalism are
often held separate, either explicitly or implicitly. For example, the
recent spate of writings on the liberal's supposedly foundational
concern with neutrality is almost entirely about political liberalism.
Economic liberalism through most of its variants is not neutral with

---

[15] John Stuart Mill, *On Liberty*, in Mill, *Essays on Politics and Society*, ed. J. M.
Robson, *Collected Works of John Stuart Mill* (Toronto: University of Toronto Press,
1977), xviii, ch. 1, para. 9.

[16] Mill, *On Liberty*, ch. 1, para. 12. For a clear and important discussion, see John
Rawls, *A Theory of Justice* (Cambridge, Mass.: Harvard University Press, 1971),
407–16.

respect to values. It tends strongly to favour welfarist values that can be enhanced through production and exchange. Economic liberals may be neutral with respect to who gets welfare, but they are not neutral on what counts as the central value, which is welfare. If other values are to come into consideration, most of the writers in the long Anglo-Saxon tradition of economic liberalism would have to bring these other values in by treating them as components of welfare. They might even have to make Mill's move of treating these other values as he did free speech, of making them valuable as means to greater welfare.

Incidentally, it seems clear that even in what one might argue is his commitment to economic liberalism, Hobbes has little in common with many contemporary libertarians. Libertarian theory is often deontologically grounded in intuitions about specific rights, such as rights of property ownership and rights to voluntary dyadic exchange. For Hobbes, rights have force or interest only if they are positively backed by a coercive government. Moreover, although it is somewhat tendentious to claim Hobbes has a clear position on an issue he did not explicitly recognize, he seems to have been moved to value property and exchange for their welfare effects, not for their prior rightness in some other sense.

Libertarians often argue from dyadic relations exclusively, not allowing any move that trumps these.[17] This is supposed to follow from a deontological commitment to consent or autonomy.[18] We might more readily think we should move, with Hobbes, from the overall achievement of, say, order or welfare to the dyadic-level achievement of exchange. For Hobbes, the social construction of welfare obviously overwhelmingly trumps what individuals can accomplish. If Hobbes was right about his implicit sociological claim here, then libertarian economic liberalism is, at its base, wrong in its individual and dyadic focus. It, too, must be pragmatically grounded in the larger social achievement. Moreover, we might wonder with Mill why dyadic agreements must trump collective concerns, as in early state interventions in unionized worker relations with business.

One way to characterize the difference between utilitarianism and libertarianism is to say that the utilitarian would consider the value of the overall result of dyadic choosing to be itself a potential matter

---

[17] Robert Nozick, *Anarchy, State, and Utopia* (New York: Basic Books, 1974).
[18] See further, Russell Hardin, 'To Rule in No Matters, To Obey in None', *Contemporary Philosophy*, 13/12 (Nov.–Dec. 1991): 6–12, esp. 7–8.

for collective choice. Some libertarians would commonly rule out such a move. In his paradox of liberalism, Amartya Sen virtually defines liberalism as a matter of what *at most* dyads would do.[19] In this paradox, each of two players has one right only, and the only additional choice rule is a requirement of unanimity that, whenever both agree, their choice will be the social choice. With these radically limited choice rules, we can still produce what Sen takes to be a paradoxical result, as follows.

You have the single right to have pink walls; I have the single right to have next Sunday free from labour. I hate your pink walls so much, however, that I am willing to spend Sunday painting them chartreuse. You hate chartreuse and have a right to keep your walls pink, but you would enjoy seeing me work all day.[20] We agree to my painting your walls. But that violates your right to pink walls and my right to the day off. Or so Sen perversely argues. Most commentators on this result seem to find no paradox. In ordinary life—no theorist's cute contrivance—I have a right to keep my money from you and you have the right to keep your car from me, and yet we may both happily engage in a trade. Hence, the usual liberal economic right to exchange is strategically an instance of Sen's supposed paradox (if there are no other people affected by our exchange). *Any putative liberalism that would make voluntary exchange paradoxical is of no interest.*[21] Sen's earliest examples of his paradox typically blend material and non-material welfare considerations. In later defences, Sen implicitly argues that it matters what the content of the violated rights is. He then resorts to particular intuitions about rights that presumably are not grounded in welfare and that he thinks should trump individuals' willingness to trade when the trading would violate these rights.[22] This move puts us in the land of

[19] Amartya Sen, 'The Impossibility of a Paretian Liberal', *Journal of Political Economy* 78 (1970): 152–7.

[20] Political philosophy ranges from the sublime to the ridiculous.

[21] If elaborated in this way, Sen's paradox requires a fourth condition. In addition to having two individual rights and the principle of dyadic agreement (Sen speaks of unanimity), he now adds the random intuition about the wrongness of a particular outcome. That these conditions cannot universally be satisfied is no paradox. For discussion of further problems with Sen's paradox, see Hardin, *Morality within the Limits of Reason*, 108–13. In particular, Sen speaks of unanimity when what he means is agreement of two people in a two-person society. In such a society, rights talk is pointless.

[22] See e.g. Amartya Sen, 'Liberty as Control: An Appraisal', in *Social and Political Philosophy*, vol. vii of *Midwest Studies in Philosophy*, eds. Peter A. French, Theodore E. Uehling, Jr., and Howard K. Wettstein (Minneapolis: University of Minnesota Press, 1982), 207–21.

whimsy. Heaven help us if I have the trumping intuition that no one should have pink walls. You say my intuition does not trump? You are wrong.

An alternative seeming justification of liberalism could be read from an alternative vision of it, a non-welfarist vision. One of the vocabularies of liberalism is of rights, as in Locke's early discussion, and some liberals conceive the range of liberalisms as merely a range of rights. For example, T. H. Marshall conceived liberalism as a succession of citizenship rights from the legal and political realm to the social realm.[23] Citizenship cannot be properly exercised without suffrage, equality before the law, and finally what one might call equality of political power. The latter requires substantial controls on the uses of wealth and substantial social welfare programmes to give individuals the intellectual and economic resources to participate well.[24] At some point, this vision must deal with the possibility of trade-offs between political equality and other concerns. The alternative would be simply to assert political equality as the overarching moral constraint. But full political equality is impractical in many ways. For trivial example, if we must have representative government, then those who are elected to office will be more than equal. Nevertheless, we would want to have representatives in order to achieve various purposes. Hence, we have to trade the greater hope of achieving those purposes against full political equality.

Strategic Structures

The problems that the two liberalisms address are strategically quite different in senses to be spelled out below. Some involve protections of individuals, some of dyads, some of collectivities. Their role, however, is the same: to make social interaction and life better. To do this well, the major methodological task that each must resolve is to generate information that can direct what the economy and society produce. The liberal market works in such a way that it does not even require aggregate accounting of its achievement, although better

[23] T. H. Marshall, *Citizenship and Social Class* (Cambridge: Cambridge University Press, 1950).
[24] See further, Thomas Christiano, *The Rule of the Many: Fundamental Issues in Democratic Theory* (Boulder, Colo.: Westview Press, 1996).

information may help agents make better decisions and plans. A liberal polity does require aggregate accounting. Trivially, for example, if it is democratic, it requires accounting of votes. But it may typically require even some central economic accounting, as it might in attempting to correct for non-marketable external effects of various economic activities, such as pollution (much of liberal debate has focused on nuisance law).

For both liberalisms, the role of the state and government seems itself to be collective—in a given polity, we all have the same government. Hence, one might say that government is a collective issue in liberalism and one might say that one class of relationships in a liberal society is that between the individual and the government. But the issues government addresses need not be collective. For example, for Hobbes the establishment or maintenance of a sovereign is a collective result but the purpose of this collective resolution is protection of individuals and dyads. For Locke, government is a device for resolving or managing issues, such as the protection of my property. The strategic structures of liberalism that I wish to discuss in the limited space here are those of the issues government is to address, not the structure of creation or maintenance of government itself or of the relationship of individuals or groups to government.

Hobbes

Let us simplify the problems of political and economic liberalism as merely the maintenance of certain civil and political liberties for political liberalism and the protection of the market for economic liberalism. To see that these need not be logically tied, although they might be causally related, consider the theory of Hobbes, arguably the greatest of all political theorists. Although Hobbes is not always counted as a major font of liberal thought, he is particularly interesting for understanding liberalism because he made material, more-or-less economic concerns paramount and he generally deplored political liberty as likely to interfere with the order necessary for economic welfare. Hobbes did not have an articulate economic theory but only an economic purpose: welfare. Only later, especially in the works of Mandeville and Smith, was there a compelling theory to connect welfare to economic liberty.

Hobbes's solution of the problem of economic liberalism and related material concerns (pre-eminently survival, but also stable expectations and material accumulation) entailed wholesale violation of political liberalism. He proposed orderly suppression of political activities by an autocratic sovereign. Contrary to the association more commonly assumed today, Hobbes evidently thought that political liberty is causally associated with the violation of economic liberty. At its extreme, political liberty could produce anarchy and chaotic violence that would destroy economic activities. Even modest efforts at political reform can start a society on the slide into chaos.

In brief, Hobbes's solution of the economic problem is as follows.[25] What we all need to enable us to construct good lives for ourselves is police protection for stable expectations and enforceable agreements. With these, we can escape the constant fear that others will take from us and the associated incentive to harm others preemptively; we can have property; and we can faithfully enter into exchanges, even over time.[26] As a result, we can make our own lives better. This is a very simple set of requirements, which many possible forms of government could meet. Indeed, given how little we know about the workings of different forms of government, we cannot even say with great confidence that one form is better than others. Hobbes thought the balance favours monarchy, unless we already have some other form.

It is often assumed that the basis of Hobbes's theory is consent, because he spoke of a social contract to resolve the problem of anarchy. But he also spoke of conquest and other usurpations of accidental history as means for achieving sovereignty that works. For him, it did not matter whether we constructed our government or had it imposed on us. What really matters is only this: that government provide order. His tale of the social contract is a just-so story that many readers illicitly turn into a normative canon by ignoring his acceptance of conquest and usurpation on an equal footing with deliberate construction of government, which he openly supposes may never have happened.

The order we want is an order that allows each of us to enter into exchanges with others as we choose and not to be coerced or harmed by others. We want orderly dyadic relations. Such relations will tend

---

[25] For a fuller account, see Russell Hardin, 'Hobbesian Political Order', *Political Theory*, 19/2 (May 1991): 156–80.
[26] Hobbes speaks of enforcing promises. The vocabulary of exchange is a later efflorescence.

to be very productive in the long run in ways that Mandeville, Hume, and Smith focused on in their own visions of economic liberalism. This is the core of the problem Hobbes's theory was intended to resolve: dyadic interactions in which order and general benefit require that only certain moves be allowed. The allowed moves are those in which both parties gain from an exchange, not those in which one party takes and the other loses. We may split this category into two: dyadic exchange and individual property ownership. Some theorists make exchange a part of ownership, but one might read Hobbes as making ownership derivative from protecting against coerced exchange or theft. In any case, the problem Hobbes resolved was the protection of each individual in potential interaction with each other.

In Hobbes's vision, our problem of sovereignty, of a powerful authority that can impose order, is not itself an exchange problem and we therefore cannot resolve it by merely making a deal to be cooperative hereafter. There is no one to enforce our agreement if we do this. The problem is to succeed in achieving *coordination on one of the possible forms of government* that could give us order in our dyadic relations by, when necessary, coercively blocking coerced exchanges and theft and by guaranteeing that we fulfil our contractual agreements when we cannot exchange immediately but must spread our exchange over time. In Hobbes's sociology, achieving this order is a virtually pure coordination problem in which we all share the same interest.

This is a striking vision to anyone who thinks of politics as inherently about conflict of interests (or who thinks of Hobbes as the pre-eminent conflict theorist). Perhaps Hobbes implicitly agreed that that is what politics more broadly is about but also supposed government should stay out of such politics and concern itself with order. His actual argument, however, is merely the following two steps. First, if we are in a state of anarchy, as during civil war, our ignorance of the likely details of various governments lets each of us treat some set of these as indifferently equally good and as enormously better than continued anarchy. Secondly, if we are under a working government that some now think to be not as much in their interests as some other might be, still we should all recognize that any effort to improve it a little bit has too great a risk of tipping us into anarchy. Hence, again, we all share an identical interest in maintaining the current regime, so that we face merely a pure coordination with a single universally best outcome. This is the easiest of all strategic interactions to resolve if all are properly informed.

There have been many apparent Hobbesians in political power. Such military coup leaders as Park in South Korea and Pinochet in Chile, and the drab, mortmain leadership of China that quashed the democracy movement in 1989 may have cared primarily about economic development and performance. They abridged political liberties in order to maintain a firm hand on the order that they believed would bring economic prosperity.

Hobbes has given us an economic justification for having a regime or even for keeping the regime we have. But we cannot use that justification to argue for what a regime ought to do, because once we delve below the level of justifying the grand regime, we cannot suppose many of the important problems are merely pure coordinations. Eventually, economic and political concerns merge in many areas. The finer points of contract or other law may not be matters of mere coordination. Adopting any particular rule may systematically advantage one class of parties over another. Hence, in its detail, law is not a simple matter of coordination even if the choice of what form of general regime to have was, as Hobbes argued, such a simple matter.

Having a political system available to resolve the details of law may be a matter of mere coordination. But the issues that system itself faces are typically not merely coordination problems. For example, in an issue on which law is unsettled, settling it one way or another is likely to benefit one class of parties relative to another class or to apportion benefits in one way rather than another. The recommendation of contemporary law and economics in many contexts is to assign an unsettled right in the way that is productively most beneficial overall, for example by assigning the right in the way that minimizes transaction costs.[27] One might imagine it eminently reasonable *ex ante* to adopt this principle for settling new problems and we might all happily coordinate on this rather than any other rule. Yet in an actual application of the principle, there is no longer a matter of pure coordination. I may lose much of what you gain.

---

[27] For a clear statement and argument, see A. Mitchell Polinsky, *An Introduction to Law and Economics* (Boston: Little, Brown, 1989, 2nd edn.), 13.

Locke

Both liberalisms—political and economic—can be achieved through collective devices. But, as noted in the opening section above, early political liberalism required collective resolution, whereas economic liberalism could partially work its way without collective resolution. Locke shared much of Hobbes's vision of the need for collective protection of property and exchange and was an economic liberal. But he was especially exercised by the political problems of religious diversity.[28] Locke supposed, in part for epistemological reasons familiar from later utilitarian social theorists, that the best way to organize society was on weakly democratic principles. If people—for Locke this was restricted to a few—participate in their own governance, their interests are likely to be better addressed.

This requirement is inherently collective. It is not merely about dyadic relations, but about group relations, as when, for example, religious beliefs create group interests. The problem is how to incorporate groups into the polity. For a Hobbesian or even a traditional monarchist, this was not a problem: religious groups need not be incorporated; they need only be controlled or suppressed. But for Locke, incorporation was inherently required by democratic commitment. Locke's way of incorporating religious groups was itself, however, almost Hobbesian. He simply required that they leave their religion out of politics. By implication, Catholics could not be incorporated in England, because their religion gave them an alternative political authority outside England. Hence, their religion was inherently political.[29]

Locke's economic liberalism was intellectually messier than his political liberalism. It focused on property, which was a very broad notion for Locke, including one's body and life, as well as external material holdings. It is a loose category that he used very loosely. His readers may fail to read the term as broadly as Locke did, however, because his central discussion of coming to own something by mixing one's labour with it is largely about external holdings, such as apples. Although there are welfarist sentiments laced through his argument, his principal justification of ownership seems to be deon-

---

[28] Locke, *Toleration*.
[29] Locke, ever careful, wrote of Mahometans rather than Catholics (*Toleration*, 51–2). Also, atheists could not be trusted because they could not bind themselves with an oath whose violation would bring punishment after death (ibid., 52).

tological. Subject to the constraint that I leave enough for others, I own what I work over. In his own time, Locke seems to have thought this theory could apply to America but not to England. In our time, it cannot apply to anything but philosophical history and, until a few decades ago, Antarctica. Locke was the first major philosopher to advocate both economic and political liberalism, but he made no claim for their being logically or empirically related. Such claims reach their fullest development in the work of Ludwig von Mises and Friedrich Hayek after the rise of the Soviet state.

Smith

Smith went beyond Hobbes's concern with protection of my own property and my own stable expectations that would justify my developing it. He argued further that each individual's welfare depends on the productivity of others. If this is true, then letting people pursue their self-interest is the way to enhance not only their own welfare but that of others. While this might seem to be merely an economic theory, it is inherently also a liberal political theory because it implies that cutting people free from economic constraints imposed by government makes them all better off.

Smith, as Mandeville before him also did, turned the tables on the notion that our well-being depends on beneficence to say, on the contrary, that a truly beneficent government would generally leave us to follow our own self-interests. Economic liberalism is a moral political theory that paradoxically has at its core Mandeville's private vice of selfishness. This seeming rot at the core of Anglo-Saxon liberalism has been the focus of much of the criticism of it and even the cause of scorn for it. But the association of self-interest with collective good is strongly reinforced by Smith's sense that economic knowledge is decentralized and not well mastered by government.

This issue is not a matter of rotten character on the part of the economic actors but is rather merely a matter of the limited epistemology of government or any other single institutional actor. It has become the central concern of twentieth-century Austrian economics, which is arguably a more important and perspicuous political than economic theory. Epistemological limits played a role in Hobbes's conclusion in favour of an all-powerful sovereign, but for the Austrians such limits argue for a very weak government, at least in economic affairs. A weak government in economic affairs is apt to

Liberalism

imply weak government in general, because a government with great power to control any particular thing is apt to be able to use that power in far more general ways. Control of politics might be separable from control of economics in principle, but they are apt to go together in practice.

Madison

Madison, his fellow conventioneers, and his co-authors of the *Federalist Papers*, were engaged in making liberalism work and were therefore concerned with institutional structures. They were the workers on the ground who made sense of the theories of Montesquieu, Locke, Smith, and others. Of these men, Madison was singularly the deepest thinker and the greatest architect of the new constitution. He clearly thought Montesquieu fundamentally mistaken in the latter's central claim that only a small republic, with its homogeneity of interests and opinions, could hope to have stable government. Madison held, on the contrary, that the worst threat to liberty in the United States was from the state governments. He thought a national government would give better protection against the tyrannies of petty, local majorities.[30] He therefore wanted a strong national government, but that meant strong relative to the state governments. He mainly wanted to break the power of the states, which he might as soon have eliminated. He had no vision of a government as strong as, say, that of France in the seventeenth and eighteenth centuries or of any advanced nation today. Arguably, his intention was to create a government that would have *less power* overall in domestic relations than the collection of states plus the weak government of the Articles had had while it would have *more power* in international relations, especially with respect to trade but also with respect to national defence.

Madison clearly saw the states as being arbitrary, which in his vocabulary is virtually the opposite of liberal. This was a problem because he

---

[30] Madison's argument in *Federalist*, 10 is perhaps the strongest refutation we have of Montesquieu. For a superb recent account of Madison's liberalism, see Samuel H. Beer, *To Make a Nation: The Rediscovery of American Federalism* (Cambridge, Mass.: Harvard University Press, 1993), 244–340. Beer attributes some of Madison's arguments to David Hume, 'Idea of a Perfect Commonwealth', in Hume, *Essays Moral, Political, and Literary*, ed. Eugene F. Miller (Indianapolis: Liberty Press, 1985; 1st pub. 1752), 512–29 and to James Harrington, *The Commonwealth of Oceana*, ed. S. B. Liljegren (Heidelberg: 1924; 1st pub. 1656).

thought Montesquieu was wrong in supposing that small republics would be homogeneous enough not to have conflicts.[31] Madison thought on the contrary that they would be small enough to have vicious majority-versus-minority conflicts. He argued that the larger nation would not so readily be sundered into such vicious conflicts. It appears Madison was right, Montesquieu wrong. Furthermore, Montesquieu thought coalitions of interests could not work; Madison thought they could. Again, Madison was right, Montesquieu wrong. In creating the larger nation he further attempted to design institutions that would prevent the national government from being arbitrary. The government he helped design has probably been the most successful major government in guaranteeing political and economic liberalism to most of its populace (slaves and women long excluded). Part of the cost of that success is that that government is remarkably often incapable of addressing some problems—most notably, the problems of slavery, race, and poverty, but also perhaps violent crime.

Madison's was not a theoretical but a practical contribution, although one can claim that he was a better sociologist than Montesquieu. And his core ideas were often about how to deal with the peculiar situation of the thirteen American states. This is not a broadly generalizable problem. Its solution does not even apply to some of the later federations of states, such as the Argentine federation, the Yugoslav federation of quasi-autonomous states, the Belgian quasi-federation, or the Soviet and Indian empire federations. It would be only moderately applicable to the Canadian and Australian federations. But of all the great liberal thinkers, Madison was the most effective. When he went head-to-head with the Anti-Federalist exponents of Montesquieu's views during the ratification debates, he won the day. He won the intellectual debate overwhelmingly and he and the Federalists won the political debate by sometimes narrow margins but still with finality.

Mill

Hobbes was centrally concerned with dyadic economic relations and the protection of individual well-being. Locke added his concern with large-group political relations. Smith sought general social

---

[31] James Madison, Letter to Thomas Jefferson, 24 Oct. 1787, in Philip Kurland and Ralph Lerner, eds., *The Founders' Constitution*, 5 vols. (Chicago: University of Chicago Press, 1987), i. 644–7, at p. 647.

benefits through the protection of individual initiative. In his *On Liberty*, John Stuart Mill turned the focus of political liberalism back down to the individual, both for the good of the individual and for the good of the entire society. Often he argued forcefully for the protection of various civil liberties merely for the benefit of the individual. As did Hobbes and Locke, Mill argued from epistemological failings. He supposed we should presume each individual has inherent epistemological advantages in knowing what is in her interest. The presumption could be shown false in certain cases, such as the cases of children and the mentally incompetent, but it is very strong in many other cases.[32]

In addition to defending individual liberties for reasons of the individual alone, Mill sometimes resorted to a collective-level defence of political liberties. In particular, he defended them on grounds of their general effect on others. For example, one reason for protecting your right of free political speech is that your exercise of this right increases the chance that others will know what they need to know for their own political choices. Apart from the strategic move to collective resolution of individual and small-number problems, this may be the most remarkable move in the long development of welfarist liberalism. In this Benthamite move, *collective benefits are secured though protection of individual liberties*. I might actively want to have my liberty. But this is not the whole story. *I also want others to have it because their exercise of their liberty is good for me.* Therefore the systematic protection of the liberty is justified. This is parallel to Smith's argument for economic liberty (as discussed above, section on 'Smith').

Hence, Mill gave defences of individual liberty in political matters that paralleled those Hobbes and Smith gave in economic matters. He shared Hobbes's concern with the individual *per se* and Smith's concern with society overall.

Mill was even more democratic than Locke, and he shared Locke's concern with political liberalism at the level of incorporating, rather than suppressing, various groups, such as fundamentalist religious groups. And he was a master of political economics who shared Hobbes's and Smith's basic concern to enable exchange and pros-

---

[32] Mill seemed to assert the individual's right to be left without interference even more strongly than this presumption might warrant. Perhaps he had a theory of human welfare that gave autonomy central place. Or perhaps he had a deontological vision of individual liberty.

perity. However, the changing economic structure of his time, at the
height of the industrial revolution, made economic liberalism seem
to be no longer merely a dyadic matter. He began to analyse it at the
group level, as in his discussions of unions and of restrictions on the
length of the working day.[33] It would be wrong to say that the problems Mill saw so clearly were entirely new in the factories of his time.
For example, there had been sailing vessels with significant numbers
of crew members even in Hobbes's time and Mill's argument could
have applied as well to them as to later factories. But there was
growth in the pervasiveness and prominence of collective issues in
the market in the centuries between Hobbes and Mill.

The Complex View

Although the problems addressed by political and economic liberalism are quite different in structure, the form of resolution in many
areas is the same for both problems. Political liberalism involves
enforced *laissez-faire* with respect to religious views and practices
and with respect to opportunities for participation in political decisions. Economic liberalism seems to work best when it too involves
enforced *laissez-faire* to a large extent. Libertarian anarchists sometimes have a very optimistic view of the prospects for cooperative
exchange without enforcement, while Hobbes seems to have had a
very pessimistic view. Hobbes's actual view may have been relatively
modest despite his violent vision of the state of nature. He supposed
that, without enforcement, the few who would take adverse advantage of others would finally drive others to be too defensive to enter
into beneficial relations that they might readily have sustained without the threat of the few.

Political liberalism therefore has a complex structure. It was collective (Locke's modal concern in his treatment of religious toleration) and individual (the great concern of Mill's *On Liberty*). Before
the utilitarians it was almost entirely addressed to individuals either
alone or in aggregate, but Benthamite utilitarians began to elevate to
first concern the aggregate or total welfare. This was not even a
plausible idea for Hobbes and Locke.[34] Economic liberalism is also

[33] John Stuart Mill, *Principles of Political Economy*, ed. John M. Robson (Toronto:
Toronto University Press, 1965; 1st pub. 1848), book 5, ch. 11, § 12.
[34] See further, Russell Hardin, 'Efficiency', in *Companion to Contemporary
Political Philosophy*, eds. Robert E. Goodin and Philip Pettit (Oxford: Basil Blackwell,
1993), 462–70.

complex. It has a three-fold focus: individual, dyadic, and collective. It is individual as in Hobbes's and virtually all Anglo-Saxon views of the value to the individual of the stability of property. Indeed, even a Crusoe on a frontier wants no theft even when he has no expectation of exchange or collective benefit. It is dyadic as in Hobbes's and the later political economists' concern with exchange, which dominated the nineteenth-century heyday of the rights of contract. It is group-level as in Mill's concern with the economic liberty of groups of workers acting as groups. And it is societal-level in Smith's concern with the wealth of nations and in Mill's concern with the social benefits of individual liberty.

In the developments from Hobbes through Locke, Smith, and Mill, there is also a steady decline in the justified power of government. Hobbes wanted all-powerful government to prevent turmoil. He included dictatorial determination of religion in the purview of the sovereign. Locke wanted less power over religion but wanted it hived off from politics. Smith wanted weaker control over economic relations. And Mill wanted weaker control over individual values of various kinds in a virtual end to paternalism towards full citizens. Smith argued that limiting government control over the economy would enhance productivity and, hence, wealth. At least in modern economies, this conclusion appears to be roughly right, as the doleful experience of the Communist world suggests (see further, Chapter 6). One could add to claims for all of these trends the contingent claim that government power to control either economics or politics is not easily kept separate from the power to control the other. Hence, if less powerful government were recommended for political liberty while more powerful government were recommended for economic welfare, we would have to forgo either some liberty or some welfare. Therefore, we should be pleased if both liberty and welfare depend on less rather than more powerful government.

It is interesting that Locke's arguments for religious toleration are primarily welfarist, while his arguments for the ownership of property seem chiefly deontological. For example, Locke argued for excluding religious issues from politics because they would disrupt the peace we need for individual prosperity. This anti-deontological principle seems to say one should not do what one believes is right if that harms welfare. Yet Locke's strangely irrelevant and even more strangely captivating concern with the morality of appropriating property through mixing one's labour with it gave a very early deontological twist to economic liberalism and provided the moral foundation for one branch of libertarian thought. Hence, Locke's positions were virtually the opposite of much of the later development, with at least the line of economic liberalism that goes through Smith basically welfarist and the arguments for political liberties, including even many by Mill, increasingly deontological.

Collective Resolution

Locke and Mill more or less take for granted that the defence of political liberties is a matter for government. That is, the resolution of both the collective and the individual problems is itself collective, as was Hobbes's resolution of his individual-level and dyadic problems. Why should collective resolution be so readily favoured for resolving all of these classes of issues? For dyadic problems of economic liberty and individual problems of political liberty, it seems natural strategically to resort to collective devices to correct problems that cannot be corrected dyadically or individually. But it is not merely that it makes strategic sense to resolve dyadic problems by going to the collective level. More important is that the principle of a strong form of collective protection is mutually advantageous. For Locke's collective issue of the incorporation of groups, it is a defining characteristic of a resolution that it be collective. The collective issues in economic liberalism that interest Mill are issues in part because they are governed by contract and other laws that derive from dyadic principles. Those laws are centrally collectively enforced; to change them by enabling collectives to enter into contracts requires collective devices.

Collective devices might have greater stability than spontaneous devices. But they may also have potential for far greater effective variance, so that a collective regime might be capable of extraordinary harm. One might suppose that the great value of democratic politics lies in its supposed capacity to produce best leadership when needed through competitive elections, as though Condorcet's jury or truth theorem were as applicable to government as it might be to juries. This theorem says, roughly, that, if the average person is at least slightly more likely to know the truth than not, then the

likelihood that the majority of a jury will find the truth in their deliberations rises with the number of jurors. But juries seek factual truth
with interests ostensibly ruled out of court. Governments seek compromise in the face of conflicting interests, and there is little reason
to suppose they find a relevant truth.[35]

The real magic of liberal democracy often lies in its tendency—
sometimes overcome—to decentralize decisions, to make its government less capable of acting, not more capable. Tocqueville saw this
characteristic in democratic government: 'Not what is done by a
democratic government, but what is done under a democratic
government by private agency, is really great'.[36] As Mill noted,
Tocqueville was too quick to attribute what he found in America to
democracy when much of it merely followed from civilization or
from commerce—or, one might add, liberalism.[37] Clearly, it is not
democracy *per se* that has the character Tocqueville here praises but
specifically liberal democracy—there could be, for example, a democratically favoured government of enforced religious belief. The
French historian François Guizot explained the stunted growth or
short life of many civilizations by their focusing on one element of
human improvement more or less to the detriment of all others.
Hence, 'the community, after accomplishing rapidly all which that
one element could do, either perished for want of what it could not
do, or came to a halt, and became immoveable'.[38] A liberal society
leaves it open to individuals to develop in manifold ways. In a liberal
society, Karl Marx, John Stuart Mill, and Herbert Spencer can share
the same library and each can find a publisher.

This magic is analogous to the magic of the market. Hence, political and economic liberalisms share a single causal structure.
Decentralized decision-making in the market, however, solves a vir-

---

[35] See further, Geoffrey Brennan and James M. Buchanan, *The Reason of Rules:
Constitutional Political Economy* (Cambridge: Cambridge University Press, 1985),
38–40.

[36] Quoted in John Stuart Mill, 'De Tocqueville on Democracy in America, II', in
Mill, *Essays on Politics and Society*, ed. J. M. Robson, *Collected Works of John Stuart
Mill*, xviii (Toronto: University of Toronto Press, 1977), 153–204, at p. 171. The trans-
lations by Henry Reeve in Alexis de Tocqueville, *Democracy in America* (New York:
Knopf, 1945; 1st pub. 1835 and 1840), i. 252, and by George Lawrence (New York:
Harper and Row, 1966), 244, are less elegant and less forceful.

[37] Mill, 'De Tocqueville on Democracy in America, II', 191.

[38] ibid., 197. Mill refers to François Guizot, *Cours d'histoire moderne: Histoire
générale de la civilisation en Europe, depuis la chute de l'empire romain jusqu'à la
révolution française* (Paris: Pichon and Didier, 1828).

tually impossible information problem, as Hayek and the Austrian school argue.[39] Many complain of the inefficacy of contemporary democratic governments in the face of domestic and international problems, especially problems of welfare and distribution. But the benefits of this incapacity arguably may outweigh its costs. The diffusion of power in liberal democratic forms of government often blocks capacity for decisions that ignore the interests of many. Under an autocratic regime, the issue of abortion, for example, might be relatively quietly and effectively settled even in a society with diverse views. Under liberal democracy, the issue of abortion may not be settled for generations, because views cannot be quietly blocked or overridden. An anarchist might well conclude that democratic liberalism is a reasonably good second best.

A mild form of the difference between autocratic and liberal democratic governments may even be exhibited by more centralized democratic regimes as compared to the relatively decentralized federal regime of the United States. In the centralized British system, it was relatively easy to require seat-belts in vehicles at the overall national level. In the United States, libertarian objections to such legal requirements on behavior could be focused at the state level to slow down the adoption of seat-belt laws. In the face of a well-organized and well-financed industrial lobby, on the other hand, national governments in both the United States and the United Kingdom were long unable to take very strong action against tobacco and its use, although their day may come. (Autocratic Nazi Germany was already able to act strongly against smoking two generations ago.) The decentralized American system, however, allows effective action to be taken at lower levels of government.[40] Local governments have even gone so far as to outlaw smoking at public beaches and other outdoor areas. The eventual success of state governments in suing big tobacco companies induced those companies to try to pre-empt state-level attacks by cooperating in the drafting of national legislation against smoking.

Economic liberty evidently leads to the growth of powerful commercial organizations, especially firms. Given their power and

---

[39] Friedrich A. Hayek, 'The Uses of Knowledge in Society', in Hayek, *Individualism and Economic Order* (Chicago: University of Chicago Press, 1948; reprinted by Gateway, n.d.; essay first published 1945), 77–91, esp. 86–9.
[40] Howard M. Leichter, *Free to Be Foolish: Politics and Health Promotion in the United States and Great Britain* (Princeton: Princeton University Press, 1991), 257.

relative autonomy, these may become the locus of protection of other liberties for some members (even as they may also have become a source of problems for liberalism). Hence, economic liberty may compete with and therefore constrain government in its regulation of liberties. Twentieth-century trends that increasingly bring property under governmental regulation undercut this constraining power of property.[41] Historically, we have tended to assume that liberties—political and economic—must be defended by central government against the particularistic values of various local groups and interests. This assumption may usually be correct. But it is an empirical, not an a priori, matter. A varied collection of liberties may enjoy decentralized support from business, communities, religious organizations, and other local institutions. Perhaps we gain more liberty in trumping these institutions than we lose. But we may also increase the likelihood of great variance in achieving protection of liberties.

Finally, the achievement of economic and political liberalisms in a common collective government brings the two together even though they need not be conceptually related. Groups may use liberal political devices to intervene in economic relations. This is typically a problem during economic transitions or during the East European effort to introduce democratic and then economic reforms (Chapter 5, section on 'The Dual Task of 1989', and Chapter 6, section on 'Economic Transition in a Constitutional Democracy'). If political liberties are sociologically correlated with economic performance, we may expect governments to have strong incentives to promote liberties. This motivation did not trump lesser urges in Ne Win, Papa Doc, Pol Pot, Idi Amin, and many others.

Causal and Conceptual Links

In the views of many writers, political and economic liberalisms were historically linked in the long process of breaking the hold of views of the primacy of the community over the individual. Henry Sumner Maine, in his account of the movement from status to contract, Karl

---

[41] See Jennifer Nedelsky, *Private Property and the Limits of American Constitutionalism: The Madisonian Framework and Its Legacy* (Chicago: University of Chicago Press, 1990).

Marx, in a discussion of the relation of political and economic liberalism and how the latter guts the former, Herbert Spencer, in an extension of Maine's arguments, and L. T. Hobhouse all argued, usually in other vocabulary, for this thesis.[42] Liberalism was about emancipation or liberation from the fetters of feudal, often familial, control over individuals. It was all one: a 'religious, political, economic, social, and ethical' protest against an authoritarian order.[43]

In communal organization, the entity that matters first is the community, and individuals can be used in various ways to serve the community. This view might make compelling sense in the context of the ancient Greek city state. There, as Hobhouse wrote, 'It was no feat of the philosophical imagination, but a quite simple and natural expression of the facts to describe such a community as an association of men for the purpose of living well'.[44] In such a society, if Socrates is deemed to disrupt the community by leading its youth astray, then he must be expelled or put to death. Despite Socrates's own claim of the importance of obedience to the law of Athens and therefore his not fleeing his capital sentence, this was not an act of law. This was a decision on behalf of the community.

Such communal precedence over the individual made less sense in the time of Hume and Smith. In their 'community' the king awarded a monopoly to a particular family, perhaps merely as a reward for loyalty. A modern might think this unfair to others who would be excluded. Hence, economic liberalism would appear to be, as political liberalism was, emancipatory. Against this view, Hobbes saw economic liberalism not as emancipatory but as enabling. We need the state to protect us from *each other*, not from the lord of the manor, so that we may exchange. Later, Smith and other critics of mercantilism argued that mercantilism was bad for almost the entire society, because it made almost everyone worse off than they would be with competition instead of monopoly. In Smith's view, therefore, economic liberalism was about enabling the wealth of nations rather than about emancipation of individual economic actors.

[42] Henry Sumner Maine, *Ancient Law: Its Connection with the Early History of Society and Its Relation to Modern Ideas* (London: John Morrow, 1906, 10th edn.); Karl Marx, 'On the Jewish Question', Part I, in David McLellan, ed., *Karl Marx: Selected Writings* (Oxford: Oxford University Press, 1977); Herbert Spencer, *The Principles of Sociology* (New York: Appleton, 1884), ii. e.g., 244–8, 568–78, 603–21, 637–40, 648–61; L. T. Hobhouse, *Liberalism* (Oxford: Oxford University Press, 1948; 1st pub. 1911).
[43] Hobhouse, *Liberalism*, 19.   [44] Hobhouse, *Liberalism*, 12.

The two liberalisms are sometimes run together in the thesis that the—or an—important function of private property is as a bulwark against political power. Jennifer Nedelsky attributes this view to James Madison, and she argues that property under constitutional developments in the United States no longer has this function, because it is now too pervasively subject to legal constraints.[45] C. E. Lindblom criticizes this view for almost the opposite reason that private property can only contribute to the liberty of the very few who own corporations.[46] Again, Smith's view, as represented in part in the epigraph to this chapter, of private property is, rather, that it allows the incentive for gain to play its role of producing for the market, thus making all of us better off. His is a welfarist, not a political liberal, justification of property.

Independently of the thesis that animates the critiques of Nedelsky, Lindblom, and many others, I take economic liberalism to be represented in the vision of Smith. In that vision, it is not tied virtually by definition to political liberalism. The two liberalisms make different contributions to welfare, and they might make their contributions independently. But they can be strategically tied together with either one playing a causal role in determining the other. For example, those who want political liberalism may resort to economic moves, such as strikes, to force a regime to liberalize politically. Moreover, a regime that is committed to high levels of economic productivity and growth may find little point in using illiberal political devices to maintain power when political suppression leads to economic disruptions.

One of Hobbes's seemingly most outlandish claims is that any kind of sovereign government—monarchy, oligarchy, democracy—would do for order. Yet this claim seems to be true enough for economic liberalism, which has arisen under quite varied regimes. Or perhaps the claim is only true during early stages of economic development. Marxist regimes that assumed economic liberalism was the source of problems they wished to resolve have, of course, been openly hostile to economic liberalism. But that is a result of their ideological position on economic liberalism and not of their authoritarian political structure *per se*. Economic liberalism has come to be associated with liberal political regimes in the views of many the-

[45] Nedelsky, *Private Property and the Limits of American Constitutionalism*.

[46] Charles E. Lindblom, *Politics and Markets: The World's Political-Economic Systems* (New York: Basic Books, 1977), 45–51.

orists other than Marxists. But, to the limited extent that the association holds, that is generally because the liberal political regimes have followed the prior establishment of liberal economic regimes.

Today, we have the opportunity to watch the reverse order, with liberalizing politics in some nations of Eastern Europe before liberalizing economics—as well as some instances of simultaneous political and economic liberalization. Many observers evidently think it an open question whether liberal economics must follow liberal politics. Why? Because more-or-less democratic politics may work against long-term collective interests. One who thinks that in the long run free trade will be mutually beneficial may also think that for the nearer term protection is in our interests. Or the producers in a declining industry may be able, through democratic politics, to secure their jobs through protections and subsidies that violate liberal economic principles (see further, Chapter 5).

It is a common misunderstanding of the Pareto principle—itself supremely liberal—to conclude that if all exchange is consensual, no one will be made worse off by generally free exchange. Suppose that in one state of affairs no one is worse off and one or more are better off than in a second state of affairs. Vilfredo Pareto supposed that the first state of affairs is unarguably superior to the second. Consensual exchange seemingly should produce only better-off people unless there are external costs of production imposed on others, for example, through pollution. But if I have a modest restaurant and you open another across the street from me, within days your superior cooking may drive me under. All exchanges that take place in this sad story may be fully consensual. My loss is that I participate in too few of them, although I once participated in many. The dismal fate of my restaurant may await most entrepreneurial activities. For example, American Airlines not so inadvertently drove Braniff under by making its fares extremely competitive for the summer of 1992. American did not need to violate the Pareto principle, narrowly conceived at the level of dyadic exchanges, for Braniff to lose badly.

Some of the most spectacular losses among major corporations are the losses of entire industries as the technological capacities and demands of economies change rapidly. Among the most productive enterprises in Eastern Europe and the former Soviet Union are very large firms in industries that a short-sighted Stalin thought important in the more advanced economies of his time and on which he improved by making his even larger scale. Those industries have been in decline for decades in the West and they will plausibly go through even more rapid decline in the East. Declining industries include steel manufacturing, coal mining, and much of the rest of heavy industry in Poland, the Czech Republic, Slovakia, and much of the former Soviet Union (as well as in much of the industrial world). In addition, agriculture is in relative decline as it becomes more efficient and as it becomes an ever smaller part of the overall economy as wealth rises. Hence, the eastern economies must make a twofold transition: from a discarded central to a market organization and from obsolescent industries to dynamic industries. Most discussion of their problem in the American press focuses on the former transition, while the latter may be the greater obstacle if they try to make a gentle, piecemeal conversion.

Economically threatened groups—such as farmers—have long pushed through anti-liberal economic policies in democratic societies, yet we would generally think those societies have tended to maintain basically liberal economies. In the Eastern European experiments of our time, the protectionist politics of groups does not merely threaten to reduce the quality of economic liberalism. Rather, group politics over economic issues has threatened to block the introduction of economic liberalism. That would be a perverse causal connection between political and economic liberalism.

There may also be a causal connection between domestic and international possibilities that drives all nations towards market devices in order to stay comparatively viable. For example, the educated élite, who might have options elsewhere, may leave if their nation chooses egalitarianism, collective ownership, or other major policies that block entrepreneurial possibilities. Such policies may virtually require anti-liberal policies on freedom of political activity or on migration in order to block the options of voice and exit in a personally disagreeable context. Hence, anti-liberal economics may lead to anti-liberal politics. In a nation that was isolated and autarkic, this result need not follow. But for a nation with economic and personal ties to a larger competitive world, it might follow with a vengeance (see further, Chapter 5). For example, a nation that gives up 1 or 2 per cent of its potential annual rate of economic growth in order to achieve egalitarian distributions might find itself reduced to relative poverty in a generation or two.

At its extreme, we may wonder whether Hobbesian political autocracy, by suppressing political liberties, might boost economic performance. It may sound incredible today, but around 1960, when military juntas took power in both nations, Burma and South Korea had similarly impoverished per capita incomes. (General Ne Win seized control of the government of what was then Burma in 1958 and General Park ended relatively democratic government in 1960 in South Korea.) After three decades of autocracy, South Korea has very nearly entered the ranks of the wealthy industrial world while destitute Burma (now Myanmar) has arguably even declined from its earlier position.[47] During that same period, North Korea, with its autocratic Communist regime, may have achieved greater equality than South Korea. But if it did, it did so at a very high cost in productivity. Both these comparisons may be poor cases for present purposes, because South Korea's growth may have been stimulated very much by its special relationship with the United States or by some other special feature. Many Korean observers, however, think that the authoritarian imposition of order plus protection of economic liberties did the trick. Debate largely turns on whether specific, inegalitarian, entrepreneurial policies hastened or slowed economic growth. In any case, autocratic governments that are hostile to political liberties can evidently have dramatically different economic effects. Somewhat crude and probably inconsistently measured data put per capita GNP at $200 in Burma in 1986, $3,450 in South Korea in 1988, and $1,180 in North Korea in 1985.[48]

Against the vision of a resplendent autocracy, note that autocracy is not typically a choice. It is more nearly like life. It is what happens to us when the autocrat comes in from the wings, typically with military force. Hitler and Khomeini were unusual cases of autocrats who were relatively popular choices.

One Unified Liberalism?

Do the long lines of welfarist liberalism in English political and economic thought cohere? In particular, is the complex liberalism of

[47] From 1967 to 1989, gross domestic product per capita in Burma rose 31 per cent from 946 kyats to 1,239 kyats (in 1985 prices), for a dismal annual rate of growth of slightly over 1 per cent (International Monetary Fund, *International Financial Statistics*, 1991).

[48] *The Statesman's Year-Book 1991–92*, ed. Brian Hunter (New York: St Martin's, 1991), 254, 781, 787. Such figures must be taken as very crude. The income for North Korea seems very likely to be overstated.

Mill consistent with the earlier political liberalism of Locke and with the economic liberalism that grew from Hobbes to Smith? To answer such questions, we must look to the major turns in the development of liberal thought. First, there were the strategic focuses of various liberalisms, from Hobbes's economic individuals and dyads and Locke's political collectives through to Mill's political individuals and economic collectives, as discussed above. Then there has been the sometimes acute, sometimes mild concern with religious toleration, which often brings in a value that might give welfarists trouble, and which merits further brief discussion. Finally, there have been historical changes in capacities for addressing many of the economic issues that drove Hobbes and Locke. With rising wealth, political and economic concerns seem to have merged, perhaps inextricably.

Religious Toleration Again

Hobbes and Locke both confused the issue of the separation of material and non-material welfare when they addressed religion. Hobbes willingly supposed we must suppress, banish, or kill certain fundamentalist believers. The very issue of survival that Hobbes invoked to justify government he oddly ignored for the fundamentalist. Locke similarly ruled religious issues off the political agenda while counting material issues as acceptable subject-matter for a political theory. Their moves against certain fundamentalists are not a matter of mere coordination or of mutual advantage—it is not to the advantage of the fundamentalist to be depoliticized, suppressed, or killed. Implicitly, Hobbes and Locke made substantive value claims that the economic well-being of most people outweighs the religious values of some people. This argument would not survive even in implicit form if they were addressing a severely divided society.

There is a conundrum in the liberal guarantee of freedom of religion. For example, the discussion of the establishment of religion and the freedom of religious practice in the first amendment to the US Constitution seems to be internally contradictory. Each person may worship as her beliefs dictate—this sounds like neutrality. But the state will not support any religion.[49] If one's beliefs dictate that

---

[49] Nor can there be any religious test required as a qualification for any office or public trust under the US Constitution (Art. 6) although often such a test is imposed by the electorate.

one have a religious state (some of the original American colonies were religious states with the death penalty for such minor infractions as taking the deity's name in vain), what is one to do?

One might suppose Mill faced a similar problem when he pushed economic liberalism into collective issues of the rights of groups involved in the market, as opposed merely to the rights of individuals. But, in so far as he had a utilitarian value theory for aggregating welfare, he could escape the automatic inconsistency that troubles the arguments of Hobbes and Locke.

Chief among the interests on which most people in liberal polities have been prone to want to coordinate have been economic prosperity, personal liberty or autonomy, and national defence. These are almost inherently popular concerns whose modern articulation has accompanied the rise of democratic thought and practice. There have been at least two other major focuses for coordination that have mobilized nations: religious orthodoxy and expansive, xenophobic nationalism. (There have also been major focuses for coordination of subgroups within nations, such as economic and ethnic groups.) Nationalism can evidently fit with coordination on domestic prosperity and liberty. Religious orthodoxy clearly conflicts with liberty.

One could infer from modern political history that liberty tends to win over religious control. There are potentially important asymmetries between coordinating on religious restrictions and coordinating on individual liberty. First, if we coordinate on the former, many individuals may find themselves at odds with the restrictions in their own lives. If we coordinate on the protection of individual liberty, there may be opponents of the regime of liberty, but their opposition will primarily be to the liberty of others. Occasional true believers might be as strongly motivated to restrict others as anyone might be to gain their own liberty, but typically we may expect those who chafe from restrictions on themselves to be harder to control than those who chafe from lack of restrictions on others. Secondly, to coordinate successfully on restrictions requires a demanding level of consistency. Thirdly, when a polity coordinates on a set of restrictions, its members coordinate both against outsiders and against their own future inclinations for deviation from the current beliefs. Such a coordination seems likely to be tenuous. Indeed, the very idea of requiring religious restrictions implies systematic concern with spontaneous violation of the religious norms. Historical defences of the protection of liberty have primarily been addressed to protections against officials, not suppressions of spontaneous individual actions.

Historical Changes

The separation of economic and political liberalism makes less sense in very productive modern societies than it once did. Why? Because the separation of contributions to welfare into the relevant material and non-material categories makes less sense than it once did and less sense than it might still make in much less productive societies today. The change derives from a combination of causal and conceptual changes.

Conceptually, my valuations of matters covered by political liberties are not decoupled from my valuations of material benefits. This is trivially true for valuations of political liberties to try to affect economic policy in my own interest. But it is true more generally in any value theory with roughly the form of the indifference-curve utility theory of modern economics. In this theory, the more I have of any desirable thing, the more of it I am willing to trade for other desirable things. At some point in the increasing consumption of, say, bread, I will finally be willing to trade off some further bit of bread for some non-material good. Despite this fact, however, the level of my consumption of such things as bread may be so low that I never reach the point of willingness to trade off bits of them for many non-material goods. If I am very well off—I get all the bread I could want—I would even trade a large amount of it for beluga caviare or a night at the opera. Suppose my government says that Mikhail Baryshnikov cannot do modern dance, because such dance is a manifestation of bourgeois decadence. Now I, who have no worry about the adequacy of my food, housing, and clothing and who can afford to indulge my cultural tastes, may suffer a direct loss from this lack of political liberty. It affects what I can consume, just as taking money away from me affects what I can consume. Many of the peasants who made up the vast bulk of the populations of Europe until this century would have suffered no direct loss from comparable restrictions on political liberty in their time.

Unfortunately, if we see political and economic liberalism as joined in our value theory, then we no longer have available an a priori argument such as Locke and early defenders of religious toleration used. Material and non-material interests were relatively decoupled in seventeenth-century England. These finally blend with non-material interests and an effort to hold them separate for the citizen of a modern, wealthy state may be wrong-headed.[50] We cannot hive off religion and let government and social choice focus entirely on material interests. Hence, separate programmes of economic and political liberalism make less sense in very productive modern societies. Material and non-material interests were always coupled in principle in our value theory or our value commitments. Their coupling now intrudes more frequently or urgently into our opportunities. We now want additional liberty of, say, lifestyle and other choices in part because such choices are now broadly affordable.

Hobbes, writing in a period of grim turmoil, put survival as the individual's first concern in having government. Locke, taking survival for granted even in a state of nature, put material interests first. It would be silly to suppose that survival and material interests would not be major concerns in justifying states, but non-material interests play a larger role as the other concerns are increasingly well addressed. But that means—if we may generalize from observed phenomena—that conflicts over what governments ought to do and to protect may get worse in many areas even while the grand economic policy conflict of this century seems to have been almost universally settled in favour of the market.[51] With survival and material interests comfortably secured, we can afford—literally—to fight it out over religious and other divisive issues. David Braybrooke argues that welfare policy should be designed to let needs be satisfied in order that wants might flourish.[52] This is what has happened for the upper reaches of the middle class in Western societies. Hobbes, however, might shudder at the thought of what could follow in the train of this flourishing, especially if some people happen to want murderous religious policies.

---

[50] As argued by Kent Greenawalt, *Religious Convictions and Political Choice* (New York: Oxford University Press, 1988), esp. ch. 3.

[51] Even India has abandoned much of its socialist economic programme. *New York Times*, 29 Mar. 1992, sect. I, pp. 1, 9.

[52] David Braybrooke, *Meeting Needs: Studies in Moral, Political, and Legal Philosophy* (Princeton: Princeton University Press, 1987). Also see Robert E. Goodin, *Protecting the Vulnerable: A Reanalysis of Our Social Responsibilities* (Chicago: University of Chicago Press, 1985).

Centralized Intelligence

John Dewey supposed we needed merely to bring intelligence to bear at the centre of government to redress the depredations of private power, which he held responsible for impositions that have detrimental effect on individual liberty and welfare, including the continuing poverty of his time.[53] I will not attempt to give an account of what we need for that purpose, but I think what Dewey suggested—he did not spell it out—is not what we need. We do not need massive central planning. He commended the use of intelligence to redesign economic institutions. No one could argue for the use of unintelligence. But one can sensibly argue against the supposed use of intelligence to contrive a central plan for the economy. Indeed, the implications of more than two centuries of economic liberalism is that a central plan is an unintelligent idea. If, during the past 250 years, England, the United States, or some other developing capitalist nation had adopted any of the reigning economic theories of their day and had seriously enforced them, our best retrospective view must be that the result would have been to slow down that nation's development. Hamilton's mercantilism or the later populist efforts to secure old-style farming through politics when it was being demolished by economic changes could have been disastrous.

The slow-down would not merely have been in levels of economic performance but also in the spread of the benefits of liberalism through the society. Any state that had the forces in place to control commerce could have let those forces spill over into the control of other things as well, such as social hierarchy, mobility, and religion, as states commonly have done. It is hard now even to comprehend the harm, for example, that came from the Elizabethan poor laws that eventually were articulated into a perverse set of constraints on geographic mobility that must have ruined thousands of lives. In Elizabeth's time, the laws were intended to guarantee support for the indigent by making communities responsible for them. In the end, the result was one of the most grotesquely illiberal, complicated institutions of its era. Yet, analogues of some of those laws are occasionally suggested as useful devices for controlling the dispropor-

[53] John Dewey, *Liberalism and Social Action*, in *The Later Works of Dewey, 1925–1953*, xi (Carbondale, Ill.: Southern Illinois University Press, 1987; 1st pub. 1935), 1–65.

tionate flow of impoverished seekers of welfare assistance into certain communities, such as New York City and Wisconsin.

Sometimes good would have come of central control—for example, defenders of the arts in past times sometimes note that it was often despots who sponsored artistic productions which now count among the great treasures of the world, treasures that we might now think of as held in common. And occasionally there must have been a genuinely benevolent central government that would have improved the lives of most of its citizens in many ways. But the variance in what central, autonomous authorities do is appalling and few of us would wish to take the risk of having central control in the hands of others than ourselves. The claims of the old political liberalism have not faded in our time. We still want constitutional, institutional, and popular constraints on government. One of the strongest institutional constraints is the existence of private agencies, including private economic firms.

Scepticism about applying intelligence to the design of central controls for social and economic development does not merely turn on the Austrian economists' view that we cannot amass the information we would need, information that is inherently diffused among the millions of producers, consumers, and auxiliary agents of the economy.[54] Moreover, the scepticism is not merely a worry that it would be wrong or a violation of anyone's rights to use central control. Rather, the scepticism is that we simply do not have the theory to do it well. Further, even if someone among us now does know how to do it well, there are others who know how to do it differently. The difficult political problem, then, is for political leaders, who are almost certain to be atheoretical, to decide which way is the right way. (As though to underscore this point, the Brazilian president, Fernando Henrique Cardoso, is a theorist who has gone both ways.[55] Some might say at least he learns. Others could say he follows the fad of his time and role, and that he does not clearly act from good theoretical understanding. One hopes the fad that governs his political leadership happens to be right or nearly so.) Even

---

[54] There are numerous statements of the problem of centralizing information on the market. See F. A. Hayek's last, somewhat florid statement in *The Fatal Conceit: The Errors of Socialism* (Chicago: University of Chicago Press, 1989; 1st pub. 1988), 71–88; an accessible standard statement is Michael Polanyi, *The Logic of Liberty: Reflections and Rejoinders* (Chicago: University of Chicago Press, 1980; 1st pub. 1951), esp. chs. 8 and 10.

[55] *New York Times*, 20 Nov. 1994, 4.7.

supposing there is a right way licenses a strong leader with, say, Yeltsin's tendency to suppose he should personally run things to attempt to do so. Again, the variance from having politicians bring holistic theories to bear argues against entrusting them to do it.

Concluding Remarks

In the end, perhaps a unified welfarist liberalism is an incoherent programme. The unification of economic liberalism, which is most focused at the dyadic level, and political liberalism, which is focused at the collective and individual levels, may demand too much complexity. But if that is true, the incoherence is more than merely in liberalism. First, it is in the conflict between society and the individual. Our relations are too intertwined for a theorist to cut out a part of our problem and analyse it alone as Hobbes, Locke, and others have tried to do. And, secondly, the incoherence is in our plausible value theories, welfarist and non-welfarist. Unless we can appeal, as Hobbes, Locke, and Mill did at crucial moments,[56] to our fundamental ignorance of parts of our problem, we may not be able to prune the thicket enough to untangle it.

Historically, the two liberalisms were not related ideologically. Hobbes was a nascent liberal in economics but not in politics. Indeed, Hobbes's solution of chaotic anarchy was an all-powerful sovereign, a solution that might well achieve economic order but that violates political liberal values. For Hobbes the point of politics was to secure order that economy might flourish. It is prima facie a contingent matter just how far towards political liberalism or how far away from it a society can go without grossly harming economic relations.

In our time, economic relations are commonly attacked in the name of political liberties (and other, non-liberal concerns, such as fundamentalist religious beliefs) or through the institutions of political liberalism, which can offer losing economic groups an alternative route to welfare. The most striking case of this phenomenon in our time may occur in the Eastern European and former Soviet nations in which economic groups whose livelihood depended on prior ways

---

[56] One could add Mandeville, Hume, Smith, and others in the long lines of economic and political liberalism to this list.

of doing things or on the prosperity of senescent industries strive to maintain their positions through political actions. But finally, it seems increasingly difficult to hold separate the values that Hobbes, Locke, and other early writers cavalierly separated. If our vision is welfarist and, at the same time, subjectivist, we cannot a priori rule particular values, such as social, communal, or religious commitments, out of someone's welfare.

Finally, there have been uses of the appealing term 'liberalism' that go beyond the traditional economic and political liberalisms discussed here. I canvass several of these in the Appendix. The earlier liberalisms focused on constraints on or even elimination of government control over citizens' activities. The newer so-called liberalisms typically require the use of government power to block other controls—of social conventions or of non-governmental institutions, such as business organizations—or even actively to do things for people. Some of these liberalisms cannot realistically be expected to be sociologically mutual-advantage principles and they therefore do not belong in the main discussions of this book. If any are sociologically mutual-advantage principles, we might expect them simply to be adopted as government policy.

3

Constitutionalism: Contract or Coordination?

Ingenious men will give every plausible, and, it may be, pretty substantial reasons, for the adoption of two plans of Government, which shall be fundamentally different in their construction, and not less so in their operation; yet both, if honestly administered, might operate with safety and advantage.

Caesar (1787)[1]

Institutions and Choice

A constitutional regime can be put in place to manage and protect both liberalisms of Chapter 2. The regime can back political liberalism with institutions to protect individual liberty and to promote education. And it can enable economic liberalism by maintaining economic infrastructures of a currency and a legal system, especially to govern property and contracts. In a constitutional regime, institutions have two distinct roles. The most obvious, perhaps, is to enable, to make various actions and results possible. We need specialization and organization to get many things done at all. For example, if we wish to establish and maintain law and order, we will need to have various institutional structures, including police and judicial powers. The second role of institutions is to block, to raise the cost of instant coordination on many possible actions and results, sometimes to make such coordination prohibitively difficult. The alternative to blocking instant coordination in many contexts is mob rule. Under mob rule, law and order are reduced to vigilantism and lynching, or

---

[1] Caesar, no. 2, 17 Oct. 1787, in Philip B. Kurland and Ralph Lerner, eds., *The Founders' Constitution*, 5 vols. (Chicago: University of Chicago Press, 1987), i. 60–1.

even to something as grim as the French revolutionary Terror. In their two functions, institutions both enable and block not only piecemeal changes but also the popular will. The tension between enabling and constraining democracy is therefore the heart of democratic constitutionalism.

Liberal thought has roots in the overtly illiberal arguments of Hobbes. Hobbes's concern was to control spontaneous actions by individuals to harm others rather than actions by government officials, whom he wished to empower seemingly to the point of enabling the sovereign to act from whim. But his central claim is that, given a choice between a protection of all against all and no protection, we would virtually unanimously choose the regime of protection. Hobbes excepted from the unanimous agreement those who are glory seekers—those, mostly aristocrats, whose life was in fighting, even just for the thrill of it—and religious fanatics for whom religious rectitude was more important than worldly peace. He did not attempt to construct an argument for why it was really in the interests of these people to submit to order. Rather, he merely concluded that the many who wished to live in an orderly world should suppress the few who would prefer disorder. Later liberal thinkers added to Hobbes's concerns the worry over abuses not by one's fellow citizens but by officials (perhaps especially Hobbesian officials). Hence, such liberals as Benjamin Constant, Wilhelm von Humboldt, and John Stuart Mill wished to constrain the government whose function was in large part to constrain individuals.[2]

Both the Hobbesian and the later liberal constraints are part of a two-stage choice. We generally coordinate on creating institutions for constraining certain classes of behaviour and then the institutions implement the constraints. In an extreme statement of this dual structure of choice, James Madison argued that an advantage of the particular form of representative government proposed for the United States in its new constitution was '*the total exclusion of the people in their collective capacity* from any share' in the government.[3]

---

[2] Benjamin Constant, *Principles of Politics Applicable to All Representative Governments*, in Constant, *Political Writings*, ed. Biancamaria Fontana (Cambridge: Cambridge University Press, 1988; *Principles* 1st pub. 1815), 171–305; Wilhelm von Humboldt, *The Limits of State Action* (Cambridge: Cambridge University Press, 1969 (written 1791–2; 1st pub. 1854)); John Stuart Mill, *Principles of Representative Government* and *On Liberty*, any edns.

[3] *Federalist*, 63, para. 14, emphasis in original. Madison here refers to the role of representatives. They should actually legislate and not merely report what their constituents want. Montesquieu makes a seemingly similar claim that the people are

That is to say, popular sovereignty stopped at the adoption of the constitution. It must seem perplexing to anyone committed to popular sovereignty that this was an argument made in public to win popular support for the constitution.

In one sense, constitutionalism is democratically easy while working out the details is democratically very hard. Constitutionalism requires merely coordination on big issues of general structure and protections. Coordination on any detailed programme is virtually out of the question. We might successfully hammer out a compromise in some committee or legislative arena, but we cannot mobilize a large polity behind all the details. We can put up a relatively detailed constitution for a vote and expect it to be voted up or down, but we cannot thrash out the content of the constitution at the popular level. Once we have a constitution and relevant legislative institutions in place, working out details may then be facilitated, although it need not be very democratic. It would be empirically preposterous to suppose that a large polity generally agrees with the detail of public policy or law in any area or that it would ever be likely to agree with it.

In another sense, constitutionalism can be exceedingly difficult. It works at all only if there is relatively wide agreement on core issues, such as the agreement of the American political elite on the need for something like the Commerce Clause to enable the growth of an American economy through the creation of an open American market under the US Constitution. In polities in which there is no such general agreement, constitutionalism cannot work well. Indeed, it is plausible that the only government that can 'work' in many contexts is authoritarian government (see Chapter 7). To take an extreme example, straight constitutional democracy has little or no chance of working today in Burundi. Even attempting it during 1993 led to grotesque slaughter and a nearly instant reversion to autocracy under the minority Tutsi.

competent to elect but not to govern (Charles le Secondat, baron de Montesquieu, *The Spirit of the Laws* (Cambridge: Cambridge University Press, 1989; 1st pub. 1748), book 2, ch. 2, p. 12). But Montesquieu held that the people were incompetent to understand what the more qualified governors could understand. Madison's constraint on voters is motivated by representative democratic theory rather than by a judgement of the weak character of the masses. See further, Samuel H. Beer, *To Make a Nation: The Rediscovery of American Federalism* (Cambridge, Mass.: Harvard University Press, 1993), 227.

Before turning to the strategic structure of the constitutional problem, consider an issue that in a sense is one that the American constitutionalists would not even have recognized but that is often an issue today. We might view a constitution or the rules or the institutions that it sets up as either regulative or constitutive. In its strongest form this distinction might be invoked to ask whether constitutional architects are interested in merely regulating some range of conflictive issues or in more substantially defining the nature of the nation they create with their constitution. Plausibly, one might argue that the issue for some of the Anti-Federalists was that the constitution proposed in 1787–8 would constitute a nation of a kind in which they preferred not to participate. This might have been true of Richard Henry Lee and others whose views are cited below. For Madison and for Andrew Hamilton, however, that constitution merely regulated interactions that the Articles of Confederation handled badly in a nation that was already constituted. For them, the Commerce Clause and therefore the constitution was regulative, not constitutive. Of course, at some level, it was constitutive of the government which it entailed, but its modal purpose for most of the Federalists was merely to make an already functioning society work better.

Contract or Coordination?

One of the oldest and most honoured traditions in political philosophy is the odd claim that a constitution or the very act of forming a government is metaphorically a big contract. There are at least two kinds of force that proponents of contractarianism in political theory seem to expect to gain from this persuasive definition. First, there is the descriptive and explanatory force one might get from relating the creation of a constitution to an act of contracting as implied in the commonplace but fundamentally wrong term, the social contract. Secondly, there is the normative force of using contract theory in the analysis of social institutions to give a justification for them. If we can say that people agreed to certain constitutional arrangements, as they generally do to contracts under which they are legally obligated, we supposedly can go further and say that they are politically obligated to abide by these arrangements. After centuries of arguing that

people must obey monarchical government because the monarch
was put there by god and god's will must be obeyed, the rise of government from the polity rather than by appointment from god
seemed evidently also to need a ground for stipulating the obligation
to obey. During the twentieth century, this urge to find a ground of
obligation was muted into much lesser urges, but consent theory has
somehow managed to live on.

I wish here to argue against the first of these theses to show that
constitutions are not even metaphorically speaking sensibly seen as
contracts. If we wish to explain either the origin or the working of a
constitution, we must jettison this metaphor. I think both the
explanatory and the normative contract theses are false but if one can
first show that constitutional arrangements are not the simple product of agreement in the sense in which contracts are, even hypothet-
ically, the normative thesis loses most of its interest.[4] I will attempt
to establish the first thesis through consideration of the US
Constitution and of the understandings of its rationale and role at the
time of its writing and adoption, with special reference to *The
Federalist Papers* of Hamilton, Madison, and John Jay, writing
jointly as Publius.[5]

What is the difference between a contract and a constitution in
political life? The latter is prior, in the following sense. We all coordinate in having a practice of promising and a law of contract that
make life better for us. A typical contract resolves an exchange or a
prisoner's dilemma problem (which is the game-theoretic representation of exchange, as further discussed below). But the commonplace view that creating a constitution or establishing a government
is equivalent to contracting to cooperate or to live at peace, as though
this were similarly an exchange problem, is wrong-headed. A constitution does not resolve a particular exchange or prisoner's dilemma
interaction. It regulates a long-term pattern of interactions. It establishes conventions in the sociological or strategic sense that make it
easier for us to cooperate and to coordinate in particular moments.
Creating a constitution is itself primarily an act of coordination on
one of many possible ways of ordering our lives together, not an act

---

[4] One might wish to argue, as some contractarian moral theorists do, that we are
bound by those morals that we rationally would assent to. See e.g. David Gauthier,
Morals by Agreement (Oxford: Oxford University Press, 1986).
[5] References to *The Federalist Papers* will be by number in the text. Any standard
edition should suffice for reference.

of cooperating in an exchange or prisoner's dilemma. In the general case over the long term, roughly speaking, we must have one regime: for example, general enforcement of contracts or no enforcement, general protection of property or no protection. Many of us have an easy choice in this general case: we prefer coordination on a regime of enforcement of contracts and protection of property to coordination on a regime of no enforcement or protection.

It is important to keep clear what is the issue here. One can renege on any given contract and plausibly still keep open the opportunity for mutually beneficial contractual relations with other potential partners. But one cannot will away the whole institution of enforcing contracts and then still expect mutually beneficial contractual exchanges with anyone to work. A constitution is not a contract; indeed it creates the institution of contracting, which would be *de facto* impossible without a constitutional or other strong order to back it. Hence, again, its function is to resolve a problem that is prior to contracting by first coordinating us. If we set up a rule that all should coordinate by using the metric system, and we begin to follow that rule, then all will be likely to find it in their interest to do so thereafter. There will be no cheating, no taking advantage of others *by using a different system*. In Hobbes's vision of the creation of an all-powerful sovereign, the problem similarly is one of mere coordination.[6] We all want to have order that will let us prosper through our own efforts and through exchange with others. Once we establish a sovereign or government, we individually find it in our interest to be orderly.

As discussed in Chapter 1, in coordination theory the issue is not that we did agree but that our incentives and those of virtually everyone are to go along once a particular coordination is established. *Coordination theory is primarily a theory of workability*, not of normativity or obligation. A constitution that takes the form of a contract is likely to be less workable because it will not be self-enforcing. It will be subject to renegotiation or even violation any time any group can gain from renegotiating or violating it. Therefore, in contractarian theory, the object is often to give a *normative grounding* for the order established by bargaining, for example, to claim against those who would violate the contractual constitution that they are obligated to it by their prior agreement. In coordination theory,

---

[6] Russell Hardin, 'Hobbesian Political Order', *Political Theory*, 19 (May 1991): 156–80.

there is little explicit attention to normative justification. But one may generally infer that a coordination is good to the extent that it does secure interests while giving incentives to follow it.

The US `vonstitution of 1787–8 was clearly a successful coordination at its core. The core was the elimination of tariff and other trade barriers among the thirteen states, as guaranteed in the Commerce Clause (as discussed further in Chapter 6). It was this issue that brought the conventioneers to Philadelphia, and in its resolution they chose to exceed their mandate and to write a wholly new constitution to replace the Articles of Confederation. The possibilities were either essentially free trade or willy-nilly barriers to trade by the individual states. Some of the Anti-Federalists may have been incoherent in their views, because their estates depended on commercial profits from their produce and they therefore wanted essentially free trade to some extent.[7] Yet, they opposed a national government, which may have been the only way to guarantee free trade. Although Anti-Federalists opposed the values of a larger nation that might dominate local communities, the conventioneers and the later state conventions to ratify the constitution clearly favored re-coordinating from willy-nilly barriers onto free trade. Their choice essentially settled that issue for the next two centuries and presumably still for a long time to come.

There are at least three major ways in which a constitution fundamentally differs from a contract. I wish briefly to discuss each separately below. These are the following. First, the strategic structures of the modal interactions governed by contracts and constitutions are different. A contract typically resolves an immediate prisoner's dilemma interaction (usually, an exchange between two parties); a constitution typically resolves an immediate coordination interaction (the creation of a particular set and form of government institutions). Secondly, a constitution has a far less significant element of agreement behind it than does a contract. This problem has given rise to a remarkably obtuse and unenlightening literature on tacit consent, hypothetical consent, implied consent, and so forth. In practice, acquiescence is more important than agreement for the working of a constitution, while agreement is crucial for obligations under a contract to make sense. Thirdly, and finally, the sources of support for a contract and for a constitution differ radically. A contract is gener-

---

[7] Jackson Turner Main, *The Antifederalists: Critics of the Constitution, 1781–1788* (New York: Norton, 1974; 1st pub. 1961), 117.

ally backed by external sanctions; a constitution is more nearly backed by default, by the difficulty of re-coordinating on an alternative arrangement. A constitution, if it is to work in bringing about and maintaining social order, must be self-enforcing. As Caesar, a pseudonymous colleague of Publius, bluntly put it, what is required of most people is that they 'proceed without mutiny'.[8]

The first of these three claims is about the initial creation of a constitutional order. The claim is simply that the strategic structure of the problem resolved by a constitution is not the prisoner's dilemma. The other two claims are about the way a constitution (with its order), once adopted, works. Their establishment further shows that the interaction at issue—abiding by a constitution—is not a matter of maintaining cooperation in a prisoner's dilemma.

If constitutions are not analogous to contracts, they might seem to be analogous to contracts by convention in which a pattern of prisoner's dilemma interactions gets resolved cooperatively through the rise of a convention that regulates behaviour in future interactions, as will be discussed more fully below.[9] Again, there are elements in common here, but in general a constitution is distinctively different from a contract by convention, primarily in that it generally governs a large-number society, even in the hundreds of millions, while a contract by convention governs ongoing interactions in a dyad or a very small-number group. A constitution for a society of two people would be silly.[10]

The most important element a formal constitution and a contract by convention have in common is that both depend on sanctions not from some external power, as legal contracts typically do, but on sanctions and incentives internal to the group governed by them. Moreover, a constitution must work and be interpreted conventionally, with its content changing over time. But, still, a contract by convention is similar to a simple contract in that it governs a small-number exchange relationship, and is therefore not like a constitution. The incentive structure of a dyadic exchange relation is dramatically different from that of a large-number exchange relation, and it is that incentive structure that allows an individual in a dyadic

[8] Caesar, no. 2, in Kurland and Lerner, *The Founders' Constitution*, 1: 60–1.

[9] For the definition and account of contract by convention, see Russell Hardin, *Collective Action* (Baltimore, Md.: Johns Hopkins University Press for Resources for the Future, 1982), chs. 10–14.

[10] See further, discussion of Amartya Sen's so-called paradox of liberalism, Chapter 2, section on 'Deontological Additions'.

exchange that is iterated over time to sanction a defaulting partner by simply refusing to cooperate further with that partner. Indeed, this is the issue in the logic of collective action. If we are involved in a large-number collective action that requires the participation of all of us, as social order or the adoption of a constitution virtually does, we cannot simply sanction violators of that order by refusing to cooperate with them.

Once we are clear what a constitution is not, we may then wonder why we want one. I will conclude with a brief discussion of what one might call the strategic functions of a formal constitution.

Finally, note that, once it is in place, a constitutional government can regulate all types of problems: conflict, exchange, and coordination. At that point, the coordination is, in a sense, *in medias res* rather than *ab initio*. The spontaneous coordination that it takes to create a constitution is likely to be more demanding than the coordination required to maintain it thereafter. This follows from the fact that the burden of undoing the constitution and putting something else in its place, that is to say, of re-coordinating, is likely to be the chief obstacle to change. This will be a central consideration in Chapter 6, which addresses how a constitutional regime manages economic and demographic change. For the present chapter, the focus is rather on *initial spontaneous coordination to create a constitution.*

The Strategic Structure of a Constitution

To make the case against seeeing a constitution as a metaphorical or real contract as transparent as possible requires some technical discussion of the game-theoretic structures of the two. This can be done, however, without any heavy machinery. We may characterize all strategic interactions between two or more actors as of three types. If preference orderings over outcomes are strictly opposing, a two-party interaction is *pure conflict*. If preference orderings over outcomes are identical, an interaction is *pure coordination*. All other interactions involve a mixture of both conflict and coordination, with some outcomes in opposing orders and some in identical orders. These are *mixed-motive* interactions.[11] The prisoner's

[11] Many interactions that are technically mixed-motive are approximately pure conflict or pure coordination because the only outcomes of interest to the parties to

dilemma is the most studied and discussed of all mixed-motive interactions, largely no doubt because it represents the strategic structure
of an exchange interaction.[12]

The modal purpose of a traditional contract is to regulate an
exchange, hence to resolve a prisoner's dilemma interaction. The
modal purpose of a constitution is to resolve a coordination interaction. Two-person versions of these two kinds of interaction are represented in Figures 3.1 and 3.2.[13] In these figures, the payoffs to each
player are strictly ordinal. That is, the outcome with a payoff of 1 is
the player's first choice, or most preferred outcome, that with a payoff of 2 is the player's second choice, and so forth.[14] In each cell of
the matrices, the first payoff goes to the row player and the second
to the column player (in the mnemonic Roman Catholic convention). Hence, the top left cell of the first game (prisoner's dilemma)
gives both players their second-best outcomes. Resolution of a prisoner's dilemma inherently requires the creation of relevant incentives, usually in the form of threatened sanctions, to get both players
to choose their cooperate rather than their defect strategies.
Resolution of a coordination game typically requires little more than
signalling, for example, to get both players in Figure 3.2 to choose
their strategies I or their strategies II.

		Column	
		Cooperate	Defect
	Cooperate	2, 2	4, 1
Row			
	Defect	1, 4	3, 3

FIG. 3.1. Game 1: prisoner's dilemma or exchange

the interaction involve either conflict or coordination but not both. In general, what
is of interest in large-scale social contexts is that an interaction involves coordination
for enough important groups that they can find a mutually beneficial order for themselves, an order that cannot be upset by any remaining, less efficacious groups.

[12] Russell Hardin, 'Exchange Theory on Strategic Bases', *Social Science
Information*, 2 (1982): 251–72.

[13] One should beware of generalization from two-person games to the interactions
of whole societies or even larger groups. I will generally be concerned with interactions between large groups, so that the two-person analogy should not be misleading.

[14] Such representative games are more commonly presented with cardinal payoffs,
e.g., in dollars. Cardinal representations are, however, often grossly misleading. For
arguments about social arrangements, ordinal representations are often to be preferred.

		Column	
		I	II
	I	1, 1	2, 2
Row			
	II	3, 3	1, 1

FIG. 3.2. Game 2: coordination

It would be wrong to say that there are no similarities between the two kinds of interaction. Obviously, the reason a prisoner's dilemma is worthy of *joint cooperative* resolution is that it has a large element of coordination within it: all parties to it prefer the all-cooperate to the all-defect outcome. If we analytically define all games for some number of players, we will generally find that most of them include elements both of coordination and of conflict. Moreover in a time of constitutional creation or revision one might generally expect to find genuine conflicts of interest over the form of certain of the constitutional provisions. For example, Hamilton objected to the US Constitution that it did not provide for life terms for senators and for the chief executive. His opponents accused him of wanting to impose an aristocracy and a monarchy. Hamilton might have answered that they were right but that an aristocracy and a monarchy would produce better government than would a relatively free-wheeling democracy with rapid turnover in higher offices.[15] But he might also have supposed that, while any strong national government was preferable to a weak national government, still an aristocracy with a monarchy would better serve *his* interests than would a more open democracy. Hence, there was perhaps in part merely a disagreement over the facts of how different forms of government would work. But in part there may also have been a partial conflict of interest, as there is in a prisoner's dilemma.

To the extent that there was a genuine conflict of interest as between possible coordination outcomes, the interaction was more nearly analogous to the unequal coordination in game 3 (see Fig. 3.3) than the Coordination in game 2 (Fig. 3.2). In game 3 there are two outcomes that both of us prefer to both of the other outcomes. But I prefer one of these, say, (1, 2), to the other, (2, 1), while you prefer (2, 1) to (1, 2). Whether we should now see our interaction as essen-

---

[15] He declared as much at the Convention, 18 June 1787 (in Kurland and Lerner, *The Founders' Constitution*, 1: 254–7, at pp. 255–6).

tially one of coordination rather than of conflict turns on how the differences between 1 and 2 compare to those between 2 and 3 in our estimations. If 1 and 2 are negligibly different while 2 and 3 are radically different for each of us, ours is predominantly a coordination interaction. If the converse is true, ours is essentially a conflict interaction. Even if 1 and 2 are substantially different, 2 may still be radically better than 3. In this case we may face a problem of persistent disadvantage for one party if we successfully coordinate one way rather than the other so that our final coordination may seem exploitative.[16] But this is still a coordination problem and not a prisoner's dilemma problem. If it were the latter, it would have to be true that, once the choice of, say, government without a monarchy was made, there would still be reason for Hamilton to try to free-ride on the coordination on not having a monarch by enjoying the benefits of that social order while still going his own way with a monarchy. But that is incoherent. Those who insist that Hamilton contracted over this issue should explain the meaning of his then free-riding on that agreement.

		Column	
		I	II
	I	2, 1	3, 3
Row			
	II	3, 3	1, 2

FIG. 3.3. Game 3: unequal coordination

Some degree of conflict of interest is inherent in a constitutional arrangement just because the arrangement establishes institutions that can be used for narrow purposes, such as assisting me in securing my interests against you. As Hamilton noted of the US Constitution, it affected many 'particular interests' (*Federalist*, 1). He had earlier noted that any measure 'will operate more to the benefit of some parts, than of others', but had argued that that was silly ground for opposing measures whose tendency was generally

[16] Russell Hardin, 'Political Obligation', in Alan Hamlin and Philip Pettit, eds., *The Good Polity* (Oxford: Basil Blackwell, 1989), 103–19, at pp. 114–15; Edna Ullmann-Margalit, *The Emergence of Norms* (Oxford: Oxford University Press, 1977), 134–97.

beneficial.[17] Clearly, Hamilton supposed that, at worst, the problem is one of unequal coordination. If it is fundamentally a prisoner's dilemma—rather than a coordination interaction with several coordination outcomes, some of which you slightly prefer, others of which I slightly prefer, and so forth—then it must be true that some outcomes that are *best for some* of us are *worst for others*. There must be outcomes analogous to the (1, 4) and the (4, 1) outcomes in Fig. 3.1 in the view of major groups. If it is fundamentally a coordination interaction, this is not true.

The factual question here for 1787 in the thirteen states is one that *The Federalist Papers* suppose admitted of none but the simple answer that *no one could sensibly have thought it better to have no Union rather than some moderately powerful government*. (Of course, some of the Anti-Federalists disagreed—evidently, they were not sensible.) Madison argued that even a strong faction must want protection of *all* parties (*Federalist*, 51). Some people clearly preferred a weaker government to the one promised by the Constitution and perhaps some preferred strategically to block the Constitution in order to get a new negotiation for some other form of government, whether weaker or stronger. Hamilton, perhaps with some exaggeration, argued in the opening *Federalist* that the choice was of 'an adoption of the new Constitution or a dismemberment of the Union' (*Federalist*, 1, final para.). As discussed further below (in the section, 'Incentives to Abide by a Constitution'), there was no general incentive for anyone to enter the agreement in the hope of later cheating and refusing to cooperate, as one might well do with a contract or a promise to resolve a prisoner's dilemma.

All of these points would follow from the supposition that the payoff from coordination swamped all other possibilities, a supposition that must have seemed compelling to the Federalists. Although there were different plausible coordination outcomes with some perhaps preferring one and others preferring another, there was not likely to be any major group that could seriously suppose that some outcome was the analogue of the (1, 4) outcome of Fig. 3.1 with itself getting the most preferred payoff and some other group getting the

---

[17] Kurland and Lerner, *The Founders' Constitution*, i. 477–9, at p. 479. This was a constant theme for Hamilton, who, for example, justified excluding an explicit provision on paying off the national debt in the Constitution 'from the impolicy of multiplying obstacles to its reception on collateral details' (letter of 26 May 1792 to Edward Carrington in Max Farrand, ed., *The Records of the Federal Convention of 1787*, 4 vols. (New Haven: Yale University Press, 1937, rev. edn.; 1st pub. 1911) 3: 366–7).

least preferred payoff instead of both getting some intermediate compromise. For example, Hamilton and other financiers could not have supposed they would be best off when Thomas Jefferson and other plantation agrarians were worst off. Rather, both must have supposed that for either to prosper the other would also have to prosper. If either were very badly off, the other would also be badly off. The same would be true for Madison's other pairings of conflicting interests in *Federalist*, 10.

Let us consider this last point in greater detail. A contract generally regulates an exchange. What is at stake in an exchange between us is the trading (1) to me of something you have that I value more than I value what I have and (2) to you of something I have that you value more than you value what you have. That is a clumsy but full statement. If I can take what you have while keeping what I have, the outcome is best for me and worst for you: (1, 4). One could say we increase value if, instead, we make the exchange but it is more perspicuous simply to say that we both are made better off—that is, exchange is mutually advantageous. What a stable government that backs contracts, property, various kinds of cooperative organizations, collective decision-making capacity, and other arrangements does is give us the stable expectations to justify longer-term efforts to create values, to specialize in ways that would not benefit us except for the strong expectation of being able to trade what we produce for other things that we could not so readily or efficiently produce. It will do this by blocking (1, 4) outcomes in which we do not exchange but I merely take from you. It may also create so-called public goods that make virtually all of us more productive, as when it dredges harbours and rivers, maintains roads, or builds bridges, to cite the mundane examples of Adam Smith.

The most important very early effects of the US Constitution were to eliminate military insecurity between the states (*Federalist*, 9) and to increase the scale of the market in which entrepreneurs, farmers, and plantation owners in the states could trade (*Federalist*, 11, 23). The Constitution was, in Clinton Rossiter's words, seen as 'an open door to prosperity, and a shield to independence'.[18] The problem of insecurity was not as idle as it now might seem, not least because the states were in severe competition for control of new territories to the west. Union under a strong national government took away most of

[18] Clinton Rossiter, *1787: The Grand Convention* (New York: Macmillan, 1966), 296.

the point of such competition and eased the way to development without conflict. The Commerce Clause of the Constitution prohibited taxes on interstate commerce and let the national government generally bring about uniformity in certain laws that made trade and other activities easier and more beneficial.

The object of this clause had been the early impetus to the Philadelphia Convention. The Annapolis Convention of September 1786 was called by several states to consider ways to regulate trade and commerce more harmoniously. Because it was attended by delegates from too few states, the Convention merely recommended a further convention to consider the broader range of problems with the Articles of Confederation. Two of the twelve commissioners in Annapolis were Hamilton and Madison.[19] Madison claimed that the Commerce Clause of the new Constitution was really the only new power that that document gave to the new government (*Federalist*, 45). The purpose of the clause had such popularity that designing the rest of the constitution to hang around it was the chief task of the Philadelphia Convention. The point was to coordinate the thirteen states on an institutional structure that would enable more productive trade relations. The point was not to bargain for any trade in particular but to ease the way to such bargains by eliminating the wasteful transaction costs entailed in interstate tariffs. Literally *nothing* was exchanged by the conventioneers. They were not involved in interstate trade at all although the object of their deliberations was interstate trade. They merely coordinated on an institutional structure that eased the way to such trade.

Why then do some writers seem to think that the problem to be resolved by the creation of government is like that of the prisoner's dilemma so that its resolution requires something like a contract? Perhaps the error is merely the trivially wrong supposition that, because the class of issues to be resolved in the future in the larger society was exchanges, anything that helped in resolving them must have been an exchange. This is merely illogical and false. For example, setting up a communication system could help us make exchanges, but it need not be the product of an exchange.

There is also perhaps a logical slippage that is more subtle. At times the proponents of the view that creating government must be

---

[19] 'Proceedings of Commissioners to Remedy Defects of the Federal Government', in Kurland and Lerner, *The Founders' Constitution*, i. 185–7; also see accompanying documents, ch. 6 in ibid.

a big bargain seem to run two seemingly inconsistent views together. One of these views is that our problem is one of merely maintaining what we have, as though it were virtually a problem of pure conflict. I want everything I have plus everything you have—and you do, too. The other view is that there are in a sense mutual gains to be had (or mutual benefits to be maintained) by securing one allocation rather than another. The combination of these views of the issue makes it appear to be a prisoner's dilemma, in which the pair of outcomes (1, 4) and (4, 1) is in conflict, while the pair of outcomes (2, 2) and (3, 3) sets up a potential for mutual advantage if we move from the latter to the former.

What makes the problem of coordination rise above the conflict in my wanting everything and your wanting everything is the tremendous prospect for production and mutual gain from allowing each of us to keep some of what we have and produce. If we successfully coordinate on a governmental structure to establish order and regulate exchange, our outcome is not then worse for me than the state in which I get everything we already have and you get nothing. It is radically better than that outcome. It is an outcome that only a productive society could provide for any of us. The best state for both of us is then (1, 1); the state of nature allocation of everything to me or to you is (2, 4) or (4, 2); and the status quo in the state of nature is (3, 3), as represented in Figure 3.4. Coordination on a constitutional order takes us out of the state of nature. It does not merely regulate our relations while we remain in the dismally unproductive conditions of the state of nature. Hobbes clearly saw all of this. It is odd that many of his readers today and many students of the so-called social contract, who have the simplifying advantage of knowing a bit of game theory, fail to see it.

		Column	
		I	II
Row	I	1, 1	4, 2
	II	2, 4	3, 3

Fig. 3.4. Game 4: constitutional coordination
Note: First outcome is *far* superior to second-best outcome.

Thinking of the so-called state of nature is grossly misleading in this respect because it tends to focus our attention on what we already have rather than on what we may produce under the relevant regime of coordination. The central value of government that makes it easy to assent to is that it enables us to coordinate in the production of enormous gains.[20] If its chief value were to prevent our conflicts over what we already have from turning violent, its rise would be the mystery that many writers try to solve. Indeed, not only is it true that constitutional coordination takes us to our best outcome, but that outcome is radically better than the second-best outcome for any one of us, in which one merely has all that is available in the unproductive state of nature. The differences between the second and third outcomes is extremely small in comparison to the difference between the first and second outcomes, which is enormous. The latter difference is analogous to that between the average condition in a very primitive subsistence economy and the average condition in a richly productive modern society such as Sweden. There is simply no way for one member of the primitive society to become wealthy by absconding with what others in that society have.

Many actual constitutions do have the character of contracts at their core. They cover the agreed resolution of a bargaining process in which interests compromise. Unfortunately, constitutions that include contracts at their core are typically unstable. Unlike ordinary contracts within a legal system, they lack the benefit of an outside enforcement agency. If a constitution is to be stable, it must be self-enforcing, it must be a coordination, because the nation cannot go to a supranational agency to enforce its citizens' contractual agreement with each other or with their government. With an ordinary contract, I may be able to say it is in my interest to have the whole package of your action and my action *plus* some confidence in enforcement against either of us if necessary. Therefore, we contract. If later it appears that enforcement will not happen, you or I may no longer see it as in our interest to comply with the original agreement. A constitution that has the form of a contract immediately faces this problem of how to motivate compliance without enforcement.

The Anti-Federalists envisioned the Articles of Confederation as a contract and the constitution as something very different. Surprisingly, they had a more cogent grasp of the issues than most later commentators have had. They argued specifically for a contract between the states *against* the national union of the constitution.

[20] See further, Russell Hardin, 'Bargaining for Justice', *Social Philosophy and Policy*, 5 (Spring 1988): 65–74.

They held the view, common for centuries, that a contract in the state of nature could be abrogated at will. Hence, under a contract between sovereign states, secession was a natural move, because such a contract is unenforceable by a superior power. Their view on this point was shared by Madison, who therefore wanted a constitution that would coordinate (Madison spoke of 'concert') the states on a national government.[21] The traditional view was an odd view of contracting. According to it, the Articles of Confederation were not even the result of a bargain. They were merely a prior agreement by the states to do whatever they subsequently unanimously agreed to do. The chief causal effect of the Articles was to establish a forum in which to try to reach the later unanimous agreements. This is not in itself a useless purpose. In the days of the Cold War, the United States and the Soviet Union created a standing consultative commission in order to have a forum for reaching modest agreements on oversight of arms control. Still, the Anti-Federalists were right to hold that the Articles were not a constitution and that the proposed constitution was not a contract.

There were bargains in 1787, such as that over how to count slaves and eventually to end their importation. But these were bargains that would be enforceable *only by the government which got its power from the fundamental coordination of most interests* in organizing economic relations across the states of the union. The issue of slavery was revived when the innovation of adding new states to the union threatened the possibility of a constitutional amendment to abolish slavery. Such an amendment would have cost many southerners more than they expected to lose from the breakdown of free trade among the states. The threat of such a change therefore broke the initial coordination and broke the union. But after that conflict was settled more or less irrevocably, the constitutional arrangements again were essentially coordinative.

Finally, note that there were two groups in 1787–8 who plausibly saw their interests as essentially opposed to those of the Federalists. Many of the Anti-Federalists seemed to prefer the breakup of the Union to strong government. And the slaves, who were not party to the constitutional decision, may similarly have seen it in their interest not to have union under a constitution that perpetuated their

---

[21] James Madison, 'Vices of the Political System of the United States', Apr. 1787, in Kurland and Lerner, *The Founders' Constitution*, i. 166–9. See Beer, *To Make a Nation*, 222–4, 239–40.

condition. Hence, both these groups may clearly have preferred the status quo, even if it entailed collapse of union, to the creation of a strong national government under the Constitution. If this is a correct view of their interests, it follows, of course, that from their perspective, the issue of the Constitution was essentially one predominately of conflict with the Federalists. They were in neither a prisoner's dilemma nor a coordination interaction with the latter. This must be an accurate account of at least the *statement* of the position of the relatively anarchistic opponents of the Constitution and of those, such as Brutus and Cato, who thought no republic of such size as the thirteen states together could be anything but despotic.[22] But we may reasonably doubt that this was the actual view of some of them (for example, George Clinton of New York) once the rhetorical moment of debate passed and they had to decide whether to join or stay out of a union that was going to happen with or without them. Adoption of the Constitution by the nation in general did not serve the interests of the Anti-Federalists as they saw them. But, once it was adopted by enough states to create a nation, living with the Constitution did serve the interests of the Anti-Federalists. Whether it also represented the interests of the slaves turns on what one would have expected to issue from the failure of the Constitution.

Consider the Anti-Federalist opposition more extensively. This opposition focused on the size of the proposed House of Representatives, which, from a concern to keep it small enough to allow genuine debate, was made too small to give genuine representation to various communities and groups. Philip Kurland and Ralph Lerner conclude that this issue eclipsed all others during the ratification debates.[23] The Anti-Federalists supposed that government could be genuinely representative only if each group or community were represented proportionately by its own members. Through such passive representation, as opposed to representation by mandate, the legislature could be expected to take community interests into account. As Brutus noted, 'the representatives ought to be intimately acquainted with the wants, understand the interests of the

---

[22] See essays by Brutus and Cato, in Kurland and Lerner, *The Founders' Constitution*, i. 124–7. Hamilton goes a long way towards demolishing their claims in *Federalist*, 9 and Madison addresses them further in *Federalist*, 10, 63, and, less persuasively, in the famous no. 51.

[23] Kurland and Lerner, *The Founders' Constitution*, i. 386.

several orders in the society, and feel a proper sense and becoming zeal to promote their prosperity'.[24] Again, once they lost this debate and the constitution was in place to govern the creation of a government, the debate was virtually a dead letter.[25] There was no forum in which the Anti-Federalist vision could be successfully articulated. Madison's defence of the small size of the House in *Federalist* 55 ignores this concern and clearly focuses on two issues: the effectiveness of a smaller body in having intelligent debates and reaching decisions, and the greater likelihood that a very large body would become oligarchic.[26] The first claim was no defence at all for the Anti-Federalists, who did not want effective national government. The second claim was one that would have motivated both sides, if they agreed with Madison's sociological analysis.

It is also plausible that some of the Anti-Federalists opposed a national government that would diminish their own local power and that others merely misunderstood their interests through 'the honest errors of minds led astray by preconceived jealousies and fears', as Hamilton supposed (*Federalist*, 1). Both these classes of opponents must then also have seen themselves in simple conflict with the Federalists.

Did the Federalists actually see their problem in resolving the weakness of government under the Articles of Confederation as essentially one of coordination? Many of their statements indicate that commonly they did. *The Federalist Papers* are laced with this view, as in Hamilton's opening and closing comments that the issue was Union under the Constitution or dismemberment, 'the very existence of the nation' (*Federalist*, 1, 85). George Washington strongly advocated a convention to revise the Articles of

[24] Brutus, Essay 3, in Herbert J. Storing, ed., *The Complete Anti-Federalist*, 7 vols. (Chicago: University of Chicago Press, 1981), 2.9.42. For a very good discussion of the ratification debate on this point, see Bernard Manin, *Principes du gouvernement représentatif* (Paris: Calmann-Lévy, 1995), 143–70.

[25] One constitutional issue that arguably was related to this issue was the Supreme Court decision in *Baker v. Carr* that required states to equalize the populations of congressional districts. But opposition to *Baker v. Carr* turned rather on issues of states' rights than on defence of small communities *per se*. See *Baker v. Carr*, 369 U.S. 186 (1962).

[26] Madison had a grasp of the 'iron law of oligarchy' in organizations, and, as the House of Representatives grew, his argument has proved true. He must also have supposed a body as large as today's House of Representatives (435 members) to be too large to have intelligent debates. Again, he may have been right. On the iron law, see Robert Michels, *Political Parties: A Sociological Study of the Oligarchical Tendencies of Modern Democracy*, ed. S. M. Lipset (New York: Free Press, 1966; 1st pub. 1911).

Confederation and, further, advocated expeditious rather than ideal change.[27] His role in Philadelphia was, outside all debates, to stand only for the final document and its eventual government. Caesar wrote explicitly that quite different constitutions might be equally acceptable (in the epigraph to this chapter).[28] Indeed, had the Articles of Confederation merely been changed to allow for amendment by a supermajority of, say, three-quarters rather than by unanimity, it might well have survived as the US Constitution and might have worked about as well as the one drafted in Philadelphia to replace it. Replacing it avoided the great difficulty of getting past the unanimity requirement for changing the amendment procedure. Madison pre-empted the focus of the debates in Philadelphia by bringing in his proposed Virginia Plan, a full-scale constitution, at the beginning of the convention. He evidently had no intention of letting the convention do only what it was legally constituted to do.

There might have been other, substantially different constitutions that could have been defended as cogently as that which the Philadelphia Convention proposed. Under the circumstances, however, once many of the most important political leaders of the thirteen states spent a few hot months in Philadelphia hammering out a rescue of the Union, they effectively selected one from all plausible points of coordination. To this extent, James Wilson's claim before the Pennsylvania ratifying convention that the drafters of the Constitution 'exercised no power at all' is surely false.[29] They forced the selection of a particular constitutional order to stand as the sole effective alternative to the dismemberment that Hamilton posed as the alternative to accepting the Constitution. In the concluding number of *The Federalist Papers* Hamilton observed, with eminent plausibility, that the prospect of 'assembling a new convention, under circumstances in any degree so favorable to a happy issue, as those in which the late convention met, deliberated, and concluded' was nil (*Federalist*, 85).

---

[27] George Washington, Letter to Henry Knox, 3 February 1787, in Kurland and Lerner, *The Founders' Constitution*, i. 188.

[28] Caesar, no. 2, in Kurland and Lerner, *The Founders' Constitution*, i. 60–1.

[29] Speech excerpted, in Kurland and Lerner, *The Founders' Constitution*, i. 202.

Coordination on and under a Constitution

In claiming that a particular constitution is a device for coordination we could be making two quite different claims: that the choice of the content of the constitution was itself a matter of coordination or that the constitution works by successfully coordinating actions under it. The US Constitution was a coordination in both senses, although it took political contrivance to get coordination on its initial content and ratification, and there was substantial opposition throughout both stages. It was successful because it did generally benefit all major interests to go along with it—not to mutiny—once its government was in place. Indeed, it generally benefited most major groups to go along with its adoption once it was virtually assured of being the only choice to make. Hence, once enough other states ratified it, opposition in Virginia was finally overcome to let Virginians such as Edmund Randolph, who had refused to sign the document at the Philadelphia Convention, vote for it. In the end, even North Carolina and Rhode Island, despite strong, arguably large majority sentiment against the Constitution, voted narrowly for it in preference to being left out of the new nation. Randolph was criticized as inconsistent, but wrongly. What he wanted in Philadelphia was national union under a different constitution. But by the time of the Virginia Convention, there was no chance that there could be such an outcome because national union under the Philadelphia Constitution was virtually certain. Therefore his choice had been reduced to that between national union under that constitution with Virginia in it or national union without Virginia.

How did the initial coordination get contrived? There were three large groups interested in the outcome: plantation agrarians, commercial and financial interests, and communitarian rural citizens, many of whom were eventually the Anti-Federalists. The plantation agrarians and communitarians shared commitments to rural values. But the plantation agrarians also shared commitments with the commercial interests to larger, easier markets. Plantations were, after all, in the business of mass production, not merely of self-sufficiency. Bringing these two together gave a majority to the programme of a national government with jurisdiction over commerce. Together, they dominated the convention.

Their domination was heightened by the fact that the rural communitarians so opposed the purpose of creating a stronger national government that they did not participate fully in the convention. The two communitarian delegates from New York withdrew, thereby removing one hostile state's vote against strong national government from all votes at the convention on matters taken after 10 July, which is essentially when the detail of the constitution began to be determined. The state of Rhode Island refused even to send delegates to the convention. Had Rhode Island sent delegates, it seems most likely they would have been similarly hostile to strong national government. Hence, the communitarians were in default at the convention by two full votes out of thirteen.

The loss of these two states is only part of the story of communitarian default. When asked at the Virginia state ratifying convention why, although elected as a delegate, he had not attended in Philadelphia to influence the design of the document, Patrick Henry retorted, 'I smelt a rat'.[30] The Federalists must have been grateful for his olfactory judgement, because he might have been a formidable orator at the convention. Several men who were elected as delegates declined to serve, and eight who were elected but did not evidently decline to serve nevertheless did not attend. Jackson Turner Main concludes that at least four of those who declined were probably Anti-Federalist, none evidently Federalist. Of the eight who did not attend, two were Federalist and one was Anti-Federalist.[31] Defaulters from Virginia may have given that state's vote to Madison and friends. The defaulters therefore virtually handed the initial victory in defining the constitution to the nationalist combination of plantation agrarians and commercial interests. There were reasons other than opposition to the proceedings for not attending, reasons that may also have worked against communitarian representation. Those who attended virtually had to be wealthy to pay their way and somewhat idle or able to turn their affairs over to others for the duration for a whole summer.[32] Many of the communitarian farmers

---

[30] Farrand, *Records of the Federal Convention*, iii. 558 n.

[31] Main, *The Antifederalists*. The details are scattered throughout his account. Anti-Federalist decliners included Richard Henry Lee, Patrick Henry, and Thomas Nelson of Virginia (pp. 177 and 224), and Willie Jones of North Carolina (p. 35). Anti-Federalist Abraham Clark of New Jersey did not attend (p. 195), nor did Federalists Henry Laurens of South Carolina and John Pickering of New Hampshire (pp. 212, 222).

[32] Gordon S. Wood, 'Interests and Disinterestedness in the Making of the Constitution', in Richard Beeman, Stephen Botein, and Edward C. Carter, II, eds., *Beyond Confederation: Origins of the Constitution and American National Identity* (Chapel Hill, NC: University of North Carolina Press, 1987), 69–109, esp. p. 72.

might not have wanted to neglect their modest enterprises during the summer season.

Further, to exaggerate, but only somewhat, the two dominant interests at the convention simply left their own conflicts with each other out of discussion.[33] In part, this was because Hamilton, the most adamant of the commercial party, was weakened when the departure of his fellow New Yorkers denied New York a formal vote in further proceedings, and because Jefferson, among the most adamant of the plantation agrarians, was not at the convention (although his absence may not have mattered much because Jefferson lacked the gift for public speaking).

In part, however, it was because the two parties may have misjudged enough of the future economic developments that they did not adequately attempt to secure their interests with constitutional safeguards (this issue is discussed more extensively in Chapter 6, where the focus is on the later workability of the Constitution). Madison, for example, seemed to expect that the economy would remain primarily agrarian into the far distant future, so much so that he held the Malthusian view that population growth must soon be limited by the supply of arable land.[34] Hence, the conventioneers were able to coordinate on a relatively limited national government with the power to regulate trade and to unify the nation in international relations but without a specific economic charge. Or rather, the clear majority of the conventioneers were able to coordinate. Indeed, in the end, almost all of those who remained to the end of the convention accepted the draft constitution as an improvement over the Articles of Confederation, in comparison to which it served their mutual advantage, and they were the politically effective group who could get it written and put up for adoption.

[33] Thornton Anderson divides the delegates into three groups: nationalists (such as Hamilton and Madison), state Federalists, and defenders of state sovereignty and equality. From interesting factor analyses of votes taken at the Philadelphia Convention, he finds that much of the debate focused on the division of the first two groups. In essence, the state Federalists were the centrists who therefore got much of their way in forging the details of the constitution because their votes tipped the scales one way or the other. See Anderson, *Creating the Constitution: The Convention of 1787 and the First Congress* (University Park, Pa.: Penn State Press, 1994).
[34] See his speeches of 26 June and 7 August, Farrand, *Records of the Federal Convention*, i. 421–3, ii. 203–4. He also had republican agrarian leanings: 'It follows, that the greater the proportion of this class [those who provide at once their own food and raiment] to the whole society, the more free, the more independent, and the more happy must be the society itself' (Madison, 'Republican Distribution of Citizens', 5 Mar 1792, in Kurland and Lerner, *The Founders' Constitution*, i. 680–1.

Charles Beard has argued that support for the Constitution was a clear function of economic interests.[35] The prosperous business and plantation classes were for it; small farmers were against it. One could break this thesis into two stages: writing the Constitution and ratifying it. On the account above of the convention debates, it seems transparent that the thesis is roughly correct for the first stage. Moneyed interests and trade carried the day, not least because they were substantially overrepresented—it was their issue, after all, that brought the conventioneers together. The thesis also seems to be correct for the second stage, although even here it may have taken extensive political contrivance and no little luck for the advocates of the constitution to win.[36] If the bulk of the small farmers, who constituted the large majority of male property owners, were opposed, then adoption of the Constitution required their failure to vote. In essence, they acquiesced to letting the Constitution govern them even before that Constitution was in place.

At both stages, the Constitution and the object of the Commerce Clause were grand coordinations for those who stood to benefit from them. These people gained control of the convention and, as Evelyn Fink and William Riker argue, they also gained control of the ratification process, largely through controlling the agenda and timing of the votes.[37] By staging votes in the states where there was little or no opposition first, the Federalists were able to make the votes of later states a matter of joining the coordination or accepting a world even worse than that of the Articles of Confederation, a world in which they would be outside the nation and unable to enjoy the benefits it offered and, just possibly, at risk of war from the more populous new nation. Presumably, even many Rhode Islanders could see that that was an easy choice. The Federalists were also greatly helped in coordination on ratification by the failure of most eligible voters to vote—from the beginning US democracy has not been very participatory.[38]

[35] Charles A. Beard, *An Economic Interpretation of the Constitution of the United States* (New York: Macmillan, 1935; 1st pub. 1913).

[36] See e.g. Cheryl L. Eavey and Gary J. Miller, 'Constitutional Conflict in State and Nation', in Bernard Grofman and Donald Wittman, eds., *The Federalist Papers and the New Institutionalism* (New York: Agathon, 1989), 205–19.

[37] Evelyn C. Fink and William H. Riker, 'The Strategy of Ratification', in Grofman and Wittman, *The Federalist Papers and the New Institutionalism*, 220–55.

[38] Fink and Riker, 'The Strategy of Ratification', 221.

A dozen years later, the concurrence of commercial and plantation interests had broken and the communitarians seemingly became part of the Jeffersonian hegemony.[39] But by then, the commercial constitution was in place and few if any groups could benefit from not going along with its coordination of the society. And even then, the communitarians lost their programme forever in the 'agricultural empirialism' that the Jeffersonians thought justified the purchase of Louisiana and that made the nation so grand that the possibility— and until recently, the very idea—of communitarianism was buried.[40] Thereafter, all parties seemed able to coordinate on nationalist urges. It took the conflict over slavery finally to break the force of that coordination and yet, even then, the coordination had led to the growth of enough power in the national government for the constitution to prevail by force. The Constitution and the government it created were massively successful at coordinating the nation, at reinforcing themselves.

Agreement and a Constitution

Agreement to a contract and to a constitution differ in two important respects: whether one agrees at all and, if one does, what one agrees to. To come into being or to be effective, a constitution does not require universal or even widespread agreement. Indeed, one of the appeals of proposing a new constitution in 1787 rather than proposing amendments to the Articles of Confederation was that the former could be done without the destructive 'absurdity' of the unanimity required by the latter, especially when unanimity could be blocked by tiny but obstinate Rhode Island (*Federalist*, 40). In many contexts a constitution does not even require majority support, it merely needs lack of sufficient opposition.

[39] On Anderson's account, one might suppose that the two factions of state Federalists, and defenders of state sovereignty and equality were united in the Jeffersonian party, with state Federalists still holding the middle, swing vote and finally breaking from its partial coalition with the nationalists. That would mean Madison either was an opportunist going with the winner or was no longer a nationalist. Anderson, *Creating the Constitution*.

[40] Charles A. Beard and Mary R. Beard, *The Rise of American Civilization*, 2 vols. (New York: Macmillan, 1930; 1st pub. 1927) i. 391–436.

The US Constitution was adopted in the most grudging of ways. Two of the eventual states first rejected it and only later accepted it after it had taken effect as the result of the ratifications of enough other states. Although Rhode Island's licence plates do not proudly proclaim it the last to hold out, Rhode Island voters rejected the Constitution in a statewide referendum by the resounding margin of 2,711 to 239; more than two years passed before a Rhode Island state convention ratified the Constitution—after Washington had already been the first president of the new nation for more than a year. North Carolina's first constitutional convention refused to ratify the Constitution; a second convention ratified it more than a year later—again, after Washington entered office as president. Some states ratified the Constitution by large majorities—Delaware, New Jersey, and Georgia even by unanimous consent of their constitutional conventions. But several others voted for it by narrow margins.

Of the three crucial large states in the middle of the proposed Union—New York, Pennsylvania, and Virginia—only Pennsylvania ratified by a comfortable margin. New York, indeed, elected to its state convention a substantial majority of delegates opposed to ratification. Hamilton privately threatened that New York City would secede from the state if the state refused to join the Union. Perhaps this threat turned the convention by convincing enough of the conventioneers of the opposite of their belief that there would be no Union without New York—namely, that there would be no New York without Union.[41] Had the Anti-Federalists not put off the convention on ratification out of hostility to it, they might well have voted by a large margin against and might then have tipped other states against, thereby killing the constitution. Instead, they were forced to vote after ten states, one more than necessary, had already ratified. Several weeks after Virginia's vote as the tenth state to ratify, the Anti-Federalist majority at the New York Convention caucused and decided that some of them should vote for ratification, but

---

[41] Rossiter, *1787*, 294. See also, Forrest McDonald, *We the People: The Economic Origins of the Constitution* (Chicago: University of Chicago Press, 1958), 287–8. For a summary record of the ratification, see Michael Kammen, *The Origins of the American Constitution: A Documentary History* (New York: Penguin, 1986), pp. xxviii–xxix. For a more discursive account, see Rossiter, *1787*, ch. 14. The New York City threat may not have been idle. After Rhode Island seven times defeated calls even to hold a ratification convention, Providence seceded and, at last, Rhode Island, long after the new nation was under way with its first government, called a convention and barely voted to ratify.

only enough to make a bare majority.[42] Of the eleven states that ratified in time to participate in the formation of the new government, Rossiter supposes at least four could easily have been lost, thereby killing the Constitution, but for the shrewdness of the Federalist advocates and some accidents of timing, such as that in New York, one of the most important states.[43]

Despite this grudging acceptance, the US Constitution has had an extraordinary impact on social and political relations in North America. In this respect, a constitution is clearly like a convention in the strategic sense: It may not give you the best of all results, but it gives you the best you can expect *given that almost everyone else is following it.* Can one imagine in a like fashion a contract that bound those who had in no sense agreed to it? The Constitution is not so pristine as the driving convention that induces people in North America to drive right, that arguably even morally requires them to do so; but it is very imposing even for those who would never have voted for it.

Geoffrey Brennan and James M. Buchanan say that 'The rules of political order . . . can be legitimately derived only from the agreement among individuals as members of the polity'.[44] The word 'legitimately' suggests that this is intended as a normative claim. I do not wish to discuss the normative claim here except in so far as to note that an agreement cannot be binding if it is not feasible. It is the implicit feasibility claim that I wish to consider. Or perhaps one should speak of the implicit claim of the meaning of agreement. How do we derive the rules of political order from the agreement among individual members of the polity? For a trivial example, consider the rules that govern debate and voting in Congress. These are spelled out in the popularly available version for use in other deliberative bodies in *Robert's Rules of Order. Robert's Rules* stipulate that the parliamentarian, whose task is to invoke the relevant rule, should not be elected but appointed by the president of the group. 'It is absurd and also embarrassing to elect an advisory officer, when that adviser may know less about the subject than the officer he is supposed to advise.'[45] What the parliamentarian must know is merely the

[42] McDonald, *We the People*, 287–8.

[43] Rossiter, *1787*, 296.

[44] Geoffrey Brennan and James M. Buchanan, *The Reason of Rules: Constitutional Political Economy* (Cambridge: Cambridge University Press, 1985), 26.

[45] Henry M. Robert, *Robert's Rules of Order Revised* (Chicago: Scott, Foresman, 1951), inside back cover.

distillation of past precedents, many of which do not flow from any evident principles and might therefore have been otherwise. That distillation fills about three hundred pages.

Robert's Rules are like the Common Law. They have grown without a lot of guidance and certainly without a lot of popular control. The polity lets the rules prevail but it does not often in any stronger sense express its agreement to them. If academic deliberative bodies, such as departmental meetings, are typical of the larger society in this respect, many members of the polity must find many of *Robert's Rules* peculiar, unfamiliar, and even quite disagreeable. It is therefore the case that those who master the rules of order, as the late Senator James B. Allen did, can shrewdly manipulate legislative deliberations to their advantage. We let these and many other rules prevail largely because we cannot easily act collectively to influence them. General Robert has coordinated us on his version of the Congressional system of rules and we are stuck. We might spontaneously or collectively overturn them, but we can be fairly confident that we will not, as students of the free-rider problem and the logic of collective action know all too well. That we do not is no proof of our agreement with these rules.

Perhaps one could simply alter the terms for what counts as agreement in the case of a *collective* institution that has to govern all of us at once. It is not necessary for all to agree in any meaningful sense; it is only necessary for enough to agree or even merely to acquiesce for us to move ahead with our collective arrangements. Clearly this is what is done *under* a constitution in most cases: some fraction of those qualified to vote on an issue is all that is required to decide the issue. Those who lose in the vote might be said to suffer an externality.[46] Many who are not signatories to ordinary contracts similarly suffer externalities from the result of others' reaching agreement. But there is much more at stake than this in the formal creation of a constitution. We virtually all benefit from having constitutional regulation of our interactions in a sense that could not plausibly apply to any ordinary contract.

Many of the people of Rhode Island presumably only wanted a constitution that would have been more advantageous to themselves than that put to them for a vote. They presumably did not want to

<hr>

[46] This is the view of James M. Buchanan and Gordon Tullock, *The Calculus of Consent: Logical Foundations of Constitutional Government* (Ann Arbor: University of Michigan Press, 1962).

refuse union altogether. Hence, after voting against the Constitution relatively early, Rhode Island voted for it when the Union was a *fait accompli* that Rhode Island could either join or not join. The vote of the convention of Virginia came after eight of the required nine states had ratified.[47] In the last speech of the Virginia convention on ratification, Edmund Randolph, who had refused to sign the Constitution when it was proposed at the Philadelphia Convention, observed that 'the accession of eight states reduced our deliberations to the single question of *Union or no Union*'.[48] That was Hamilton's opening and closing question in the *Federalist Papers* (1 and 85). Randolph voted in Richmond for what he had refused to sign in Philadelphia. There was no point in not coordinating on what was by then the best of likely outcomes.

Eloquent testimony to how little a people must agree to a constitution for it to prevail is the fact that the deliberations of the constitutional convention of 1787 were essentially secret and that the secret was maintained until after the death of all the conventioneers (Madison was the last to go, in 1836). It is, as Rossiter remarks, 'one of the intriguing facts of American constitutional history that the people in whose name and by whose power the great charter of 1787 was proclaimed should have had to wait more than half a century to learn how it came to be written'.[49] In fact, of course, virtually all of these people had died by then so that those by whose power the government was established had little idea how it had been done.

Three centuries of talk about tacit consent and hypothetical agreement notwithstanding, many cannot plausibly be thought to have agreed *to* the US Constitution on any meaningful account. What is it that they did not agree to that others did? Brennan and Buchanan claim that a constitution is a social contract that creates rules to commit one's later selves and later generations to various specific things, for example, to payment of agreed upon taxes.[50] Clearly this is the wrong way to put the issue. A constitution does not commit the way a contract does. Rather *it merely raises the cost of trying to do things some other way through its creation of a coordination convention.* Moreover what it commits to is open to evolution and change in a far

[47] Actually nine had ratified, thereby creating the new nation. But news of New Hampshire's ratification did not reach Virginia before the Virginians voted.
[48] Quoted in Rossiter, *1787*, 292.
[49] Rossiter, *1787*, 332. Madison's extensive notes on the convention were first published in 1840. Quite fragmentary bits from other participants had appeared earlier.
[50] Brennan and Buchanan, *The Reason of Rules*, esp. ch. 2.

more expansive way than is the expectation of action under a contract. Signing a contract similarly raises the cost of then going against the agreement, but it does so in a relatively clearly specified, well understood, and predictable way. Typically, in a contract, enforcement and the costs of enforcement come from outside parties, not from the parties to the agreement.[51] And the scope of the sanction that can be applied to one who reneges from fulfilment of a contract is generally well defined.

A constitution involves a much broader gamble than this, as both the advocates and the opponents of the US Constitution recognized (*Federalist*, 85, final paragraph). One of the major debates of the time was *whether* the presidency would evolve into a virtual monarchy and the Senate into a virtual aristocracy. Even the president as created was 'a bad edition of a Polish king', according to Jefferson.[52] It is only the hubris of retrospect that makes such debates seem misplaced. Those debates gained their sense and their urgency from the fact that changes in the constitutional provision or failures to abide by it could not be appealed against to a higher contract enforcer once the Constitution was ostensibly in place. If the order it led to was different from the way that the initial designers intended or expected, they might still be organized by and forced to abide by the different order despite the fact that they had not agreed to it.

We speak of the intentions of parties to a contract and of the meaning of a law. Indeed, as in the secrecy of the debates of the 1787 conventioneers, Lon Fuller argues that the *intentions* of the law makers are of little or no interest after the law has been in effect for a while.[53] Madison agreed, writing in 1821 that, 'As a guide in expounding and applying the provisions of the Constitution, the debates and incidental decisions of the convention can have no authoritative character'.[54] The generations that have followed Madison and the other constitutionalists of 1787 have not rewritten much of the original text of the Constitution, but they have surely redefined many of its meanings. Jefferson presciently said of his own time that he did not

[51] Those who deal with each other repeatedly or who depend on their reputations may successfully enforce their own agreements by contract by convention and may therefore be able to avoid the irritations of legally contracting.

[52] Quoted in Rossiter, *1787*, 284.

[53] Lon L. Fuller, *The Morality of Law* (New Haven: Yale University Press, 1969 rev.; 1st pub. 1964), 86.

[54] James Madison, Letter to Thomas Ritchie, 15 September 1821, in Kurland and Lerner, *The Founders' Constitution*, i. 74.

fear tyranny from the presidency but rather from the legislature, that the day of presidential tyranny would come in the distant future as the nation grew and its government flourished.[55] Perhaps he was drawing on the analogy of Roman history rather than on keen insight. But either way, he sensed clearly enough that the document would not govern, elected officials would, and that the content of the document would be determined by the electorate and the people elected to its offices—some of whom these days are blacks and women, contrary to the original intent and words of the conventioneers in 1787. 'All new laws', Madison wrote in *Federalist*, 37, 'are considered as more or less obscure and equivocal, until their meaning be liquidated and ascertained by a series of particular discussions and adjudications'. How much more must this be true of a new constitution.

Incentives to Abide by a Constitution

A final crucial difference that shows that the constitutional problem is not generally a prisoner's dilemma is that, once we have settled on a constitutional arrangement, it is not then likely to be in the interest of some of us to try to renege on the arrangement to be freeriders. Our interests will be better served by living with the arrangement. And this is generally true not because we will be coerced to abide if we choose not to but because we generally cannot do better than to abide. To do better we would have to carry enough others with us to set up an alternative, and that will typically be too costly to be worth the effort. Hence, our constitutional arrangement is self-enforcing and is not subject to free-rider problems.

We abide by a contract in large part because there is the shadow of sanctions to be brought against us if we do not and, indeed, we often choose not to abide by a contract when the sanctions are likely to be less costly than fulfilment would be. The sources of the costs of defection in the constitutional and the contract cases are strategically very different. For the contract case, the ultimate source is sanctions from an external body; for the constitutional case, the ultimate

[55] Thomas Jefferson, Letter to James Madison, 15 March 1789, in Kurland and Lerner, *The Founders' Constitution*, i. 479.

source is the internal costs of collective action for re-coordination or, in Caesar's word, mutiny.

The generally coordinative aspect of the Constitution may be lost in certain fundamentally conflictive contexts, as in that between some of the Anti-Federalists and the Federalists and between slave-owning southerners and anti-slavery northerners in the mid-nineteenth century. An effect of successful coordination can be the creation of great power. Successful coordination of the United States under the Constitution has led to extraordinary power of a kind and scale that one could not expect in North America without union. This was, of course, a major issue for the Anti-Federalists. That their fears were justified, even though their hopes without union may not have been, is suggested by the use of the power that came from coordination to resolve a major conflict through military force in the Civil War. The tilting of the Congress and the presidency towards a relatively mild anti-slavery position in the election of 1860 finally convinced many southerners that their benefits from further coordination with the North were outweighed by the potential costs of conflict. Hence, they saw the interaction as no longer essentially one of coordination but one of conflict. The North evidently continued to prefer union to no union with the South even at the cost of a grisly war, but the South now preferred no union to union.[56] Earlier, many Federalists shared the fear that such conflicts could arise and would be settled forcibly, even tyrannously, but saw the balance in favour of coordination nevertheless.

Contracts Not Like Contracts Either

Contemporary vocabulary has distorted or expanded the use of contract to cover virtually anything that has some element of agreement in it. Contract is such a good word with such positive connotations that it naturally gets called into service at the slightest hint of its possible relevance. In the era of the doctrine of social contract, the clear implication of contract was genuine mutual agreement between two parties for some kind of exchange. The whole point of invoking the

---

[56] Note that the view of the southerners could not plausibly be represented as a prisoner's dilemma either before 1850 or after. It was coordination before and conflict sometime afterwards. Whereas they had seen the outcomes that involved union as better than no union before, they saw no union as better afterwards.

term 'social contract' is to assert the voluntarism of our participation in society under its governments. From voluntarism obligation supposedly follows. This is arguably the biggest single point of debate in all of sixteenth to eighteenth century political philosophy when the collapse of a unified church and the growth of the independent state (not the term they used; they spoke rather of political society) forced reconsideration of the source of political obligation (as briefly discussed in Chapter 1). But here consider three possible objections to the claim that constitutions are not metaphorically like contracts, objections that, in a sense, say that after all contracts are not like contracts either.

First, one might suppose the marriage contract is a counter-example to the distinction between a contract and a constitution. Alas, however, it is only anachronistic usage of today that makes marriage a contract. Even today it generally has few if any of the trappings of a contract between two families but is merely a legally prescribed arrangement over which the parties have little control beyond entering or not entering it. Before his marriage to Harriet Taylor, Mill wrote a document clearly explaining why he objected to the legal prescriptions that mostly gave him powers and her liabilities and he essentially complained that if the law would allow he would contract with her for a more reasonable arrangement.[57] Since the law would not allow him to do that, or would not recognize such an action, he could only assert his strong intention to behave as if their union were governed by such an agreement between them, as though it was legally binding on him even though it was not. However, there is increasing use of genuine contracts to govern financial arrangements in marriages today, especially in second marriages. These contracts are commonly and rightly called pre-nuptial agreements or contracts rather than marriage contracts because they primarily cover pre-marital issues of prior wealth or achievements, and they cannot regulate some things specifically governed by law, such as child custody in the event of divorce.[58]

Secondly, such complex arrangements as labour–management agreements are described as multiparty contracts that look for all the

---

[57] John Stuart Mill, 'Statement on Marriage', in John M. Robson, ed., *Essays on Equality, Law, and Education*, xxi of *Collected Works of John Stuart Mill* (Toronto: University of Toronto Press, 1984), 99. (The 'Statement' was unpublished in Mill's lifetime.)

[58] *New York Times* (7 Nov. 1993), 9.10.

world like constitutions. The analogy does not hold, for two reasons. The first reason is that labour–management agreements are in fact very detailed, specific two-party agreements for relatively short terms. Indeed, the early history of Supreme Court interference in labour law was based on the claim that union agreements would violate the rights of individual workers to contract for the terms they chose. That this view was arguably heinous in its intent does not run against its partial coherence with the actual views of the day. In fact, the issue for the Court was whether the labour union could be counted as a person. It had long since decided, under a peculiar fiction, that corporations could count as persons (in order, of course, to enable them to enter contracts). The heinous side of its views in turn-of-the-century union and strike cases was that it somehow supposed that corporate bodies organized around capital could be fictional persons while corporate bodies organized around people or their labour could not be.

The second reason that the analogy between a worker–management agreement and a constitution fails has to do with the actual role of the individual workers or stockholders in such collective agreements. This is a major concern in the contemporary death-of-contract debate of Grant Gilmore, Ian Macneil, and others.[59] These observers note that contractual devices are being displaced by regulatory, substantive laws that stipulate what the content of various interactions must be. You and I cannot contract away certain rights or regulatory requirements. Macneil resolves the issue by speaking of the *new* social contract. Because all of his observations about the decay in the use of traditional contract devices and their substitution by directive laws are quite compelling, he should arguably have stuck with his own traditional contract notions and used a different term for what he thinks we now have. What he puts under the new social contract, however, is not the labour–management agreement, but rather the regulatory and case-law implications of such a contract for workers, stockholders, other employees, and the general public, all of whom are implicated and bound in certain ways by the actual contract even though they have not signed it and may object to it. This does sound rather more con-

[59] Grant Gilmore, *The Death of Contract* (Columbus, Oh.: Ohio State University Press, 1974); Ian Macneil, *The New Social Contract* (New Haven: Yale University Press, 1980).

stitutional than contractual. The parties are constrained to do what the law mandates rather than what they agree to.

Finally, many long-term contracts are self-enforcing in ways that constitutions are also. Hence, they are not so dependent on enforcement by an external authority as traditional contracts might be thought to be. This is a very complex claim worthy of substantial discussion to show how the self-enforcements of the two arrangements genuinely differ. The relevant similarity here is that constitutions and long-term contracts both typically imply strategic manipulation of future incentives. They do so in different ways largely because *they are based on different strategic structures.* The self-enforcing long-term contract is a contract by convention; a constitution is not.

When we are involved in a repeated interaction of the form of the prisoner's dilemma, we commonly discover a convention for cooperation that resolves the instances of the interaction well rather than letting them all, one after the other, end in a failure of cooperation. It makes sense to call this process of the emergence of a convention a *contract by convention*, as discussed above, because it resolves prisoner's dilemma interactions, as contracts do, but it does so by the creation of a convention, by coordination on a pattern for resolving the interactions, rather than by a literal contract that is externally enforceable.[60] It is enforced, in a sense, internally, that is, by the parties to the convention, either of whom can stop cooperating immediately if the other does. This process can be spontaneous and not regulated. Deliberate creation of a constitution is clearly different from this and yet in some ways strategically similar. It is neither a formal contract nor a spontaneous convention.

Note that the establishment of a constitution, as in the United States in the two years 1787–8, is a relatively singular act in the way that the establishment of a convention often is not. Much of its import is, of course, open to interpretation over time, but there is a certain fixedness in the creation itself. A major difference between contract by convention and the creation of a constitution is this. The latter is a very general move made very much in ignorance about the future range of choices that it will help to govern. It is, as noted above, a large gamble. A contract by convention grows piecemeal out of a very clear class of interactions. It is a small gamble because, like a contract in the state of nature, it can be abrogated at will. It is

---

[60] Hardin, *Collective Action*, chs. 10–14.

unlikely to gain anything approaching general scope, although it may serve as an example that will influence the way other, similar patterns of interaction get resolved. By contrast, a constitution is initially little more than a commitment to go on to resolve various interactions that involve some conflict as well as some that perhaps do not, that are virtually pure coordination problems in which little more than centralized signalling is required for successful coordination. The initial commitment can, however, create institutions that take on a commanding life of their own.

This is the truth in the common view that we can often agree on the procedure for deciding an issue even when we cannot so readily agree on what decision to make on the issue itself. This view is even more compelling for establishing a procedure well in advance of addressing any specific issues.[61] Indeed, one of the most compelling considerations in defence of a particular procedure is merely that it has been in use for a while already. This is often the persuasive force of, say, *Robert's Rules of Order*, which may be invoked to settle debate in some peculiar circumstance. People who strongly disagree on how to proceed typically desist from debate immediately when shown some arcane rule in this tedious book borne of long experience.

In formally adopting a constitution we can agree to coordinate one way rather than another. But we may still not have full control over what happens because we may steadily fall into doing what works instead of what we agreed to do. This is one of the beauties of conventions as devices for social regulation: they need not be constrained by mistaken ideal conceptions; they can accommodate a far wider input of understanding and experience than would be available to a particular group of constitution drafters such as that in the State House (now Independence Hall) in Philadelphia in 1787. The range of likely uncertainty in most contracts is therefore radically less than what one should expect from a new constitution. Taking a gamble on such uncertainty will seem worthwhile if we suppose that gains from coordination that we might achieve will outweigh the stakes in conflicts that we might face. One may sensibly read as the lesson of economic progress that this is generally true.

---

[61] Brennan and Buchanan say that 'The scope for potential agreement on rules is *necessarily* wider than that for agreement on outcomes within specified rules' (Brennan and Buchanan, *The Reason of Rules*, 29, emphasis added).

Bargains in Philadelphia

The arguments above clearly establish that the constitution of 1787 was a coordination rather than a contract. Nevertheless, there are many writers who hold that it was a grand contract and that, therefore, the sessions in Philadelphia were largely dedicated to bargaining over the compromise content of the final agreement. In part, the sessions were, indeed, given over to bargaining over specific provisions of the constitution. But most of these provisions covered relatively minor points that arose *just because there was consensus on establishing a genuine national government that would rise above the states for commercial purposes*, unlike the supposed government under the Articles of Confederation. Even on more detailed issues of how to organize the nation, as Benjamin Wright notes, 'many of the most difficult decisions confronting any constitutional government had, in effect though not by any specific action, been made before the Federal Convention met' as a result of the multiplicity of state efforts to work out these issues in their constitutions.[62]

We may divide the issues in debate into two categories: substantive issues of what the government was to do and structural issues of how it was to work. The bulk of discussion at the convention was on the latter because the core of the former was in agreement (the New York majority and some individual delegates from other states disagreed). Some matters cross these categories. For example, Madison famously wanted a federal veto over state legislation. This was not allowed and Madison saved face by saying it became clear that the task would overwhelm Congress because there would be far too many laws to review. Madison was attacked as really wanting an all-powerful national government. He was, however, plausibly concerned only to make the overall system of state and national government coherent by making its laws consistent. In the end, he won much of his purpose when the Supreme Court took its mandate to include judicial review of the federal constitutionality of state laws, as was deemed only natural by Hamilton in *Federalist*, 80 and 81. Moreover, the actual convention debates on all these issues were transmuted into debates about the structure of the national government.

---

[62] Benjamin F. Wright, *Consensus and Continuity, 1776–1787* (Boston: Boston University Press, 1958), 21.

There were three apparently major splits on *substantive issues* in the early US constitutional debate. First, there was the split between Anti-Federalists and Federalists. Secondly, there was the split between agrarian and commercial interests, as represented in the persons of Jefferson and Hamilton. And thirdly, there was a grudging devil's bargain on the part of many northerners to accept slavery as the price of including the southern states in the new nation. Only the last of these was the subject of extended debate at the convention because only it immediately affected the design of the institutions of government. But by far the biggest issue in debate at the convention was the representation of states in the national legislature with a presumption of conflicting interests between large and small states. This was essentially a *structural issue* of how to make the government work. As Madison later wrote to Martin Van Buren, 'the threatening contest' at the convention was whether and how states were to be represented in the new national legislature. 'The contests & compromises, turning on the grants of power, tho' very important in some instances, were Knots of a less "Gordian" character.'[63] Let us consider these four divisions, beginning with the structural issue between large and small states and then turning to the three substantive issues.

Large versus Small States

Ironically, one of the more grievous issues in the Constitutional Convention in Philadelphia was the supposed conflict between the interests of small states and those of large states. Indeed, Madison wrote that this conflict 'created more embarrassment, and a greater alarm for the issue of the Convention than all the rest put together'.[64] This was essentially a false conflict that made coordination harder just because people wrongly believed in it. Rhode Island, the last to hold out, was one of the small states fearful of dominance by such states as Massachusetts, Pennsylvania, and Virginia, as was Delaware, the first state to ratify the Constitution.

The Articles of Confederation had been designed in part to reduce the prospects of war between various states, especially to reduce the prospects of attacks by larger states on smaller states. That issue was still alive in 1787 if the Articles were to collapse but, in the prospect

---

[63] Farrand, *Records of the Federal Convention*, iii. 477.
[64] James Madison, Letter to Thomas Jefferson, 24 Oct. 1787, in Kurland and Lerner, *The Founders' Constitution*, i. 644–7, at p. 647.

of a new order, the possibility that large states might come to dominate small states in a fully representative government was the major concern. That issue was addressed with the device of the two-tier legislature, with populations represented in the House of Representatives and states in the Senate.

There has still not been any significant conflict between small and large states as such since the ratification of the Constitution. One might therefore conclude either that the structure of the Constitution resolved the conflict or that this widely perceived conflict was in fact of little or no concern. In particular, one might suppose that the constitutional allotment of two senators to each state, irrespective of population, and the preclusion of ever changing this provision by amendment, secured the interests of the small states. A constitutionalist could ask for no happier result.

It seems more plausible, however, that it was the very general fact of the Constitution that protected the interests of the small states. The issue was essentially a matter of misunderstanding. Small states had something to fear from large states only if they had systematically different interests on anything. The only issue on which they might have had systematically different interests was the earlier one of the threat of conquest, an issue that was settled by the creation of a workable constitutional order (Article 1, section 10, which reiterated the concerns of the Commerce Clause, also blocked the use of military force by any state acting on its own). National union meant that head-to-head conflict between two states ceased to be a real issue, so that inequalities in resources, especially in population, ceased to matter for security. Successful creation of a national government was the best safeguard of the interests of small states. The gamble the constitutionalists and their opponents thought they were taking on this issue was in fact no gamble at all. Imagine a similar debate today at the international level if there were a prospect of world federal government. It would be naive for small nations to worry that such government would actually put them at a greater disadvantage *vis-à-vis* large nations than does their status without such government. Even at the lower level of European unification, the very small Benelux nations have typically been among those most strongly in favor of strengthening the European Union.

The supposed conflict between small and large states was a chief point of contention at the constitutional convention in Philadelphia. Yet, as Madison said there, it was of no real concern because, once the new constitutional order was in place, the issue would disappear. It would disappear because there was in actual fact unlikely ever to be an issue that united small states against large states.[65] The actual sides in conflict would, in contemporary social science jargon, not correlate with sizes of states.

This conclusion seems to be transparent and unarguable. Certainly, it has been factually true for more than two centuries. Perhaps the only issue at all that could make the large-versus-small state conflict manifest would be a proposal to end the advantage that small states have in the Senate. Why then was there such great concern in 1787? An especially plausible explanation is the following. The states had only recently been individual colonies without a joint government, and during the colonial period, many people must have worried about conflicts with other colonies. A conflict between Massachusetts and Rhode Island, for example, would probably have been hopeless for Rhode Island. During the revolutionary war, forces of the Continental Congress marched on Quebec with the intention of subduing the British there and incorporating Canada in the confederation of states. Massachusetts alone might similarly have been inclined to conquest. Instantly to recast one's mind to think of states in a nation rather than *de facto* nations in the maelstrom of international politics may have been very difficult, especially in a context in which Anti-Federalists were arguing that the states were sovereign even in the United States.

By thinking analogically from the past, however, the representatives of the small states very nearly wrecked the most natural route to their safety. The electorate of Rhode Island, the lunatic fringe of their time, held out against union until long after the first government was solidly in place. This was only one of several severe mistakes in understanding that twisted constitutional deliberations and led to misjudgements about the way the nation would go under the constitution.

Anti-Federalists versus Federalists

The principal group of those opposed to the constitution were the Anti-Federalists.[66] Their chief objection to the new union was that it

---

[65] Letter of 13 May 1828, in Farrand, *Records of the Federal Convention*, i. 486.

[66] This designation, following Storing, is now the conventional name for the opponents of the Federalists. Storing, *The Complete Anti-Federalist*, i. 79–80, n. 6.

would create a large and fractious nation that would be incapable of addressing the interests of particular communities. They argued that a republic must be small to work because it must have a small enough citizenry to have *homogeneous interests and commitments*. This is an odd thesis in the context of even a moderately commercial society in which *the division of labour is the source of general welfare*. Division of labour means *heterogeneous interests*. Yet the Anti-Federalists were remarkably consistent in making this empirically incoherent argument.

It would be implausible to suppose that this widespread, essentially communitarian, but illogical view came individually to the minds of people in dozens of communities around the nation. By what genius did these Anti-Federalists come to have such articulate, uniform views? Chiefly by the genius of reading or, more likely, by hearing the ideas of Montesquieu, who laid out arguments for small-scale republicanism that are no longer compelling today but that were well received by many of the Anti-Federalists. They argued that a republic of large size would be subject to tyranny from easily misled majorities, that it would require military force to keep those more distant from the government in line, and that it would reduce everyone to uniformity. Madison held, on the contrary, that small communities would be more readily subject to arbitrary tyranny from local majorities, that a large nation would be more peaceful and would better allow individual liberty. As was typical, Madison had the better insights. In one sense, the debate was very odd, because it was very abstract and little grounded in actual experience other than opportunistic references to past societies that, with sometimes gross simplifications, fit one or the other argument. Yet the arguments were essentially sociological and they therefore needed empirical support, which no one bothered to give. The political tradition of making empirical arguments without empirical support has ancient roots.

In a second line of argument, the Anti-Federalists were, in many cases, concerned with the *moral* nature of their communities and they wanted to block political and economic arrangements that might override the autonomy of these communities. They were the Amish of their time. They held, with Richard Henry Lee, that 'the Spirit of Commerce is a Spirit of Avarice', and they wanted no part of a constitutional arrangement that furthered that spirit.[67] Lee and

---

[67] Richard Henry Lee, Letter of 10 Oct. 1785 in Kurland and Lerner, *The Founders' Constitution*, ii. 482.

many other communitarian Anti-Federalists missed the central claims of Montesquieu that commerce would sweeten life and make people more civil. They took the bad, small-republican half of his thesis and ignored the good, spirit-of-commerce half. The Federalists were primarily concerned with economic opportunities and, perhaps, with a quest for national grandeur. Both groups were strongly committed to individual liberties, but they disagreed sociologically on how these could best be secured.

The communitarian opposition to the constitution and the kind of nation that they thought it would be likely to support is well framed in Lee's comment. Indeed, moral theory throughout the medieval era and down to about the time of David Hume and Adam Smith was predominantly a variant of virtue theory, in which the moral categories are certain personal virtues, such as honesty, charity, and piety. Under Christian influence, charity was elevated to first among the virtues. Its counterpart vice was, of course, avarice, which was therefore the worst of all vices.

Bernard Mandeville flouted this morality with his book, *The Fable of the Bees*, in which he eloquently put forward his thesis that avarice is good in a subtitle: *Private Vices, Publick Benefits*.[68] This was the overwhelming lesson of the emerging market economy. Mandeville was reviled but he helped to move moral theory away from its concentration on the virtues. Charity soon tumbled from its vaunted position at the top of moral theory and more or less fell out of discussion.[69] Indeed, the function of charity—to help those in need— was largely taken over by the state and therefore taken out of individual morality. The hold of Christian virtue theory did not immediately pass, however, and even Hume framed his own essentially utilitarian theory in virtue terms. That Lee and many others in the new nation were still under the sway of the powerful view that avarice is the supreme vice is not surprising. But in what was soon to be the most commercial and avaricious of all societies, they were of fading importance. Politically, they were a residue.

The communitarian Anti-Federalists were soundly defeated in the constitutional convention, where, by their own default, they were

---

[68] Bernard Mandeville, *The Fable of the Bees: Private Vices, Publick Benefits*, ed. F. B. Kaye (Oxford: Oxford University Press, 1924; 1st pub. 1714; reprinted by Liberty Press, 1988).

[69] J. B. Schneewind, 'The Misfortunes of Virtue', *Ethics* (1990) 101: 42–63; Russell Hardin, 'Altruism and Mutual Advantage', *Social Service Review* (1993) 67: 358–73.

ill-represented, as noted earlier. The Federal Farmer deplored the failure of 'many good republican characters' to attend the convention despite being appointed as delegates by their states.[70] That is the sad fate of communitarians. They must band together to stop general anti-communitarian hegemony, but banding together into a larger entity is itself against the small-scale ideology of communitarians. After the convention, despite their often articulate opposition to the Constitution during the ratification debates, the Anti-Federalist communitarians were demolished in the overwhelming ratification—eventually by all thirteen states—of the Constitution and its structure of national government.

One might suppose that the natural constituency of communitarianism would be farmers, who are, in Marx's extreme account of the French peasantry in the mid-nineteenth century, genuinely alike in their interests, their customs, and their values.[71] Since the overwhelming majority of the population of 1788 were farmers, one may wonder why the Anti-Federalists lost the vote on ratification. In Rossiter's assessment of the geography of support for and opposition to the ratification of the constitution, supporters were urban and coastal, opponents were rural and inland.[72] Yet, although farmers were the bulk of the enfranchised population of the United States at the time of ratification, still they failed to elect state conventions hostile to the Constitution, with the apparent exceptions of New York and North Carolina and belatedly perhaps Rhode Island. Actual voting turnouts were dismal, but they were dismal in general and not merely among farmers. On Beard's account, there were only 160,000 votes from a population of about three million, so that less than a third of the eligible adult males voted.[73]

In Main's analysis of the conventions in the three states of Pennsylvania, Connecticut, and New Hampshire, farmers were only 21 per cent of the delegates (24 per cent were of unknown occupation). Of these, on the limited biographical evidence available, 34 per

[70] *The Federal Farmer*, 1, in Storing, *The Complete Anti-Federalist*, ii. 223–30, at p. 228. The Farmer numbered eight or nine men who failed to attend and noted (at p. 227) that those especially interested in changing the government 'seized [the moment] with address'.
[71] Karl Marx, *The Eighteenth Brumaire of Louis Bonaparte* (New York: International Publishers, 1963; 1st pub. 1852), 123–7.
[72] Rossiter, *1787*, 295–6.
[73] Beard, *An Economic Interpretation of the Constitution*, 253.

cent were Anti-Federalist and 14 per cent Federalist.[74] This fits the supposition that farmers should be relatively communitarian and therefore hostile to a strong national government, at least on matters of social and political control. In a more comprehensive statistical analysis of characteristics of delegates to the state conventions, farming has been found to be not statistically significant as a predictor of ratification votes.[75] These are contrary findings, but in either case, farmers form a remarkably small percentage of the delegates as compared to their likely percentage among the electorate. Hence, farmers defaulted on voting for their interests if they were Anti-Federalist just as Anti-Federalist leaders defaulted on attending the Philadelphia Convention to attempt to influence its deliberations.

It is a peculiar and apparently unanalysed fact of the politics of ratification that farmers, the only substantial group that genuinely could have fitted the rhetoric of the Anti-Federalists, were not mobilized against the constitution. One plausible reason for this is that few farmers might have identified the interests of the leading Anti-Federalists as their interests. The leading Anti-Federalists were, after all, commonly lawyers and estate holders, people as foreign to the sensibilities of real farmers as Madison and even Hamilton. Moreover, unlike Madison and Hamilton, they were the people with whom the farmers had to deal, with whom they must often have been in economic conflict. They might have seen their communities as oligarchic rather than idyllic. Only the communitarian élites could see the idyll in the oligarchy.

Hobhouse's censures of community governance of lives, discussed in Chapter 2, must have been a natural concern of small farmers living under the sway of such Anti-Federalists as Governor George Clinton of upstate New York. Madison was worried that small communities (even as large as the individual states) would be at risk from tyrannous majorities. Those less élite than Madison might more naturally have worried that they would be subject to oligarchic rule. It was a signal failure of the Anti-Federalists, as it is of élite academic communitarians today, that they failed to think through the darker

[74] Main, *The Antifederalists*, 289–90. These percentages become 28, 45, and 19 per cent, respectively, of those whose occupations are known.
[75] Robert A. McGuire and Robert L. Ohsfeldt, 'Public Choice Analysis and the Ratification of the Constitution', in Grofman and Wittman, *The Federalist Papers and the New Institutionalism*, 175–204, at p. 194. Perhaps there was self-selection that led farmers who favoured national government to be more likely to go to the state ratifying conventions.

implications of their vision for the bulk of the people who would have to live that vision.

In the ratification debates, the Anti-Federalists' position was taken somewhat seriously by Madison in *Federalist*, 55, in which he argued against their complaint that communities would be inadequately represented in the too-small House of Representatives. But he showed either lack of understanding or lack of sympathy in *Federalist*, 56, in which he countered their complaints with essentially universalist arguments, which were precisely what they opposed.

After a sympathetic reading of the Anti-Federalists, Storing concludes that they lost the day 'because they had the weaker argument. They were, as Publius said, trying to reconcile contradictions. There was no possibility of instituting the small republic in the United States.'[76] Surely, however, having bad ideas is no guarantor of political defeat. The Anti-Federalist communitarians had their minor role in political theory despite their bad ideas because the ratification debate was inherently a debate for or against the Constitution. Only Anti-Federalists were against on that issue. Even then, they were taken seriously only because it was not possible to know confidently what was the distribution of communitarian and federalist views—it was conceivable that the communitarians could muster the votes in, say, New York, North Carolina, Rhode Island, and maybe Virginia, thereby wrecking the project by leaving the potential nation with gaping holes. Therefore they gave the Federalists reason to write some of the best political theory ever produced by Americans and they themselves contributed one of the most articulate, but still deeply flawed, bodies of writing in defence of small communities. They and their progeny, however, have done little more than squeak up in national political debate since ratification.

Slavery

The devil's bargain over slavery turned it into a structural issue of how representation for slave states was to work. There was a genuine element of coordination in arranging the Constitution to allow the most committed slave states—the Carolinas and Georgia—to join the new nation, because the larger nation was likely to be more

[76] Storing, *The Complete Anti-Federalist*, i. 71.

prosperous. There was also the likelihood of conflict over western lands if the slave states were not included in the nation. Still, there was a large element of bargaining. The northerners had to swallow hard to live with slavery and the southern states had to yield some control over their future to an uncertain arrangement. And there was a structural bargain over the way slaves were to be counted and a substantive bargain over the date of the end of the slave trade (constitutionally set at 1808).[77]

Already at the convention it was recognized that the principal conflictive division of the states was into those having and those not having slaves, as Madison said.[78] In defence of his principle of concurrent majorities, under which the southern and northern states would both have to vote by majority in favour of legislation for it to be passed, John C. Calhoun cited the protection of small against large states as a precursor.

When the Constitution was formed the impression was strong that the tendency to conflict would be between the larger and smaller States, and effectual provisions were accordingly made to guard against it. But experience has proved this to have been a mistake; and that, instead of being as was then supposed, the conflict is between the two great sections.[79]

Oddly, Madison, who evidently despised slavery, had already considered a way of accomplishing the protection that Calhoun later wanted.[80] But in the end in 1861, the conflict over slavery transcended the mutual advantage that the conventioneers had seen in unifying the slave and non-slave states. The Constitution, which had worked well enough for two or three generations, then failed massively.

[77] The formula for ending the slave trade was unusually obtuse: 'The Migration or Importation of such Persons as any of the States now existing shall think proper to admit, shall not be prohibited by the Congress prior to the Year one thousand eight hundred and eight' (Art. 1, sect. 9). The conventioneers knew how despicable slavery was and hesitated to call it by name.

[78] Farrand, *Records of the Federal Convention*, i. 486.

[79] John C. Calhoun, *Discourse on the American Constitution*; 1st pub. 1853, excerpted in *A Disquisition on Government and Selections from the Discourse* (Indianapolis: Bobbs-Merrill, 1953), 101.

[80] He thought of apportioning representation in one branch of the legislature according to the entire population of slave and free and in the other branch according only to the free population (Farrand, *Records of the Federal Convention*, i. 486–7).

Plantation Agrarian versus Commercial Interests

The split between plantation agrarian and commercial interests lurked in the background but did not become the focus of debate at the convention. The issues were perhaps badly understood. Had the agrarians foreseen their long-run fate, they might have balked at national union of any form. And the proponents of commercial interests, who may also have misjudged their own eventual significance from too easy generalization from their then minor significance, were prepared to coordinate on any union that increased economic coordination among the states.

Both the plantation agrarian and the commercial interests were content to leave their conflict out of the Constitution. Perhaps the plantation agrarians expected to carry the day without government assistance anyway, as they soon did during the long Jefferson–Jackson hegemony, when plantation agrarians were joined in a coalition with other, far more numerous agrarians. The mercantile position was disfranchised early at the convention because John Lansing and Robert Yates of New York opposed Hamilton's views in favour of a strong national government to replace the Articles of Confederation, and state delegations voted by absolute majority as a block. When Lansing and Yates withdrew from the convention in July, they left Hamilton alone and therefore without a vote. (I will discuss the commercial-agrarian split more extensively in Chapter 6, where its role in the working of the constitution, rather than in adopting it, is at issue.)

Ex Ante *Justification*

The argument for constitutionalism is inherently an *ex ante* argument. This raises a difficult normative question: why should we give preference to *ex ante* over in *medias res* assessments? In many contexts it would seemingly be wrong or irrational to do so. For example, I might decline *ex ante* to do something you invite me to do that I would enormously enjoy *in medias res* once I started doing it. In such a case, one might suppose that my *ex post* evaluation would fit my *in medias res* view against my *ex ante* view. I might then be talked into the activity by having it pointed out to me that I would be glad I had done it *ex post*.

This problem suggests a messy argument in which we might easily get lost. Perhaps we could make the reverse argument for an institutional or constitutional constraint. *Ex post* we would rather we had been prevented *in medias res* from doing something against the constraint. This *ex post* judgement might be experiential, as my *ex post* evaluation of doing what you invite me to do would be. For example, we might come to understand our action as we do it and realize that we acted irrationally and might retrospectively wish we had not done it. But the *ex post* judgement might seem to be merely a variant *ex ante* judgement about how to handle like cases in the future. Either way, the concurrence of *ex ante* and *ex post* judgements seems to give some preference to the *ex ante* judgement over a contrary *in medias res* judgement. Of course, for the *ex post* consideration, there is no popular sovereignty in taking action but only retrospective approval of action taken, even though it was not taken with popular approval. Hence, we prefer *ex post* not to have had sovereignty *in medias res*. That seems to ground a normative claim against full-blown popular sovereignty, contrary to its superficially compelling ring.

The defence of *ex ante* principles is compromised by the fact that many of the *ex ante* devices to constrain our present choices were not our devices but those of earlier generations. We constrain ourselves, as the generation of the American constitutionalists did, and we are constrained by what past generations did. The second of these may sound less rational than the first. But, in fact, we are broadly constrained and also enabled by what past generations have done. Our generation has vaccination, electronics, plentiful food, and countless benefits from the past, including many institutions that make life easier and more congenial. We also have more limited options of many kinds, less pristine land and water, fewer of many resources, and, of course, institutions that often get in our way. All of these leavings of the past are the result of human action. There is nothing inherently less rational in our living with constraining institutions from the past than in our living within the other general constraints we face, even including the physical constraints of gravity and of the availability of land and resources. If we can coordinate to revise or replace our constraining institutions, we may do so, as the constitutionalists of 1787–8 did.

The defence of *ex ante* devices is also complicated by the frequent problem of their vagueness. Part of what made the near-consensus at

Philadelphia possible was the lack of full appreciation of what would eventually happen once the government was under way.[81] As discussed in Chapter 5, neither the commercial nor the plantation agrarian interests knew enough to guess at the spectacular economic changes that they might have wanted to control if only they had known enough to do so. Those changes eventually destroyed one of the two groups in the core consensus: the plantation agrarians. Without the support of major plantation agrarians, including the first, almost necessary president, the Philadelphia Constitution would never have come to govern a United States that included Virginia and the Carolinas.

A decision theorist might say that it was plausibly rational that the men of Philadelphia and of the ratifying conventions chose according to their best lights in the face of massive uncertainties. A moral theorist with contractarian leanings might add that it was then right to hold them obligated to what followed from the constitution they supported in their uncertainty. Most social theorists, however, would be likely to agree substantially with Jefferson's moral observation that the world belongs to the present generation and that they cannot be bound by what was decided decades or generations before. And most practising politicians and citizens might suppose that, if they once got it wrong, they now are entitled to try to get it right. *Ex ante* arguments are insufficient to carry the day, or at least not sufficient to carry for all days to come.

In the actual life of a constitutional order, contingent factors are enormously important, just as they are important in getting a constitution in place to begin with. Coordination on the US Constitution may have required failures of foresight. There were two big failures of foresight that gave that constitution a chance. First was the failure to guess future economic changes. Had the constitution been written to handle those by embodying a relevant economic theory, it might eventually have failed before the force of economic change. Hence,

---

[81] In many contemporary cases, there may be greater confidence in the predictability of what conflicts might arise, because the nations now writing constitutions have greater experience of their manifold interests and because they can plausibly infer results from other constitutional experiences that have gone further. Perhaps this is why the current constitutions run to 150 pages in South Africa, and more than 200 pages in Brazil. India's amended constitution is now more than 500 pages (*New York Times*, 30 Nov. 1997, 4.3). Such detailed documents may be more precise than the US Constitution, but they may also be less coherent and they may finally not be supple enough to fit with further economic and social development.

as argued in Chapter 5, it was constructive that the US Constitution did not embody an economic theory at all, because if it had done so, it would have been a bad theory—perhaps as bad as Jefferson's agrarianism or Hamilton's mercantilism.

Alas, however, that Constitution did embody a bad social theory with its constitutional protections of slavery. And the constitutional order failed badly only once: over this bad social theory. Even this issue was inadequately understood in an important causal sense. Neither the northern opponents nor the southern supporters of slavery adequately foresaw the impact that extension of the nation into new territories, with the creation of new states, would have on the standing of slavery. Nor did they sense the eventual economic importance of slavery. Even decades later, Madison still supposed slavery could be eliminated by buying the slave's freedom.[82]

Rousseau argued 'that the more important and serious the deliberations are, the closer the prevailing opinion should be to unanimity'.[83] The evidence of Chapter 7 is that this maxim is correct if we are to have open, democratic government. On the most fundamental issues we must be relatively coordinated. On the evidence of Chapter 5, it may also be true for many issues that the more vague or uncertain they are, the more likely we can reach unanimity; hence, the more likely we can coordinate on a central government. Arguably, successful coordinations must be over points that are clearly indifferent (such as driving right or left) or points that are of such vague definition that one cannot tell what difference they would make. A constitution falls in the latter category for many issues, or approximately so.

The Anti-Federalist Brutus argued that the Philadelphia Constitution was overwhelmingly in the latter category and that it essentially left the central matters to the full discretion of the government that the Constitution would license. He objected especially to the vague delegations of power in Article 1, section 8, paragraph 18: the power 'to make all laws which are necessary and proper for carrying into execution the foregoing powers'. Brutus wrote: 'No terms can be found more indefinite than these, and it is obvious, that

---

[82] See Marvin Meyers, *The Mind of the Founder: Sources of the Political Thought of James Madison* (Hanover, NH: University Press of New England, 1981 rev. edn.), 313–36.

[83] Jean-Jacques Rousseau, *On the Social Contract*, trans. Donald A. Cress (Indianapolis: Hackett, 1983; 1st pub. 1762), book 4, ch. 2, p. 82.

the legislature alone must judge what laws are proper and necessary for the purpose'.[84]

The trouble with Brutus's complaint is that it would have been hard to construe the language in an adequately restrictive way while accomplishing the purpose of enabling the nation and its people to prosper. There was inadequate theory to say what would be the best way to go in the longer run, or even in the relatively short run. What the conventioneers in Philadelphia and eventually in the thirteen states were coordinating on was in large part a hope that the government would behave reasonably well. They had of necessity to leave the actual governance of the nation up to the eventual government. They could do little better than that because they could not say more specifically what they wanted the government to do. Again, had they known better, they might not have been able to coordinate.

Why a Written Constitution?

It would be wrong to think of the creation of constitutional procedures as simply devices for conflict resolution. They are far more profoundly devices for enabling us to act and constraining us in relevant ways. This is also true of the devices that make contracting useful. What I do when I contract is to bind myself in certain ways, but I bind myself in order to be free to accomplish certain things.[85] More generally, what it means to commit oneself to action A is to block oneself from taking actions B, C, D. It is through constraint that we are enabled in our strategic interactions with others to achieve outcomes that require joint action. (Indeed, it is trivially true that even in order to act alone one must forego other actions.) The point of a constitution is to tie our hands in certain ways in order to discipline them to more productive use. This point was considered 'paradoxical' by no less an authority than Publius in *Federalist*, 63. There it was argued that too quick a response of elected officials to changes of view among the electorate would lead to inefficient changes in

---

[84] Brutus, no. 5, in Storing, *The Complete Anti-Federalist*, ii. 388–93, at p. 389.

[85] As Thomas Schelling notes, it is by constraining oneself to be subject to suit under various contingencies of one's own actions that one can enter beneficial contracts. (Thomas Schelling, *The Strategy of Conflict* (Cambridge, Mass.: Harvard University Press, 1960), 43.)

policy. Therefore, legislators should not have too short terms in office because short terms, not to speak of constant referendums, would not be in the interest of the electorate.

This view is sometimes supposed to imply that Publius, in this case apparently Madison, distrusted the electorate and was somewhat anti-democratic. On the contrary, the view seems merely to reflect common sense. Even in one's individual decision-making, the power to make a decision and then to get on with life rather than to keep the issue permanently open is beneficial. Decision costs can be made so high as to leave no benefit from deciding. Hence, that constraints are enabling is not a logical paradox even though it may seem odd on first statement. Anyone who has come to understand the modern economist's view that virtually everything is a matter of trade-offs should no longer view it as odd or paradoxical—it is the heart of learned good sense. To put it negatively, the point of establishing a constitution and of creating particular institutions is to put obstacles in our way in order to force us to move along certain paths and not others. It enables us the more readily to organize ourselves for progress rather than to dissipate our energies in random directions.

Suppose one grants the central claims in the sections above. Still, one may wonder why anyone would go to the trouble of creating a constitution if there were not something vaguely like a contractual purpose. Clearly, we can live by conventions for which no one has ever voted. Indeed, one might exaggerate and say that the English Constitution is only a constitution so-called—it is really a set of conventions that have developed over time and that now seemingly prevail.[86] In this respect, it is similar to the peculiar rules of the English road that prevailed in England before they were made the law of the road. (Many of these 'conventions' are politically adopted documents as much as any constitution is.) Moreover, the law of contracts and their enforcement preceded the US Constitution through the conventions of common law courts. So why a written constitution? Obviously in order to hasten the establishment of relevant conventions and to direct them in certain ways rather than others by getting people to commit themselves immediately rather than bumbling

---

[86] This is, of course, an old thesis. For a recent account of the state of the conventions that govern England, see Geoffrey Marshall, *Constitutional Conventions: The Rules and Forms of Political Accountability* (Oxford: Oxford University Press, 1984). A reading of Marshall should suggest just how much of the American and any other constitutional system is similarly a matter of convention.

through to a result, a result that might have been the rise of a tyrant by force.

But one cannot simply commit oneself and then have it stick. This is the whole point of Hobbes's ridiculing the possibility that a sovereign can be governed by the laws that the sovereign passes and enforces. One cannot boot-strap oneself into doing what, when the time comes, one would not want to do. Contract works not because I say today that I will pay tomorrow but because I submit today to an authority who can force me to pay tomorrow.[87] The sovereign cannot submit to the sovereign in the same external sense but must boot-strap future action from present commitment. Neither can one's signature on a document or one's vote for it thereby generally make one's commitments under or to it stick.

Is Hobbes's argument somehow beside the point here? Yes. What one can do is commit oneself and then *arrange* to have it stick. That is what Ulysses did when he wished to hear the Sirens and yet survive and that is what we all do frequently. Indeed, many—most?—of us arrange to have some of our commitments stick in just the way the pre-citizens of the United States arranged to have their commitments stick. We set ourselves up in public to be made fools or worse if we do not follow through on our supposed commitments. If enough of the states had not ratified the Constitution two centuries ago, conventions and perhaps other formal arrangements would still have regulated their relations, or life in the states would have become nastier and shorter. Once enough of them did ratify, however, reneging became difficult, and increasingly difficult as time passed and the convention of coming under the governance of the Constitution became stronger. Eventually the southern states discovered during the Civil War just how difficult reneging might be. Today one need not 'love it' but if one wishes to renege one must 'leave it' or become criminal.

Arguments about commitment in this context are often framed as though they were individual problems, as in the problem of Hobbes's sovereign, who supposedly cannot self-commit. Pascal wrote of devices that one could individually use to bring about one's

---

[87] In this respect, contrary to a substantial tradition that runs contract and promise together, promising is quite different in typical uses of it. Promises are usually between people in ongoing relationships that give them an incentive to be reliable, to keep their promises to each other. Contracting is used in those contexts in which promising would not be self-enforcing in this way.

commitment through a kind of psychological habituation. Ulysses used external, non-psychological devices in having himself tied to the mast. The forms of commitment that are especially important for constitutional and even for conventional social choice, however, are those that derive *from the difficulties of collective action and of re-coordination from one coordination outcome to another*. These are not merely problems of internal psychological discipline and they can be powerfully effective in securing a system because they typically make the costs of changing the system radically higher than the costs of simply abiding by or even submitting to it. They may occasionally be overcome, as they were in 1787–8 when the Constitution was substituted for the Articles of Confederation in the United States and as they have been in many revolutionary contexts. But they can be a grand block to taking certain roads rather than others. Moreover, they can apply to someone whom Hobbes might have thought sovereign, which for him meant being able to change one's mind at a whim and to have the power to back the whim.[88]

The Constitution of 1787 worked in the end because enough of the relevant people worked within its confines long enough to get it established in everyone's expectations that there was no point in not working within its confines. Perhaps the most important single action by anyone under the US Constitution in its first decades was President John Adams's resolute departure from office after the victory of Jefferson and his Republican Party in the elections of 1800, an action that made the nascent American democracy meaningful in a way that must be at the core of any sensible definition of democracy. Those who lose elections leave or stay out of office; those who win enter or stay in office.

Adams's action, which seems ordinary today but which must have seemed remarkable to many people everywhere at the time, also reinforced the Constitution. Naturally, he did his best while still in office (in those days for more than four months after the election, as opposed to more than two months today) to have his political vision survive his time in office with post-election judicial appointments and other actions. But then, at the height of one of the bitterest periods in all of American political history,[89] he simply left and went home to Massachusetts when his time was over. That was arguably

---

[88] Russell Hardin, 'Sanction and Obligation', *Monist* (July 1985) 68: 403–18.
[89] See Edmund S. Morgan, 'Pioneers of Paranoia', *New York Review of Books* (6 Oct. 1994): 11–13.

the most important single action by anyone in all the history of constitutional government, because that action showed not merely that the principle of rule by the Constitution trumped rule by any person or party but, far more important, that rule by constitution could actually work even at such apparently high political cost to one of the parties to it. It was able to work in that case because even the losing party in 1800 had more to gain from continuing to live with the new constitutional order than by attempting to upset it. That is, it worked because keeping it in place served the mutual advantage of the principal parties to it better than trying to undo it would have done.

This was clearly the view of Alexander Hamilton, loser with Adams, who used his waning power to make sure that Jefferson and not Aaron Burr was made president. This was an issue because of a flaw in the Constitution, whose designers had not anticipated the invention and use of political parties to control elections. The president was to be chosen by the College of Electors, in which each elector was to cast votes for two candidates. The candidate with the largest number of votes, if it was by a majority of the electors, was president; the candidate with the next highest number, if by a majority of the electors, was vice-president. Jefferson's party voted for him and Aaron Burr in order to block the possibility that the vice-president would be a member of the opposing Federalist Party. That meant Jefferson and Burr tied, and the tie had to be broken in the House of Representatives, in which the Federalists controlled the outcome. Hamilton convinced his colleagues that a competent Republican was better than a rogue as president and Jefferson was elected. Hence, the two most influential Federalists, Hamilton and Adams, made it possible for the leading Republican to take office as president. Again, mutual advantage carried the day.

The agreement of certain people to it may have been important for those people to work within the US Constitution, but agreement was not the only or even an especially important motivator. Many must have worked within the Constitution simply because it was the most useful thing for them to do in their own interests. They might as soon have continued to work within the Articles of Confederation and their respective state constitutions or within the framework the Anti-Federalists might have established. Most of us most of the time are not political or politically motivated. We merely make the best of our lives in the world in which we find ourselves.

There were frequent efforts to undermine the Constitution in minor ways from the very beginning and such efforts seem likely to continue so long as some group has interests that could be furthered somewhat better by a slightly different constitutional order. There have even been what one could reasonably call unconstitutional efforts to strengthen the reach of that Constitution, as when Thomas Jefferson, avowedly one of the most democratic of the early constitutionalists, so democratic that he was ill at ease at the adoption of the Constitution, chose autocratically to overreach his authority as president to purchase the Louisiana Territory. No group of serious political consequence today appears to think its interests better served by a radical overthrow of the order that has grown out of the Constitution of 1787, although the southern states after the election of 1860 and various other groups at other times have wanted and even attempted such an overthrow, and there may be others to come, such as today's anti-government militia groups.

Benjamin Franklin remarked that 'Our Constitution is in actual operation; everything appears to promise that it will last; but in this world nothing is certain but death and taxes'.[90] In part it has since lasted two centuries and to some extent that fact makes it seem virtually certain in our lives. But the more impressive implication of that survival is its role in explaining our incentives under the Constitution. The long survival of the Constitution and the government it spawned gives force to the expectations we have that it will continue to survive and the strength of those expectations is among the chief of the reasons that it probably will continue to survive. Hence, it generally makes sense for us individually to coordinate on the order that the Constitution has helped to bring about. This suggests the strategic basis for the conservative dogma that what is is good, at least sometimes to some extent.[91]

Buchanan and his co-authors frame their requirement of unanimity at the constitutional stage as a contractarian moral principle. Unfortunately for their view, few people would accept this requirement. This fact seems to damn it as a *contractarian* principle.

[90] Benjamin Franklin, Letter to Jean Baptiste Le Roy, 13 Nov. 1789, in Albert Henry Smith, ed., *The Writings of Benjamin Franklin* (New York: Macmillan, 1907), x. 68–9.
[91] Russell Hardin, 'Does Might Make Right?' in J. Roland Pennock and John W. Chapman, eds., *NOMOS*, 29: *Authority Revisited* (New York: New York University Press, 1987), 201–17.

Some argue that the size of the majority required for constitutional choice should be the same as the size for subsequent choices under the constitution. Often, this too is framed as a moral principle as though it followed from a principle of insufficient reason. But there is a strong, even defining reason for having different requirements for constitutional moments and for subsequent quotidian moments under the constitution. *We want the constitution to be and to remain a successful coordination because then it will be self-enforcing.* A successful spontaneous coordination can happen only if there is relatively broad consensus, as on the Commerce Clause and on the general desire for order. Subsequent choices under the constitution can be successful even when they are merely bargains and compromises, because these can be enforced by the power that is created by the constitutional coordination.

If we cannot coordinate on the constitution—for example, if it is just a bargain as in an ordinary contractual arrangement—it will not be self-enforcing and we cannot expect constitutional constraints on subsequent choices to have much force. Alas, whether we can coordinate is largely a matter of luck. Argentines could not coordinate during the first half of the nineteenth century because the sharing of the customs collected in the single national port of Buenos Aires could not be governed by a mutually advantageous self-enforcing arrangement.[92] Rwandans could not plausibly coordinate today. And perhaps no advanced society can coordinate on thorough-going egalitarianism.

The elements of luck in the American constitutional coordination are discussed more fully in Chapter 6, where the focus is on the workability of a constitution once it has been put into operation and faces economic changes. Part of the luck of the thirteen states was that, unlike Argentina, they had numerous well-developed natural ports, one in every state except New Jersey and North Carolina. Hence, they needed coordination to stop competitive underpricing of import duties. Making the customs a national function was part of the purpose of the Commerce Clause that was itself the main purpose of the Constitution. With a like distribution of ports, Argentina's constitutional history might have been radically different. At the very least, Buenos Aires would not have had such a

---

[92] Julio Saguir, 'In Search of Institutional Design: A Comparison between the Constitutional Processes of Argentina and the United States', a Ph.D. thesis at the University of Chicago, 1991.

rankling role to play. The multiplicity of ports was a reason for initial coordination in the United States; the uniqueness of the port of Buenos Aires was an obstacle to initial coordination in Argentina.

It is the failure to grasp the self-enforcing quality of a successful constitution that makes the vision of the constitution of government as a contract, as though our fundamental problem were to overcome a prisoner's dilemma, so exasperating to those who hold to that vision. Because it is not a contract but a convention, a constitution does not depend for its enforcement on external sanctions or bootstrapping commitments founded in nothing but supposed or hypothetical agreement. Establishing a constitution is a massive act of coordination that creates a convention that depends for its maintenance on its self-generating incentives and expectations. Given that it is a mystery how contracting could work to resolve our constitutional problem, we should be glad that that problem is such that we have no need of a social contract.

4

Democracy: Agreement or Acquiescence?

> When a new form of government is fabricated, it lies within the
> people at large to receive or reject it . . . By what conduct do
> they discover that they are sensible of their own interests in this
> situation? . . . by a tractable and docile disposition, while others
> . . . are constructing the bark that may . . . carry them to the port
> of rest and happiness, if they will embark without diffidence
> and proceed without mutiny.
>
> Caesar, no. 2 (17 Oct. 1787)[1]

Consent

A central question in Chapter 3 was whether a constitution is somehow analogous to a giant contract. Clearly, it is not. The argument
was entirely about the different natures of contracts and constitutions, about descriptive and strategic issues. But there has been
another use of the contract metaphor in political philosophy in the
contractarian *justification* of political order and, especially, of
democracy. Democracy grounds political order in the consent of the
governed. But this is an inherently bifurcated notion. We are forced
to consider when consent should determine outcomes. In constitutional or in governing moments? *Ex ante* or *in medias res*? Although
usage and logic are not consistent in the huge literatures on consent
theory, popular sovereignty and the doctrine of the social contract
make sense primarily in constitutional moments. I will reserve the
term democracy for decisions taken under a constitution or, rather,
for *some* of the decisions taken under a constitution, namely those

---

[1] Caesar, no. 2, 17 Oct. 1787, in Philip B. Kurland and Ralph Lerner, eds., *The
Founders' Constitution* (Chicago: University of Chicago Press, 1987), i. 60–1.

that are put to the vote in some way. As argued in Chapter 3, constitutions typically restrict the scope of democracy—otherwise there would be little need for creating the many blocking institutions that constitutions typically mandate.

Hence, we could divide consent theory into two branches: constitutional and post-constitutional. Popular sovereignty and social contract theories fit largely into the first branch; democracy fits into the second. One might appeal to popular sovereignty or contractarian consent in proposing to change a constitution. In actual practice, however, even constitutional design must be done by some kind of procedure that would hardly fit a full consent account. For example, in the standard amending process in the United States there is merely a requirement for an odd kind of supermajority of states, which can happen with the backing of a minority of voters, so that amendment is handled by democracy, not by appeal to popular sovereignty or a social contract. And one might appeal beyond standard democratic procedures in certain vastly important initiatives for which popular commitment is required if they are to succeed, as might be true for fighting a major war. But for most matters that arise under a constitutional regime, one would appeal only to majoritarian democratic claims, not to claims of anything vaguely like universal consent. As L. T. Hobhouse wrote, 'In point of fact it is only now and again on some great and simple issue that the people, as a whole, can be said to have a will'.[2]

Admittedly, political rhetoric need not be constrained by logic. For example, after winning by a very narrow majority of a minority of eligible voters in 1994, leaders of the Republican Party in the House of Representatives claimed to have a 'mandate' to legislate their programme as though they spoke with the consent of the sovereign people behind them. This is a common part of democratic politics. Perhaps there is no part of political vocabulary that is more subject to the distortions of hortatory and self-boosting rhetoric than the vocabulary of consent. Not even justice is so grossly abused. But I will focus here on what one might coldly call the analytical structure of the issues rather than on the political heat that often animates them.

[2] L. T. Hobhouse, 'Government by the People', in Hobhouse, *Liberalism and Other Writings*, ed. James Meadowcroft (Cambridge: Cambridge University Press, 1994; essay 1st pub. 1910), 123–35, at p. 127.

Although there is a large literature on the nature of a sovereign, there is not a grand modern tradition of writing on popular sovereignty, which is perhaps more commonly a term of political discourse than of political theory. Democratic theory is a major enterprise, especially since the rise of the modern democratic state, but also long before from at least the time of Athenian democracy.[3] Social contract theory is also the subject of a vast and, surprisingly, despite its frequent analytical vacuity, growing literature. As discussed in Chapter 3, such theory has, over several centuries, moved from actual contract, through tacit consent, to rationalist contract, and now to so-called reasonable-agreement versions. Actual contract is still invoked, perversely, as a metaphorical model of constitutionalism but is otherwise a dead political theory. Actual contract and tacit consent ground justification in objective consent of some kind. Rationalist and reasonable-agreement contractarianisms ground it in hypothetical consent, in what we would have agreed to (or, less restrictively, could not have objected to) if we had considered the matter under relevant constraints.[4]

As is true of the moral-theoretic programmes of utilitarianism, deontology, and virtue theory,[5] and of most other major theoretical moral and political programmes, democratic theory and contractarianism are movements rather than single, focused theories. Democratic theory started perhaps as a theory of direct participation but it is now almost entirely about representative government. There have been numerous contractarian theories, many of them crafted in response to cogent criticisms of prior theories in the movement. Contributors include Hobbes, Locke, Rousseau, Kant, Mill, and many contemporary theorists.

Arguments from social contract, popular sovereignty, and democracy are all parts of consent theory. The signal difference in these three labels is that one can construct a strictly practical democratic

---

[3] Bernard Manin, *Principes du gouvernement représentatif* (Paris: Calmann-Lévy, 1995).

[4] See e.g. Brian Barry, *Justice As Impartiality* (Oxford: Oxford University Press, 1995), esp. ch. 7. But see Russell Hardin, 'Reasonable Agreement: Political Not Normative', in Paul J. Kelly, ed., *Impartiality, Neutrality and Justice: Re-reading Brian Barry's Justice as Impartiality* (Edinburgh: Edinburgh University Press, 1998): 137–53.

[5] Utilitarianism is a theory in which the good is people's welfare and in which actions are judged by their effects on welfare; deontological theories are typically about rules for moral action; and virtue theories are about the virtues that individuals, sometimes as determined by their roles, should have.

theory that focuses wholly on procedures and practices and not on justification. The other two labels seem almost inherently in large part about justification.[6] This difference fits the constitutional and post-constitutional roles of the theories. However, the bulk of normative theory on democracy has itself been contractarian in the sense that the use of majoritarian procedures is justified from claims of *ex ante* consent. Increasingly, the bulk of explanatory and descriptive theory is from the rational-choice perspective.

Finally, there is one other conception that one might wish to put under consent theory: coordination. However, there is a sense in which coordination depends far less on anything that sounds like genuine consent that is at all conscious or articulate than on merely not opposing whatever order there is. Once a constitutional order is in place, coordination is a matter of not engaging in mutiny, as the Federalist Caesar remarked in the epigraph for this chapter. Unlike the other categories of consent, coordination fits on both sides of constitutional order, both *ex ante* and *in medias res*. If we cannot coordinate, we cannot create a working constitution. And if it does not coordinate us enough after we have one, it will fail.

A successful constitution shares with many norms the fact that it is maintained by coordination by enough people to make mutiny by a few too costly to entertain.[7] It is in this sense self-enforcing. Madison, Tocqueville, and others have worried pervasively that democracy will produce a tyranny of the majority. Robert Dahl concludes against this concern that 'the more relevant question is the extent to which various minorities in a society will frustrate the ambitions of one another with the passive acquiescence or indifference of a majority of adults or voters'.[8] Caesar was right, Madison was wrong in the light of the actual facts of American history.

Coordination and its force are at issue in all of the discussions that follow and they will not be treated separately. In their justificatory uses, consent, contractarianism, and popular sovereignty are taken to

[6] One might similarly have a strictly applied theory of 'popular' sovereignty at least in international relations. Popular sovereignty of nations is a matter of practical law-making and policy. It is a sometimes deplorable notion that includes the supposition that the Idi Amins, Pol Pots, and Papa Docs of the world represent the sovereignty of some people whom they are murdering or otherwise grossly harming.

[7] On the maintenance and enforcement of norms of exclusion, see Russell Hardin, *One for All: The Logic of Group Conflict* (Princeton: Princeton University Press, 1995), 88–90, 102–4.

[8] Robert A. Dahl, *A Preface to Democratic Theory* (Chicago: University of Chicago Press, 1956), 133.

mean that we all agree with the rightness of our order. In a coordination, we merely recognize individually that it is in our individual interest to acquiesce rather than to mutiny, and there need be no belief or claim that it is in our collective interest to do so nor any claim of articulate agreement. One might call it tacit agreement, but if this is what tacit agreement means, it has none of the moral force that Locke wanted to derive from it.

In what follows, I will discuss contractarianism in its various guises as applied to democratic theory. Then I will discuss the general problem of popular sovereignty. After that I will take up constitutionalism as part of a two-stage application of democracy to public choice, and I will discuss justice as order as the clearest and perhaps most important case in which we would normatively want democratic choice to be brought to bear *only ex ante* and not *in medias res*. Then I will turn to the factual impossibility of extensive popular control of government with a discussion of the unplanned nature of government institutions. I will then discuss rational-choice problems with the application of democracy,[9] and alternative visions of democracy. Finally, I will discuss the inherent difficulties of representation.

Contractarianism

Surprisingly, after it had seemingly passed into the history of thought, talk of the social contract has come back to haunt us again in the work of many people who take no part in the earlier debate: such scholars as James Buchanan, Thomas Scanlon, David Gauthier, Brian Barry, and, under some interpretations, John Rawls.[10] Part of the reason may have been to rescue deontological arguments for political philosophy from the general trouncing they had taken from utilitarian arguments over the past couple of centuries.[11] The larger reason may be to give force to the view that we are morally obligated to support actions taken by our government because we are like

[9] I discuss these problems with relevance to the present argument in Russell Hardin, 'Public Choice vs. Democracy', in John W. Chapman, ed., *NOMOS*, 32: *Majorities and Minorities* (New York: New York University Press, 1990), 184–203.

[10] See further, Russell Hardin, 'Contractarianism: Wistful Thinking', *Constitutional Political Economy*, 1 (1990): 35–52.

[11] H. L. A. Hart, 'Between Utility and Rights', in Hart, *Essays in Jurisprudence and Philosophy* (Oxford: Oxford University Press, 1983; essay 1st pub. 1979), 198–222.

those who voluntarily enter contracts, as traditionally conceived. As argued in Chapter 3, a constitution such as that of 1787–8 is most certainly *not* a social contract as that term is generally used, and such terminology is therefore misleading.

In the social contract metaphor of Hobbes, Locke, and uncounted others, you give up some power to government in exchange for my doing likewise. If enough of us enter this exchange, government is possible and we can have order and we may even have collective provision of many constructive benefits. Interestingly, Hobbes apparently saw the practical impossibility of this move in his *De Cive*, where he notes that 'no man can transferre his power in a naturall manner'.[12] In *Leviathan*, which was published in the same year as Hobbes's own English translation of *De Cive*, however, he dodged the problem and simply asserted of our newly chosen sovereign that 'by this Authoritie, given him by every particular man in the Common-Wealth, he hath the use of so much Power and Strength conferred on him, that by the terror thereof, he is inabled to forme the wills of them all'.[13]

Gregory Kavka and Jean Hampton clearly understood that the problem of empowerment is severe and that, even if we contract, we still face the grim logic of collective action when our new sovereign attempts to bring us to order.[14] As Jürgen Habermas writes, 'rationally-motivated

[12] Thomas Hobbes, *De Cive*, ed. Howard Warrender (Oxford: Oxford University Press, 1983; 1st pub. (Latin) 1642; (English) 1651), 2.5.11, p. 90.

[13] Thomas Hobbes, *Leviathan* (1651), any standard edition, ch. 17: 87–8 in original edition. For further discussion, see Russell Hardin, 'Hobbesian Political Order', *Political Theory*, 19 (May 1991): 156–80, esp. 168–71. Locke blithely supposed that his social contractors 'must be understood to give up all the power, necessary to the ends for which they unite into Society, to the *majority* of the Community' (John Locke, *Two Treatises of Government* (Cambridge: Cambridge University Press, 1988 student edn.; 1st pub. 1690), 2.99, p. 333).

[14] Gregory S. Kavka, *Hobbesian Moral and Political Theory* (Princeton: Princeton University Press, 1986); Jean Hampton, *Hobbes and the Social Contract Tradition* (Cambridge: Cambridge University Press, 1986). Hampton seemingly resolves the problem of instant empowerment in her argument that Hobbes mistakenly views interactions in the state of nature as essentially one-shot prisoner's dilemmas, whereas they must often be iterated (pp. 75–8). Since it is rational to cooperate in iterated prisoner's dilemmas, she supposes that the state of nature is less grim than Hobbes thought. Against her argument to get rational contractarianism off the ground, however, it is typically rational to cooperate in iterated prisoner's dilemma only for two or very few players. Hobbes seems to have recognized the rationality of cooperating in ongoing relationships but he supposed that the chief problem in the state of nature was interactions with the many when few of these could be ongoing as dyadic interactions. Two of us would not need a state in order to cooperate; the many cannot cooperate without external coercion. Hence, the need for the state.

agreement on goals and programmes remains ineffective until the corresponding resolutions empower and simultaneously bind the executive bodies involved'.[15] Hobbes realized that power was necessary for order and that power cannot be conjured up by mere consent. But he did not know how to resolve this dilemma to make the social contract work to put a state in place. Nor has any other contractarian evidently ever resolved the dilemma.

One might suppose that because Hobbes realized the practical problems in this move, he therefore concluded that government need not be founded in such a contract but might rather be the result of conquest or usurpation. In fact, however, the problem that drove Hobbes's account was the revolutionary turmoil of his own time. This was not resolved by a social contract, nor did Hobbes argue that it should be. Rather, he argued that we should be obedient even to a state that has come about by conquest or coup. One might object that ordering a population by conquest is just politics while contractarianism is philosophy. But politics was Hobbes's central interest. He wished to motivate obedience to the state, to argue against insurrection merely for the sake of improving one's lot. His justification was simply that it could seldom if ever be in one's interest to attempt revolution. He needed no recourse to moral argument or to a moralized notion of obligation. Interest and obedience were sufficient. Hence, he was not genuinely a social contract theorist.

For his view that government by conquest can be good, Hobbes is sometimes ridiculed, especially by the contractarians who otherwise take him to be an early advocate of their views. More often he is simply ignored for this view. We should, however, give him the honour he is due for the view. In this century, two of the greatest democracies, Germany and Japan, were forged out of two of the most disastrous and heinous fascist states by their conquerors' imposition on them of a democratic order. In the case of Japan, the constitution that has governed the nation since World War II was written by a committee overseen by General Douglas MacArthur on an American naval vessel and then it was imposed forcibly by the United States.[16]

---

[15] Jürgen Habermas, 'Towards a Communication-Concept of Rational Collective Will-Formation: A Thought Experiment', *Ratio Juris* (July 1989) 2: 144–54, at p. 146.

[16] The actual working of MacArthur's constitution has, of course, been heavily determined by the Japanese, even, to a remarkable degree, by the Japanese language into which the constitution had to be translated. That version and the English version, both official, differ because the languages did not have equivalent terms. See Kyoko Inouye, *MacArthur's Japanese Constitution* (Chicago: University of Chicago Press,

Similarly, the Western allies created West Germany out of the ruins of Nazism and war. In both cases, armies of occupation lingered until the governments seemed to be running well. These imposed governments have produced extraordinary prosperity for their peoples and, what is more remarkable, they have been about as genuinely liberal as any governments that were ostensibly created by their own peoples. A dictator's imposed constitution might eventually be seen to have served Chile about as well. Finally, we might ruefully note that turning the Philadelphia Convention into a constitutional convention was beyond the mandate of the conventioneers. But when going beyond a mandate works and is eventually accepted, we tend to forget that it was possibly criminal. As Hobbes held, workability and success in serving its polity and not its origin should be the criterion for the judgement of the goodness of a political order.

Hobbes's fable of the social contract was a sociological, not a moral move, and it was evidently a sociological failure even in his own view. When a man transfers a right to another, as when he contracts, 'then he is said to be OBLIGED, or BOUND, not to hinder those to whom such Right is granted'. He transfers the right by signs, but 'these Signes are either Words onely, or Actions, onely . . . And the same are the BONDS, by which men are bound, and obliged: Bonds that have their strength, not from their own Nature, (for nothing is more easily broken then a mans word,) but *from Feare of some evill consequence upon the rupture*'.[17]

The sociologists Talcott Parsons and Ralf Dahrendorf have therefore seen Hobbes as a conflict theorist rather than a theorist of value consensus. Parsons therefore thinks him misguided; Dahrendorf therefore thinks him profound.[18] As noted in Chapter 1, I think Hobbes is rather a coordination theorist. But Parsons and Dahrendorf are right not to see Hobbes's theory as fundamentally

1991). For similar problems in Africa, see Frederic C. Schaffer, *Democracy in Transition: Understanding Politics in an Unfamiliar Culture* (Ithaca, NY: Cornell University Press, 1998).

[17] Hobbes, *Leviathan*, ch. 14, p. 65 in original edn., emphasis added. The most plausible reading of Hobbes's 'obligation' is as a rational or interest term, not a moral term—we fear evil consequences, as when we have an all-powerful sovereign to keep us in line. For him to say we are obligated is to mean we are obliged by our own interest. See further, discussion in Chapter 1, section on 'Political Obligation'.

[18] Talcott Parsons, *The Structure of Social Action* (New York: Free Press, 1968; 1st pub. 1937), 89–94; Ralf Dahrendorf, 'In Praise of Thrasymachus', in Dahrendorf, *Essays in the Theory of Society* (Stanford: Stanford University Press, 1968), 129–50.

normative. Many commentators have too readily ignored much of what Hobbes wrote and touted his supposed contractarianism above his concern with coordination on any regime that works.

The dismissal of the practical analogy between a contract and a constitution in Chapter 3 suggests the implausibility of a genuine social contract. Partly in the light of Hume's demolition of the myth of any such contract to back the supposedly legitimate governments of history, philosophers in our time have taken social contract theory in a very different direction.[19] As did Kant, they assert the inherent rationality of agreement on government and call this a contract. They are *rationalist contractarians.*

Rousseau argued for a general will that unifies a polity against the varied self-interests of its members. His claim for such a will seemed to come at a moment in history in which the seemingly necessary conditions for it had passed in many places and were soon to pass almost everywhere. He spoke of the general will in the small city of Geneva, which was relatively united in a strong religion and in which the belief in a single right way to live and be governed was still conceivable although dubious. Kant blended Rousseau's vision with the traditional contract vision. He said it is not necessary that our 'original contract' in fact brings us all together to form a common will ('and, indeed, it is utterly impossible') nor that there has been any actual agreement by our forebears for us to be bound by such a contract. 'Instead, it is a *mere idea* of reason, one, however, that has indubitable (practical) reality.'[20]

In recent decades, rationalist contractarianism has lost its metaphysical tone and whatever coherence it may once have had. Contractarianism is now more commonly backed by the claim that we should submit to *reasonable agreement.* These words are the open sesame and the shibboleth of much of contemporary political theory. We want government to be based on consent, as in the contract theories of earlier centuries. But we cannot plausibly believe there has been anything vaguely like contractual consent to undergird our governments and we doubt that there could be. Alas, we are

---

[19] David Hume, 'Of the Original Contract', in Hume, *Essays Moral, Political, and Literary*, ed. Eugene Miller (Indianapolis: Liberty Press, 1985; essay 1st pub. 1748), 465–87.

[20] Immanuel Kant, 'On the Proverb: That May Be True in Theory, but Is of No Practical Use', 1st pub. 1793, in Kant, *Perpetual Peace and Other Essays* (Indianapolis: Hackett, 1983, trans. Ted Humphrey), 77 (viii. 297 in the Prussian Academy of Sciences edn. of Kant's works).

also no longer metaphysicians, at least with respect to public life, and we do not believe in a rationally deducible correct way to organize ourselves politically. If we can only believe that, under relevant circumstances, we *would* agree on something, then we may think government can be grounded in something morally analogous to consent.

Still, we wish to avoid supposing with Kant, Alan Gewirth, and many others that we can derive the correct principles to which every rational person *must* consent.[21] All our talk of consent would then be camouflage for a purely rationalist theory of the rightness of government and the rightness of acquiescence to its actions and demands. In his *Theory of Justice*, John Rawls is transitional between rationalist contractarianism (in the tradition of Rousseau and Kant) and the more recent arguments from reasonable agreement. His argument from behind the veil, where there is only one representative person, appears to be a rationalist argument. The one representative person can find the form of government to which we would all agree. Rawls forcefully asserts that his argument is political, not metaphysical, but this position may not be coherent because it leaves his actual arguments for his theory unmoored.[22]

Contemporary contractarians assert that all we can really expect is reasonable agreement, not deductive rationalist agreement. Left undefined, 'reasonable' becomes a declaration of hope that something lurks there. We avoid rationalist derivation of consent by resort to normatively constrained objective agreement. That is to say, reasonable agreement is ostensibly what we would agree to if we first submitted to certain normative constraints on the choices that we make or the procedures for choosing that we use. For example, in Charles Beitz's discussion of voting, the role of 'reasonable' is merely to cover the concern that we enter discussions with the desire to reach agreement on political institutions.[23] Sometimes, this criterion is shifted to define reasonable agreement as *what we could not object to*, although this formulation leaves open a potentially large array of reasonable agreement points. Thomas Scanlon calls this approach contractualism to distinguish it from the earlier contrac-

[21] Alan Gewirth, *Reason and Morality* (Chicago: University of Chicago Press, 1978).

[22] John Rawls, 'Justice As Fairness: Political not Metaphysical', *Philosophy and Public Affairs* (Summer 1985) 14: 223–51.

[23] Charles R. Beitz, *Political Equality* (Princeton: Princeton University Press, 1989), 100.

tarianism.[24] One might associate this vision with Habermas's normative prerequisites of discourse.[25]

An Oxford moral philosopher has reputedly parodied the notion of reasonable agreement in an academic commentary addressed to a reasonable-agreement Harvardian. He asked his audience to imagine a ride on a train from London to Oxford. In the compartment are several people, including a skinhead and a Harvardian who does not know certain people exist. The Harvardian opens a political discourse: 'What kind of ideal association would you prefer?' he asks. The skinhead gives his nearly universal response to all queries: 'Fuck off'. Clearly, this conversation has failed the test of the normative prerequisites of discourse and whatever other normative constraints one might require for philosophically adequate political discourse. Unfortunately, however, it is not clear at what point it has failed the test.[26]

No reasonable-agreement theorist is an actual contractarian. Hence, there will generally be no actual discussions leading to agreement except when—for example, in political philosophy or normative jurisprudence—we pose the question whether a set of institutions is justified. The test of justification turns not on whether we have such discussions but on whether our institutions are such that we could not reasonably reject them in the event of discussions. (It would be unreasonable to reject them merely because, for example, I would be better served by some other set of institutions.) Reasonable, rational, or some other such qualifier seems to be necessary if a consent theory is not to have the implication of the old contractarianism that agreement *constitutes* the right or the good. This suggests a perplexing feature of the new contractualism. We would reach agreement because what we would agree to is somehow right or good. But we need a non-rationalist contractarianism just because we no longer believe there is a rationally deducible right or good that we are all compelled to agree with. We think different individuals may have different rights and goods that are all valid. Then why

[24] Thomas Scanlon, 'Contractualism and Utilitarianism', in Amartya Sen and Bernard Williams, eds., *Utilitarianism and Beyond* (Cambridge: Cambridge University Press, 1982).

[25] In Jürgen Habermas, *The Theory of Communicative Action*, i: *Reason and the Rationalization of Society*, trans. Thomas McCarthy (Boston: Beacon, 1984).

[26] I have this account second hand and, in the details, I may do an injustice to all concerned. I leave the parties unidentified to protect the guilty.

should we expect we would agree? Experience suggests we would not. Theory so far has had nothing of interest to say on this question.

Hobbes realized we could expect agreement on survival and prosperity only if we could rule out religious fanaticism and glory seeking as politically acceptable goods. People have not significantly changed since Hobbes's time, although one might think vicious egoism a greater problem today than glory seeking. The criterion of reasonable agreement has no bite for us as democratic or other theorists if we cannot say fairly firm things about what one could expect others to think. If one could believe reasonable agreement is possible from a large collection of diverse people, one might also believe those people must share similar fundamental moral intuitions. But two centuries of raging dispute between various schools of moral theory suggest we can be expected to disagree with hostility about every important fundamental moral principle. (Until the efflorescence of communitarianism, one might have said universalism was a universally shared moral principle. Now it, too, is under attack.) Unless someone can convince us of something none of us now believes— that we all concur enough in our visions of political order that we could reasonably agree—contractualism is a vain wish. At best it reduces to the possibility of coordination on relatively general principles, as in the argument for the logic of a constitution in Chapter 3.

Popular Sovereignty

Democratic choice is commonly supposed to be a form of popular sovereignty over political results. In any complex polity, however, this supposition is at best metaphorical, as the large post-war literature on democratic theory suggests.[27] In typical contexts, popular sovereignty is an empirically and perhaps a conceptually incoherent notion. A constitutional regime may be 'controlled' only to the extent that it is constrained by mutually advantageous coordination of important groups in the polity on the maintenance of various

[27] Robert A. Dahl, *A Preface to Democratic Theory* (Chicago: University of Chicago Press, 1956); Stanley I. Benn and Richard S. Peters, *Social Principles and the Democratic State* (London: George Allen and Unwin, 1959), reprinted as *The Principles of Political Thought: Social Foundations of the Democratic State* (New York: Free Press, 1965). There is a broad, representative selection in Philip Green, ed., *Democracy* (Atlantic Highlands, NJ: Humanities Press, 1993).

institutions. The long-run success of constitutional government depends on such coordinated interests. It might be conceptually sensible to say that there is popular control in some societies over certain relatively vague aspects of politics on which almost everyone might have an interest in coordinating. For example, we might all agree roughly on commitments to economic prosperity and to general protection of individual liberties. But there cannot be popular control over much of what government actually does.

(The term sovereignty is invested with heavy meaning in much of the writing on constitutionalism, political theory, and international relations, as well as in political debate. The heavy meaning is typically incoherent and the term is therefore often misleading. One could use the term, almost pointlessly, as merely an atonal label for what is decided by whatever procedures there generally are. I will not use it in this way.)

It is a commonplace in the history of political thought that appeals to popular sovereignty have typically been a ruse to shore up rule by élites who were not at all beholden to the larger polity. Roman emperors, Holy Roman emperors, and medieval Italian communal rulers claimed to have their power from the people, and most of them were despots.[28] Parliamentary claims to embody popular sovereignty in England during the turbulent seventeenth century were merely a somewhat larger élite's railing against Royalists. Edmund S. Morgan argues that popular sovereignty in the days of the American constitutional debates was also largely a fiction.[29] Still today, claims of popular sovereignty serve more as rhetorical legitimization than as description of democratic government.

In *Anna Karenina*, Tolstoy's *alter ego* Levin is frustrated with his half-brother Koznyshev's invocation of the people's will: 'That word *people* is so indefinite', Levin says. 'Clerks in district offices, schoolmasters, and one out of a thousand peasants, may know what it is all about. The rest of the eighty millions . . . not only don't express their will, but have not the least idea what it is they have to express it about! What right have we then to say it is the will of the people?' Koznyshev agrees that voting would not express the

[28] See e.g. discussions of debates during the Renaissance and Reformation in Quentin Skinner, *The Foundations of Modern Political Thought*, 2 vols. (Cambridge: Cambridge University Press, 1978), many passages. Benn and Peters, *Social Principles and the Democratic State*, 299–325, give a general survey of ideas.

[29] Edmund S. Morgan, *Inventing the People: The Rise of Popular Sovereignty in England and America* (New York: Norton, 1988).

people's will but blithely supposes the notion still has meaning that can be found in 'the unanimity of the intelligent world'.[30] Men of thought express public opinion, he adds later, as though to give content to his vacuity.[31]

Appeals to popular sovereignty have also been part of modern revolutionary rhetoric. The revolutionary French *Declaration of the Rights of Man* of 1789, declared that 'The principle of all sovereignty rests essentially in the nation. No body and no individual may exercise authority unless it emanates expressly from the nation.' In the French Constitution of 1946, 'the nation' is more aptly rendered as 'the people'.[32] The US Constitution opens famously, 'We the People . . .'. Manifestos from numerous colonies insisting on independence have appealed to the sovereignty of the relevant people to decide their own fate. In the French case, the people who were sovereign did not include vast numbers of those who were to be suppressed by the nation's new regime. In the US and many other cases, the people was not an inclusive label. Sovereignty is evidently a mess.

Rather than contend with the rhetoric of popular sovereignty and its mismatch with reality, however, I wish to deal with the apparent impossibility of popular control of government. Popular control fails in principle for two quite different reasons. First, there are the standard problems of social choice, that popular views will commonly not aggregate into a collective view and that individuals will be motivated neither to understand public issues well enough to act on them nor to take action even when they do understand them (as discussed below under 'The Logic of Democracy'). Secondly, there is the nature of institutional government. To be effective, government must work through institutions. But the structure and eventually the actions of institutions are substantially unintended consequences, the result of growth and not the outcome of popular choice or even any systematic choice at all (as discussed below in the section on 'Government as Grown').

The term 'popular sovereignty' is commonly used in political philosophy with a dual signification: descriptive and normative. As a descriptive notion popular sovereignty involves a fallacy of composition that Hobbes at least implicitly understood but that many

[30] Leo Tolstoy, *Anna Karenina*, 2 vols., trans. Louise and Aylmer Maude (London: Oxford University Press, 1939; 1st pub. (Russian) 1875–7, i. 426–7.
[31] Tolstoy, *Anna Karenina*, i. 428.
[32] Benn and Peters, *Social Principles and the Democratic State*, 395.

modern writers ignore. A monarch can be sovereign in the sense of being able to decide on an action and then following through on it. A group of people cannot as readily be sovereign in this sense. The group might not be able to agree enough to decide anything and also might not be able to follow through on anything even when it does agree.

Those concerned with how it would work, rather than with the ideal, have commonly seen the practical incoherence of the notion of popular sovereignty. For example, John Adams, writing in defence of the proposed Constitution in 1787, was provoked by Marchamont Nedham's claim that the people 'are the best keepers of their own liberties . . . because they never think of usurping other men's rights'. Adams contemptuously asked, 'But who are the people?' He then went on to demolish Nedham's fallacy of composition and the silliness that followed from it.[33]

A second descriptive problem has received far more attention. Hobbes supposed that sovereign governors cannot be bound by any of their own laws because they can, if genuinely sovereign, simply choose in the moment of enforcement to change the law. Hence a sovereign is above the law in two senses: the sovereign makes the law and the sovereign cannot be bound by the law. This characterization clearly fits the logic of an individual sovereign, such as a monarch, as it fits Dostoevsky's god, who makes the law and for whom there is therefore no law.[34] But there is a sense in which a corporate sovereign, such as a legislative body or a polity, can be bound by the law individually.[35] A legislature as such cannot be bound not to change 'its mind', but the individual members of the legislature can be bound to abide by whatever the legislature honours as the law. Hence, a corporate sovereign need not be above the law in the second sense. Still, it could be above the law in that sense if it simply exempts its members from coverage by the law. For example, the Chicago City Council in 1987 exempted its members from coverage

---

[33] John Adams, 'Defence of the Constitution of Government of the United States', in Kurland and Lerner, *The Founder's Constitution*, i. 59. Jefferson, Adams's sometime friend and sometime nemesis, may have shared in Nedham's fallacy of composition. In a letter to Madison he wrote, 'Above all things I hope the education of the common people will be attended to; convinced that on their good sense we may rely with the most security for the preservation of a due degree of liberty' (letter of 20 Dec. 1787, in ibid. i. 677).

[34] Fyodor Dostoevsky, *The Brothers Karamazov* (Harmondsworth: Penguin, 1958; 1st pub. 1880), 764.

[35] Russell Hardin, 'Sanction and Obligation', *The Monist*, 68 (July 1985): 403–18.

by the ethics ordinance that governs all other Chicago government office holders.

Turn now to the normative signification of popular sovereignty. It is often asserted that what the sovereign wants is right or, more typically in modern times, what the sovereign people want is right or at least ought to be done. Rhetorical appeals to the fiction of popular sovereignty are presumably motivated by the sense that popular sovereignty carries great normative weight. This was presumably the force of the elliptical chant in the streets of East Germany in 1989: 'We are the people'. Obviously, if there are difficulties with descriptive sovereignty, then there will be difficulties in drawing normative inferences from it. Popular sovereignty is of central concern, of course, in democratic theory. When sovereignty is not popular but is autocratic, it is not incoherent. An all-powerful monarch, for example, is not subject to the fallacy of composition that undercuts claims for group coherence. Unfortunately, no matter that the notion is incoherent in most contexts, popular sovereignty has a compelling normative ring that gives it extraordinary rhetorical force.

Much of the normative criticism of popular sovereignty and democracy is that it would not be good even if we had it. The standard conservative criticism is that it would be like capricious and pernicious mob rule. Against this criticism, Philip Green argues that we need more democracy, not less. He argues that the large direct actions of suffragists and others in the West and of democratic activists in Eastern Europe during the remarkable year 1989 were among the finer moments of modern democracy.[36] The 1989 actions were moments that, in a sense, created democratic government. Green wishes for more direct action to enliven democratic participation under ongoing governments. Against his wish, reality may argue that the chief moments for popular choice are constitutional moments when large, structural choices are to be made and, even then, only if there is relatively broad coordination on what choices to make. Quotidian moments hold little opportunity for the exercise of popular sovereignty.

---

[36] Philip Green, 'Introduction: "Democracy" As a Contested Idea', in Green, *Democracy*, 2–18, at pp. 15–18.

Constitutionalism and Democracy

If constitutionalism depends on coordination of the populace on core issues, should it not follow that in a successful constitutional regime popular sovereignty reigns? Yes, but only in a relatively vague and overarching sense. Suppose we have coordinated on a system of government that now decides policies for us. Is it then correct to say that because we collectively settled on that system of government, what it does is now what we want done? No. The two-stage decision process pre-empts what 'we' want done at the second stage. We need not even have evidence of what we want done at that stage. Indeed, what we want done is often the result of what political leaders and institutions have done. For example, the American populace was ambivalent about going to war over the Iraqi invasion of Kuwait until President Bush took the nation into war. Then the public was overwhelmingly supportive. Popular sovereignty generally might determine much of how we do things while determining little or nothing of what we do.

In constitutional moments the people have a voice—or at least the choices in those moments, whoever makes them, must fit the people's interests in some strong sense of coordinating them if the choices are to be at all binding. In other moments, although the people may have opportunity for voice, it is much less crucial that the choices made fit their interests or coordinate them well. It is sufficient then that the procedures for making the choices coordinate the people sufficiently well that the choices do not wreck the constitutional coordination. This is commonly a relatively mild constraint on choices so that government is relatively free to decide over a wide range of possibilities.

In the two-stage account of constitutional government in Chapter 3, we would want to establish institutions for handling various problems in order to achieve good resolutions of them because we could not sensibly expect to handle the problems well without specialized division of labour. This is a very general problem of institutions and not merely a problem of democracy. Within an organization, we assign roles to various individuals, who then are expected to act according to their role definitions and not according to what they individually conceive in each moment to contribute best to the goal of the organization. Organizations are valuable, even necessary, for achieving many of our common purposes because independently acting individuals could not do as well as properly designed institutions.[37] For example, we might design organizations to achieve utilitarian or deontological results. But the actors within these institutions would not directly attempt to produce utilitarian or deontological results. Rather, they would follow the dictates of their roles in acting jointly with others to produce the relevant results.[38]

Similarly, our democratic choice should often be invoked in determining the design of institutions, not thereafter in determining the particular actions these institutions take. Decisions by institutions that are not directly made by democratic choice are not in principle in conflict with the overriding principle of democracy. This two-stage account of democratic determination of results is evident in the creation of a constitution. For example, the US Constitution includes many direct constraints on government agents that would block majoritarian actions on specific cases. There is a direct constraint on Congress that it may not pass bills of attainder, which are *de facto* legislative convictions of individuals for their actions without the need of going through court procedures. This clearly blocks democratic votes on 'punishment'.[39] But this is not a violation of democratic norms if we would actively, democratically want to block such actions *ex ante*, as the Constitutional Convention in Philadelphia and the state ratifications of the constitution imply we would.

It is an odd abuse of contractarian political argument that it is often applied to single details *and* to overall structures by the same theorist despite recognition that *the point of overall structures is to be the means for resolving single details*. But typically, contractarians recognize the two-stage structure of political justification that was canvassed in Chapter 3. Hobbes and Locke wrote of the social contract to establish government but then left governing to that government. James Buchanan and Gordon Tullock want unanimity at the constitutional stage and then some degree of majoritarianism at the

[37] See further, Russell Hardin, 'Institutional Morality', in Geoffrey Brennan and Robert E. Goodin, eds., *The Theory of Institutional Design* (Cambridge: Cambridge University Press, 1995), 126–53.
[38] Russell Hardin, *Morality within the Limits of Reason* (Chichago: University of Chicago Press, 1988), esp. chs. 3 and 4; Russell Hardin, 'International Deontology', *Ethics and International Affairs*, 9 (1995): 133–45.
[39] Technically, attainder applies only to capital cases. Bills of pains and penalties are for lesser punishments. Both are blocked in the US Constitution, Art. 1, sect. 9.

second stage of making policy choices.[40] John Rawls's theory of justice is about the structure of overarching institutions, which will then make actual distributive and other choices.[41] (Often, the argument for the first stage is normative; for Hobbes it is simply pragmatic— we need government in order to get on with other things.)

Among reasonable-agreement theorists, Beitz holds, for example, that we cannot argue for specific details of democratic participation without first establishing an overall institutional structure. It is this structure that we must justify from the standpoint of reasonable agreement. Individuals' concerns for their own fair treatment are incorporated in that systemic justification. Hence, an individual has no further ground on which to base an appeal against the correct working of the system.[42] In particular, the individual cannot turn the criterion of reasonable agreement against details of procedure or outcome once that criterion has been successfully applied to the overall structure of institutions.

Justice as Order and Democracy

Note how democracy may seem to conflict with the two-stage account. Contemporary liberal politics is driven by several principles that do not always fit together comfortably. Liberal politics and liberal political theory are simultaneously committed to democracy and to individual liberties or autonomy. It is specifically with respect to the protection of individual liberties that criticisms of mob rule are commonly directed, because a popular decision on whether some individual's liberty should be constrained or ignored can be highly idiosyncratic and personalized. Mobs might convict individuals for who they are rather than for what they have done. This is the history of mob actions against, for example, Japanese-Americans on the West Coast in 1941–2 and against uncounted blacks in much of the United States. The overwhelming focus of much of constitutional and political theory is on constraining democratic decisions to

[40] James M. Buchanan and Gordon Tullock, *The Calculus of Consent: Logical Foundations of Constitutional Government* (Ann Arbor: University of Michigan Press, 1962).

[41] John Rawls, *A Theory of Justice* (Cambridge, Mass: Harvard University Press, 1971).

[42] Beitz, *Political Equality*, 191.

protect individual liberties, typically through procedural protections that take the application of the law out of the hands of popular bodies such as the polity or the legislature. Many constitutions are about democratically choosing *ex ante* to constrain certain classes of decisions.

Procedural protection of individual liberties has often been characterized as 'justice as order' and is an important part of any discussion of justice. Indeed, the term justice is often used to mean merely justice as order and not to include distributive justice.[43] In general, it is hard to see justice as order as an end in itself. Utilitarians see justice as order as a *means* for achieving general welfare, not least because it secures expectations that enable individuals to take future-oriented actions with reasonable confidence in the relevant future. Libertarian and other autonomy theorists see it as a means of protecting liberty.

That justice as order can conflict and typically often does conflict with democracy probably requires little discussion in one sense. We might democratically decide every issue as it arises. For example, we might take a vote on whether someone is guilty of a crime, as the Athenians did for Socrates, whose crime was teaching his philosophy. But this is only superficially a problem for any democracy that is coherently conceived. It is essentially an issue of where or when democratic choice is to be exercised.

Liberal societies are those in which there is fairly broad consensus on Hobbes's values of survival and welfare—even if there is little consensus on many other important matters, such as religious beliefs, moral principles, or the constitution of the good life beyond mere survival and basic welfare. It is that core consensus which allows *ex ante* agreement on individual protections and, to some extent, on *ex ante* empowerment of government. However, the latter has often been in contest in many liberal states and especially in the United States. Indeed, the central empowering move of the US Constitution was to turn the regulation of interstate commerce and foreign trade over to the federal government, a move that could sen-

---

[43] The term 'justice as order' is taken from Henry Sidgwick's criticism of Hume's view that distributive justice was not a proper object of government policy (Sidgwick, *The Methods of Ethics*, 7th edn. (London: Macmillan, 1907), 440). For further discussion, see Hardin, *Morality within the Limits of Reason*, 36. Many modern conservatives agree with Hume that attempts at distributive justice are pernicious. See e.g. Bertrand de Jouvenel, *Sovereignty: An Inquiry into the Political Good* (Chicago: University of Chicago Press, 1957, trans. J. F. Huntington), esp. 139–65.

sibly be seen as rather a deliberate disempowerment of the state governments. In this sense, it was generally a constraint on government rather than an empowerment (as discussed in Chapter 6).

In the two-stage understanding of the structure of democratic control over matters of justice as order, there is no conflict between democracy and justice as order. There is only conflict between *ex ante* and *in medias res* application of democratic choice. If *ex ante* choice is to govern, it must block *in medias res* choice by putting institutions in the way. If *in medias res* choice is possible, it overrides *ex ante* choice and makes it irrelevant because not determinative. Constitutionalism is all about *ex ante* empowerment and constraint. *Ex ante* choices will tend to be systematic and abstract rather than individualized. Hence, they will tend to be universalistic.[44]

It is, of course, psychologically possible for me to want both to have a general constraint on the legislature not to pass bills of attainder against me while also wanting the legislature to be able to pass them against you. But I cannot practically commend an argument for such a biased system that would pass democratic muster. Therefore, the best I could hope to get adopted is either the general constraint against such bills or the lack of such a constraint.

The Terror of the French Revolution was so grisly and destructive because it was democracy *in medias res* without strong *ex ante* democratic constraints. Hence, it turned into mob rule, in which decisions tipped instantly from one position to another, fully behind Robespierre one day and executing him the next. It was politics without principles, without even democratic principles.

Government as Grown

What one generation decides constitutionally, future generations face mainly as a set of enabling and constraining institutions. These may not easily be altered to fit what the later generations might want even if they could coherently think the issues through and agree on

---

[44] For all its heavy sound, universalism is a very commonsense principle. Margaret, the heroine of Cathleen Schine's *Rameau's Niece*, expresses the principle well: 'If people expect anything of me, I resent them and feel incompetent and ill at ease. And yet I expect so much, and if I don't get it, I feel only contempt. I'm sort of an asshole,' she thought' (Schine, *Rameau's Niece* (New York: Penguin, 1993), p. 34).

their resolution. Moreover, changes that occur in the constitutional order will often not be democratic. For example, they have seldom followed the standard quasi-democratic amending process in the United States.[45] Rather, they have been intra-institutional and evolutionary, often opportunistic and conflict ridden. Massive economic changes between the Civil War and World War II provoked profound changes in the form of American government that were only vaguely democratically determined. And, of course, those changes aggressively removed much of government policy-making even further from the first stage of democratic decision into the second stage of non-democratic decision. For example, the rising power of business provoked the creation of institutions that took politics over these popular concerns out of the popular arena and sheltered it in a bureaucratic world that business interests could more readily dominate.

Recall Hobbes's supposition that sovereign governments cannot be bound by any of their own laws. This supposition has suggested a putative paradox to many thinkers. If I am sovereign, I should be able to bind my own future actions. But if I can be bound in the future, then I cannot be fully sovereign. Hence, as a matter of temporal logic, I cannot be sovereign at all. This conundrum has led in English jurisprudence to a long-standing, somewhat arch debate over whether Parliament is truly sovereign if the current Parliament cannot bind future Parliaments. Alas, if it could, then future Parliaments could not be sovereign because they could be bound in some ways. Hence, if Parliament is sovereign, then it cannot be. The English debate on the sovereignty of Parliament is historically little more than cute.[46] But the problem at its core is the nature of ongoing government, which must develop over time in ways that cannot be fully controlled by anyone, let alone the polity acting as such. Hence, in practice, not even the overall form of government can be determined fully democratically.

[45] Stephen Griffin, 'The Problem of Constitutional Change in the United States', in John Ferejohn, Jack Rakove, and Jonathan Riley, eds., 'Constitutional Culture and Democratic Rule', book manuscript, Tulane University, 1998.

[46] It might be rendered more than cute if an actual issue arose. For example, today's Parliament could enact legislation, such as a bill of rights, with a proviso that it could be amended only by a supermajority in any future Parliament. A later, amending Parliament would have to decide whether to ignore the supermajority requirement. For legislation on a minor issue, a future Parliament would presumably dismiss the supermajority requirement with impunity. Would it consider itself bound in the case of a bill of rights?

In the last number of the *Federalist Papers*, Hamilton argued cogently against complaints that the constitution should be perfected before it was voted into force. He quoted Hume:

To balance a large state or society, whether monarchical or republican, on general laws, is a work of so great difficulty that no human genius, however comprehensive, is able, by the mere dint of reason and reflection, to effect it. The judgments of many must unite in the work: Experience must guide their labor: Time must bring it to perfection: And the feeling of inconveniencies must correct the mistakes, which they inevitably fall into, in their first trials and experiments.[47]

Implicitly, Hamilton recommended that voters turn their government over to future developments. They should use their putative sovereignty to renounce at least most of their sovereignty.

Benjamin Constant made Hume's point even more forcefully:

Constitutions are seldom made by the will of men. Time makes them. They are introduced gradually and in an almost imperceptible way. Yet there are circumstances in which it becomes indispensable to make a constitution. But then do only what is indispensable. Leave room for time and experience, so that these two reforming powers may direct your already constituted powers in the improvement of what has been done and the completion of what is still to be done.[48]

Thomas Christiano argues that the institutional structures we use for implementing our general choices need not themselves be created democratically in order for them to be part of a democratic government.[49] Indeed, since institutions are, at least in large part in their details, typically unintended consequences, there is no escaping from having our democratic choices implemented through institutions we have not democratically created. On such an account, even the grown common law could be consistent with democratic government.

Independently of whether one wishes to call grown government democratic, it is clearly true that much of government typically is grown rather than chosen. In what way then can we say that the

---

[47] *Federalist*, 85, final para. The quotation here is taken from David Hume, 'Of The Rise and Progress of the Arts and Sciences', in Hume, *Essays Moral Political, and Literary*, ed. Eugene Miller (Indianapolis: Liberty Press, 1985; 1st pub. 1742), 111–37, quote at p. 124.

[48] Benjamin Constant, *Political Writings*, ed. Biancamaria Fontana (Cambridge: Cambridge University Press, 1988), 172 n.

[49] Thomas Christiano, *The Rule of the Many: Fundamental Issues in Democratic Theory* (Boulder, Colo.: Westview Press, 1996).

polity over which a government has grown is nevertheless sovereign over that government? True, the polity could commonly, at least in principle, change the grown elements of its government. But it cannot mandate that there be no such elements. And it cannot plausibly root out all such elements as they grow. Hence, to some large extent the polity cannot be fully sovereign. Moreover, it should not want to be sovereign in so far as having grown elements of government may be necessary if government is to be effective in carrying out many of its purposes.

Consider an important element of grown government. In nineteenth-century utilitarianism, especially in the writings of John Stuart Mill, concern with getting the populace to understand and agree with principles of government (and morality) was a major topic. For Mill the issue was to make government work, and he supposed that it could not work well if the citizens were averse to or failed to understand its policies. His principle of publicity—that the rules be understandable and known—was a principle of efficacy, a natural matter for utilitarian accounts. (In contemporary political theory, discussions of publicity are often sufficiently abstract as to fail to meet their own criterion. Empirically, the larger concern with efficacy in our era has been more the focus of social psychology than of political theory as in, chiefly, the account of the importance of procedural fairness in motivating acceptance of the law.)

Does procedural justice conflict with democracy? In an odd way, it actually fits better with retrospective than with *ex ante* understandings. Part of the impact of procedural concerns for an individual caught up in the system of justice as order depends on experiential understanding. Most of us might give little actual attention to how the system ought to deal with people beyond some fairly obvious objections to torture, brutality, and so forth. A designer might devise a good set of procedures. But it is more likely that an actual set of procedures will be as good as the result of tinkering by relevant officials in the justice system over long years in the light of experience. Procedures will be more nearly cobbled together or grown than designed. While the experience of ordinary citizens might affect the content of the procedures, those procedures will not be the product of democratic choice except in the most indirect sense that democratically elected officials will have had many hands in their growth. A working system of procedural fairness is likely therefore to resemble common law more than statute law.

Procedural fairness will, of course, potentially conflict with democracy in the way that justice as order will. The procedures might block popular views on what should happen in a particular case. This might seem merely to be another instance of the *ex ante* versus *in medias res* concern with how democratic choice is to be brought to bear. But if the procedures in place were not *ex ante* determined democratically, and if democratic choice were to run against the procedures, then procedural fairness would openly conflict with democratic choice at all points. In general, it seems implausible that all rules of procedural fairness actually in place in, say, the United States would stand the democratic test. In particular, it seems likely that popular views would support more draconian police impositions and would tend to accept prosecutors' choices without allowing procedural devices for escaping conviction. Hence, procedural fairness as practised may in fact conflict with democratic choice. Despite this conclusion, procedural fairness might still make democratic laws more supportable, as Tom Tyler and others argue.[50] Hence, while democratic choice might oppose actual principles of procedural fairness, both democracy and justice as order might work better because of them.

The Logic of Democracy

In Anthony Downs's *Economic Theory of Democracy* there are two coordinate theses.[51] The first, the median-voter model, concerns the rational choices of candidates for office: in a two-party system, candidates must locate themselves at the centre of the policy space or they will be outflanked, leaving them with only minority support. The second thesis concerns the rational choices of voters. At one level, there is no problem in rationality for voters. Voters should merely vote for the candidate whose positions are nearest their own. The problem comes before this stage. Should rational voters take the trouble to vote at all? And should voters take the trouble to become sufficiently well informed to know which candidate's positions are

[50] See e.g. Tom R. Tyler, *Why People Obey the Law* (New Haven: Yale University Press, 1990).
[51] Anthony Downs, *An Economic Theory of Democracy* (New York: Harper and Row, 1957).

nearest their own? These are, for Downs, rational questions of self-interest. But they also underlie normative questions of what more broadly one ought to do.

If individuals have no reason to participate, because they cannot affect outcomes, then they would have no reason to know enough to participate wisely if they did participate. This fact has several normative implications. First, it implies that the limits to democracy entail limits in individual responsibility in the role of democratic citizen. Secondly, it affects—perhaps drastically—arguments for the autonomy of democratic participation. And thirdly, it undercuts contractarian claims for the rightness of democratic, ostensibly consensual results.

Limits on Citizen Responsibility

Democratic citizens may have responsibilities that are limited in ways that reflect natural limits and constraints on democracy. There are at least two classes of problems: those that follow from systematic actual conflict with majority decisions and those that follow from the nature of democratic participation. The first class represents failures of democracy that follow from applying it to deeper conflicts rather than merely to marginal issues. Such a failure raises questions about the responsibilities of citizens to abide by democratic decisions. The second class represents logical implications of the likely mismatch between individual citizen's incentives and the requirements for democratic procedures.

For an example of the first class, consider the 1993 election that democratically brought Hutus to power in Burundi. They were sure to keep that power indefinitely if democratic majoritarian preferences were followed because, on the evidence of the votes cast, they outnumbered Tutsis by about two to one. Suppose that the democratically elected government imposed discrimination against the minority Tutsis, perhaps gross discrimination.[52] It would then be hard to argue that the mere fact of democratic election of this partially malevolent government commands from Tutsis their loyalty to the government until the next election. Arguably, Tutsis would owe

---

[52] In fact, Tutsis rebelled pre-emptively to destroy the government before it could organize well enough to have much power. They understood, at least implicitly, Hobbes's problem of empowerment of a new regime.

it no allegiance whatever, no more than Hutus might have owed allegiance to the prior, autocratic Tutsi government.

A similar conclusion may follow for either farm labourers or large plantation owners in many contemporary agrarian states that face or have recently faced land reform. It might also follow for some minority language groups, although not for many others. Many minority language groups gain far more from being quasi assimilated in a particular society under its government than they could possibly gain from any other option they might have. One might argue that they should nevertheless be given linguistic privileges or special consideration, but that would be a matter within the ambit of democratic decision inasmuch as it is a marginal issue against the background of generally beneficial order and even wealth.

Turn to the second class of problems—the mismatch of individual incentives with democratic requirements. The crux of citizen responsibility in a democracy is the causal efficacy of the role of citizen and the individual's justification for acquiring relevant knowledge. If the role is entirely inefficacious, there is no social reason to acquire knowledge and the citizen might rationally remain ignorant. As Schumpeter wrote, 'without the initiative that comes from immediate responsibility, ignorance will persist in the face of masses of information however complete and correct.'[53] I may have reason to acquire knowledge because it gives me pleasure, but not because it will be useful in my causing good public effects through my role as citizen.

It is conceivable that we would all be better off if we all participated democratically. We might therefore fine individuals who fail to vote, as many nations have done. But that would be inadequate to guarantee that they vote intelligently or even at all knowledgeably. We might somehow require some evidence of relevant study of the issues. But then we begin to risk having the state decide what counts as relevant knowledge. Hence, although we might overcome the problem of lack of participation, *we probably could not overcome the problem of uninformed participation.*

Might it be true that we would all be better off if we did all just invest time in understanding the issues of elections in order to vote intelligently? At the margin, surely, most individuals would not be better off from their own sole efforts to be informed. But perhaps I

[53] Joseph A. Schumpeter, *Capitalism, Socialism and Democracy* (New York: Harper, 1950, 3rd edn.; 1st pub. 1942), 262.

would be better off from having everyone better informed. For one perverse reason, I might not be. That perverse reason is that having people better informed might turn every election into something more nearly like a group census. But that would make politics more divisive and might destroy the possibilities for continuing democratic government.

Apart from this possible perversity, suppose that being informed means, typically, investment of an hour every weekday in learning about current politics (not merely the lurid tales of sexual escapades, but the stuff of policy). That hour could come from work time, leisure time, entertainment time, family time, or sleep time. Most likely there would be real losses to compensate for the redirected effort. Even then, most of the newly informed citizens would be pitiful amateurs in comparison to numerous bureaucrats, elected officials, and specialists. If that were not so, we could change the latter at will. This discussion is itself amateurish—not least because the problem seems not to have been seriously addressed in the literature on citizen responsibility. In the end, if we are to claim that citizens have a responsibility to know more than they typically do, we will need a justification for the claim. And that justification will have to take into account the likely trade-offs of citizens' knowing more. *It seems plausible that there will be no justification that stands against such a test.*

Kazuo Ishiguro's butler, Stevens, argues that,

Up to a point, no doubt . . . in a country such as ours, people may indeed have a certain duty to think about great affairs and form their opinions. But life being what it is, how can ordinary people truly be expected to have 'strong opinions' on all manner of things . . . And not only are these expectations unrealistic, I rather doubt if they are even desirable. There is, after all, a real limit to how much ordinary people can learn and know, and to demand that each and every one of them contribute 'strong opinions' to the great debates of the nation cannot, surely, be wise.[54]

Stevens may have overdone his ignorance when he worked for a Lord who had Nazi sympathies, but his scepticism is sensible.

The condition of rational ignorance is not blameworthy or somehow immoral or irresponsible. It is a natural implication of the division of labour that makes life richer for us. We all share the disability

---

[54] Kazuo Ishiguro, *The Remains of the Day* (New York: Vintage, 1990; 1st pub. 1989), 194.

of Saul Bellow's Mr Sammler, who says, 'I am more stupid about some things than about others; not equally stupid in all directions; I am not a well-rounded person'.[55] If I am a typical citizen, I specialize in manufacturing goods, farming, offering professional services, making music, or whatever. I may be very good at what I do but I may be virtually incompetent at delivering professional services, making music, or any of a vast array of other things, all of which I could do, if at all, only at a much lower level of competence than I do my chief occupation. As Schumpeter noted, I might similarly drop down 'to a lower level of mental performance' as soon as I enter the political field. I might argue and analyse 'in a way that [I] would recognize as infantile within the sphere of [my] real interests'.[56] If I put some years of preparation and forty hours a week into it, I might do politics quite well. But the whole society would lose if I did that rather than what I have chosen to do.

Schumpeter's observation is cited by virtually every contemporary writer on democratic theory. And no one has yet offered more than wishes about how to change the fact. The fact is not easily changed because it is so eminently reasonable that it is the fact. It might be overcome in small contexts such as many of those that April Carter and other theorists of direct action discuss, such as whether there should be a stop sign at an intersection at which children are at risk.[57] And it might be overcome in certain very large contexts in which evidence finally seems overwhelming, as in the later days of the war in Vietnam when Americans of varied political persuasions came to agree that the war was, at the very least, not worth what it was costing, and as in the heady days of 1989 in Eastern Europe.

It follows not only that we can make at best limited claims for the responsibilities of citizens to participate in democratic government, but also that democracy cannot be justified by appeal to its grounding in substantial citizen participation. Despite the origins of the word and the way it is typically used in popular and academic discourse, either democracy cannot entail massive citizen participation or it is irrelevant to actual practice in modern polities.

---

[55] Saul Bellow, *Mr Sammler's Planet* (Harmondsworth: Penguin, 1977; 1st pub. 1970), 88.
[56] Bellow, *Mr Sammler's Planet*, 88.
[57] April Carter, *Direct Action and Liberal Democracy* (New York: Harper and Row, 1973).

Individual Autonomy

Democracy is often supported because it is thought to contribute to the development of individual autonomy or because it is supposed to be the ideal form of government for a society of autonomous individuals. Because prosperity, security, and various other aspects of well-being also play very large roles in developing autonomy, government must secure these things as well as democratic participation. Indeed, arguably it should see to it that these things are secured first and then worry about democratic principles, because these things, and not political participation, are the *sine qua non* for autonomy for most people. For obvious causal reasons, political participation cannot be a significant part of the autonomy of the vast majority of individuals in a nation as large as the United States—or even Sweden. One doubts that it counts for much even in tiny Iceland or Luxembourg. As the butler Stevens concluded in the passage partially quoted above, 'It is . . . absurd that anyone should presume to define a person's "dignity" in . . . terms' of their mastery of political issues.[58] Hence, either autonomy is a repugnantly narrow concept or it does not heavily depend on participation.

The claim that democracy is good for the reason that it enhances personal autonomy or character independently of its effects on the public business is attributed to Mill. But the argument that democracy is good because it contributes to our personal development is odd even in Mill's own discussion of it. He disqualified the claim in his account of the need for causal efficacy if our actions are to have meaning:

A person must have a very unusual taste for intellectual exercise in and for itself, who will put himself to the trouble of thought when it is to have no outward effect, or qualify himself for functions which he has no chance of being allowed to exercise. The only sufficient incitement to mental exertion, in any but a few minds in a generation, is the prospect of some practical use to be made of its results.

The test of real and vigorous thinking, the thinking which ascertains truths instead of dreaming dreams, is successful application to practice.[59]

With these claims, Mill gave full force to the Schumpeter–Downs argument that most citizens do not even have adequate reason to

[58] Ishiguro, *The Remains of the Day*, 194.
[59] John Stuart Mill, *Representative Government* (any complete edn.), ch. 3, paras. 2 and 17.

know enough to vote intelligently, because he recognized that 'all cannot, in a community exceeding a single small town, participate personally in any but some very minor portions of the public business', so that they have insufficient incitement to mental exertion over politics.[60]

One might be committed to democracy independently of whether it works in some other sense. Some writers, especially in popular media, occasionally assert commitment to democracy as an absolute value, as though it must trump all other values when it conflicts with them. This is not a credible position nor need it be discussed with great seriousness. Virtually no one insists on democracy even for all political decisions. The standard, trivially obvious examples, are the need for secrecy in making policy during warfare and the preference for justice over opinion or interests in court cases. The form of the Allied invasion of Europe at the end of World War II was not a subject fit for democratic decision. Nor is the question of someone's guilt for a crime a subject fit for such decision.

In addition to these standard examples, it is plausible that the rise of administrative government over the past century is largely a response to the inability of democratic forms to handle vast areas of government policy. In the United States, as in many nations, democracy has been reduced to relatively weak and limited oversight in many contexts. Many critics think this development is a corruption of democratic forms. Libertarians hold it to be normatively wrong because it entails coercion without prior agreement. But almost no one proposes serious alternative ways of handling the relevant problems.

The chief practical complaints and recommendations are about marginal problems in the administrative state, such problems as what might generously be read as an agency's going beyond its legislative authority. One might think it a deeper problem that the very existence of the agency goes beyond constitutional authority. Somehow, we seem democratically to have consented to the radical change and de-democratization of government—although there were no genuine votes on the matter other than such votes as to elect and re-elect the people who underwrote these revisions of the governmental structure. In the vocabulary of the Federalist Caesar, we have merely acquiesced—by now, for several generations.

---

[60] Mill, *Representative Government*, ch. 3, final para. See further, Carole Pateman, *Participation and Democratic Theory* (Cambridge: Cambridge University Press, 1970), 28–35.

It is not necessary to argue that there is another *form* of government that beats democracy to show that democracy is not always the way to go. In general, democracy might be the best form of government under certain circumstances (as outlined above) even though its forms might be better violated on occasion such as, perhaps, in the administrative state. But under some conditions, including our own, relatively limited democracy might be generally, not just occasionally, preferable to full-scale democracy.

The Right Result

Many democratic theories are themselves deduced from particular moral principles, such as utilitarian or Kantian principles. In these theories, it is possible to pass independent judgement on the rightness of a democratic outcome. A utilitarian, for example, might think it true that the least fallible device for achieving utilitarian outcomes is democratic decision procedures. But the device is merely contingently the least fallible—it is not infallible. Hence, the utilitarian might conclude that, in a particular application of such procedures, the wrong result was reached.

In contractarian theories, however, it might actually follow that what we choose is the criterion of the right—there is no independent criterion.[61] In many discussions of democracy there is the seeming assumption or implication that whatever we democratically choose is therefore right. Perhaps these conclusions derive from an implicitly contractarian view. Often, however, they may be grounded in little more than an intuitive sense that democracy is good and therefore what it accomplishes is the measure of the good.

Unfortunately, any contractarian theory that sets agreement as the criterion of the right or good is on very shaky ground for a modern polity. In a nation of even modest size, there is, again, little or no chance that typical citizens have sufficient reason to master the issues open to democratic decisions well enough to contribute intelligently to their resolution. And even if they do master the issues, they have little or no prospect of using their mastery to influence the democratic choice. The odds against their votes ever making a difference are overwhelming. There was a tie vote in a local election in New Jersey in 1994—this otherwise trivial vote became national news

---

[61] Hardin, 'Contractarianism: Wistful Thinking'.

because it was the exceedingly rare case of a tie in which one more vote could have made a difference.

There have also been votes that were *de facto* ties in larger elections in which the counting error is too great to know who really has won in a very close count. In the New Hampshire election for the US Senate in 1974, Louis Wyman and John Durkin were virtually tied at about 111,000 votes each, with various agencies giving the slight edge to the Republican Wyman and others to the Democrat Durkin during the contest over the vote. Eventually, the Senate declared the election undecidable and it was rerun as a special election. Ordinarily, a special election might have benefited the Republican because turnouts would be lower and more nearly dominated by the middles class. Instead, turnouts increased substantially and Durkin won by a large margin. Clearly, therefore, merely for practical reasons of the impossibility of counting votes accurately, one more vote is unlikely to make a difference in an election even in as small a polity as New Hampshire. The individual voter essentially does not count.

Hence, if responsible citizens who have mastered the issues wish to influence policy, they will not do it by voting, which is almost the whole story of the participation of many citizens. Rather, they will have to undertake actions to influence those who have got elected, those who might run for office, or those who might not vote the right way without efforts to mobilize them. These are relatively demanding and costly efforts. Most people do not ever undertake such efforts at any serious level. A large proportion of those who do undertake them may be intending to build political careers, so that these efforts are investments towards a future benefit and not merely a public-spirited contribution to some greater good. Perversely, then, for the democratic theorist who measures the good by the results of participation, personal career interests must often—even typically—be more important than regard for the outcomes of democratic choice. (The historian William L. O'Neill finds this a distressing aspect of American politics during World War II.[62] Alas, it was merely politics as understandably usual.)

One might argue for an ideal conception of democracy, in which all or most citizens knowledgeably participate. But that ideal cannot be used to justify or practically criticize the results of an actual

[62] William L. O'Neill, *A Democracy at War: America's Fight at Home and Abroad in World War II* (New York: Free Press, 1993).

democracy in which participation is heavily subject to the accidental whims of individual interest. Indeed, one might argue for the goodness of a democratic system that has denatured participation, a system that fundamentally violates the ideal. Such a system may also denature many potential conflicts, the very conflicts that, if acute, make democracy unworkable. *What makes democracy work makes it fail the test of the ideal conception.*

It does not follow that citizen ignorance *per se* is good. Indeed, because of citizen ignorance, a scurrilous and vicious politician such as Slobodan Milosevic can have enormously destructive influence on opinion and commitments. What is good is the background fact that most individuals can see their interests as elsewhere than in politics. Hence, they are not motivated to participate with intensity and, therefore, not motivated to know enough to participate well. Politics might enrich or impoverish us, might elevate or demolish us—it has done all of these things to a single generation of Germans in this century. But we generally have insufficient interest to try to affect these results. Moreover, we should be glad of that fact, because we cannot suppose a democracy of millions, even 280 millions, should take up a great part of the lives of those millions. Everyone should be able to specialize substantially, and high or even chief among our specializations should be our own lives. With specialization, we achieve the division of labour that is necessary for substantial creation and well-being.

In a sense, our individual lives are marginal to the larger political result. We want our lives to be lived against a relatively good and stable background of government and order, of economy and society, and we want all of these to leave us scope for individual creativity, pleasure, family, or even personal involvement in politics. But personal involvement in politics cannot be the *sine qua non* of life unless most people are to have no life or unless politics is disastrously intrusive. For most of us, sufficiently intense participation in politics over a long time guarantees the dismal result that we lose our individual lives, we become diminished in the name of a nation, a party, an ethnic group, or a cause. The 1930s memoirs and letters of Europeans who were not specialists in politics or journalism often provoke depressing sadness at the extent to which the person gets submerged in the politics of the day, often down to the level of the most tedious specific issues.

Alternative Visions

Philosophical liberalism has developed in various directions in the twentieth century, many of them increasingly removed from the real prospects of our growing mass society. John Dewey argued for an ethics of self-realization.[63] Contrary to his pragmatism and common sense, he thought this could come in part through democratic participation: 'Suffrage stands for direct and active participation in the regulation of the terms upon which associated life shall be sustained, and the pursuit of the good carried on'.[64] This has been an American theme ever since—or perhaps one should call it an American dream. If any significant share of our self-realization must come from political participation, we must be woefully unrealized humans. The claim of Tocqueville, cited in Chapter 2, is a correcting tonic for the vacuity of claims for citizen discourse and participation: it is not what democracy does for us but what happens under it through private agency that is the beauty of democracy.

Oddly, indeed, it is plausible that more lives were realized through political 'participation'—often in samizdat—in Eastern Europe *before* 1989 than in any Western democracy. In Eastern Europe, illiberalism provoked intense reactions. To twist Mill's claim, America has no need of participation—and American politics does not usually provoke intense participation. The great exception to this was the brief period of debating and ratifying the constitution, when quite ordinary people became articulate and thoughtful at levels most people never achieve and when Madison and a few others became great thinkers. There was intense participation, right and left, during the anti-communism craze of the 1950s, in the Civil Rights Movement, and in the anti-war movement of the Vietnam years. But the thought of ongoing intense participation is generally absurd and, when it is not absurd, depressing.

Tocqueville and Mill were bothered a century and a half ago by the trend towards a large bureaucratic state and a civilization in which conventional sameness would rule.[65] To put their worry in

[63] John Dewey, *Ethics*, vol. v of *The Middle Works, 1899–1924, of Dewey* (Carbondale, Ill.: Southern Illinois University Press, 1978; 1st pub. 1908), 351–7.

[64] Dewey, *Ethics*, 424. See further, Richard Schusterman, 'Pragmatism and Liberalism between Dewey and Rorty', *Political Theory* (Aug. 1994) 22: 391–413.

[65] Alexis de Tocqueville, *Democracy in America*, 2 vols. (New York: Knopf, 1945; reprinted Vintage, 1990), ii. book 4, ch. 6: 316–21; John Stuart Mill, 'Civilization' and

perspective, recall that, in the century before 1914, the typical citizen in England knew the state almost only from the post office and the police. The federal government of the United States was chiefly supported by customs revenues before the introduction of the income tax just before World War I. In the time of Mill and Tocqueville, government was responsible for a small fraction of national expenditures. Today, government has become responsible for a large fraction, in some liberal democracies even for more than half, of national expenditures. Yet Mill and Tocqueville were already then bothered by the growth of bureaucratic government. They would quail at the scale and intrusiveness of government today.

If government and democracy have the effects that Mill and Tocqueville expected, we must find a devastating trend towards conventional sameness in the advanced democracies today. But it would be very hard to determine what the trend towards sameness has been, in part because of contrary causal changes. Rural life must have been a greater force for sameness than urban life, and rural life is nearly gone in the advanced societies. In addition, the mixing of diverse peoples has been pronounced in many of the advanced societies, especially in North America and Australia, but also in the United Kingdom and much of Europe. Mill agreed with von Humboldt that individuality requires freedom and 'a variety of situations'.[66] The social advances that have brought on larger government have also brought manifold exposure to varied situations, not least in removing the bulk of the population from the stultification of the life of subsistence agriculture and in exposing many to cultures different from their own.

In our time, the Mill–Tocqueville thesis of a deteriorating sameness has been echoed by many thinkers, left, right, and centre. At this moment in the United States, it is a special theme of an oddly antiliberal kind of social conservative. Conservative visions include that of Allen Bloom, *The Closing of the American Mind*, which is sometimes rudely parodied as *Thoughts of a Closed Mind*. The earlier vision of Mill and Tocqueville might best be captured in Robert Musil's *The Man without Qualities*, which, aptly, goes on inter-

'De Tocqueville on Democracy in America, II', in Mill, *Essays on Politics and Society*, ed. J. M. Robson, *Collected Works of John Stuart Mill*, xviii (Toronto: University of Toronto Press, 1977), 117–47, 153–204.

[66] Mill, *On Liberty*, ch. 3, para. 2; Wilhelm von Humboldt, *The Limits of State Action* (Cambridge: Cambridge University Press, 1969; 1st pub. 1854), 16.

minably and was left unfinished with hundreds of draft pages of fragmentary additions. That is how we are, lacking in qualities and scattered to oblivion rather than coming to a rounded end. Bloom's complaints are expressed in a more elevated and less petty fashion by some of Saul Bellow's fiction. Communitarians attribute our supposed cultural and moral decline and malaise to urbanity and the loss of small, close-knit community and to the decline of religious attachments. They, of course, commonly prefer to live in urban America and the academics among them typically prefer the best of worldly universities. Their seeming hypocrisy does not make their views wrong, but one must wonder.

At the amorphous centre, pop psychologists attribute our supposed degradation to television, spectator sports, and, less frequently now, bureaucracy.[67] As usual, the centre is less interesting than the left or the right, but it is more specific.

From the left, we are urged to mimic the *élan* of the creation of a new civic culture in Eastern Europe, especially Czechoslovakia and, after its breakup, the Czech Republic. Against the supposition that this is somehow a natural state that we could all attain as a matter of normal life, von Humboldt slyly observed that 'the care to secure freedom is more satisfying than the actual enjoyment of it'.[68] The Czech *élan* was driven by a purpose: to create a liberal society. To what purpose people in already liberal societies should mimic the Czechs beyond merely the thrill and the jointness of the enterprise is not clear. Purposeless *élan* would be degrading. Madison, Tocqueville, and Mill wanted democracy because they wanted to make government more attentive to facilitating the choices of citizens and less given to making those choices for them. Some on the participatory left want democracy to take greater control of government in order that government can take greater control of our lives. Some evidently merely want more democracy independently of what it does. The praise of participatory discourse seemingly involves far more discourse than politics does or is likely to do in any but such extraordinary moments as 1989 and in moments of great crisis, such as the Vietnam era in the United States. The cure for the ills of democracy as we have known it so far is supposed to be more

---

[67] Television is commonly cited as the biggest factor because it takes such a large fraction of citizens' time. See e.g. Robert D. Putnam, 'Bowling Alone: America's Declining Social Capital', *Journal of Democracy* (Jan. 1995) 6: 65–78, 75.

[68] Von Humboldt, *The Limits of State Action*, 10.

active democracy—not more and better ideas about what politics our
society needs, but merely more participation in doing what we do.

Sweeping claims about what democracy does or should do must be
weighed against the possibilities of what it can do. It evidently cannot
even do what Madison thought it would do: limit government.
Criticisms of its larger impact should also be tempered by consideration of its constraints. Because democracy is in the class of mutual-
advantage theories, it cannot be expected so clearly either to cause or
to prevent conventional sameness in a society. Rather, it can only be
expected to work so long as there is a relatively important background coordination on sameness in values and demands from
government. Mill rightly criticized Tocqueville for too readily
attributing to democracy aspects of American society that were the
results of the developing commercial life of America. Much of the
contemporary criticism ostensibly directed at democracy and liberalism seems rather to be a complaint about life in a large and economically productive society. One should perhaps agree with many of
those complaints, but one should see them as existential, not political.

Virtual Representation

The American colonies rebelled from English rule because their citizens were not represented in the Parliament that decided their fate.
Thomas Whately, an official in the British Treasury, which oversaw
the collection of taxes in the colonies, rebutted their claims. The
colonists, Whately wrote, suffered no greater liability than the vast
majority of the English population, who also had no vote but who
were 'virtually represented' in Parliament. 'All *British* Subjects are
really in the same [situation]; none are actually, all are virtually represented in Parliament; for every Member of Parliament sits in the
House, not as Representative of his own Constituents, but as one of
the august Assembly by which all the Commons of *Great Britain* are
represented.'[69]

[69] Thomas Whately, *The Regulations Lately Made Concerning the Colonies, and
the Taxes Imposed upon Them, Considered* (London, 1765), 109; quoted in Samuel H.
Beer, *To Make a Nation: The Rediscovery of American Federalism* (Cambridge, Mass.:
Harvard University Press, 1993), 172. See further, Gordon S. Wood, *The Creation of
the American Republic, 1776–1787* (Chapel Hill, NC: North Carolina University
Press, 1969; reprinted Norton, 1972), 173–81.

Whately's view that even those who are denied the vote are nevertheless represented in their government is, functionally, merely a corruption of the argument for the divine right of kings. Yet this view was commonly held in England in Whately's time.[70] Francis Plowden, a lawyer writing in 1794 after the tumultuous debates over representation in the United States, insisted that English government was based on the 'free will and consent of a free people'.[71] Deplorably, under the principle of Locke's doctrine of toleration, Plowden, as a Roman Catholic, was not allowed to vote, so that his consent or lack of consent was a matter of irrelevance to Parliament. He seems not to have been distressed by the illogic of his defence of English representative government.

The peculiarity of the view of virtual representation, apart from its perverse illogic, is that it seemed to sit easily beside an overtly contrary view that to be ruled by laws in whose making one had no hand was to be a slave. 'What, my lord, is the definition of a slave?' an Irish barrister asked Lord North in 1780. 'Is it not where a man is bound by laws, to which he never assented, and lies at the mercy of a power over which he has no controul?' John Phillip Reid supposes that 'North and every other political leader in Great Britain or the colonies would have answered yes'.[72]

The irony of the rejection of Whately's view of virtual representation by John Adams and others in the colonies is that they set about creating a government that merely freed some people—moderately élite males—while leaving the overwhelming bulk of the population still, by their own lights, enslaved under a system of virtual representation. But Whately's view and the contrary view that one is a slave who has no part in making the laws are still with us today. It is, after all, a matter of the nature of the case that most individuals in modern democracies have nothing more than a formally defined but actually hollow role in determining the content of the laws under which they live: they are at best virtually represented in Whately's sense.

Indeed, the American constitutionalists added a new and especially reprehensible wrinkle to the possibilities of virtual representation that presumably not even Whately would have approved. They

[70] Beer, *To Make a Nation*, 164–8.
[71] Quoted in John Phillip Reid, *The Concept of Representation in the Age of the American Revolution* (Chicago: University of Chicago Press, 1989), 12.
[72] Reid, *The Concept of Representation*, 20.

allotted to those more abjectly enslaved only three-fifths virtual representation. And even that was handled by their white masters who, therefore, were *de facto* overrepresented in the national legislature and who could use their overrepresentation to defend their control of their virtually represented slaves. The standard argument for virtual representation was that, say, the people of Liverpool do not need to be directly represented in Parliament because they share interests with the people of Bristol, whose representatives therefore virtually represent the people of Liverpool by speaking for their interests. While southern slave holders were soon extolling the benefits to the slaves of being owned by them, most observers would think southern white representatives did not represent, even virtually, the interests of slaves.

More important than the formally defined constructive role for most citizens is that they do not coordinate in opposing their government, that they do not mutiny. Indeed, in enabling government, the failure to coordinate in mutiny is the fundamentally important contribution of citizens. This is the empty meaning of consent. As Reid concludes, the debate over consent is laced with dilemmas.[73] Yet, in the normative defence of constitutionalism and democracy, consent is by far the most frequent argument. The reign of consent theory is an old and remarkably varied charade. In the actual contexts of the liberal constitutional democracies of our era it is of necessity, although not of vocabulary, a matter of virtual consent. It is as phony and grossly irritating as Thomas Whately's defence of taxation without representation was to the American colonists.

How does such a charade charm us? I am probably not the person to answer this question because the charade of consent theory does not charm me. It is a game with too few delights to justify the effort of participating. If I were a Bostonian in 1773, I might want to throw the writings on consent theory overboard as though they carried a tax on serious discussion imposed by a capricious foreign power or—more likely—a cabal of metaphysicians. An uncharitable explanation for the livelihood of consent theory would be that consent theorists are engaged in an effort to justify states that they like. This argument might fit Whately and many others, but it is probably wrong for most contemporary consent theorists, many of whom are critical of what states there are. An alternative explanation is that

---

[73] Reid, *The Concept of Representation*, 137–46.

contemporary consent theorists are, after all, theorists and as such they have a tendency to abstraction that lifts them off the ground on which they actually live.

If our arrangements are only virtually those of liberal constitutional democracy, how do we justify them? Surely we must agree that representation is at best virtual for most of us most of the time; indeed, for most of us *all* of the time. If we are to justify our arrangements, therefore, the justification is not likely to depend on the fact that some of us have somehow chosen them or acquiesced in them. This might be evidence for some kinds of justification, such as a justification from utility or autonomy or liberty. But, by itself, the seeming claim of democracy fits too poorly with what actually can happen to yield a justification directly. Arguments from consent for real governments are finally abstract and irrelevant.

Concluding Remarks

Any democratic choice must be either *ex ante* or *in medias res*, about institutional structures or about immediate policies, and these two can and probably often do conflict. Democracy must therefore be constrained into a two-stage theory or it will be incoherent in practice. Even then, there is not likely to be very much democracy except in the first, ostensibly democratic stage of institutional design. Appeals to popular sovereignty are therefore apt to be merely rhetorical and to have little or no content in the normal course of politics.

George Kateb writes that, for the American constitutionalists, there were values higher than majoritarianism.[74] This does not follow from their anti-majoritarian arguments about specific matters. They merely placed higher value on constitutional than on post-constitutional majoritarianism. Kateb further writes that 'The very idea of living politically by a written constitution offends' the majority principle.[75] Unfortunately, the majority principle is not independent of time. We can invoke it *ex ante* to cover future actions or we

---

[74] George Kateb, 'The Majority Principle: Calhoun and His Antecedents', *Political Science Quarterly* 84 (Dec. 1969): 595–617. Reprinted in Green, *Democracy*, see esp. 301–2.
[75] Kateb, 'The Majority Principle', Green, *Democracy*, 298.

can invoke it *in medias res* to change our past decisions. We can even invoke it *ex post* to defend *ex ante* barriers to choosing *in medias res*.

One of the most compelling statements of at least limited popular sovereignty is in the so-called oath of Aragon: 'We, who are worth as much as you, take you as our king, provided that you preserve our laws and liberties, and if not, not'. The implied popular sovereignty is limited in several ways: It applies only to recall, it covers only extant laws and liberties, and it is invoked by only part of the populace. As beautiful as the oath is, it is sad that it is evidently an invention of the sixteenth century rather than the actual oath of the centuries earlier Kingdom of Aragon.[76] Oddly, however, if the oath could have had any force it would have been unnecessary, because the Aragonese could simply have deposed any king who violated their liberties. In most societies today, no such oath could have any force, because we the people could not expect to act together to enforce it (although a rump group of assassins might claim to enforce it).

Rough agreement on commitments to economic prosperity and to general protection of individual liberties is arguably the central core of popular views in the United States and many other liberal polities. Popular sovereignty has been exercised, if at all, primarily to adopt a constitution and amendments to it to effect these commitments. It has perhaps also been roughly exercised in taking the nation into a few wars and in pulling it out of a couple of wars (Korea and Vietnam). In the rump nation immediately after the Civil War it was also exercised to impose changes on the southern states. In all of these, it was at best roughly exercised because in actual fact there were large elements of opposition to these actions, although the level of support in some of these cases may have been far greater than the level of support in any national elections after the time of Washington. There are today sizeable minorities who would happily restrict many of the civil liberties or who might claim with great force that they have not benefited from the regime of economic prosperity.

Appeals to popular sovereignty, a social contract, and democracy are as beautiful, perhaps, and often as false as the Aragonese 'if not, not'. They usually are based in fiction and they have no analytical bite. But they evidently motivate nevertheless. When they actually

[76] Ralph A. Giesey, *If Not, Not: The Oath of the Aragonese and the Legendary Laws of Sobrarbe* (Princeton: Princeton University Press, 1968), 181.

could be sensibly invoked, that is because in the relevant context they coordinate us. In this, the greatest value of institutionalizing democratic procedures for many realms is that they break—or at least weaken the prospect of—any coherent control of the agenda and policy by oligarchic leaders. They do not strictly hold leaders accountable, but in crucial moments or over major issues they can disrupt leader's best-laid plans and force them to acquiesce in our general coordination.

5

Liberalization and its Discontents

> When I went to Venezuela . . ., I realized something about my
> own country which I had not previously seen there: the ideal-
> ism which is inherent in what I had experienced [in the United
> States] as materialism and individual self-seeking. I saw that for
> Venezuelans, for whom economic development had just begun
> . . ., the democratizing of material consumption and the open-
> ing up of opportunities—*for those able to seize them*—was a
> truly liberating idea.
>
> Lisa Peattie (1969)[1]

Transition to the Two Liberalisms

As there are two liberalisms, so also there are two major liberalizing
transitions that non-liberal polities may make. They may become
politically liberal and they may become economically liberal. It is
possible that eventually a society must be both politically and economically liberal if it is to be either, although, despite many arguments in defence of this supposition, evidence suggests that, at least,
politically illiberal societies can be relatively liberal in their economic
management for decades and maybe longer and politically liberal
societies can have very strong central control of their economies.[2] In
this and the next two chapters, I wish to discuss the prospects of successful liberalization in many societies. In this chapter I will address

---

[1] Lisa Peattie, 'Cuban Notes', *Massachusetts Review* (Autumn 1969): 673–4;
quoted in Albert O. Hirschman, *Shifting Involvements: Private Interest and Public
Action* (Princeton: Princeton University Press, 1982), 130, emphasis added.

[2] A related issue is whether economic growth is more likely with political liberal-
ism or with relative autocracy. For a thorough survey of evidence, see Adam
Przeworski and Fernando Limongi, 'Political Regimes and Economic Growth',
Journal of Economic Perspectives (Summer 1993) 7: 51–69.

the problems of initial liberalization, which is a matter of essentially spontaneous re-coordination from one form of government order to another. In Chapter 6, I will discuss the problems of managing economic change under a constitutional regime, which is the trick that successful constitutional regimes in North America and Western Europe have managed, in some cases for centuries. This is a matter of institutionalized coordination under a going regime. Then, in Chapter 7, I will discuss the problems of democracy in societies in which the broad coordination on overarching political institutions that constitutionalism requires is difficult or even not likely.

In recent years there have been many efforts at political liberalization in Spain, Latin America, Eastern Europe, and the former republics of the Soviet Union. There are three main discontents in the liberalizations of the societies of the Eastern nations. They are the difficulties involved in economic reform, the dispiriting rise of group conflict, including violent ethnic conflict, and the loss of the programme and hope of egalitarianism. The first two of these may pose obstacles to liberal constitutionalism; the third may be a cost of liberalization. All of these could become much worse problems as time passes, and many fear that one or the other of them will. They are typically interrelated. It is economic reform that kills the—perhaps already forlorn—hope of egalitarianism. And group conflicts are often centred on and motivated by economic conflicts that are forced to attention by reform policies.

Remarkably, the one task many of these societies resolved most expeditiously was political liberalization with the nearly instantaneous creation of democratic, nascently constitutional governments. Adam Michnik reports a quip from a French friend, who said that 'there were two ways for Poland to emerge from its appalling crisis. The first would be through common sense: . . . angels would descend to free Poland from Communism. The second would be through a miracle: the Poles—including both the Communists and the opposition—would come to an understanding with one another.'[3] To the surprise of everyone, the miracle happened. Western social science was caught flat-footed by this extraordinary achievement in a region on which the United States had trained 20,000 nuclear warheads and about as many intellectual heads. Adam Przeworski commented that this change, which came with astonishing ease, demonstrated the

[3] Adam Michnik, 'The Two Faces of Europe', *New York Review of Books* (19 July 1990): 7.

intellectual bankruptcy of the discipline of comparative politics.[4] Albert Hirschman noted that, given our utter lack of understanding of what was possible in 1989, 'utmost modesty is in order when it comes to pronouncements about the future of human societies'.[5] Modesty is perhaps too much to expect.

My purpose is not to explain or ruminate on the failings of comparative politics or on the initial changes in the East. I suspect those changes have depended very heavily, at least for their timing, on Mikhail Gorbachev, whose first move was to begin the demolition of the radically overwrought nuclear deterrent system. His second, equally astonishing move was to abolish the Soviet empire virtually overnight. With the removal of their Soviet military underpinnings, the regimes of the East European nations of the Warsaw Pact collapsed in the face of demands for political and economic liberalization. The obvious question now is whether the new regimes can succeed in establishing stable liberal orders. After briefly surveying the rise of liberalism and the nature of constitutionalism that were discussed in Chapters 2 and 3, I will turn to the varied difficulties the Easterners face in liberalizing politically and economically.

One of the two main obstacles to liberalization in many of the Eastern nations is immediately evident to anyone who hears news of ethnic conflict across these nations, although there is a misleading tendency to characterize such conflict as irrational.[6] My task will be to relate such conflict to liberalism and to constitutionalism. The nature of the second potential obstacle has been in debate for more than a century. Among others, Karl Marx, Joseph Schumpeter, Milton Friedman, and Mancur Olson have addressed the ways in which economic and political liberalisms may interact.[7] On this

[4] In conversations at the University of Chicago during early 1990.
[5] Albert O. Hirschman, 'Good News Is Not Bad News', *New York Review of Books* (11 Oct. 1990): 20–2, at p. 20.
[6] Dismissing the ethnic conflicts and violence as merely irrational is far too simplistic. See further Russell Hardin, 'Contested Community', *Society*, 32 (July/Aug. 1995): 23–9; *One for All: The Logic of Group Conflict* (Princeton: Princeton University Press, 1995).
[7] Marx addresses such problems throughout his works. In particular, he relates the odd politics of the French peasants to the misperception of their economic interests in *The Eighteenth Brumaire of Louis Bonaparte* (New York: International Publishers, 1963; 1st pub. 1869), 123–9. He also discusses potential conflicts within industry and between labourers; Joseph Schumpeter, *Capitalism, Socialism, and Democracy* (New York: Harper, 1950, 3rd edn.; 1st pub. 1942); Milton Friedman, *Capitalism and Freedom* (Chicago: University of Chicago Press, 1962); Mancur Olson, Jr., *The Rise and Decline of Nations* (New Haven: Yale University Press, 1982).

issue, my concerns will be with how politics may constrain the market when liberalization of politics and economics are carried out in tandem and with whether economic liberalism may be successfully constitutionalized.

By comparison to the current liberalizing nations, the United States in 1787 was in a remarkably different position. The miracle of the creation of the new nation under its present constitution was largely a matter of fortuitous timing and of its being spawned by a society that was already a liberal society, both politically and economically. As Tocqueville said, the United States did not experience a democratic revolution—it did not need one.[8] Because it was already doubly liberal, its citizens were nearly united in their concern for order and for a working economy. The illiberal, communitarian Anti-Federalists were against such an order on a large scale. But this was the only conflict: scale. The Anti-Federalists wanted democracy at the level of the village in which there might be near unanimity on moral and political issues, but not at the level of a large nation that might override the village mentality.

Constitutional Liberalism

Let us briefly bring the issues of Chapters 3 and 4 together to focus on the problems of liberalization. Modern liberalism arose historically in two parts: economic and political, as discussed in Chapter 2. Economic liberalism, or market organization of economic activities and choices, arose without general design or plan in Europe, especially in England. When such expositors as Bernard Mandeville and Adam Smith came along to argue for it, the market was already working to a large extent, so that their task was principally to describe and make sense of what existed. Political liberalism had a somewhat different history. It was partly invented to address particularly difficult problems of inequality, as addressed by the Levellers, and religious conflict, as addressed by Locke. Locke's *Letter Concerning Toleration* was a theory of and a plea for liberalism, not

---

[8] Alexis de Tocqueville, *Democracy in America*, 2 vols. (New York: Knopf, 1945; reprinted Vintage 1990), ii. book 1, ch. 1: 7. See further, Daniel Brühlmeier, 'Demokratische Revolutionen', in Karen Gloy, ed., *Demokratie-Theorie: Ein West-Ost-Dialog* (Tübingen: Francke Verlag, 1992), 64–83.

a description of the actual politics of his time.[9] Locke wished to push religious differences out of politics in order to achieve greater political peace. As a Protestant, of course, he thought religious beliefs an individual, not a collective, matter. Some of the contemporary transitions in the East have nearly the opposite character: the political transition has been spontaneous and largely from below, while the economic transition is being managed from above. In Russia, arguably both transitions have been brought in from above, by Gorbachev and Yeltsin in turn. Gorbachev's introduction of democratic principles and dissolution of the Soviet empire led almost immediately to his being pre-empted in the national leadership.

It is sometimes said that there is no political liberalism without economic liberalism. This is at least partly a distortion of the facts. Until recently, India, for example, had an extensively, though not wholly, socialized economy.[10] Yet it has also been one of the most politically liberal of all contemporary nations, with what for the Third World is an unusual history of democratic politics. As was true for the United States after 1800, India had a single dominant party for several decades, and that may have contributed to the stability of its constitutional order. Still, it may be true, as Friedman argued, that there is a strong causal connection between having a market economy and having strong civil liberties, although perhaps less strong than he thought.[11]

The creation of conditions for economic success and, essentially, mutual advantage through production and exchange was the central concern of Thomas Hobbes's theory of the autocratic, all-powerful sovereign. Hobbes supposed such a sovereign is virtually necessary for the maintenance of civil order, without which economic prosperity is impossible. Moreover, Hobbes was openly hostile to political liberalism, which threatens rebellion and disorder that might undermine prosperity and even safety. In the twentieth century,

[9] John Locke, *A Letter Concerning Toleration* (Indianapolis: Bobbs-Merrill, 1950; 1st pub. 1689).

[10] That may now be changing very quickly. See Edward A. Gargan, 'A Revolution Transforms India: Socialism's Out, Free Market In', *New York Times* (29 Mar. 1992), sect. 1: 1, 9.

[11] Friedman, *Capitalism and Freedom*, esp. ch. 1. One statistical study of the relationships between economic and political liberty found that 'where economic liberty exists, political liberty matters and where economic liberty does not exist political liberty does not matter', although this is hard to square with Indian, Swedish, and other experiences. See F. Vorhies and F. Glahe, 'Political Liberty and Social Development: An Empirical Investigation', *Public Choice*, 58 (1988): 45–71.

there has been a massive turn to Hobbesian principles. Communist rule in much of the world was politically illiberal in various regimes' efforts to drive economic and social goals. Fascist rule similarly was directed in part at political suppression in support of economic order and racist dominance. And various Third World regimes, often military, have used illiberal politics to control economic and military order, although many others have used illiberal politics for no apparent social purpose or advantage. The world of Islam has been ruled by nearly universally disastrous autocracies with little or no economic vision or understanding.

Many of the politically illiberal regimes have finally failed even at achieving their economic goals, and they have failed in the very compelling sense that they have done worse than politically freer regimes in much of the world. But some of these regimes have seemingly succeeded. Nazi Germany might have succeeded had its programme not been overwhelmed by the Nazi urge for war and conquest. South Korea, Taiwan, Singapore, Hong Kong, Chile, and others succeeded for about a generation while China has succeeded for more than a decade and some of these may continue their success despite periods of malaise. In some cases economic successes may finally have blunted revolutionary political efforts to bring in dramatically different systems. For some of these nations, the movement from illiberal, autocratic politics to relatively democratic politics may come almost as a reform rather than as a revolutionary change. For example, the grudging reintroduction of democracy in Chile and the apparent growth of democracy in Taiwan have seemed almost easy and uneventful, as nearly like a change of parties in power as a change of regimes: the autocrats simply lost elections that they had called.

In Eastern Europe and the Soviet Union, the autocrats often withdrew without even so much as an election, with less political violence in some nations than the United States suffered during the height of the Vietnam war or than France suffered in the late 1960s. Although there were violent confrontations in Lithuania and especially in Romania, the real violence has followed the end of autocracy in some of the successor states. Georgia, Nagorno-Karabakh, and Chechnya have added woeful pages to the annals of political murderousness. For some of these areas, Hobbes's view that any government that can maintain order is better than the risk of reform may be compelling, at least for the short run.

The chief task of the liberalizing regimes of Eastern Europe and the former Soviet Union is to create stable structures that strongly support liberal practices. Because one cannot rely on the commitment or integrity of particular persons to maintain liberalism, these nations generally must establish constitutions that design government institutions that will last. In theory, this requires only one thing: to match incentives with liberal institutions. If it is in everyone's interest to support liberal institutions and to behave as these institutions stipulate, the institutions will prosper. If it is in no one's interest to do so, they will founder quickly.

When incentives match, we may say that a constitution or institution is self-enforcing, because its design secures its support. A self-enforcing constitution gives a complex answer to the old but seemingly simple question: which is better, a government of men or a government of laws? The best form of government is one in which persons govern but they do so in a setting in which laws and institutions match their incentives as closely as possible to the purposes of their government.

If we are to understand the liberalizing constitutional experiences of formerly autocratic states today, we would do well first to look at whether their chief constitutional problems are to compromise on an unenforceable contract or, contrariwise, to coordinate on a mutually beneficial set of arrangements that will be self-enforcing once in place. Often, these nations face a twofold problem of constitution-making. They must achieve both political and economic liberalism. If their constitutions are to be self-enforcing, these must successfully coordinate major interests on both liberalisms.

Ethnic Conflicts

Why are there such great differences in successful political liberalization? Several of the nations of Eastern Europe and the former Soviet Union seem genuinely to face a relatively simple coordination problem. If one of these nations can only agree on a constitution, its population will have no incentive to violate the constitutional arrangements. Virtually every significant group shares an interest in general order. Within a regime of order all groups and individuals could pursue their own advantage to the mutual advantage. One of these nations, such as Poland, might have chosen a quite different constitution that might have been roughly as good as the choice it has made. The initial task was merely to coordinate on a single constitutional arrangement. This was the position of the United States during the constitutional convention of 1787.

The former Czechoslovakia, Ukraine, most dramatically Yugoslavia, and many other nations of the East have not so clearly faced such an easy coordination problem. The only easy coordination that many of the Eastern nations faced was toppling their old regimes. But they could do this without what the Germans call a constructive vote of no confidence, in which a government falls only if an alternative government can win the vote of a majority of the parliament. The East Europeans could dispossess an old regime without simultaneously creating a new regime. By breaking their task into these two parts, they could easily coordinate on resolving the first part of the problem.

In many of these nations perhaps the chief obstacle to simple coordination for mutual advantage beyond ending the old regime is ethnic division. The Azeris of Azerbaijan could coordinate easily enough on a mutually beneficial constitutional arrangement. But the Azeris and the Armenians of Azerbaijan together evidently could not. During the constitutional debates in the United States, the Anti-Federalists opposed a strong central government, while financial interests, plantation agrarians, and nationalists supported it. In the end, the Anti-Federalists had no programme to oppose to the Federalist programme—hence their name by default. Even more important for the success of the Federalists' constitution, however, was that once it was in place and working, the Anti-Federalists had nothing to gain from trying to undo it. The constitutional arrangement became self-enforcing, and Anti-Federalism virtually disappeared from American politics. A reasonably well-designed constitution in Poland, Hungary, or Russia might similarly be self-enforcing, at least with respect to problems of political liberalism. But there may be no plausible constitution that would be self-enforcing in Yugoslavia or Azerbaijan because there is no mutually beneficial order on which all could coordinate. Of course, after sufficient destruction on both sides of any conflict, coordination on ending the destruction might finally suffice to bring order.

Political liberalism has long faced the conundrum: can tolerant liberalism tolerate illiberal political movements? For example, must a liberal government allow Nazi racists to march in a Jewish community such as Skokie, Illinois? At some point, when the potential harm is great enough, the answer must finally be no. But it is too easy to suppose that such a point has already arrived. Locke thought Catholics should not be fully tolerated because they were loyal to a political authority outside England, the Pope in Rome—or perhaps to King Philip of Spain, who subsidized the Catholic James II. In the United States in this century, German-Americans, Japanese-Americans, Nazis, and Communists have all been treated illiberally for a similar reason or for the mere suspicion that they might be disloyal. Popular racism against Germans, Japanese, and, during the recent Gulf crisis and war, Arabs revealed hostility to liberal ideals. But it is state-sponsored actions to intern or suppress some of these groups during the two world wars and the Cold War that are the analogue of Locke's problem with Catholics.

Unfortunately, however, popular illiberalism and state sponsorship of illiberal policies may come together. When this is true, there may be no easy argument for popular government. This is not the commonplace claim that perhaps we must fight illiberalism with illiberalism, as in the suppression of a Nazi party or the Ku Klux Klan. It is the theoretically more distressing claim that liberal political devices may produce illiberal policies and even government. For example, relations between Armenians and Azeris were relatively civil throughout the illiberal reign of Communism. They became actively murderous only with the dissolution of autocratic power, with the opportunity for popular political expression and localized suppression.

In many areas of the world today, such ethnic conflict has the political status of the religious conflict of Locke's England. But there is a striking difference. Beliefs were in conflict in the religious wars of the Reformation, as they are to some extent in many parts of the world today, especially in the Middle East and Myanmar (formerly Burma). Because beliefs led to war and conflict, interests were also at stake in the earlier religious conflicts. But this was a contingent result of the conflict itself; it was not the cause of the conflict. Today, in manifold ethnic conflicts, interests are causally important because they are in conflict even before there is warfare or political fighting.

It is commonly asserted that nationalist and ethnic conflicts are the product of irrational hatred or remembered conflict from the past. For example, Armenians and Azeris have a long history of conflict, with the Azeris on the side of their cousins, the Turks, in occasional suppression of and even genocide against the Armenians. Hence, we can supposedly expect only irrational, self-destructive conflict between the two groups. Against this shallow assertion, we should also look for the interests at stake in this and other seemingly intractable conflicts.[12]

What are the interests at stake? Nagorno-Karabakh is a territory within Azerbaijan that is an Armenian enclave. The Azeris of Azerbaijan, or at least its leaders, think they will be losers if the territory of Nagorno-Karabakh becomes part of Armenia, and the Armenians of Nagorno-Karabakh and perhaps those of Armenia as well will be losers if the territory does not become part of Armenia. It is, of course, conceivable that all will be losers compared to either of these outcomes if there is a long and hard war over the territory. But even if this is true and if both sides recognize it is true, it does not follow that either side has an incentive to cede the issue to the other side. To win control of Nagorno-Karabakh, either side may have to persuade the other side of its irrationality, of its willingness to lose more in the long run through war rather than less in the short run through giving up its claim on the territory. National leaders may therefore stimulate mob actions and declarations, which the naive may then read as merely the product of natural emotions. It is possible that the Armenians living in Nagorno-Karabakh commonly believe their future under the Azeris is worse than their shorter run future in all out war against Azerbaijan, so that they need not demonstrate irrationality to convince others of their commitment to fight long and hard.

In cases of conflicting interests, we often are able to reach a compromise in which we share the benefits that are at stake. In conflicts between states, compromise often fails because both sides strive to hold out for everything. When national commitment is the main requirement for successfully holding out, even to give a signal that compromise might be acceptable is to give the other side an incentive to assert its irrationality in never assenting to less than everything. Where information is not relatively complete to begin with, discussion of the options is not a neutral strategic move. But it is only when information is not complete that discussion may have value.

---

[12] See further, Hardin, *One for All*, esp. 56–9.

Perhaps it is true that a compromise in which the Armenians of Nagorno-Karabakh are given relatively autonomous status within Azerbaijan would make everyone better off than they would be after a bloody conflict. But this is not a stable compromise; it is not self-enforcing. If the Azeris later decided to rule the Armenians more viciously, the costs of Armenian intervention may have risen to make Armenian success seem even less likely, even more costly than it might be if fought for today. Hence, the Azeris might not have adequate incentive to honour the mutually beneficial compromise. Similarly, the Armenians might someday think they could readily prevail in a moment of Azeri weakness to undo the earlier compromise.

Hence, as with many contractual bargains, such a compromise might be credible only if there were some external power, such as the United Nations, to enforce it. There was relatively little violent conflict between Azeris and Armenians during the years of Soviet hegemony.

Moving borders and peoples might make a contemporary compromise more readily workable than one that left the Armenians of Nagorno-Karabakh surrounded by Azeris and might eventually contribute to a self-enforcing status quo. Unfortunately, one might suppose that redrawing borders and relocating some people to make Armenia and Azerbaijan more nearly ethnically homogeneous would lead to eventual recidivist hostilities between the two nations. The United Nations could plausibly oversee the stability of national borders to ward off conflict between hostile ethnic groups in different nations. But internal political arrangements cannot so readily be guaranteed by an external power with strictly limited authority, such as the United Nations. One might have viewed the former Soviet government as an external power in the regulation of potential conflicts between, say, Armenians and Azeris. But its success in suppressing conflict probably depended on the pervasiveness of its authority to act and even govern. It is specifically the introduction of popular, liberal political devices that now gives the conflict room to grow by making it subject to allocative political decisions keyed to the groups.

Economic Conflicts

For this discussion, let us stipulate that, in the long run, market organization of an economy is generally more productive than command organization. Central command of very important parts of an economy might be better than market organization. For example, central provision may be more effective and more efficient for the short-term problems of wartime in any society or early industrialization in a backward economy, or even for the long-term provision of certain functions, such as highways or health care. We might suppose the market should generally determine what gets produced and consumed (perhaps subject to constraints to counter external costs), but that the market alone should not determine incomes. But still, let us stipulate that basically letting the market work is better than attempting centrally to control it in fine detail.

We might also stipulate that the transition from a command to a market economy will impose costs on many who will be short-term losers and some who will be long-term losers.[13] Hence, although one might argue that the market in the abstract is more efficient than a command economy, one cannot claim that *switching* to the market is efficient in Pareto's sense of making some better off while making none worse off. If losses in the transition were randomly distributed, all might face expected gains on average, so that the switch could be a unanimous choice and, hence, *ex ante* efficient. But if some of the long-term losers are identifiable *ex ante*, the transition cannot be efficient. Democratic politics virtually assures that no deal can be made with losers to guarantee them some of the gains of greater productivity because no future democratic choice can be fully bound by a present agreement.

The possibility of loss in the transition provokes concern with what contemporary Germans call *Besitzstandswahrung*, which can be broadly translated as protection (*Wahrung*) of what one has (*Besitzstand*) or status preservation, as though it were a matter of personal property, an entitlement that follows merely from occupancy of the position or status for some period of time. *Besitzstand*

---

[13] Adverse effects in Russia and much of the rest of the former Soviet Union have included a sharp decline in living standards and deterioration in mortality and morbidity. Michael Ellman, 'The Increase in Death and Disease under "Katastroika" ', *Cambridge Journal of Economics* (Aug. 1994): 329–55.

involves both of what in English would be called status and property. It has more the character of Locke's notion of property than of
the modern English notion. Employees of public firms in Germany
have opposed privatization because it would be accompanied by the
loss of their status as public officials, with all the protections and
privileges of that status. A big economic transition necessarily
changes status and holdings. That is much of its point or, rather, its
method. Illiberal economic policies create specific statuses and holdings, specific implicit entitlements. Liberal policies undo these.

There are two related accidental facts that run against the long-run
prevalence of massively illiberal economic policies. First, nations are
not autarkic and cannot generally close themselves off from economic competition from other nations. If a nation attempts to stay
out of international economic markets, its populace is likely still to
be psychologically influenced by visions of greater wealth elsewhere.
Hence, more liberal nations may prosper better than others and may
tend to affect economic policies in less liberal nations. Secondly,
technological innovations can take a nation's economy out of areas
in which the market is encumbered into new areas not yet illiberally
regulated. But in the short run of a generation or less, these two correcting forces may not work to push an illiberal regime into liberal
economic policies. *Constitutional arrangements to protect the market may therefore not be self-enforcing in the short run.*

Unfortunately, for the newly liberalizing nations of the defunct
Soviet empire, the short run is the hard problem, because it is in the
short run that they must make the transition to market economics. It
may be that the greatest hope they have is the relative incapacity of
their governments. If these governments cannot regulate the nascent
markets beyond maintaining order and backing contracts, they cannot prevent the spread of market devices. But suppose popular government is more successful than this in responding to popular
demands. Then liberal political devices may produce illiberal economic policies. In particular there may be Luddite protection of
workers in dying and dead industries and there may be price controls.

With governments subject to democratic control, the short-term
costs of economic reform may block long-term gains. As an Indian
opposition party leader friendly to market reforms remarked,
'Economic reform will have long-term advantages, but the disadvan-
tages have to be bearable'. With the closing of bankrupt state-owned

enterprises, 800,000 workers were slated for unemployment. Powerful unions not committed to economic liberalism were an obstacle to the government and its policies.[14] Vaclav Klaus, characterized as the fist in the velvet Czech glove, wavered before some of the groups that his stated policies, if actually carried through, would harm.[15] Pinochet's finance minister, who is given credit for the current Chilean free-market economic miracle, claimed that other nations seeking free-market reforms must first go through the chaos Chile suffered before Pinochet's grisly dictatorship: 'Only after hitting bottom will the general population accept major transformations'.[16] Even then, a population may be more likely to 'accept' transformations backed with draconian military force.

In the United States and other industrial nations, economic change has finally destroyed the historical dominance of agriculture over other economic activities. This has happened despite massive public efforts to enable farmers to remain on the land while staying abreast of the larger society's gains in welfare. In the United States, which is only a slightly extreme case, less than 3 per cent of the workforce is now in agriculture but produces enough food to make the nation a net exporter of food. Most of the eventual nations of the Soviet empire should approach that figure. But farm interests in Poland and much of the former Soviet empire now threaten economic progress, because the massive reductions coupled with the rational end of huge subsidies entail massive agony.[17] Earlier reductions in the United States and other industrial nations, where the agony was not conspicuously a matter of deliberate policy by popular government, were also politically hard fought.

Of course, in these nations farm interests are not alone. Heavy industry, most of which is obsolescent, state agencies of many kinds, and long-protected groups, such as older workers and bureaucrats, all want strong government protection to continue. Economic change, one of the two great motors of the current revolution, cannot proceed well while major failures of the past are protected and

---

[14] Gargan, 'A Revolution Transforms India', 9.
[15] Jane Perlez, 'The Fist in the Velvet Glove', *New York Times Magazine* (16 July 1995): 17–19.
[16] Jonathan Kandell, 'Prosperity Born of Pain', *New York Times Magazine* (7 July 1991): 14–18, 33, 35, quote p. 18.
[17] Karen Brooks, J. Louis Guasch, Avishay Braverman, and Csaba Csaki, 'Agriculture and the Transition to the Market', *Journal of Economic Perspectives*, 5 (Fall 1991): 149–61, esp. 154–5.

maintained. Nations such as the Asian Tigers may have outper-
formed nations that were already more advanced than they were in
large part because they had no *Besitzstandswahrer*, defenders of their
status.[18]

One of the cruellest of major short-term policies of the twentieth
century has been land reform, which has given small farms to millions of previously dependent rural workers. The cruelty of the boon
is that it came in a sector that has been doomed to steady decline. In
The Eighteenth Brumaire of Louis Bonaparte, one of the most compelling works of nineteenth-century sociology, Marx analyses the
stultifying quality of traditional subsistence farming in France. His
picture is of a non-Hobbesian world in which, although there is a
stable order and there is no murderous conflict, life is still nasty and
brutish. The great humanitarian impulse of land reform has generally
backfired and produced prolonged, multi-generational agony. Marx
wrote that Napoleonic land reform had reduced the French peasantry to troglodytes within two generations.[19] In many nations, land
reform has also produced a massive interest group whose presence
has distorted and damaged economic development.

In agriculture, Poland, the Serbian parts of Yugoslavia, and India
are more like Latin America than like the nations of the former
Soviet Union. Collectivization ended in Poland in 1956, and
Yugoslavia and India have both had land reform to some extent.
These nations now have vested interests in an outmoded agricultural
economy. The other nations of Eastern Europe have been able to
couple land reform—in the form of privatization—with economic
reform of agricultural and food policies. Prices had been set artificially low (below costs of production), but farm labourers had nevertheless been heavily subsidized. Farm populations and food
consumption were therefore artificially high. In a sense, therefore,
private ownership and higher food prices have been traded for the
elimination or reduction of subsidies. Consumption should now fall
somewhat, production should become more efficient, and, by
painful implication, farmers must become impoverished or their
numbers must drop substantially and soon. An alternative, at least in
principle, is export of agricultural products. Working against this
alternative are the facts that many of these nations have poor land
and climate with only lower labour costs to help them to be compet-

[18] This is in essence the thesis of Olson, *The Rise and Decline of Nations*.
[19] Marx, *The Eighteenth Brumaire of Louis Bonaparte*, 127.

itive and that much of their potential market is protected against import of agricultural goods. In the short term, ownership has probably made economic reform palatable. But will it stay palatable when 10 to 20 per cent of the workforce is far too large for agricultural production at world market prices and normal demand?

This is a more generally compelling question. There are large workforces in many areas that are not likely to be competitive in a market organization of an economy today. In Chapter 6, I discuss the use of so-called shock therapy: making the transition from a centrally controlled to a market economy almost instantly. There the focus is on the longer-run changes in the economies of the Eastern nations and how those changes might affect governmental stability and liberal politics. Here, consider briefly the impact of a policy of transition on a democratic government in the short term. In the short term the task of the government is to switch from institutional control of the economy from above to spontaneous generation of economic activity from below.

The economic conflicts between various groups are real, so that simple coordination on mutually advantageous arrangements that deal only with these issues is not possible. As with the political problem of ethnic conflict, the potential for illiberal economic policies is the result of liberal political devices. Anne Krueger has surveyed policies for economic development in the developing countries from the 1950s era of imposed controls to the 1980s era of reforms to undo many of the controls. This is not fully equivalent to proposals by many observers that reform in the Eastern nations should be gradually managed by central government, but it is instructive. In Krueger's study, once a group or industry was protected by, say, a tariff, that group or industry grew and the constituency for maintaining and extending the protection grew while opposing forces were weakened. Over and over, Krueger tells of the insidious and varied implications of attempts to control economic performance from state bureaux. Every intervention, no matter how admirable its purpose, seemingly had its perverse corollary effects. The problem was one of politics rather than of economics but the result was growing economic distortions. The result is autonomous bureaucratic states or, if one has a harsher view, autonomous predatory states.[20] When Rajiv Gandhi attempted to reform the system in India in 1985,

[20] Anne Krueger, *Political Economy of Reform in Developing Countries* (Cambridge, Mass.: MIT Press, 1993), 62.

there were 17 million bureaucrats whose interests were at stake. This is a peculiarly collective variant of Margaret Levi's theory of predatory rule: a predatory *bureaucratic* state.[21]

This is a familiar story, almost an inference from theory. Mancur Olson argues more generally that the historical growth and empowerment of special interest groups trammels coherent economic policy.[22] To the extent that Olson's view is right, one may expect Poland to have greater problems with agriculture than other Eastern nations, because Poland empowered farmers long ago, letting them opt out of state ownership. Outside the formerly Communist world, India may have a particularly hard time with privatization and freeing the market. Decades of democratic participation and political organization have produced powerful groups that may readily block reforms that entail short-term costs.

The problem with mere coordination for market institutions today is far more difficult than that in 1787 North America. Then, government institutions at their best were sure to be relatively weak, and they were sure to have a relatively poor grasp of the state of affairs in the economy. Today, government institutions are much stronger and more pervasive and they have command over extensive bodies of relevant economic data. Governments today typically spend a third or more of the gross domestic product of their nations. In 1787 such a level of government expenditure was almost inconceivable. Governments could not even tax adequately to consume a large fraction of the national product. The so-called defence budget of the United States today consumes a larger share of gross domestic product than did the entire national government for most of national history. The government of the United States was funded primarily by customs duties for more than a century before corporate and personal income taxes displaced the customs levy in importance in the twentieth century. The world has known less than a century of pervasive, modern government.

Although governments today have great power, they lack the theoretical understanding to gain real control over economic developments beyond gaining some control over fiscal policy, the currency, the rate of inflation, some aspects of investment, and various welfare programmes such as retirement protections. Indeed, economists lack

[21] Margaret Levi, *Of Rules and Revenue* (Berkeley: University of California Press, 1988).
[22] Olson, *The Rise and Decline of Nations*.

such understanding.[23] But there are some things governments can do quite effectively. In particular, governments can increase the welfare of some small group in the society, at least for the short term of the careers of the group's current members, by simply laying out the necessary funds or by intrusively regulating relevant parts of the economy (for example, with protective tariffs, entry restrictions, or *de facto* grants of monopoly). The effort might be woefully inefficient in its dispensation of funds, consuming as much as it dispenses, or in its larger impact on the economy, but such policy is within the competence of the government of a typical industrial state. Hence, any government of such a state today is capable of distorting liberal market performance.

The government of the United States in its first decades had much less capacity for such distortion apart from distortions from differential tariffs. Beyond that, it could be seen as likely to do little more than provide the framework of order within which individuals and groups could engage in mutually advantageous endeavours and exchanges. But that just means that the Constitution of the United States could originally be seen, as far as its role in the economy was concerned, to coordinate the society on a government that could provide such order. The potential for distortion was itself not a major concern of those who sought economic order two centuries ago. Indeed, the chief appeal of the Constitution for its major supporters was that it would eliminate the distortions of customs duties on interstate trade, that it would effectively create a national market.

The specific difficulty of major economic policy changes in the industrial world today, East and West, is that such changes cannot be seen as merely serving mutual advantage. They are rightly seen as inherently conflict ridden. Economic policy now is too detailed to serve mutual advantage. There is not merely order and the granting of special privileges. There are policies to govern the conditions under which corporations can go bankrupt, merge, release workers, invest, or use certain technologies. Intervention in the relatively highly developed economies of Eastern Europe to replace the

---

[23] In *Democracy, Capitalism, and Ralph's Pretty Good Grocery* (Princeton: Princeton University Press, forthcoming), John Mueller argues that economists have now just about reached the point of sophistication that, when government gets economic advice from them, the advice is more likely to be beneficial than harmful. If true, this would be a major turning-point, roughly comparable to the point about a century ago when doctors began to be more likely to help than to harm their patients (a point many people are not yet convinced has been reached by their own doctors).

command economy with a market is not like creating a market in a primitive economy. Moving to a market might make almost everyone better off in their own lifetimes in an economy as primitive as that of, say, South Korea in 1960 or China in 1980. But many Russians who are already 50 years old might reasonably expect to be losers for the rest of their lives from the successful introduction of the market.

Productivity may generally be self-enforcing in a market that is kept free of extensive political intervention—there should be a strong tendency for selection of the fittest producers. But the market itself cannot be isolated from politics and therefore cannot be self-enforcing. Economic liberalism is not subject to easy self-enforcement when government is available to intervene in market relations to protect the backward and unproductive. If my group lost in the last round of policy, it may struggle for revision now. And the revisions that groups often want are revisions that override market forces to benefit themselves. But, by Hobbesian definition of the situation in which we find ourselves, there can be no very successful market without government. Indeed, normal markets may fail if they have no more stable legal system than the former Soviet Union had.[24] Hence, we are in a logical bind that virtually guarantees the sometime failure of economic liberalism.

Egalitarianism

The concern with *Besitzstandswahrung* is not a matter of fairness across the population but only of 'fairness' over the continued lifetime of each particular person, with fairness defined merely as a matter of continuing expectations. In *Democracy in America*, Tocqueville was concerned with the equality of condition that he thought was 'the fundamental fact from which all others seem to be derived'.[25] On Tocqueville's account this condition is intimately, causally connected with democracy (although this may have been a

[24] See further, John M. Litwack, 'Legality and Market Reform in Soviet-Type Economies', *Journal of Economic Perspectives*, 5 (1991): 77–89.

[25] Tocqueville, *Democracy in America*, i. 3. See also, Claude Lefort, 'From Equality to Freedom: Fragments of an Interpretation of Democracy in America', in Lefort, *Democracy and Political Theory* (Minneapolis: University of Minnesota Press, 1988; trans. David Macey), 183–209.

definitional rather than causal point for him). It was in their striving towards equality of political condition—as in, for example, equality before the law—that the old regimes of Europe approached democracy in Tocqueville's time. In our own time, the egalitarian urge has more typically been intellectually associated with economic condition and hence with socialism, which has been associated in actual politics with non-democratic government. Indeed, the rhetoric of defenders of Soviet-style political regimes has often suggested that authoritarian government by the Party was necessary to protect people against the inegalitarian ravages of liberal democracy and the market.

The central problem of any striving for egalitarian economic results is that economic productivity thrives on variance in ways of achieving results. We want many different approaches to the resolution of various demands in order to let us sift through them to achieve a good or, plausibly even, the best resolution or to let some of us choose one resolution while others choose other resolutions. The first question for an egalitarian is whether this result of market organization of production can be mimicked by centralized devices. In principle, at least, it might be. Unfortunately, however, the results are likely to be plagued by gross variance in the overall achievement. A small number of governors setting production and consumption policy can do the job exceedingly badly as well as perhaps very well. The experience in the East, which is limited even if extensive in the number of nations and people whom it affected for many decades, is that the variance tends towards the unproductive. In certain stages of economic development, centralized devices that can simply ape the production of more advanced economies may work relatively well in the sense of producing competitive rates of growth in productivity and wealth. In other stages of development, there may be little hope that even the best-intentioned central government could match a market organization of the economy.

We may distinguish two urges in the current reorganizations of the Eastern societies. The initial urge seems to have been Mikhail Gorbachev's—and, no doubt, other leaders'—concern to improve economic performance. The favoured solution is to introduce some degree of market economics to replace centralized economic control. The second urge is popular clamouring for political equality through democratic institutions, which supposedly fit the new economic order. The extraordinary events of 1989 are almost entirely from the second urge to create democratic institutions. Introducing the market and capitalism may take far longer than introducing new, relatively democratic regimes.

These changes may raise doubts about the possibility of a political programme of egalitarianism in incomes. The fundamental issue for the short run of a generation or two is not whether there can be Communism—there evidently cannot be for very long in a world dominated by economic competitiveness as we know it. The issue is whether there can even be socialism or a reasonable modicum of egalitarianism. It seems to be the conclusion of Soviet, East European, and Chinese leaders that there cannot be socialism in competition with capitalism. There was a slogan popular in the early days of Polish reform: Liberty, Equality, Initiative. That sounds like a minor variation on an old theme. It is not. In the new slogan, Liberty means freedom of enterprise. Equality means equality of all forms of property.[26] The new word in the slogan, Initiative, is the only straightforward term. Its force, despite the rhetoric of equality of opportunity, is radically inegalitarian.

Equality versus Efficiency

The view that equality of income and efficiency of production inherently conflict has become almost a dogma in the West.[27] In his theory of justice, John Rawls supposes that inequality can be just *if* the inequality leads to such greater production as to permit even the worst-off class or group in the society to be better off than they would be under a more egalitarian regime.[28] This is a concession on his part to the seeming likelihood that economic incentives of greater wealth and income are necessary for stimulating higher levels of production. It might appear to be a staggeringly conservative conces-

[26] Reported by Jacek Tarkowski in conversation, University of Chicago, 14 Feb. 1990.

[27] The standard treatment is Arthur M. Okun, *Equality and Efficiency: The Big Tradeoff* (Washington: Brookings, 1975); but see also Gary A. Dymski and John E. Elliot, 'Capitalism and the Democratic Economy', *Social Philosophy and Policy*, 6 (Autumn 1988): 140–64. There are numerous accounts of the inequities that follow from policies of economic stimulation in many nations that lag behind world industrial standards. For example, see Robert H. Bates, *Markets and States in Tropical Africa: The Political Basis of Agricultural Policies* (Berkeley: University of California Press, 1981).

[28] John Rawls, *A Theory of Justice* (Cambridge, Mass.: Harvard University Press, 1971).

sion. But it is no more than a concession to the moral theorist's dictum: ought implies can. It cannot be true that we ought to do what is impossible for us to do. If the economist's dogma that greater productivity requires differential rewards as incentives is correct, then we cannot have greater productivity without at least Rawlsian inequality.[29]

Until very recently the nations of the Eastern bloc proclaimed a commitment to egalitarianism. And, although their practice did not meet their proclaimed aspiration, there was much greater equality of incomes among industrial, professional, and bureaucratic wage-earners in the East than in the West. A clear implication of the current capitulation to capitalism is the freeing of wages from central determination and the introduction of personal profits that must reduce equality of earnings. Leaders may talk as though the changes will hurt no one, that even if they increase inequality, they raise the floor for everyone. If it does work this way, their move is essentially Rawlsian. Against that sanguine hope, consider just one minor group who, like many other groups, will not fit the new structures: vast numbers of teachers and professors of Marxism-Leninism have surely lost in the transition.[30] Many scientists and other well-defined economic groups have also lost.[31] And, at least in the early returns, women have lost substantially in the 'patriarchal renaissance' in what are ruefully called the new 'male democracies'.[32]

The Eastern nations provide some unique evidence for the equality versus efficiency thesis. The evidence touted at the moment is their current economic difficulties. But this evidence is very unclear. In general, the Eastern economies seemed in recent years to lag behind some capitalist economies at similar levels of development in

[29] G. A. Cohen argues against Rawls's capitulation to inequality for the sake of productivity in 'The Pareto Argument for Inequality', *Social Philosophy and Policy*, 12 (Winter 1995): 160–85.

[30] At Moscow State University in June 1989, with a group of American philosophers, I was introduced to an elegant older professor who was described to us as the greatest living Marxist philosopher. He smiled ruefully and bowed almost imperceptibly as he said, 'That is no great distinction.' In our subsequent group discussion he said he expected Marxist philosophy to descend into limbo for a century or two as Aristotelianism had done after the rise of Cartesian analytical philosophy. In the Soviet Union, he said, it was already dead.

[31] *Science* (20 Dec. 1991): 1716–19; (18 June 1993): 1744–6, 1753–8. Scientists in East Germany lost in the merger of the two Germanies in part because Eastern research departments were overstaffed by competitive Western standards (*Science* (6 April 1989): 23).

[32] There are many accounts. See e.g. *Toronto Globe and Mail*, 1 Nov. 1993, p. A8.

their rates of growth—but they shared this sad fate with most of the non-socialist economies of Latin America. In any case, the differences were not great. Indeed, the conservative American economist Herbert Stein concluded that the slight differences do not explain the capitulation to capitalism.[33] The differences might even have been transitory. During the decades of the 1950s, 1960s, and 1970s, there were many West German books with such titles as 'The Shattering of the East German Economy', 'The Collapse of the East German Economy', 'The Disastrous Failure of the East German Five-Year Plan', and so forth. These books demonstrated that, although the East Germans had got by until then, they were bound to collapse soon. As of 1989, the East German economy had still not collapsed, although it was probably not performing at the high levels attributed to it by Western intelligence agencies.

The debate over the presumed conflict between efficiency and equality in the West is generally about gross productivity, not really about efficiency in a narrower sense. It is about the role of unequal rewards in motivating people to work.[34] The Eastern economies have suffered from another problem of inefficiency: the failure to produce goods that are desired. Without greater inputs in production, consumer demands could have been better satisfied. This inefficiency results from centralized control and from the mismatch of incentives with *what* is produced.

The real evidence of conflict between equality of income and efficiency of production is less obvious. Note four kinds of evidence for the slightly peculiar case of East Germany.

First, economic pressures allowed egalitarian commitments to be severely undercut for the last couple of decades of the East German regime in letting citizens receive hard currency gifts from relatives in the West. A large fraction of East Germans received such supports in West German marks, which could be used to buy various goods and even to gain access to apartments immediately without going through normal queues that could take as long as a decade. Many of

[33] Herbert Stein, 'The Triumph of the Adaptive Society', Frank E. Seidman Lecture in Political Economy (Memphis: Rhodes College, 14 Sept. 1989), 23.

[34] The argument is not about what goods are produced, although higher incomes for some may generally imply demands for different goods. For example, high-income earners in the West commonly buy luxury cars, very expensive dinners, international travel, and vacation homes, which are seldom bought by low- or even moderate-income earners. Hence, unequal rewards are likely to affect the pattern of production.

the purchases were nominally illegal, but they were openly tolerated because of the need for hard currencies, without which nations lacking commodities for foreign sale cannot enjoy the benefits of world markets. Getting hard currencies benefited everyone, even though it benefited some more than others.

Secondly, the Eastern nations increasingly tolerated certain black markets over the decades, even legalizing some of them. Production of many agricultural goods for domestic consumption was turned over to farmers working on their own plots while earning much of their staple income from wage labour on their collective farms. Farmers who were good at their private production were well rewarded at *de facto* market prices for their efforts. Throughout industry in the Eastern bloc there were arbitrage agents who, for bribes, facilitated trade in inputs for production. Some of these activities were presumably parasitic on the system, as they often are in democratic, capitalist societies. But some of them seem to have been genuinely facilitative. The bribes are unequal rewards that give managers and others an incentive to put extra effort into making things work better.

Thirdly, in the years before the Wall, East Germany suffered substantial losses of workers to emigration, almost all of it to West Germany. The emigration was not random but was strongly correlated with occupation and potential earnings differences East and West. There was a reverse flow of about 30 per cent of the Westward movement.[35] The net movement was highly skilled and professional workers going West, low-skilled workers going East. Chile under Allende reputedly suffered a similar experience of top-heavy emigration, although the data are subjective because no one had an interest in collecting them for Chile. Similar, less dramatic experiences have afflicted the entire Eastern bloc. This problem suggests that egalitarianism faces special obstacles in a larger world in which inegalitarian incentives and rewards prevail. Alternative rewards may induce adverse exit.

For the fourth piece of evidence, return to the failings of the last couple of decades before the drastic changes of 1989. For all we know, the problems of the moment in the socialist economies would have passed and those economies would have begun to show substantial rates of growth and technological and organizational

[35] Russell Hardin, 'Emigration, Occupational Mobility, and Institutionalization: The German Democratic Republic', MIT dissertation, 1971, ch. 4.

innovativeness. The usual Western view is that innovativeness depends heavily on entrepreneurial incentive and, therefore, on some variant of capitalist ownership. That may be true, especially in new technologies, such as electronics and computing in our era. But it seems also to be true that some very large organizations, such as Dupont and Toyota, are superb innovators who lead, rather than follow, economic change. The Czech economy is smaller than that of some very innovative firms. What the Eastern economies face at the moment, however, seems to be difficulty in making the major transition from follower to leader economies just when the latter seem to have enormous advantages for growth and international domination through the subordination of all activities to the information technologies.

Leader economies did not so clearly have such advantages a few decades ago. Lacking the leadership to make a transition from the top, the Eastern nations are on the verge of trying to succeed by decentralizing economic control and even creating capitalist incentives. Had there been no capitalist world markets or if these had been less successful, however, the socialist nations would not have any incentive now to reconsider their own organization. In the 1930s, the prospects for capitalism seemed poor enough to lead to popular support for fascist reorganization of societies to create quasi-socialist economies. Stein notes that his lecture, mentioned above, on comparative economic trends in Eastern and Western economies was given two weeks before the 'sixtieth anniversary of the onset of capitalism's greatest crisis'.[36] He quotes a German economist, Moritz J. Bonn, writing in 1932:

[The] question arises in thousands of hearts and brains: Is the capitalist system any longer justified if, in the richest country in the world, it is incapable of shaping an order which will guarantee to a comparatively sparse population, admittedly industrious and capable, a subsistence consonant with the human needs developed by modern techniques, without millions being from time to time reduced to beggary and to dependence on soup kitchens and casual wards?

The real significance of the American crisis consists in the fact that today it is not merely the present economic leadership or economic policy that is being questioned, but the capitalist system itself.[37]

[36] Stein, 'The Triumph of the Adaptive Society', 1.
[37] Moritz J. Bonn, *The Crisis of Capitalism in America* (New York: John Day, 1932), 188–9, 190; quoted in Stein, 'The Triumph of the Adaptive Society', 7.

With slight changes of reference, Bonn's claim sounds familiar. Now socialism seems to have poor economic prospects and the system itself has been questioned, although its economic problems were far less grim than what capitalism suffered in the 1930s.

It may often be true of judgements such as Bonn's 1932 judgement that they are merely transitional, not fundamental. Schumpeter argued against reliance on such short-term evaluations, especially for capitalism:

[S]ince we are dealing with a process whose every element takes considerable time in revealing its true features and ultimate effects, there is no point in appraising the performance of that process *ex visu* of a given point in time; we must judge its performance over time, as it unfolds through decades or centuries. A system—any system, economic or other—that at *every* point of time fully utilizes its possibilities to the best advantage may yet in the long run be inferior to a system that does so at *no* given point of time, because the latter's failure to do so may be a condition for the level or speed of long-run performance.[38]

Still, it may be that the transition from non-competitive to competitive socialist economies would be so hard as to result in economic collapse in the short run, so that, even if the challenges were only momentary and not fundamental, making a transition instead to capitalism would still be the intelligent policy for the moment.

Oddly, the main problem may be the simple one of ossification of organizations that have strong personnel protection policies when they come to face changing technologies. *Besitzstandswahrung* through feather-bedding (keeping workers on the job with nothing to do) or its analogue becomes an obstacle to change. But this is not socialism, it is merely strategically misdesigned social welfarism. In a free-market economy, the response to ossification of old enterprises may be displacement by other firms or even industries that utilize new, more productive technologies and perhaps differently trained workers. Among the most effective forms of differential incentives that were not available in the East are bankruptcy and unemployment. Galbraith parodies the commitment of Western economists to these painful incentives with a sly twist on an old slogan: 'To each according to his ability, from each according to his need'.[39] In a centrally controlled economy, displacement of an ossified industry or

[38] Schumpeter, *Capitalism, Socialism, and Democracy*, 83.
[39] John Kenneth Galbraith, 'The Rush to Capitalism', *New York Review of Books* (25 Oct. 1990): 51.

firm requires decisive action by someone, not merely the brazen actions of a couple of teenagers working in their garage to compete with the then gigantic IBM.

Oskar Lange, John Roemer, and others have argued that socialist firms can be competitive, just as Dupont and Toyota are.[40] They merely need not to be monopolies and to face real competition. But the general point of creating private property is to give opportunity to entrepreneurs. It is entrepreneurial creativity that is fundamentally important, not property. In genuinely competitive markets—that is, markets with many sellers and many buyers—creating property may be sufficient to let entrepreneurial talent and initiative bring about much greater productivity, as has happened with vegetable farming on quasi-private plots in the Soviet Union and East Europe. But there are few genuinely competitive markets in this sense—the only ones of any significance may be vegetable farming, restaurants, and a few services. These make up a very small part of national economies in industrial states and they are not central to the problems of Eastern bloc economies in their misfit with international markets. Creating property without entrepreneurs in other industries by simply turning firms over to the current bureaucrats who manage them cannot change much in the short run and may even hinder developments in the longer run by tying up capital in sick firms, although with free trade those firms must soon shape up or go under.

Egalitarianism in One Society

Let us return to the third problem, noted above, of inefficiency in the Eastern nations under Communism. Imagine two neighbouring nations that are similar in many relevant respects. They have similar populations, levels of economic development, education, and gross domestic product per capita. But East is a nation with relatively egalitarian incomes and wealth while West is a free-wheeling market economy with unequal incomes and wealth. Successful entrepreneurs in West may amass fortunes such as those of Bill Gates (many tens of billions of dollars from his computer software firm,

[40] Oskar Lange, *On the Economic Theory of Socialism* (Minneapolis: University of Minnesota Press, 1938); John E. Roemer, 'The Possibility of Market Socialism', in David Copp, Jean Hampton, and John E. Roemer, eds., *The Idea of Democracy* (Cambridge: Cambridge University Press, 1993), 347–67.

Microsoft) or Sam Walton (who had amassed more than 20 billion dollars from his retail discount chain, Wal-Mart, before he died at a rich old age). Suppose the unequal incomes and wealth in West are produced by market forces and that there are characteristics of individuals that put them well above or well below the median income and that individuals tend to know whether they have these characteristics, if not at the beginnings of their working lives, then soon enough.

The equality in East could come about through various devices. East could have socialist ownership of production (reducing the possibilities for entrepreneurially based inequality) and of distribution. Or it might not be socialist at all but might let the market generally determine what gets produced and consumed (perhaps subject to some regulatory constraints). To achieve greater equality, it might merely have an incomes policy, effected through progressive taxation on incomes and stiff taxes on wealth.

Suppose East and West do not suppress migration between them, so that they have essentially a joint job market. We can expect that there will be a steady stream of those with the characteristics for high incomes from egalitarian East to inegalitarian West, and a steady stream of those with the characteristics for low incomes from inegalitarian West to egalitarian East. This would mirror the years (1949–61) of massive migrations between East and West Germany before the Wall was built, as noted above.[41] If it is generally true that high incomes tend to go to more productive and low incomes to less productive individuals, these migration flows would work systematically to the economic advantage of West and the disadvantage of East. The result would be slightly higher total productivity growth in the inegalitarian society, which would lead to grossly higher productivity after a generation or so. As a result, one would expect economic prospects in the egalitarian society to deteriorate steadily in comparison with those in the inegalitarian society. After a long enough period of such deterioration, one might even expect that the median welfare in the egalitarian society would fall well below the median welfare in the inegalitarian society. Political liberty of movement may therefore destroy an egalitarian society.

---

[41] Viktoria Mullova, Dmitri Rostropovich, and many others may have emigrated to the West to secure greater artistic freedom, but they may also have been motivated to emigrate to where their talents would be far better paid.

In a world of non-egalitarian societies, egalitarianism is not self-enforcing unless people are normatively motivated in favour of it. If people are predominately or even largely self-interested, egalitarianism in a competitive world with inegalitarian alternatives may require substantial, ongoing intervention to enforce it. Such intervention is likely to be costly and therefore to reduce productivity. Hence, there is likely to be a contingent connection between egalitarianism and autocracy. A nation may successfully achieve modest egalitarianism with democratic, politically liberal devices, as Sweden seems to do. But if popular approval fails, the outside world competes too strongly, or the move to equality goes too far, even a nation such as Sweden may face decline.

This is, of course, not merely a theoretical conclusion. Its truth depends on empirical relations, such as the claim that market inequalities correlate with productivity. Many social scientists and others seem to believe this claim. Unfortunately, the claim masks a conceptual problem: productivity and income are circularly related. For many things that matter to us, we can compare productivity levels in different societies if what they produce is similar enough in kind and different primarily in quantity. If very much is simply provided by the state without market measures of demand, we may have difficulty evaluating those things in comparison to other things and we may succumb to the fallacy of measuring them by the inputs to them rather than by the unpriced outputs. In the end, even the very careful comparisons of East and West German productivity grew increasingly tenuous as consumption patterns in the two societies diverged. Converting from one form of economic organization to the other would make the converted economy look bad by comparison.

In our imagined pair of nations, does East trade productivity for equality? If there are real costs of resources or lost opportunities for production that result from enforcing egalitarian distributions, then yes. East also loses productivity in its labour-force competition with West. This loss is not inherent in East's egalitarian system *per se* because it depends on the existence of a West. But it may make East's egalitarianism untenable in our world.

Egalitarianism Without Socialism

Concerns with efficiency and productivity seem to have destroyed socialism in the East. Does egalitarianism still have a voice in the world? During the rapid process of the absorption of East by West Germany, the West German novelist Günter Grass regularly appeared on television to bemoan what was being lost. Ian Buruma writes:

His constant invocation of 'Auschwitz' as a kind of talisman to ward off a reunited Germany had the air of desperation, the desperation of a man who had lost his vision of Eden. His Eden was not the former GDR [German Democratic Republic], to be sure, but at least the GDR carried, for Grass, the promise of a better Germany, a truly socialist Germany, a Germany without greed, Hollywood, and ever-lurking fascism.[42]

There may be other ways to pin one's aspirations to an egalitarian political programme than by reference to an ideal corrupted in practice. But the desperation that Buruma read into Grass's complaints may be real and understandable.

In Western usage, 'socialism' and 'communism' are distinctly different in the vernacular language of ordinary politics. 'Communism' is a denotative term that refers to the immediate past systems of the Eastern bloc, to Soviet-type economies and polities. 'Socialism' is a plausible political goal under systems quite different from those of the Eastern bloc. It is not quite utopian but it is more ideal than real, at least up to present experience. In eastern usage, 'communism' was always only a utopian aspiration at best. In the East, 'socialism' is the reified term, the 'communism' of Western vocabulary, and it has been tarred by its association with the immediate past systems. Rejection of those systems makes invocation of the term 'socialism' politically unacceptable, as though 'socialism' as a term had been fully appropriated by the Ceauşescus and the Honeckers. As Michael Walzer laments, 'Communism has given socialism a bad name'.[43]

Even in the West, socialism may lose its appeal by association with the Eastern judgement. As the Eastern societies have associated socialism with political repression and autocracy, so they seem to associate capitalism with political freedom and democracy. Both associations may be causally correct, although we have no compelling theory of why they must be, and they might only be

---

[42] Ian Buruma, 'There's No Place Like Heimat', *New York Review of Books* (20 Dec. 1990): 34–43, quote at p. 34.

[43] Michael Walzer in *Dissent* (Spring 1990); Neil Kinnock reputedly outlawed use of the word socialism in the British Labour Party (*New Yorker*, 4 May 1992, p. 91). Unfortunately, communism may also have given feminism a bad name in the East.

denotative. Many in the West share the association of capitalism with freedom and democracy and Western opponents of socialism have long touted the association of socialism with repression and autocracy as a causal law.[44] Oddly, these opponents of egalitarian policies may now draw on Eastern arguments to support their position.

Without socialism as an aspiration, it is hard to frame an agenda for egalitarianism. The English Levellers at the time of Hobbes and the Radical utilitarians at the time of Bentham and the elder Mill rallied for equality but they were unable to found lasting movements at all comparable to the politically and intellectually powerful socialist movement of the past century or more. For the near term, it seems likely that support for more nearly egalitarian incomes policies will depend very heavily on the beneficence of many who will not benefit from such policies. Recent evidence in many Western nations is that even such beneficent motivations are in decline as tax policies have become less progressive while welfare programmes have gone into decline.

On many reports there remains a strong commitment to economic egalitarianism in many Eastern nations. Indeed, Friedrich Katz thinks the acrimony against East German leaders' secret privileges was intense just because Honecker and his associates betrayed a commitment to egalitarianism that was shared by the populace.[45] But despite such sentiment, there may remain no political party for egalitarianism. Can people aspire to greater equality without socialism as a party and a possible form of political economy?

Democratic politics seems to have certain egalitarian tendencies. It may not do very well at equalizing wealth, income, or even benefits provided by governmen, but it may push for uniformity in many rights assignments. Their violation of such uniformity may be another source of East German disaffection with Honecker and Romanian disaffection with Ceauşescu. In the United States, it has become difficult for government agencies to sponsor social and medical experiments that assign subjects to different treatment groups. Various theories of the impact of welfare programmes on incentives

---

[44] For enlightening discussion of these associations, see Charles E. Lindblom, *Politics and Markets: The World's Political-Economic Systems* (New York: Basic Books, 1977). Several of the articles in the special issue of *Social Philosophy and Policy* on 'Socialism' (Spring 1989) are of interest on this issue, although, despite their recent publication, they are already badly dated by events—an unusual fate for philosophical work.

[45] In private conversation at the University of Chicago, 19 Apr. 1990.

to work could be tested by trying different welfare regimes on selected populations. Congress became hostile to such experimental tests not so much because they are experiments or because certain members of Congress thought it obvious which theory or pro-gramme was right but, rather, because many people thought it unfair, for example, to apply differential work incentives to people who were otherwise similarly situated. Similarly, tests of new drugs for treatment of AIDS have been blocked before they could reach statis-tically sound results on the grounds that it is unfair to give people different life chances. But these correlates of democracy are minor instances of equality. Historically, the propertied class has worried, as did the authors of the *Federalist Papers*, about the equalizing ten-dency of democratic government. In the modern experience of democracy coupled with great inequality of wealth and income, that issue has virtually dropped from concern. Madison might be aston-ished at how little property has been at risk from democracy in the United States.

Despite any egalitarian tendencies democracy has, ending the hope of egalitarianism poses no obstacle to current constitutional trans-itions in the East because there is no party for egalitarianism there. Egalitarianism *per se* is not an interest. The only interests that groups have is to get more and better for themselves irrespective of the effect on equality across groups. If it is a dispiriting fact that equality and productive efficiency do conflict in practice in modern societies that we know, it should be even more dispiriting that they may especially conflict under democracy.

The Dual Task of 1989

It is a striking fact of the growth of economies and polities histor-ically that none has really faced the task of the East Europeans at this moment. In East Europe, the task of creating democracy and making it work is being undertaken simultaneously with the task of creating a market, largely capitalist, economy. Although some democratic tendencies preceded much of the development of major Western economies, broad-based democratic participation and institutions have almost invariably followed the growth of market elements of the economy. The events of 1989 seem to have produced instant democracies in many East European nations with little preparation of liberal economic institutions (with the most notable exception of Hungary, in which economic reform was well under way before 1989).

It is now up to these new democratic regimes to create the new economic order. Can they do it? Can a government that needs majoritarian support afford to shut down virtually whole industries, temporarily reducing economic production while causing substantial unemployment? During the Great Depression, the complaint against President Hoover was not that he deliberately brought it about for some reason but merely that he failed to stop it sooner. In switching to capitalist organization of their economies, Eastern leaders may face the accusation that they have brought about a similar transitional disaster that ruins lives for a decade or more. The hesitations of Gorbachev may therefore rightly be shared by all the East European leaders. But, from the too short perspective of about a decade after 1989, there is good reason for cautious optimism about the prospects for success of the dual liberalizations in several of the East European nations. At the very least, there is good reason to suppose that quick retrogression to old forms will be very difficult.

An impressionistic reading of seemingly countless analyses of the economic reforms in many of the Eastern nations suggests that the more detailed accounts are more pessimistic than the less detailed general accounts. Perhaps this is in keeping with the vision of coordination, in which there may be many ways to achieve roughly the same values. In the end, the details of the arrangements do not matter so much as their general character. Nancy Bermeo has compared the pessimistic accounts of the Eastern prospects to similarly pessimistic accounts of the future of Western European nations in the 1950s and concluded in favour of cautious optimism.[46] One ground for respect for the achievements to date is the inordinate difficulty of massive re-coordination on any grand social structure. Many of the Eastern nations have overcome this difficulty, which is arguably the greatest obstacle to both liberalisms.

Still, it is a discouraging thought, but a perhaps plausible one, that China may follow its own events of 1989 with greater success in making the transition to market economics with democracy than many, perhaps most, of the East European nations are likely to have.

[46] Nancy Bermeo, 'Democracy in Europe', *Daedalus* (Spring 1994): 159–77.

Autocratic development of a market economy may be easier than democratic development of it. Of course, there may be much greater variance along the autocratic path, with some nations following something like the South Korean example and others the Romanian example.[47] But democracy may have a much better hope of survival and success if it follows successful economic change than if it has to stimulate and manage the change. That must be a discouraging worry for anyone who is committed to the priority of liberty.

Against this claim, former President Alfonsin of Argentina has asserted that 'in Latin America, the strategy of implementing economic reform before political reform has been tried over and over again. It has never succeeded.'[48] Presumably, the economic reform to which he referred was primarily reform towards socialism and, indeed, such reform has not worked in Latin America or perhaps anywhere if it was not preceded by liberal democracy, as in Sweden. The Chilean economic reform to cut the economy relatively free of government control under the autocrat Pinochet apparently did succeed—at the cost of great brutality and increased inequality and poverty—and was followed by relatively open democracy in which Pinochet was defeated in a free election. Similarly, liberalizing economic reforms in Hungary, South Korea, and Taiwan have been followed by democratic reforms and one may reasonably hope for similar successes in other nations.[49]

In the West, discussions of the market often seem to make its efficiency a dogma rather than a carefully demonstrated result. In some contexts, however, it has seemed liberating, as Lisa Peattie was surprised to learn in the newly liberalizing Venezuela, as quoted in the epigraph for this chapter. The sense of liberation that the market brings in such a case may owe as much to the freedom to be an entrepreneur on one's own as to the prospect of greater wealth. It is not so much the efficiency of the market that excites those who suddenly have a market opened to them. What excites them is more akin to the

---

[47] For discussion, see José María Maravall, 'The Myth of the Authoritarian Advantage', *Journal of Democracy*, 5 (Oct. 1994): 17–31; and Thomas Apolte, 'Democracy, Dictatorship, and Transformation: A Proposal for a Constitution-Guided Systematic Change in Formerly Soviet Republics', *Constitutional Political Economy*, 6 (1995): 5–20.

[48] Reported in Jon Elster, 'When Communism Dissolves', *London Review of Books* (25 Jan. 1990): 3–6, at p. 4.

[49] In many nations, such as Myanmar, the urge for democracy, or at least the end of military autocracy, might precede the urge for economic reform of whatever kind.

liberation that comes with political liberalism. But, while we may suppose that the wealth benefits of the market will accrue to almost everyone, no doubt unequally, in the long run, we cannot easily suppose that these 'liberty benefits' will accrue to everyone. The appeal of agricultural reform in much of East Europe was that liberalizing agriculture could be coupled with private entrepreneurial ownership, which is received as a highly desirable liberty benefit. But not everyone can be an entrepreneur in a productively efficient economy that requires a large scale for many tasks. Hence, few will benefit from liberty benefits, while many, even almost all, can benefit from the greater economic productivity that is associated with greater economic liberty.

Political liberalism similarly holds great appeal in actual experience for relatively few. Indeed, not everyone values it as much as Western rhetoric and political philosophy typically seem to suppose. Thomas Paine sometimes seemed to think it the only thing that mattered, but he was one of the oddest people of his or any other time. A. J. Ayer wrote that, although very few people would openly reject Paine's democratic pleas, 'it is only to a very limited extent that they have ever been translated into practice'.[50] Not the least reason for this is that, for many people, intense democratic participation is not of great value. For them, if there is to be an argument for great political liberty, the liberty must have general effects on the general well-being and prospects of people, including themselves. For these people, economic and political liberty are worth having if the entrepreneurs bring prosperity to others as well as to themselves and if the active political participators work generally for benign politics and policies. In some of the Eastern nations, there may be general confidence about the prospects for benign, more or less universally good effects. In others, there cannot be and we may rightly suppose that many groups in these nations could be mobilized for illiberal policies.

Adopting liberal constitutions may not put all of the East European and formerly Soviet nations on the way to liberalism. Liberalism, democracy, and capitalism could grow up together when central control of an economy was beyond the means of government. For the liberal political order, democratic input may be functional. For economic order, it may not be. There may be psychological con-

[50] A. J. Ayer, *Thomas Paine* (New York: Atheneum, 1988; reprinted by University of Chicago Press, 1990), 187.

nections between liberty and affluence, so that eventually a liberal economy will work well only in the setting of political liberalism. But the evidence of the Asian autocratic governments that long presided over booming platform economies and of autocratic China runs counter to any such connection for at least the long years of rapid economic growth.

The difficulties inherent in re-coordinating the Eastern economies are so daunting that one must stand in awe of the achievements to date in many of the these nations. The Czech Republic and maybe Russia, for example, have made regression to general central control an implausible option for any regime in the near future even though the government's share of the economy may still be relatively large. But regression would now be another massive transition that would bring massive losses initially. The public spectacles of such leaders as Yeltsin and Walesa in power are misleading because they are marred by their apparent urge for personal control of what is ostensibly a decentralized, open, non-dirigist system. Yet economic policy in Russia and Poland has moved progressively towards removal of many government controls and the dissolution and privatization of many government-owned firms.

Irreversibility of Liberalization?

A major concern in any society undergoing a transition to liberalism of any variety is whether the change will be irreversible. To some extent, of course, it cannot be causally irreversible, because there can be military coups, major disasters, devastating external wars, and major changes in interests of various groups, all of which could lead to efforts to reverse liberal arrangements. But short of major shocks or disasters, any set of institutions that are reasonably self-enforcing has good prospects of surviving. Crucial issues, then, for many of the societies currently in transition are, first, how likely they are to go far enough with liberalization to make it self-enforcing and, secondly, how likely they are to face shocks severe enough to reverse their liberalizations once they are relatively self-enforcing.

The perhaps idiosyncratic lesson of the American experience is that a very strong coordination on commercial and defence issues can be broken over a moral issue: slavery. This was not unpredictable or entirely unforeseen—Madison had already taken note of the risk at the Philadelphia Convention.[51] Jefferson, who expressed his opposition to slavery many times throughout his life, expressed his worries about the nation somewhat ambiguously in the 1820 letter in which he discussed the Missouri Compromise that extended slavery to new states under the rule of one slave state for every free state. In one of his most widely quoted images, he said 'We have the wolf by the ears, and we can neither hold him, nor safely let him go'.[52] The moral issue was particularly divisive because it had profound economic implications. Slaves were the main wealth of many southerners and slavery enabled a way of life that it was hard—although not impossible—to recast without slaves. The nearest thing to such a conflict in many nations today is ethnic conflict, which, however, it would be difficult to cast as genuinely moral, no matter what the rabid partisans of any ethnic group might claim. It is widely supposed to be visceral, as it often becomes in the face of violent encounters, but it is as grimly economic as the issue of slavery was.

Political Liberalization

In their recent political liberalizations, many nations have virtually gone all the way almost instantaneously. Several have already held second or later national elections that have turned governments out of office and brought new parties to power—all without significant extra-constitutional efforts to overturn or block the electoral choices. This is, in the astonished view of many observers, a major and promising achievement. Apart from some nations with Islamic fundamentalist parties, as in Algeria and some of the peripheral former Soviet Republics and Russia itself if its economic malaise continues, there seems little likelihood of democratic choice to end democracy and its accompanying liberalism. The chief risk, then, would seem likely to be from military or quasi-military putsches or from major social changes that break the coordination on commercial interests.

---

[51] Max Farrand, ed., *The Records of the Federal Convention of 1787*, 4 vols. (New Haven: Yale University Press, 1937, rev. edn.; 1st pub. 1911), i. 486.

[52] Thomas Jefferson, Letter to John Holmes (often entitled 'A fire bell in the night'), 22 Apr. 1820, in Jefferson, *Writings* (New York: Library of America, 1984), 1433–5. From very early, Jefferson held the hope of freeing but re-exporting the slaves, a hope later shared briefly by Abraham Lincoln.

The single most threatening social change in many of the liberalizing or potentially liberalizing nations is ethnic conflict such as has destroyed Yugoslavia and has dominated the early post-Soviet years in Georgia and Azerbaijan. Plausibly the most important contribution Yeltsin has made to the longer-run stability of a liberal regime in Russia was to break the Soviet federation—although he also attempted to hold onto a piece of Russia itself with an ugly war in Chechnya. The peoples of the late Soviet Union may have been fortunate to have had their breakup in a surprisingly peaceful way rather than through a debilitating series of civil wars. Even the relatively small-scale war over Chechnya has been very harmful to Russian progress in liberalization. Larger wars over Ukraine, Kazakhstan, and other republics would have been devastating. The actual breakup was peaceful in part because it served Yeltsin's interests in finessing Gorbachev out of power. Gorbachev's seat of power was at the supranational level and the easiest way to displace him was to eliminate that level. Opportunistic politics in this case played a beneficial role by eliminating what might otherwise have been a wrenching series of ethnic problems. Poland, the Czech Republic, Slovakia, Slovenia, and some other nations in the East similarly face no ethnic crisis.

The three former Soviet republics that seem most naturally attuned to the West and to Western economics are the Baltic states, two of which, however, face serious ethnic conflicts and which may suffer distorted politics that will take precedence over economic commitments. The presence of an ethnic conflict is inherently likely to produce an economic conflict, because the easiest way for one ethnic group to improve its lot in the short run is to harm the lot of another ethnic group. This is the appalling story of Yugoslavia, Burundi, Rwanda, and many other nations, in which any programme of economic liberalism—let alone of political liberalism—is derailed by short-term vicious greed.[53] In principle, it seems likely that the hardest issues to trump in a programme of economic liberalization are specifically economic issues, and ethnic conflict between substantial groups is, almost by the logic of the situation, typically an economic conflict. Here, therefore, economic and political liberalism may die together even if they are not logically tied together.

[53] Hardin, *One for All*, ch. 6.

Economic Liberalization

It is the economic liberalizations that raise more complex issues and that are less secure. Successful conversion to a relatively open economy cannot be established instantaneously and the possibilities of backing off or reversing initial developments are manifest. There have been second elections in Eastern Europe that were fought over complaints against various liberalization policies. Elections in Poland, Bulgaria, and Hungary have turned initial liberalizing governments out of office and brought in parties dominated by former hard-line Communists ostensibly opposed to much of the new economic programme. Yet the successor governments have continued the general programme of economic liberalization.

A strong consideration in support of confidence in continuing economic liberalization is the peculiarly negative argument that, after all, no one has any alternative theory with which to oppose economic liberalism. Every government tweaks bits of its economy; some may even tweak very many bits of their economies. Every government engages in some protectionism, both domestic and international. Every government has regulatory, tax, subvention, or other policies that distort market performance. And governments typically attempt to achieve some distributional welfare through manipulations of the economy rather than through direct transfers. But all of these are sloppy, ad hoc, unsystematic moves. They are politically motivated, not theoretically grounded. Today, no government has any compelling idea of how systematically to run an economy. And the overwhelming lesson of the past decade or two is that politicians can only tar themselves if they reach too far. In seventy-five years, the Soviet-type economies learned repeatedly that solutions to last year's problems tended to create new problems, sometimes worse than the original problems.[54]

If the central shared value in the coordination on economic liberalism is commercial prosperity, then the liberalizing government should be responsive to that order in two very different ways. First, it must dismantle the past, sometimes massive systems for control-

---

[54] There are many detailed accounts. See e.g. Peter J. Boettke, 'Credibility, Commitment, and Soviet Economic Reform', in Edward Lazear, ed., *Realities of Reform* (Stanford, Calif.: Hoover Institution Press, 1995), 247–75. Boettke canvasses Soviet reforms of the 1920s, 1950s, 1960s, and 1980s and compares them to Russian reforms in the 1990s.

ling commerce. Secondly, it must create systems for facilitating commerce. Chief among the needed systems are financial institutions and effective commercial law. The most difficult task in many liberalizing nations may be to erect a competent legal system for handling commercial relations. This is a task that must be undertaken almost *de novo*. Commercial law could be grafted onto extant traditions of law, but it might be more effective to create new courts for it.

If such problems are not resolved, it is conceivable that a liberal economy cannot finally take full root and economic performance might finally drag a government down. Some of the conditions that would help a nation make a successful transition to fairly quick prosperity are more evident in some of the liberalizing nations than in others. For example, as discussed in Chapter 6, workforce growth and changing economic structure that would supply workers to new industries are less available in Russia than in most of the other former Soviet republics, and liberalization may therefore take longer to show its benefits in Russia than in those republics or in Poland. Because the people in these nations can readily enough see the benefits that liberalization is supposed to bring—they know reasonably well how splendid life in the West can be (they may even overrate it)—the greatest risk the liberalizing regimes face may be not succeeding fast enough. Their achievement can be measured by the typical citizen.

Citizens over 50 are likely to see liberalization as not succeeding at all. Many of the younger citizens, especially those who are at the beginnings of careers, already find liberalization successful, at least for themselves.[55] With the passage of time—a decade or two—the losers fade in significance and the mass of those who are beneficiaries of the then-current state of affairs will be the chief guarantor of the continuation of democracy and the market. Both of these liberalisms would then become self-enforcing.

Concluding Remarks

As Jefferson reputedly wrote, 'the public good is best promoted by the exertion of each individual seeking his *own good* in his own

---

[55] *New York Times*, 23 July 1995: i. 1, 12; Anders Aslund, *How Russia Became a Market Economy* (Washington: Brookings Institution, 1995).

way'.[56] President Washington stated his similar view when writing to the governor of Rhode Island to welcome his state belatedly to the Union after that state finally ratified the constitution. Washington wrote, 'we are members of that community upon whose general success depends our particular and individual welfare'.[57] This is not Talcott Parsons's vision as discussed in Chapter 1; it is Smith's, and it is the vision promoted by Madison's constitution and by economic and political liberalism. It is the vision at the core of Chapter 2. It comports with constitutionalism and with democracy. It has not always driven American politics, which have often been petty and crabbed, authoritarian and illiberal, and viciously partisan and anti-democratic.

American politics has also been criticized, as by the Anti-Federalist critics, as something bordering on aristocracy—rule by a special class apart from the normal run of citizens. Until Andrew Jackson, the presidents who followed the aristocratic Jefferson were men from élite families—Madison, James Monroe (an Anti-Federalist aristocrat), and John Quincy Adams. Even today, American national political office holders are far wealthier, more urbane, and more educated than the population they ostensibly represent. Like the delegates to the Philadelphia Convention, they are dominated by lawyers. The Anti-Federalist diatribe that such people are aristocrats is accurate enough for many of them. But many made their own wealth and their own professional lives. In this, they have as much in common with Federalists such as Ben Franklin and Alexander Hamilton as they have with the Anti-Federalists.

What of other nations, especially those that are democratizing at the end of the twentieth century? It seems likely that they too will tend to be governed by wealthy, relatively educated, prominent people if government position cannot be successfully rewarded with large dollops of graft to make politics a prosperous life for the ambitious careerist from the general mass of the populace. American political leaders rose from the democratic mass most commonly in the days of the urban machines when votes and candidates could be openly bought. If there are lasting exceptions to these general trends,

[56] Quoted in Gordon S. Wood, 'Interests and Disinterestedness in the Making of the Constitution', in Richard Beeman, Stephen Botein, and Edward C. Carter II, eds., *Beyond Confederation: Origins of the Constitution and American National Identity* (Chapel Hill, NC: University of North Carolina Press, 1987), 102.
[57] Quoted in Clinton Rossiter, *1787: The Grand Convention* (New York: Macmillan, 1966), 304.

they are likely to be in nations in which democracy rules only in the sense of Parsons's Calvinists, in which a narrowly focused religious caste governs. An almost unstoppable reason for the usual trend is that good politics is like good anything else worth doing. It requires division of labour to develop talents and expertise. The constitutionalist Benjamin Rush may have overstated the case when he wrote as Nestor in 1786 to say that 'Government is a science'. But he was right to say it could not be done well by people who 'spend three years in acquiring a profession which their country immediately afterwards forbids them to follow'.[58]

Vaclav Havel is sometimes seen as the embodiment of the virtues of a civic community in our time. But if he serves his nation well, it will not be because he leads his fellow Czechs onto the path of civic virtue, which, once their nation's liberalism is well established, would be a squandering of too many individuals' talents and energies. It is because he has successfully played the coordinating role of the Czech George Washington. He has been the person who seemed to stand outside party and for unity to everyone—except certain ambitious Slovak leaders. He has coordinated politics to allow the Czechs to reorganize their society on liberal principles that enable individuals to prosper enough to make the society prosper.

Boris Yeltsin and Lech Walesa have had similar roles in Russia and Poland, although they were more ambitious personally and seemingly more imbued with pride in their own abilities to manage everything than were either Washington or Havel. All four got their status in large part from their courageous histories of standing against the powers of the past. For the liberal transitions, it may be better that Havel, Yeltsin, and Walesa stood against illiberalism than that they stood for anything in particular, because that lifted them above party. Parties have come soon enough and have taken over much of the governments of the Czech Republic, Russia, and Poland, as, under Washington, they quickly took over the government of the United States, where, to some extent, the modern political party was invented specifically to gain control of the government.

---

[58] Nestor, in the *Independent Gazetteer* (Philadelphia), 3 June 1786; quoted in Jack N. Rakove, 'The Structure of Politics at the Accession of George Washington', in Richard Beeman, Stephen Botein, and Edward C. Carter II, eds., *Beyond Confederation: Origins of the Constitution and American National Identity* (Chapel Hill, NC: University of North Carolina Press, 1987), 262.

All of these nations have also had their Alexander Hamilton working on financial stability and the enablement of liberal economic activity, as West Germany earlier had its Ludwig Erhard. Beard considered Hamilton the real genius of the American experiment and Rossiter echoed the sentiment.[59] Some consider Vaclav Klaus the real genius of the Czech experiment. Neither of these men has much hope of being fondly remembered in broad public circles, because, unlike their presidents, they made real decisions that affected interests, sometimes painfully. But Hamilton made it possible for Washington to seem to tower over the American success as Klaus may also have made it possible for Havel retrospectively to seem to be the giant of the Czech success, if it happens. Ironically, Hamilton probably depended for his success on his earlier failure to get a constitution that would allow his mercantilist dreams to be fulfilled and on his subsequent inability to push his mercantilist plan for economic development through Congress. Forced to work with more constrained powers, he was forced to be essentially an economic liberal.

Washington's prestige enabled a government of jealous and antagonistic men to collaborate for eight fundamentally important and difficult years to set the US Constitution into institutional forms that then could survive. Many of the American constitutional debaters ridiculed what they called 'parchment' barriers. They were fortunate to have eight years to turn their bit of parchment into flesh, incentives, and even stone. Havel and his government seem plausibly able to do the same for the Czech Republic. Some of the other Eastern leaders—Walesa and perhaps Yeltsin—may have been less fitted for such a task in their nations, because they made their leadership far too personal and autocratic. Yeltsin paid dearly for survival, with his military destruction of Parliament and his demoralizing war against Chechnya. And Walesa reduced himself to such pettiness that there was little chance that he would be able to regain his once impressive stature.

Those who think nations can be pulled together only by the likes of Washington, Nehru, or de Gaulle must wonder about the future of many of the Eastern liberalizations. If, however, the liberal vision is itself compelling, liberal society does not depend on collective leadership but on the mass of individuals who are enabled to act on

---

[59] Charles A. Beard, *An Economic Interpretation of the Constitution of the United States* (New York: Macmillan, 1935), 100–14; Rossiter, *1787*, 307–11.

their own, as Tocqueville eloquently asserted. Indeed, as Tocqueville and Mill supposed, American society did not need especially good leaders—once its government was well started. On this vision, Walesa, Yeltsin, and others must chiefly not get in the way but must only coordinate their societies enough that no major group soon mutinies. It is their nations that will soon provide the ultimate test of liberalism, constitutionalism, and democracy.

6

Constitutional Economic Transition

> A constitution is not intended to embody a particular economic
> theory, whether of paternalism and the organic relation of the
> citizen to the State or of laissez faire.
>
> Justice Holmes, dissent in *Lochner v. New York*

A Neutral Constitution

In his short but sharp dissent in *Lochner v. New York*, Justice Oliver
Wendell Holmes declared that a constitution is neutral on economic
policy.[1] He was wrong in general because some constitutions have
gone a long way towards embodying particular economic theories.
Even for the US Constitution, he was wrong to some extent, because
that constitution did embody a limited degree of *laissez-faire*,
enough to give capitalism at least an advantage over any other economic organization of the society if Adam Smith's theory is roughly
right. What capitalism mainly needed was free markets, and the US
Constitution went a long way towards providing that markets would
not be trammelled by the states acting for narrow interests against
farmers and producers in other states.[2]

Holmes was right descriptively, however, in the sense that the
Constitution of 1787 left it relatively open for various economic theories to prevail. One of three systems of economic organization that

[1] *Lochner v. New York*, 198 U.S. (Oct. term, 1904): 45.
[2] Benjamin Wright observed that debate in Philadelphia was silent on the question
of 'laissez-faire versus collectivism' (Benjamin F. Wright, *Consensus and Continuity,
1776–1787* (Boston: Boston University Press, 1958), 29. There was no debate because
there was no issue. The overwhelming consensus of the conventioneers was that government should not be strong or intrusive. Without strong government, collectivism
is essentially ruled out and capitalism is, as it turned out, given full scope to develop.

were favoured by different groups was plantation agrarianism. Plantation agrarianism was not constitutionally bound to fail as it eventually did. It failed economically on its own in the face of overpowering capitalism. But the framers of the constitution did not intentionally put capitalism into the Constitution. They merely designed an economically almost neutral—at least neutral between plantation agrarianism and capitalism—national government, which was virtually all that capitalism needed. And they arguably did even that without much understanding.

This statement is more or less in terms that the constitutional generation might have used. In actual fact, plantation agriculture is merely one of many industrial and other economic activities. It is therefore fully consistent with capitalism if the plantations are privately owned, as they were. It was only the agrarian ideology of the way society should be ordered that makes plantation agrarianism seem contrary to capitalism. For such an ideology, the central trouble with capitalism is that it allows whole industries to prosper or decline as economic conditions warrant. There is nothing special about any particular industry. All that matters for any industry is how it succeeds or fails in the market. The plantation agrarians believed their order would last indefinitely. The party of commerce was evidently less sure of its future—therefore Hamilton wanted a mercantilist government—but still convinced of the rightness of their views. In the cockiness of their belief in their different views, these two economic groups could collude in designing the constitution, because each group thought that merely ending state-level interference in its markets was enough for its views to prevail.

Was that an unintentionally good choice? In a fundamentally important sense, it was good for the longer-run workability of the Constitution and its government in the face of massive economic transitions over the subsequent centuries. A government too narrowly defined to handle one set of economic conditions can be a disaster when it must handle dramatically different conditions. The problem of the Eastern socialist regimes in the 1980s is that they had been designed essentially to handle the mobilization of backward economies to make them more productive quickly. Indeed, they had been designed to manage the Russian transition to an industrial economy after World War I. When the economies of these nations ceased to benefit from centrally controlled mobilization to do what was already well done elsewhere, their Communist governments were an obstacle to developing in other ways.[3] The mercantilism of the eighteenth century in France, England, and other European nations had similarly been an obstacle to economic development in the early decades of the new industrial age, as the quasi-mercantilism of the individual states was an obstacle to general development in the United States under the Articles of Confederation after the War of Independence.

The fundamentally important issue in the design of constitutions is to *enable rather than hinder economic transitions* that are not well understood in advance. The way to achieve this is essentially negative. It is the lack of an embodied economic theory that might fit badly with dynamic transitions. To enable spontaneous developments in the economy in the lack of a correct economic theory, government must be partially disempowered. Perhaps someday this claim will not hold. It is not a theory or an easy implication of a theory, but only a sceptical reading of the history of government management of economies. There are quasi-theoretical positions that stand behind the claim. For example, Friedrich Hayek and the Austrian School of economics hold that it is in fact impossible for anyone or any institution to know all of the relevant facts for managing an economy, because too many of these are distributed across the population and are inaccessible to the state. Still, it must be open to question whether a state could know enough to run an economy under some circumstances.

In the American constitutional experience, the necessary move was to break the hold of a mix of crude mercantilism and beggar-thy-neighbour competition *at the level of the individual states* and, thereby, to create a large, diverse, and relatively free market. In the current constitutional redesign of the formerly socialist nations of the East, the necessary move is to create relatively free markets where they were previously blocked. In these nations, this has to be accomplished *by demolishing a vast array of national institutions* for controlling production, distribution, and even consumption. Relatively simple coordination on a national regime sufficed for the American states. A far more dramatic transformation is required for the Eastern nations.

---

[3] The Eastern nations that already had well-developed industrial economies—East Germany, Czechoslovakia, and perhaps Hungary and Poland—were economically ill served by the industrializing Soviet model from the beginning.

Holmes supposed that a constitution could be economically neutral so that government might choose economic policy without severe constraint. He was wrong in fact for the US Constitution. Anti-Federalist communitarianism is partially an economic system that was definitively ruled out by the US Constitution. The descendants of the Anti-Federalists should probably be grateful for that fact. Holmes was also arguably wrong in the abstract for two broad classes of economic systems: it is hard to conceive a meaningful constitution that would be completely neutral as between state controlled and non-state controlled economic systems. While, as Holmes remarked, nothing so specific as Herbert Spencer's *Social Statics* was built into the US Constitution, something vaguely approaching the free market was.

At the very least, the constitution enabled capitalism, a system not well understood by the framers of the constitution, and stood in the way of a centralized command economy. It also enabled plantation agrarianism by protecting slavery, although plantation agrarianism could not finally survive the coming economic changes that would make agriculture a minor part of the economy and it was destroyed before that by the Civil War. Indeed, already from his tour of 1831, Alexis de Tocqueville saw that it was doomed to be an ever-decreasing part of the US economy and polity, not least because virtually all new immigrants went to the northern and western states, not to the plantation states.[4] They did so, of course, in part because that is where industry was, but also in part because that is where land for poor farmers was.

Tocqueville's visit came only six years after Jefferson's death and while Madison still lived. In keeping with Madison's sharp quip that he had outlived himself by then, he had also nearly outlived the era in which his constitution allowed for the easy concurrence of plantation and commercial interests on a simple protection of commerce. By the time of Tocqueville's visit, the two were in mortal contest, and plantations were doomed. One might suppose that, but for the defeat of the Civil War, they could have survived into the twentieth century as agri-business concerns. That seems unlikely, because agri-business is genuinely industrial in its reliance on machinery to replace workers. The plantation system, built on slavery, would probably have shared the fate of big steel in the face of technological

[4] Alexis de Tocqueville, *Democracy in America*, 2 vols. (New York: Knopf, 1945; reprinted Vintage, 1990), i. 361–9.

innovation even if the South had successfully seceded and had supported the plantation system indefinitely. Big Steel has had to lay off most of its workforce; the plantations might soon have had to release most of their slaves. In the end, the Confederacy would have been a relatively impoverished neighbour of the booming Union to its north. It would soon enough even have lost some of its agricultural export markets to the lusher, more productive farms of Illinois and Iowa. More generally, it would have shared the fate of most commodity-based economies of going into secular decline.

In standard capitalist economics, a central concern is stability of expectations that will give incentives to investment. Any constitution that can create stable expectations in a context of entrepreneurial freedom especially enables capitalism. There might be an economic system in which stability of expectations would not play a strong constructive role in motivating people to improve their lives, but it is hard to imagine that economies geared to production could function well without relatively stable expectations. Part of the ideology of Communism was the possibility of creating a new socialist human being, who would be motivated by social or moral commitment rather than by incentives of personal gain. Part of the method of slavery in many contexts has been the use of force and terror to motivate. Neither moral commitment nor terror seems likely to induce widespread creativity and innovation, but if either of them or if some other system not dependent on stable expectations and incentives could be made to work, then much of what I will say here might be irrelevant.

In what follows, I will discuss the role of expectations and constitutional stability in economic relations. Then I will turn to the US experience with discussions of the conflicting economic and political visions in the United States in the constitutional era, the Commerce Clause and its object of freeing trade from petty interferences by the states and foreign powers, and the working of the constitutional regime through subsequent general problems of growth and economic transition. Then I will take up the problems of the East with discussions of the contradictory symbolic vision of economic relations in the era of the hammer and sickle, the peculiarly complex problem the Eastern regimes face in combining democratic and economic transitions, and the role that demographic changes have had and could have in economic change. I will conclude with some general comparisons of the American and Eastern experiences and prospects, including elements of luck in the apparent success of their constitutional regimes. In both the American and the Eastern cases, the focus will be on the workings of the constitutional order rather than on the politics of bringing it about (which is discussed for the American case in Chapter 3 and for the Eastern cases in Chapter 5).

Expectations and Constitutional Stability

It is common in the lives of nations that they go through substantial economic transitions. Many nations today are facing merely a grander than usual transition as they attempt to move from central planning to relatively free-market organization. Large economic transitions in general may be the most important challenges for constitutional government. Such a transition might be managed without grievous difficulty by a political regime that is stable. But many of the transitions today are coupled with at least temporarily destabilizing constitutional transitions from autocratic to relatively democratic forms of government. The problems of some of these are complicated further by ethnic conflict.[5]

Stable expectations are conspicuously important in economic contexts, because investment (in capital, skills, reputation) will commonly be higher if, for a given level of average expected benefit from the investment, variance in results is less. If you can double your current wealth or lose it all on the toss of a fair coin, you are likely to prefer not to make the gamble. In social contexts, the gamble is often even worse than this, because the potential losses stagger the potential gains. For example, suppose the peasants of Vietnam can switch from one strain of rice to another to increase their average annual yields of rice—but only at the risk of a greater likelihood of complete failure and starvation in any given year. They might then reasonably opt for the less productive strain.[6] Similarly, a firm that might have its access to a market in a neighbouring state barred from one year to

---

[5] This may commonly be, in large part, a matter of failed economics. See Russell Hardin, *One for All: The Logic of Group Conflict* (Princeton: Princeton University Press, 1995), 56–9, 142–7.

[6] James C. Scott, *The Moral Economy of the Peasant: Rebellion and Subsistence in Southeast Asia* (New Haven: Yale University Press, 1976); Samuel L. Popkin, *The Rational Peasant: The Political Economy of Rural Society in Vietnam* (Berkeley: University of California Press, 1979).

the next may invest less in increasing production for that market. With such truncated expectations, one has far less reason to bank on the future.[7]

Madison argued elegantly for the value of stability in fairly straightforward economic terms. He and Hamilton discussed it many numbers of *The Federalist Papers*.[8] In *Federalist*, 62 Madison noted, first, the perverse implication of instability in government and policy: that it gave incentive to some to calculate their investments to fit the changes to steal advantage from those less calculating rather than to be productive. (This might sound like an odd criticism to the capitalists for whom that is what Wall Street is all about: making money from the foresight 'to steal advantage from those less calculating'.) Then he put the standard case:

The want of confidence in the public councils damps every useful undertaking, the success and profit of which may depend on a continuance of existing arrangements. What prudent merchant will hazard his fortunes in any new branch of commerce when he knows not but that his plans may be rendered unlawful before they can be executed? What farmer or manufacturer will lay himself out for the encouragement given to any particular cultivation or establishment, when he can have no assurance that his preparatory labors and advances will not render him a victim to an inconstant government?[9]

Hobbes supposed that the instability of the state of nature would lead us to produce only what we can consume more or less immediately. Introducing stability of expectations can substantially stimulate future-oriented actions. A working constitutional order that stabilizes expectations is therefore enormously important to economic productivity and welfare. To stabilize expectations over the longer run, such an order must enable economic developments—or at least not block them.

The long-run success of the US Constitution arguably came from its fit with the developing economy. The object of the Commerce

---

[7] Such problems might be overcome. For example, if the government could convincingly guarantee to provide minimal levels of rice even in the worst years, it could, at very low average annual cost, stimulate a substantial increase in rice production. That increase could be taxed enough to pay for the occasional rice distributions, thereby making everyone better off.

[8] A quarter of the contributions to *The Federalist Papers* address order or stability. For example, Madison takes up stability in numbers 19, 37, 49, 51, 62, and 63; and Hamilton in numbers 21, 25, 30, 71, 72, 73, 76, and 77.

[9] *Federalist*, 62, penultimate paragraph.

Clause, while important to the original thirteen states and the reason for the constitutional convention of 1787, is central to the possibility of large-scale economic organization without government control.[10] It is almost the doctrine of *laissez-faire* defanged and made operational rather than ideological, at least for the domestic economy. The proponents of the Constitution and its Commerce Clause wanted uniform national tariffs to make their then-current relations work better, especially in the context of Great Britain's divide-and-conquer trade policies with the states. Perhaps there were thinkers who had the foresight to imagine what prodigious economic changes were in store during the century after adoption of the constitution, but it seems likely that no one argued for the Commerce Clause and national government on the claim that these would enable revolutionary changes in the world the constitutional generation knew. Madison, Jefferson, and no doubt many others expected the economy to remain agrarian more or less forever. That what they designed worked through the eventual revolution of the economy was largely a matter of chance rather than of intentional design.

Incidentally, stable expectations are also of central importance in political liberalism. The obverse of stable expectations in political rule is arbitrariness. One of the strongest passages in the entire *Federalist Papers* is the passage in *Federalist*, 47 in which Madison quotes Montesquieu on the claim that arbitrary exercise of power is the core of tyranny. For Montesquieu, the point of separation of powers between the legislative, executive, and judicial branches is to reduce the odds of the arbitrariness that might follow from having any one of the branches fully in control.[11] The argument is essentially the claim that requiring multiple branches to act to deprive one of liberty adds to one's security through regression towards the mean. It is far less likely that two or three branches will coordinate

[10] See various documents in Philip Kurland and Ralph Lerner, eds., *The Founders' Constitution*, 5 vols. (Chicago: University of Chicago Press, 1987), ii. 477–528. In 1785, Madison argued especially strenuously that the national government must be made able to accomplish the ends of the eventual Commerce Clause, *if necessary by replacing it with a different government* (ibid., 481). A convention was called at Annapolis to address the issue, but too few states sent delegates, and that convention called the Philadelphia Convention that produced the Constitution. Pennsylvania had unilaterally adopted a policy of *de facto* free trade with the other states before the Philadelphia Convention (see Tench Coxe to Virginia Commissioners, 13 Sept. 1786, in ibid. 3: 473–4).

[11] Charles de Secondat, baron de Montesquieu, *The Spirit of the Laws* (Cambridge: Cambridge University Press, 1989; 1st pub. 1748), book 11, ch. 6: 157.

in an arbitrary suppression of someone's liberties than that a unified single branch will be arbitrary.

Economic and Political Visions in the Early United States

There were three visions in contest for the future of the United States during the constitutional era. These were defining visions about the nature of the society that would follow the creation of a national government. They were the plantation agrarian vision of Thomas Jefferson, the commercial vision of Alexander Hamilton, and the communitarian vision of the rural Anti-Federalists. The last of these played a central role in the ratification debates in many states, especially in New York. But it was effectively crushed by the creation of a relatively strong national government and was therefore of little political significance once the Constitution of 1787 was ratified. I will therefore not discuss it here—its role was taken up in Chapter 3, which covered the origin of the Constitution through its ratification.

There were many things that Jefferson and Hamilton each wanted, but it makes sense to restrict the labels that their names provide to central parts of their views. Each had implicit theories of how society might work once it was properly governed, but these theories need not be included in their visions. For example, Jefferson seemed to think it possible that the world could and would continue to be organized by agrarian concerns to the end of civilization. In a letter to Madison he wrote, 'I think our governments will remain virtuous for many centuries; as long as they are chiefly agricultural; and this will be as long as there shall be vacant lands in any part of America'.[12] (There has been little vacant arable land since early this century. Some of the remaining vacant lands today harbour the lunatics of various militia groups.) Hamilton generally believed that commercial progress depended on massive state action on behalf of business, on mercantilist guidance of the economy. The central, defining parts of their visions were their different views about the nature of the economy that would prosper.

---

[12] Jefferson to Madison, 20 Dec. 1787, in Kurland and Lerner, *The Founders' Constitution*, i. 677.

There was another vision that was more nearly structural and not substantive: the national vision of James Madison. This was an impressionist's vision of a unified nation that could respond to the world it faced. In essence, this vision carried the Philadelphia Convention that designed the Constitution, which then became Holmes's neutral arbiter between the economic visions of Jefferson and Hamilton while it wrecked the hopes of the Anti-Federalist vision of small communities and independent farmers in full control of their lives and their destinies.

Conceptually, the striking thing about the Constitution that Jefferson, Hamilton, and Madison all supported in the end is that it could have accommodated either Hamilton's or Jefferson's vision—and in this it clearly fulfilled Madison's vision. Factually, the most striking thing about the Constitution is that in some compelling sense it worked. In particular, it worked to get the new nation started. In the explanation of a successful constitutional regime there are two quite separate issues: (1) successful establishment of the constitution over roughly its first generation and (2) its success in guiding and constraining government in the longer run of many generations. In this era of numerous constitutional transitions, the more urgent of these two issues is the first. Most constitutions have largely or utterly failed over the few decades immediately after their adoption.

What makes a new constitution successful enough in the short run to be successful in the long run? In essence, the trick is in coordination. Adoption of a successful constitution is typically itself a matter of coordination, often spontaneous coordination (as discussed in Chapter 3). But longer-run success depends on the subsequent institutional coordination of a polity on stable expectations, perhaps especially economic expectations.

How can a constitution have accommodated two such opposing economic visions as those of Hamilton and Jefferson? Largely, it did so because the Jeffersonian plantation agrarian society and the Hamiltonian urban commercial society both required national organization of their markets and because the Constitution did not attempt to control general economic developments beyond establishing national markets. Since theories of economic developments have generally been poor and even perverse, the saving grace of the Constitution is not to have enshrined any such theory. Jefferson's vision eventually *failed* because his theory was wrong: agrarian dominance would not be perpetual. Hamilton's eventually *succeeded* because his theory was wrong: business thrives on its own without need of government direction.

Tocqueville presciently claimed that the strength of the American government was to a large extent the result of its democratic *incapacity* to run the nation and the economy as coherently and effectively as a monarchical or autocratic government might run it.[13] This is one of the sharpest insights in all of the commentary, then and now, on America's political and economic success, but it was not only democracy that produced this result. Madison's constitution was a more or less neutral referee in the economic transitions that followed the Constitution. Because of the general lack of understanding of economic futures, of what the future alignment of interests and their weights would be, the neutral constitution was relatively easily agreed to. Moreover, it was likely to be more stable than a more definite one would have been. Adam Przeworski has observed that 'Institutions adopted when the relation of forces is unknown or unclear are most likely to last across a variety of conditions'.[14] We should qualify this observation to say that a constitution is more likely to last if it does not embody a misfit economic theory. It may be less likely to embody any theory if the relation of forces is not well understood. Hence, the direct correlation between unclarity of economic theory and longevity of institutions, if there is one, may be spurious.[15]

After twelve years of tentative government, Jefferson and the Jeffersonians came to power in the United States under the still new constitution. At the time, this must have seemed to be the success of a Cincinnatus who could guarantee the stability of the agrarian party. From our retrospective vision, this would have been—at least economically—a disaster. In the long run of a century or so, business was sure to become the dominant force and Jefferson's farmers were bound almost to disappear, although no one need have understood this trend during Jefferson's lifetime. The remarkable fact then is that Jeffersonism controlled the early government, perhaps down

[13] Tocqueville, *Democracy in America*, i. 251–2.
[14] Adam Przeworski, *Democracy and the Market: Political and Economic Reforms in Eastern Europe and Latin America* (Cambridge: Cambridge University Press, 1991), 88.
[15] The belief that Islam embodies an economic theory runs counter to this possibility, and perhaps there is no good reason to expect it to be true in other contexts either.

through the presidency of Martin Van Buren (1837–41), while business interests have seemingly controlled much of the policy of American government in this century. C. E. Lindblom argues that the interests of business are now so much in tune with what government must want that business need not even overtly exert itself.[16] The transformation of the economy from an agrarian society to an industrial society was wrenching, although the twists in people's lives were spread out over generations and often appeared to be individual rather than group or national and, therefore, personal rather than political.

Hamilton and the Hamiltonians gained the dominant position in the government very briefly under President John Adams and they shared control with agrarian interests under the less clearly defined presidency of George Washington. Because the Jeffersonians held the middle, they were the swing group between Anti-Federalists and Hamiltonians. It is therefore hard to imagine Hamilton's Federalist Party could have held sway for a generation or more as Jefferson's Republican Party did. Still, we might ask, would a more equal contest between Republicans and Federalists for hegemony have meant a less stable constitutional regime? This question should be answered in two parts: for the near term and for the longer term.

For the near term, the US constitutional order may have come to work in part because one party gained hegemony for several decades. It might not have mattered very much whether the Hamiltonians or the Jeffersonians gained such hegemony. But it might have mattered whether *neither* had gained it, whether there had been consequential fighting and better definition of the partly latent conflicts. Then each party in office might have put great energy into pre-empting the other party to secure its own vision through any interregnum. In particular, the two opposing groups might have tried to impose their wrong economic theories on the government, making it less able to handle the economic transitions that violated both theories. John Adams's midnight appointments to federal offices as he and the Federalists left office in 1801 is merely a hint of what might have happened with real competition thereafter. The instability of expectations in the United Kingdom wrought by several post-war reversals between socialization and privatization of various industries is more indicative of the harm that an early ideological fight between

[16] C. E. Lindblom, *Politics and Markets* (New York: Basic Books, 1977).

Jeffersonians and Hamiltonians might have caused. In the United Kingdom, each side thought its vision was correct and the other's wrong. But both should retrospectively have agreed that frequent reconsideration was worse than stability under either regime.

Perhaps just because Jefferson and the agrarians were so comfortably in office, they might not have been concerned to attempt to secure their interests for the longer run. Because they were continuously in power, except for the ambiguous interregnum of John Quincy Adams (1825–9), the Jeffersonians could be confident of their own leadership and could forego trying to put institutional obstacles in the way of any non-agrarian vision. Early American Democracy may therefore have benefited from the relative lack of competition.

For the longer term it may have mattered substantially whether Hamilton or Jefferson prevailed. The constitution did not *proscribe* national involvement in the economy but only blocked certain kinds of involvement by the states. When Hamilton's mercantilist policies were blocked, it was because plantation and farming interests were hostile. Hamilton suffered a legislative, not a constitutional defeat. In part this was perhaps because political sides were being drawn up, so that everything Hamilton stood for provoked opposition from Jefferson and Madison.

For whatever reason it failed, the failure of government to attempt management of the economy set in place institutions coordinated against such management. Thereafter, to overcome their coordination required a massive external shock of some kind—eventually World War I temporarily (as though it were an experiment in what might be possible), but then the Depression and World War II. Hence, the failure of Hamilton's designs for central management of the economy may have been fundamentally important in keeping the government from getting in the way of later economic developments. *Hamilton's failure essentially strengthened* laissez-faire *as the default rule of the US government*. It may have been a matter of great good luck for the longer term that the Jeffersonians reacted against the years of Hamilton's mercantilist policies. That failure was forced by agrarian interests that in a few generations would be wanting federal intervention on their behalf.

Let us go back to the short term of the Jeffersonian hegemony of about four decades. Why can stability lead to stability? Other things equal, stability over a long period reduces *expected* variance, which leads to greater investment in future returns, which leads to enhanced future production, which confirms and reinforces positive expectations. Stability of a constitutional order becomes self-confirming as the order endures. Of course, other things need not always be equal, and there might be external or internal shocks that upset the trend of expectations. For example, by about 1850, the US constitutional order began to be undermined by the prevalence of Hamilton's vision over Jefferson's. Industrial production in the growing cities of the north-east and farm production without slavery in the new western states tipped the political balance away from what was previously the relatively even balance of slave and non-slave states.

The success of Hamilton's vision might have undermined the order even more than it did, but that vision needed no party to lead it to triumph. Under relatively weak government, it would succeed on its own. Business as such has received little advantage from any party, although individuals and individual firms have often got enormous advantages, sometimes through graft and special favour, sometimes through more general policies. At the extremes in the late nineteenth century, the 1920s, and the 1980s, these advantages have been sweeping, especially in making large numbers of people rich and inadvertently strengthening a bit of the Hamiltonian vision by severely undercutting subsequent government capacity.

The Commerce Clause

The Commerce Clause—assigning the federal government power to regulate interstate and foreign commerce—has been seen through many lenses to do many different, sometimes contrary things. It reputedly empowered the federal government, disempowered it, and did little or nothing. Perhaps, with the proper nuances, all these claims are true. This is the Clause in its simplicity: 'The Congress shall have Power . . . To regulate Commerce with foreign Nations, and among the several States, and with the Indian Tribes'.[17] It sounds like an empowerment. But in its time, the Commerce Clause bothered the Anti-Federalists primarily because it took power from the

[17] US Constitution, Art. 3, sect. 8.

states and gave it to the national government and to economic interests other than themselves, not because it created government power at all. As exercised by the states, that power had been destructive. States attempted to generate their public revenues from taxation on trade from other states and from tariffs. For the Federalists, the focus of the Clause—commerce—was the driving issue. For the Anti-Federalists, the objectionable issue was lodging control in a national, as opposed to local, government. The two concerns were logically inseparable. One group had to lose its issue if the other won its issue.

The Commerce Clause implies that the Federal government has the power of taxation on commerce. But it also implies the end of selective taxation on domestic commerce that happens to cross state boundaries, leaving only general excise taxes and taxation on foreign trade. Even for the latter, the government can only tax particular categories of imports uniformly, so that it cannot differentially affect competing business incentives in two or more states. For commercial interests, the constitution turned the United States into a single market.

There had been extensive prior agitation for measures to improve economic prospects by equalizing tariffs, harmonizing currencies, and developing joint waterways. Many documents leading up to the Philadelphia Convention articulate concern with the disruptive trade practices of the states under the Articles of Confederation.[18] Even a stalwart Anti-Federalist delegate to the Philadelphia Convention, Roger Sherman of Connecticut, asserted that regulating trade was one of the few principal objects of the convention—along with defence against foreign attack, prevention of the use of force among the states, and making international treaties.[19] Even more singular than the claims for the need for national regulation of the market, however, is the strongest objection to the Convention's purpose. As noted earlier, Rhode Island refused to send delegates and two of New York's three delegates withdrew from the Convention early in the proceedings. Madison attributed the obstinacy of New York and Rhode Island to their opposition to the object of the Commerce Clause. Under the Articles of Confederation, these two states benefited from the beggar-thy-neighbour uses of their ports to extract

[18] See several documents in Kurland and Lerner, *Founders' Constitution*, iii. 477–83.
[19] Max Farrand, *The Records of the Federal Convention of 1787*, 4 vols. (New Haven: Yale University Press, 1937, rev. edn.; 1st edn. 1911) iii. 133.

wealth from neighbouring states, especially Massachusetts and New Jersey.[20] Supporters and opponents alike knew the object of the convention: to end such disruptive practices.

In many respects, the Commerce Clause can be seen as reducing overall government power over the economy. Instead, at the time, it was criticized as an overreaching of federal power. But this response was an artefact of the nature of the debate, which was whether powers of the states should be transferred to the federal government. The Clause was, after all, *an imposition on the states, not on economic enterprises*. Indeed, it may have reduced overall government power in principle and it did reduce overall impositions on business and trade in actual practice. It made the states considerably weaker without making the federal government very strong.[21] Because the exercising of state power was economically disruptive in the years before the Constitution, eliminating it with the Commerce Clause would serve business more than it would serve the federal government. When he wanted to vest such power in the Congress under the Articles of Confederation, even the ultimate Hamiltonian described it as public power to do good things. Against those who argued that trade would take care of itself, he should have argued that it would— but only if the states were stopped from interfering with it. Instead, he argued that, to prosper, trade needs the regulating hand of government.[22] He was wrong. It was only the states that needed the uniformly regulating hand of national government if trade was to prosper.

The misguided nature of some of the US constitutional debate is relived today when many nations of Europe object to giving up power to the European Community. In its chief respect, this is not what those nations are doing. Rather, they are reducing overall government power over their economies. The European Community has weaker economic powers than the member nations have given up. *The chief transfer of power is from politicians at any level to business and its customers.* It may happen that, as the Community

---

[20] Madison's discussion of New York in a letter of 26 December 1826 to Thomas Cooper, in Farrand, *Records of the Federal Convention*, iii. 474; Madison's discussion of Rhode Island in his draft preface to his notes on the convention debates (1st pub. 1840) in ibid. iii. 539–51, at pp. 546–7. Also see Madison's *Federalist*, 42.

[21] It did, however, set up the possibility of later accretions of power, such as those of the Civil War, the two world wars, the Cold War, and the welfare state.

[22] Alexander Hamilton, 'Continentalist, no. 5' (1782), in Kurland and Lerner, *Founders' Constitution*, ii. 477–9.

develops and as its court interprets its powers, the Community will take on far greater powers, as the US government and many others have done over time. But initially, its effect is to reduce government power over commerce.

The Commerce Clause sounds nearly vacuous today. It does not say that states do not have power to regulate commerce, merely that the federal government does. One might suppose it virtually a logical inference to conclude that the states have no such power, because the federal government can clearly override their actions. But they do seem to have that power until the federal government overrides them. The federal government has trumping power but it does not have the only power. Part of the reason the clause sounds so vacuous today is that its point was so well understood that no one needed to state it more fully. The reason for calling the Constitutional Convention in Philadelphia was to establish national power over commerce, both foreign commerce and commerce between the states. Even the control over foreign commerce was, *de facto*, an issue of interstate trade. It was an urgent issue because most of the states favoured a uniform tariff policy but, under the single-state veto of the Articles of Confederation, they could not adopt such a policy. Hence, states that were hard on imports from Great Britain (such as Massachusetts) simply lost British commerce to some other state (such as Rhode Island), which might then transship British goods to the first state.[23]

There could not have been significant misunderstanding of the import of the Commerce Clause among those who knew the Continental Congress, the Philadelphia Convention, or the later state ratifying conventions. *This is not a normative argument from original intent to rightness*—it is merely an explanatory argument about how the Clause came to be and how it was actually understood at the time. What mattered for the initial success of the Constitution was whether it coordinated positive expectations. In the matter of the Commerce Clause, expectations were already coordinated, and the Constitution principally played the role of setting up institutions that could fulfil those expectations. Hence, it was not the actual operation of the Commerce Clause, as in later court decisions, that mattered but merely the institutional fact of the elimination of state

[23] Again, Madison attributed Rhode Island's obstinate refusal to take part in the Philadelphia Convention to its wish to continue this practice (Farrand, *Records of the Federal Convention*, iii. 546–7).

power to impose interstate tariffs and putting the power over tariffs on foreign trade in national as opposed to state hands.

The central point of the Commerce Clause, the Constitutional Convention, and the larger Constitution itself was to stop the states from exercising the commerce powers that were assigned to the federal government by the Constitution. This was so thoroughly taken for granted that it was not even explicitly written. In part, this seeming oversight follows from the haughty view the Constitution has towards the prior government under the Articles of Confederation—it largely ignores that government as though the nation were being created *de novo* by its future citizens.

There is a thesis in American constitutional history that national arrogation of commerce powers was accomplished by the Court in a series of cases that gave increasing power to the federal government. In this view, the Commerce Clause is held originally to have been a barrier to federal power. It is reputedly the 'dormant powers' of the Commerce Clause that were slowly awakened by Court action.[24] But the doctrine of these 'dormant powers' is a later embellishment that was used as justification of the Court's rulings, not explanation of them.

An alternative reading of these cases is that they made more clearly explicit what was the broad understanding of what the government could do. Part of that understanding probably was that the federal government was not to exercise capricious power over commerce as the individual states had done. The immediate force of the Clause was, after all, to end state power over tariffs on trade between the states. Again it is a mistake to see this as arrogation of power to the federal government. It reduced overall government power. Essentially, the federal government was to be relatively *laissez-faire*. Specific empowerment of that government to be proactive in the economy, as the mercantilist Hamilton wanted it to be, was deliberately denied at the Constitutional Convention, although (as discussed above) Hamilton tried to introduce it administratively and legislatively.

[24] For brief discussion, see William Eskridge and John Ferejohn, 'The Elastic Commerce Clause: A Political Theory of American Federalism', *Vanderbilt Law Review* 47 (1994): 1355–1400. They cite case-book treatments of Gerald Gunther, *Constitutional Law* (Westbury, NY: Foundation Press, 1991, 12th edn.), chs. 2–5; Daniel A. Farber, William N. Eskridge, and Philip P. Frickey, *Cases and Materials on Constitutional Law: Themes for the Constitution's Third Century* (St Paul, Minn.: West Publishing Co., 1993), ch. 7; and Geoffrey Stone, *Constitutional Law* (Boston: Little, Brown, 1991, 2nd edn.), chs. 3–4.

The later 'dormant powers' were primarily directed, as the Commerce Clause was originally, at state interventions to control interstate commerce, but through devices other than tariffs. This issue is still very much alive today in such areas as environmental legislation at the state level when, for example, California requires tougher standards on pollution control than other states do. Often, the tricky issue for the courts is to determine whether such regulations are really devices to impede interstate commerce. In these days of large national corporations with firms in many states, the issue is perhaps much less acute than it was in the early days of Commerce Clause jurisprudence.

Hence, the view that the Constitution limited the national government is not ungrounded. But its limits on that government are clearly not stated in the Commerce Clause. As is true of much of the US or any other Constitution, much of the import of the Clause is unwritten. The ostensibly written US Constitution is only different in degree from the ostensibly unwritten British constitution. What later came to be called the dormant powers of the Commerce Clause and the general doctrine of *laissez-faire* were both well understood and plausibly both taken for granted by the constitutional generation. It is in this limited sense that, as Samuel Beer says, capitalism was there in the Constitution.[25]

If a constitution is essentially a start-up measure rather than a compelling guide for evermore, it follows that well-understood interpretations of its meaning need not be written into it in order for it to work to establish an initial order. If initial understandings change, a partially unwritten constitution may lose its clarity over time. But, in any case, it may also cease to be an important guide to expectations, which may be increasingly grounded in extant institutions and arrangements. Many of these latter may have been given their initial form by the constitution, but they may evolve a long way away from their initial form.[26]

In guiding our own decisions, it is likely to be more important to most of us to look to the extant institutions than to their presumed genesis. It would then be true to say that the original constitutional

[25] Oral comments at the second Murphy Institute Conference on Constitutionalism, Tulane University, New Orleans, 11–12 Mar. 1995.
[26] Also see Stephen M. Griffin, 'The Problem of Constitutional Change in the United States', presented at the conference 'Constitutions and Constitutionalism', Murphy Institute, Tulane University, New Orleans, 11–12 Mar. 1995.

arrangements affect us forever after, but this is a trivial point. For example, the resolution of the small-versus-large-states conflict was, in part, to give states equal representation in the Senate. That this was not an important part of the resolution is suggested by the fact that the Senate was relatively unimportant during the first generation of its life. If the small-versus-large-states conflict had been urgent, the Senate would surely have assumed an important role at once. Instead, it was not even an attractive venue for a political career, and major contenders for national leadership mainly came from the House of Representatives instead of the Senate. The Senate rose to importance as the result of dramatic leadership efforts towards the end of the Virginia hegemony over the presidency.[27] For example, Henry Clay rose to prominence in the House of Representatives. But when, after holding national office, he later returned to Congress, he chose the newly important Senate as his home.

That the Senate exists is now an important fact of American political life. Indeed, if it had not been included in the constitutional arrangements, no one now living in the United States might have been born and the American citizenry would comprise completely different people. Both these facts are of little interest for constitutionalism. What would be important for constitutionalism would be the success of the later Senate in managing the conflicts that lay behind the constitutional debates, if these conflicts continued, or, alternatively, the success of the Constitution in getting the nation out of the small-versus-large-states conflict altogether. On the latter score, the creation of the Senate under the Constitution was important in making the document work as a start-up device, although it was not otherwise important in resolving the large-versus-small-states conflict, which simply vanished once there was national government to block military conflict between large and small states. Indeed, the issue vanished even earlier—it was not a major issue in the ratification debates. The important fact for the resolution of the once potential conflict is not how the Senate has worked to defuse the conflict (it has not done so), but in the way *the existence of a genuinely national government has made it no longer an issue at all*. Just as with the interest in making trade policy uniform, the issue of

[27] Elaine Swift, 'The Making of an American House of Lords: The U.S. Senate in the Constitutional Convention of 1787', *Studies in American Political Development* (1993) 7: 177–224, and *The Making of an American Senate: Reconstitutive Change in Congress 1787–1841* (Ann Arbor: University of Michigan Press, 1996).

peaceful cooperation between the states was a matter of consensual coordination by almost all.

The original consensus on *laissez-faire* was not as broad as that on stopping states from intruding into commerce. As implied above, Hamilton did not want *laissez-faire*—he wanted an economically activist national government that would invest in harbours and waterways and that would help in financing and managing business expansion. In *Federalist*, 85 he claimed that the anti-mercantilist views of 'a very ingenious and sensible writer'—presumably Adam Smith—had been exaggerated. Part of the great appeal of *laissez-faire* to many people, including the plantation agrarians, was that it would force business to succeed on its own without subsidy from agrarian interests. They did not want government to favour business. The Madisonian constitution was a compromise seemingly more to the advantage of the agrarians than of commercial interests. It gave the plantation agrarians almost all they could expect from national government. What it fatally did not give them was protection against their eventual economic decline, protection that they might have wanted if they had foreseen the decline. And it gave commercial interests a national market through limits on capricious state governments but not the activist, pro-business government that Hamilton at least wanted.

Oddly, both groups seem to have misread the future in which commercial interests needed little more than *laissez-faire* to enable them to dominate the nation. What the unwritten rule of *laissez-faire* did for commerce was to enable it to lead the grand economic transition from a rural agrarian to an urban industrial economy and polity. That transition might have been harder had the declining but still dominant agricultural interests been able to use greater constitutional powers over the economy to block or slow the transition. Farmers were disempowered in large part because the élitist Jeffersonian agrarians had pre-emptively and perhaps unwittingly disempowered every group in favour of relatively unconstrained individual initiative.

Economic Growth, Economic Transition

The Commerce Clause was of immediate value to both the plantation agrarians and the commercial interests, and therefore they could coordinate in creating the Constitution. While they were united in creating a national government that benefited both southern plantations and northern traders and financiers, they had dramatically different philosophical visions of the ideal future of the new nation. Hamilton foresaw cities and banks, although his vision was still tainted with the mercantilism that Smith had only recently reviled. Jefferson foresaw farms, although his vision from the crest of his little mountain of Monticello distorted these into plantations. Each group must fully enough have understood the vision of the other. Their difference was one of values and tastes, openly acknowledged.

Of course, both groups thought their own visions superior in complex causal ways as well. For example, the agrarians believed that government should be republican and that only farmers could be civic republicans,[28] and the Hamiltonians believed government should make things work well for business. However, their debate never ascended to the heights of the debate over the communitarianism of the Anti-Federalists, perhaps because no immediate choices of significance turned on the difference of views. As time passed, the agrarian vision was sorely tarnished by its seeming association with plantations, which were grounded on slavery.[29] The difference between slave and non-slave states, which was causally correlated with the difference between plantation agrarianism and urban commercialism, was itself a recognized potential conflict, as noted by Madison during the Convention.[30] But, although it inspired real debate at the convention and may have lain behind some southern doubts about the new Constitution, the slavery difference remained a minor issue to be managed by temporizing compromise. After all, the slave states needed open domestic and international commerce—they could not consume their own produce and prosper. The Jeffersonian agrarian vision was shattered by the Civil War and was then remade in the image of western subsistence farmers. Its career

[28] Madison was seemingly anti-republican in his compelling arguments in *The Federalist Papers* against the communitarian Anti-Federalists that small communities would tend to tyranny. But, by 1792 when politics against Hamilton may have made his view change opportunistically, he seemed to be republican himself. See his 'Republican Distribution of Citizens', 5 Mar. 1792, in Kurland and Lerner, *The Founders' Constitution*, i. 680–1. See discussion in Chapter 3, section on 'Anti-Federalists versus Federalists'.

[29] Some of the debate is represented in Anne Norton, *Alternative Americas: A Reading of Antebellum Political Culture* (Chicago: University of Chicago Press, 1986).

[30] Farrand, *Records of the Federal Convention*, i. 486.

fell rapidly thereafter and it has finally been reduced to the trivializing dogma of the benefits of the family-owned farm in our time, Cincinnatus having long since died.

Oddly, neither the Hamiltonians nor the Jeffersonians may have understood the causal nature of their eventual conflict, which would turn mortal. Both seemingly thought it a matter of choice which way the nation went. It was not simply a matter of choice. Commerce was sure to crush the agrarians economically if the agrarians did not first defeat commercial interests politically—that might not have been possible although it has been done in other nations. In the constitutional period there may have been no one who grasped the accelerating trend out of agriculture and into the larger economy.[31] In the constitutional period, commerce and agriculture had potential conflicts, but these were not significantly different in kind from the conflicts between certain industries or between certain agricultural interests. For example, they had the usual conflict over who should bear the brunt of the tariffs that funded the government.

The fundamental change that the United States faced was astonishing growth in wealth and consumption. There was, of course, no need for radically greater consumption of foodstuffs after 1788. Hence, the growth came from greater productivity of labour, which meant that labour could be moved off the land and into other forms of production. This trend would be the ruin of agrarian visions. Yet, the larger agrarians, especially the plantation owners, needed what the urban commercial interests needed—they needed easy, stable access to domestic and foreign markets as defined by the Commerce Clause.

Since the agrarian vision, for all its appeal, had any chance only in plantation society, Jefferson's generation of agrarians held views that could not remain tenable together in the longer run. Jeffersonian views were simultaneously conservative and romantic. They were conservative in supposing that the agrarian life could be maintained. And they were romantic in supposing that such life would be good and beautiful. Jefferson's agrarian views were inherently élitist and they conflicted oddly with his egalitarianism. He was an anomaly in American thought, an economic conservative and a political radical,

---

[31] Madison foresaw at least a change in the distribution of the population towards the commercial and the manufacturing classes by inference from some European experiences. Farrand, *Records of the Federal Convention*, ii. 124.

and perhaps therefore he has been a plausible hero to people with oddly diverse interests.

The grand estates of Jefferson and his plantation colleagues did not represent the conditions of the agrarian life for most farmers and farm workers in Jefferson's time. Most farmers struggled to achieve subsistence; they did not enjoy the cultured leisure of Jefferson and his library at Monticello. Most of these subsistence farmers had nothing to gain from the Commerce Clause in their daily lives—if they benefited from the Clause, it was through the longer-run reformation of the economy and its opportunities. But this was a benefit that many of them—perhaps almost all of them—would have opposed, because it was a benefit that came via the destruction of their way of life. Most farmers in Jefferson's America were like many workers in the failing industries and farms of the East European and former Soviet nations. Given a chance to veto the changes brought about by the industrial revolution and the Commerce Clause, they might have done so. Their veto would have had huge intergenerational effects because it could have worked only by trapping the next generations in subsistence farming.

The Philadelphia Convention focused on the conflict between large and small states. The nation and its press during the ratification debate and many constitutional scholars since then focused on the Federalist versus Anti-Federalist conflict. *But the inescapable and overriding conflict was that represented by Hamilton and Jefferson*, two eminences who were largely missing from the Constitutional Convention. In this conflict, Jefferson seemingly triumphed. Hamilton went to an ignominious early death in his duel with Aaron Burr while Jefferson created the party that held hegemony over US politics until it was broken by the slavery issue in the 1850s. But, by the time he died on 4 July 1826, the fiftieth anniversary of the Declaration of Independence, Jefferson might have been able to read from the changing facts of the nation and its demography that his agrarians were doomed. They were doomed by the eventually crossing trend lines of relatively decreasing employment in agriculture and increasing employment everywhere else.

Jefferson was an agrarian living off the surplus production of his plantation. Such agrarians can be mistaken for communitarians. Some of the prosperous farmers of upstate New York, New England, and Pennsylvania genuinely were communitarians. But Jefferson the plantation agrarian was not communitarian. With many communitarians, the Jeffersonian agrarians shared a belief in the political goodness of a society organized at the level of the local community. Such a society could support the open debate and extensive participation of civic republicanism.

In actual fact, the Jeffersonians were probably wrong about what such a society would be like. Aristotle argued that, for democracy, an agrarian society would be best, because its citizens, busy with their farms, *would be too busy to participate extensively in politics*. He said, indeed, that working is more pleasant to farmers than politics unless there are great spoils to be had from politics.[32] Aristotle's claim that an agrarian society makes the best democracy is sometimes taken out of context to suggest that something like the agrarian vision of the American Anti-Federalist communitarians is what is needed for republican democracy. The Jeffersonians were, as usual, thinking not of a farming society but of Monticello and plantation society, with the leisure it provided the head of the plantation. Aristotle would have thought such a society to be less good for democracy. The only way to construct a republican society under anything like modern economic conditions would most probably require the élitist structure of plantation society, although presumably it would not require full slavery.

In their desire for a national economy that would let them prosper despite specializing in agricultural production, the Jeffersonians differed from the communitarian Anti-Federalists. Many of the southern plantation owners may have preferred small-society government all other things equal, but they could not have lived well with it unless they secured open trade with other societies. Nothing short of a national constitution with a commerce clause could fit their interests, which were for open economic arrangements and security from military attack. Between their interests and their vague ideals of civic republicanism, they went with their interests.[33]

Suppose government had been more important in people's lives than it was two centuries ago in the United States. Perhaps we could imagine what participation and life might have been like for large numbers of people, who would have become active as Jefferson,

[32] Aristotle, *Politics*, VI.4.1318^b6–17; see also *Politics*, IV.6.1292^b25–34, IV.4.1291^b30–8.

[33] North Carolina balked until its choice was complete independence or full submission to the Constitution. With the romanticism of myriad possibilities from which to choose finally closed off when all but Rhode Island had voted for the Constitution, North Carolina submitted.

Hamilton, Madison, and many others did. But in reality, it seems utterly implausible that there could have been many more of these people. Someone had to produce things, food especially, but also the wigs these men wore and the paper on which they wrote. These active participants in governing were a leisure class—Hamilton perhaps much less than the others, which may be partly why they soon finessed him out of power.

Then what would civic republicanism have meant to that society? It could not have meant Philadelphia writ large across the life of the nation. National government did not have much to do until the Civil War and then not again until World War I and the Depression. Outside wartime and before the past sixty years, citizens regularly encountered national government only in the person of the local postmaster.[34] Indeed, A. J. P. Taylor noted that, before World War I, 'a sensible, law-abiding Englishman could pass through life and hardly notice the existence of the state, beyond the post office and the policeman'.[35] Since World War II national government has invaded our lives. In the age of Jefferson, most men could have participated heavily in politics only at the local level, which is to say, only in a relatively small-scale communitarian organization of the society. What a dismal thought—squandering the talents of Jefferson and even lesser politicos on very small local politics.

It would be false to claim that whether agrarian or business interests prevailed initially was a matter of chance. The coordination on agrarian control was not a matter of random tipping. There were many features of the situation of the late eighteenth and early nineteenth centuries that gave the agrarians great advantages. Foremost was the sheer number of independent landowners among the initial electorate. Commercial society was still nascent and business owners were few. The spectacular rise of cities was still in the future, although New York, Philadelphia, and Boston gave hints of what might come. Moreover, once Jefferson came to power, he and the Jeffersonians were able to extend the vote to incorporate many new voters into their party and thereby increase the chance that they could win future elections. And the opening of new lands to the west generally meant the expansion of farming.

[34] Jack N. Rakove, 'The Madisonian Solution', presented at the conference 'Constitutions and Constitutionalism', Murphy Institute, Tulane University, New Orleans, 11–12 Mar. 1995.

[35] A. J. P. Taylor, *English History 1914–1945* (Oxford: Oxford University Press, 1965), 1.

Similarly, the later change to the predominance of business interests followed demographic changes. The rise of business in the economy meant that workers' interests partly coincided with those of
business against those of farmers. And the demographic decline of
farmers has almost removed them from the electorate altogether.
(Less than 3 per cent of American employed persons now gain their
living from farming.) The Jeffersonian move to extend the suffrage to
all white males was complete by about 1820. That increased the proportion of farmers in the electorate and seemingly, therefore, secured
the agrarian hold. That this was not the result in the longer run may
be suggested by the very undemocratic form government took in the
southern plantation states, where the oligarchy of plantation barons
held enough control to take the region into the Civil War. They constituted no more than 10 per cent of the vote but virtually all of the
government of the region. Small, especially subsistence farmers were
of little political consequence in the South.

From our retrospective position, it appears that in the early days
of the US Constitution, business needed little more than domestic
laissez-faire from government, protection of the large domestic
market from regional or state barriers, and uniform foreign trade
prospects. The Commerce Clause largely gave it all of these.
Additionally, business could have benefited from stable monetary
policy (again, decreasing variance in expectations increases investment) and favourable tariffs for international trade and protection.
Here, of course, agrarian and business interests generally conflicted.
Farmers wanted freer money with its inflationary tendencies and
they wanted high tariffs on agricultural imports and no tariff on
industrial goods. But the Constitution gave business so much of
what it wanted that it was able to prosper under Jeffersonian government. Indeed, it could virtually explode into wealth and innovation in an industrial revolution that eventually outpaced those of
Europe.

In essence, the Hamiltonians won the Constitutional Convention.
But since the trend from agriculture to business was driven by forces
that went well beyond deliberate political and governmental plans,
they were likely to win the economic contest eventually in any case.
The stability of the US constitutional order may therefore have
depended on the constitutional protections that eased the way for
business. Those protections fell far short of interventions on behalf
of business *per se*. They were just as much protections of farmers

who could produce for markets outside their states and abroad. But they were more important for business than for farming just because business had the greater prospect of expansion.

Hammer and Sickle

The crossed hammer and sickle of the Soviet Union and its followers were the symbol of the union of workers' and farmers' interests in the Communist Party. It was an illogical symbol because it represented an essentially impossible union. Urban industrialization would bring about the ruin of agricultural life for most farmers and their progeny. By the time the symbol flew on a flag over Moscow, this fate must have been recognized by many as economically determined. When Jefferson believed in his élitist variant of the agrarian vision, the signs of its impossibility were not yet clear. By 1917, when the leading industrial nations had begun to leave agriculture behind and farmers had left the land in large numbers, the impossibility of the non-élite agrarian vision was transparent. The symbol lay in tatters at the Russian parliamentary elections of December 1993, when the residual Communist Party had split into the main Communist Party and the rump Agrarian Party.[36]

The contradictory symbolism in the Soviet Union did not matter because agricultural interests were not constitutionally empowered. Similarly, Jefferson's agrarian vision did not matter very much because it was also not constitutionalized beyond protection of the right to own slaves —perhaps because he and other agrarians took the vision for granted as merely a description of the natural state of affairs. In the US case, *the best constitution was one that left the Jeffersonian and Hamiltonian visions to be fought out in the economy rather than in the polity*. Politics could hardly affect the outcome but politics could be wrecked by the effort to affect it.

The biggest economic transition that nations typically make is that from agricultural life to greater general prosperity. It is the move that makes for modern nationhood, the move that any ardent Marxist or capitalist must want. Yet, Marxism in our time perversely became the ideology of peasant rebellions. In the United States, the agricultural

[36] Together the two parties took about 20 per cent of the vote (*New York Times*, 26 Dec. 1993), sect. I.

workforce has fallen from over 80 per cent of the total workforce to less than 3 per cent. This change occurred over about two centuries, but its modal period was the era of populism, when farmers fell from majority status and took Jefferson's party down with them. Populism was a variant of Poujadist movements that rise when a group's fate seems clearly determined and its aspiring leaders make a last-ditch effort to interrupt the downward trend. The greenback or easy-money fight in the populist era was essentially a hopeless fight against the implications of the falling relative value of agricultural production.

In retrospect, one might readily conclude that the dramatic change in the relative values of agricultural production and all other forms of production was one of the greatest benefits in human history. But at the time, it was a source of great pain for those whose opportunities in agriculture fell. Because they could not recapture the government, they could not force their momentary interests into law.

Agrarian visions and interests were central to political debate and conflict in virtually all nations until very recently. They were at the heart of the French revolutionary constitutional debates and perhaps all the great nineteenth-century constitutional efforts. For example, Argentine constitutional efforts repeatedly faltered over conflicts between agrarian interests and financial and shipping interests until the efforts finally succeeded in the 1850s.[37] Then the Argentine Constitution was broken during the period of agrarian malaise around 1930 that may have been stimulated by protectionist tariffs in the United States that led to retaliatory European tariffs. Revolutions from Mexico to China to Vietnam have been based on agrarian interests and peasant fighters. The astonishing thing about all these revolutions is that they were openly contradictory. Their agrarian focus was opportunistic and, if the revolutions were to succeed in the long run, that focus had to be betrayed. Still, peasants today back movements that, once in power, would do little for peasants other than slow down their painful transition, primarily by detaining their children in rural poverty.

It seems unlikely that constitutional debates in advanced industrial states today would spend much time on agrarian issues, although agrarian concerns are often the sore point of European Community

[37] Julio Saguir, 'In Search of Institutional Design: A Comparison between the Constitutional Processes of Argentina and the United States', a Ph.D. thesis at the University of Chicago, 1991.

debates. Just as Jefferson may have thought these issues were settled in his time, most people in advanced economies today plausibly think they are settled in our time—merely that now they are settled against Jeffersonian agrarianism. Contemporary defences of the agrarian ideal and the so-called land ethic sound more nearly quaint and irrelevantly romantic than politically of interest.[38] That ideal could become real today only after the radical reduction of the per capita national product to less than a tenth its present level and the elimination of vast urban populations. That sounds like a prescription for a heavy dose of Pol Pot.

Economic Transition in a Constitutional Democracy

The striking difference between the current Russian constitutional challenge and the earlier American challenge is that the changes to be wrought in the Russian economy may be guided by deliberate government intervention whereas the American economic developments followed very nearly from government *laissez-faire*. In Russia today, a regime of economic liberalism must be brought into existence by illiberal, central determination. In the US case, the economic changes were not extensively foreseen and were able more or less to overtake the populace and the government. In the Russian case, the economic changes that would be the result of the successful introduction of the market can be extensively foreseen and they can overtake the populace only against substantial opposition.

In the transformation of the Russian and other Eastern economies there has been heated debate over so-called shock therapy. In shock therapy, the transformation is done instantly with one big change rather than spread out over many years with small, piecemeal changes. There is immediate privatization of most public firms through sale or free distribution of stock in them, immediate distribution to individual farmer-owners of publicly held collective farms, immediate currency reform, and immediate closure of many government agencies whose functions had been to direct the economy. The initial effect is unemployment and declining production in many areas. Expectations are initially shattered, but this result is supposed

[38] See e.g. Wendell Berry, *Sex, Economy, Freedom, and Community: Eight Essays* (New York: Pantheon, 1993).

to be partially beneficial because the prior expectations were often of the wrong things. Thereafter, expectations are left to stabilize over the next several years as no further shocks are necessary.

Many Western economists advocate shock therapy for the Eastern transitions.[39] Many critics of the apparent pace of economic reform in the East argue that going more slowly would be more humane and also more effective.[40] John Kenneth Galbraith gives a clear statement of this opposition to shock therapy:

> It should not be a criticism of this transition that it is done gradually and with thought. The return to normal productive activity in Western Europe after World War II, a task less complex than that faced by Eastern Europe and the USSR, took the better part of a decade. In Britain it took seven years before sterling was convertible, and food rationing and associated price controls were similarly continued. Sudden action, once again, is for those who do not themselves suffer, do not think before acting, who proceed by formula, not fact. Only if time is allowed can there be time for thought—the thought that is attuned to pragmatic result and not to primitive ideology.[41]

This is advice that can be relevant only to a stable and therefore in all likelihood autocratic regime, such as that of Chile's Pinochet or China's 1989 gerontocracy, not the probably unstable governments of Eastern Europe after 1989.

The initial losses of welfare from shock therapy might be substantial, but supposedly the aggregate losses of welfare from piecemeal therapy would be even greater. Relatively depressed expectations would last for many years under piecemeal therapy. Hence, investment would tend to lag below the optimal level for many years, and the effects of low investment in early years would be multiplied through subsequent years. On the other hand, positive expectations would begin to develop soon after shock therapy; hence, investment would soon begin to reach a level that would reinforce positive

[39] The literature is large. Consider e.g. Jeffrey Sachs, *Poland's Jump to the Market* (Cambridge, Mass.: MIT Press, 1993), esp. ch. 2; Peng Lian and Shang-Jin Wei, 'To Shock or Not to Shock? Economics and Political Economy of Large-Scale Reforms', *Economics and Politics*, 10 (July 1998): 161–83; and Padma Desai, 'Beyond Shock Therapy', *Journal of Democracy*, 6 (Apr. 1995): 102–12.

[40] Valtr Komarek, 'Shock Therapy and Its Victims', *New York Times* (5 Jan. 1992): 4.13.

[41] John Kenneth Galbraith, 'The Rush to Capitalism', *New York Review of Books* (25 Oct. 1990): 51–2, at p. 52. As noted in Chapter 5, Nancy Bermeo draws instead an optimistic conclusion from the comparison to post-war Western Europe. See Nancy Bermeo, 'Democracy in Europe', *Daedalus* (Spring 1994): 159–77.

expectations. Among those whose expectations matter are, of course, foreign investors, who will more readily invest if they expect high rates of return—which are more likely after shock therapy than during the long period of piecemeal therapy. But even more important are the investments in personal training and careers by Russians, on whose efforts the economy must mostly build. Hence, shock therapy and economic growth do not require boot-strapping efforts to invest resources that do not yet exist; they require primarily the investment of time to create the resources of skill and reputation, and such investment will happen if expectations for return on it are good.

The advice to go slowly is strictly economic advice for the sake of reducing the harmful impacts on particular individuals. Shock therapy has in common with the Commerce Clause that it sounds like economics when it is actually politics. It is not a device for politically organizing the economy; it is a device for *ending* the political organization of the economy. *Shock therapy is mainly a political, strategic matter.* Any alternative to shock therapy is necessarily a programme that uses government to run the economy to some extent—perhaps to a very large extent. A democratic government typically cannot expect to stay in office to manage a carefully planned, gentle transition. It might, however, succeed quickly with drastic policies to eliminate institutions that block the growth of entrepreneurial activity and the market. It might even make such effective changes that it would be difficult for the next government to restore the old order. Going slowly is not a serious alternative to going quickly for any but an autocratic regime.

Hence, the serious argument in favour of speed is the hope of getting reforms established before politics intervenes to undercut longer-run developments. It may be that an advantage of land reform in some nations was to slow down the imposition of economic disaster on rural populations by giving them the false hope of prosperity and even the real hope of subsistence. A concomitant disadvantage was, as noted, to create an interest that has been hard to deal with. One of the most astonishing cases of land reform was by the Allende regime in Chile. In an economy that had developed far beyond the era of subsistence farming, Allende virtually brought back the dead hand of the past to encumber economic development. That was an anti-socialist policy by an ostensibly socialist government. In Allende's case, the short-term false hopes were very short term, because General Pinochet intervened with brutality and sufficient force to reorganize the economy to hasten the relative decline of agriculture.

The losses to individuals must in very many cases be distressing and deeply painful. Consider a couple who are approaching retirement in a now moribund firm or bankrupt collective farm. That couple has been in the economic hands of the state all their lives. One might suppose that, although there is no way to keep their firm or farm going merely to rescue them from the depressing fate of unemployment, the state still owes them protection in retirement. But the state's retirement programmes of the past have not required savings or investment in facilities. It handled such cases as theirs by simply letting them continue to occupy a state-owned apartment and by keeping them paid through their firm or keeping them fed through in-kind supports from their farm. They have (and the state has) no vested resources for their retirement. The state must now invest real money, even hard currency, in their retirement. The task is, with only a bit of exaggeration, comparable to what an American government would face if all retirement programmes had previously been handled by the corporations for which people worked and if vast numbers of those corporations now became insolvent. If that happened to the American government at a time of deep recession and huge budget deficits, it would not handle the task well.[42]

Unfortunately, the debate over the merits of shock therapy and of piecemeal reform in parts of the former Soviet Union is complicated by a logically unrelated but empirically associated problem: the destabilization of the political regime. The destabilization is not merely the initial destabilization of creating a new order but is, further and more profoundly for the economy, the ongoing destabilization of democratic vacillation over how to proceed. It is possible that most of the Eastern nations currently attempting economic conver-

---

[42] Some of the press coverage of the sad fates of losers in the transition in Russia is extremely distressing. But for readers they are also hard to assess, because they are essentially anecdotal. The press in general views understanding of great social movements and events almost only at the level of the anecdote. Despite the quip that anecdote is merely the singular of data, this is entirely inadequate for real understanding. For example, the *New York Times Magazine* ran pictures of elderly sufferers from the Russian transition. Unfortunately, similar photographs could most probably have been taken fifteen years earlier to show the wretchedness of the Soviet economy at that time. It will be hard to determine how much of the suffering is Soviet Russian and how much is transitional. See Serge Schmemann, 'How Do You Succeed in a Cashless Society', *New York Times Magazine* (27 Dec. 1998): 36–9, with pictures by Vladimir Syomin.

sion will face constant turnover of regimes and policies. Hence, one inclined to invest time and resources in developing skills, facilities, or reputation may think it optimal to do as well as possible in the short run and to leave the longer run for later worry—because the longer run is too unpredictable to risk the present for it. This general attitude would tend to make the future less good than it might otherwise be. Some of the turnovers of government, however, have led to the continuation of transitional policies, so there may be increasing optimism in some of the nations.

Groups that are already organized from before the time of the transition or that can be organized from interests related to the prior organization of the economy have an immediate political advantage over nascent, not-yet-organized interests related to the future market. A crude counting of the democratic preferences might therefore hold that the *ex ante* distribution of interests in the society should be protected. Carried to extremes, this would mean organization by *latifundia*, feudal estates, or grim subsistence agriculture with its grinding poverty at the dawn of the industrial revolution. Although stopping transitions might sound appealing to some over the short run, it is impossible and stupid over the long run for many transitions. And the long run is not even very long. Imagine that South Korean economic structure had been fixed as of 1960, when South Korean per capita income was desolate, and that further changes had been subject to the *de facto* veto of then extant economic groups.

Oddly, therefore, the focus on the short run invites a variant of the position of the English Luddites, the American populists, and the French Poujadists. These groups wanted to stop economic change in order to maintain their positions as they were. Their concern was *Besitzstandswahrung*, of holding onto their positions, as discussed in Chapter 5. They all lost the day because the changes were too massively beneficial to others to be stopped and, in any case, while groups wanted to stop the changes, their individual members and their children often chose to join in the changes. Without political intervention, the economy has one device for making a transition from outmoded to more productive activities: failure. Political intervention can rescue those who fail in one of three ways. Government can help those who fail to move into other activities, it can directly support their welfare with cash payments as they leave their failed activities, or it can indirectly support their welfare by supporting the outmoded activity. What individuals and groups commonly want is the last of these policies, which must destroy much of the benefits of transition. As neo-classical economists commonly note, recessions have a cleansing effect on a general market economy because they help to eliminate failing, outdated firms.[43] This is cold comfort to those who are 'cleansed', but such failure of firms and individuals is a major part of the success of many economies.[44]

What the reorganization of the formerly Soviet-type economies involves in many cases is a combination of Luddite, Poujadist, populist groups, and government agencies and agents in agreement on one thing: stopping the transition for the time being, roughly for the life of the current generation. The chief argument for shock therapy is that only such a dramatic move can take the focus off politics and put it on economic opportunity for roughly the life of the current generation. Active politics is useful in stimulating political change, as in ending autocracy in much of Eastern Europe and the former Soviet Union. But it can also be a drain on economic activity. It is a drain that is exacerbated in most of these nations by the current lack of demographic growth to allow quicker expansion of new enterprises through intergenerational shifts into them.

As already noted, there are serious objections to shock therapy. The most widely discussed is its harm to many in the present generation, which seems unjust. But economic transitions generally entail harm for some. The virtual death of traditional typewriters and the decline of mainframe computers in the transition to cheap personal computers has hurt IBM workers and stockholders. Should that transition therefore be blocked or slowed down? Should IBM workers and stockholders be compensated for their losses? Piecemeal therapy merely spreads the effects of the free-market transition over a much longer period, plausibly exacerbating it in the aggregate.

---

[43] Ricardo J. Caballero and Mohamad L. Hammour, 'The Cleansing Effect of Recessions', *American Economic Review* 84 (Dec. 1994): 1350–68.

[44] Cynics may rightly note, however, that government in the United States regularly rescues very large firms that are in trouble, as in the cases of Lockheed, Chrysler, large numbers of banks, and Long-Term Capital Management. The defence of such moves is that these firms are so big and entwined with other, dependent, corporations and with large numbers of individual workers that their rescue is of general value, because their failure might cascade and bring down other firms and even set back the entire economy to the detriment of almost everyone (except bankruptcy lawyers). Hard-nosed proponents of capitalism generally think such rescues are disruptive to economic efficiency and development. Hard-nosed opponents of capitalism generally think they are supportive of capitalists. Both are possibly right.

A second problem is that shock therapy may have a perverse political effect. When an industry slowly declines, workers lose their jobs a few at a time and they may tend to hold themselves personally responsible. When a firm closes outright, workers are less likely to hold themselves responsible and more likely to hold the firm and the government responsible. Shock therapy has arguably created a large block of politicized people ready to vote for someone, perhaps a militarist, a quasi-fascist, or an old-style Communist, to undo the transitional order that has harmed them.

The problem for government in the West has not been how to manage or control or cause various major transitions, but how *not to interfere destructively in them.* In part just because the full scope of the transition from agrarian to urban life was not understood, at least not at the level of active politics, governments in England and the United States stumbled through the transition without wrecking themselves on it. The problem of the formerly Communist states is that they attempted to control various transitions, especially that from agrarian to urban life. Seemingly government action is required to undo government action. We may have some evidence that strong, autocratic government can stimulate industrialization, as in the Asian Tigers and perhaps in the Soviet Union during its early decades. But we have no evidence that democratic government can deliberately manage such a transition.

A relatively democratic government cannot expect to stay in office long enough to carry out a slow, deliberate transition. If it induces a radical change, it may be able to undo enough of the centralized apparatus of economic direction and ensure that enough of a nascent market organization is in place to make it implausible to turn back. A successor regime might still bring in policies to mitigate the losses of the inefficient and these might slow the growth of the market. Groups that are already organized from before the time of the transition or that can be organized from interests related to the prior organization of the economy have an immediate political advantage over nascent, not-yet-organized interests related to the future market. A crude account of the democratic participation in the new regime might therefore hold that the distribution of interests in the society is more firmly against reform than it is. Unstable political expectations need not be harmful to economic performance *if* the economy is not being run by the state.

In sum, because democratic government is unlikely to be consistent in its policies, we have reason to doubt that it can micro-manage a long-term transition without destabilizing economic expectations.[45] That is the chief argument for shock therapy in the newly liberalizing nations that are simultaneously democratizing.

Solid expectations are not mandatory for economic growth, which can happen even in the face of short-term or shaky expectations. For example, there is a McDonald's in central Moscow, put there at some risk while things were very much in flux. But the McDonald's can do very well in the short run. And, in truth, its expectations may be genuinely better than those of a Russian entrepreneur without relevant foreign backing. The McDonald's enjoys the privileged position Lindblom attributes to American business in the United States. Its interests coincide with the interests of the Russian government in maintaining good relations with the United States and foreign investors more generally. Oddly, an unstable domestic regime may therefore give foreign investors large advantages over domestic entrepreneurs because it gives them relatively better, more stable expectations—once they are in place. Of course, all investors and entrepreneurs would be better served by better, more stable expectations, without which the economic transition is apt to be slower, perhaps much slower, sufficiently so to reduce political expectations in the new regime.

Economic Transition and Demographic Growth

Consider a simplistic model of economic transition with and without demographic growth. Suppose careers last fifty years. Without demographic growth there are, say, a million people in each decade: those who are in their twenties, thirties, forties, fifties, and sixties. With 10 per cent demographic growth per decade, there are, say, 1,100,000 in their twenties, 1,000,000 in their thirties, 910,000 in their

[45] The reform of agriculture in Mexico that is mandated by the North American Free Trade Agreement might be an exception to this observation for the simple reason that the reforms are tied into the larger NAFTA regime. That regime is backed by important groups that can be expected to constrain government in a time of political change. For an economic account of how the transition can be managed over fifteen years and of the limited impact on efficiency gains of a moderately slow transition, see Santiago Levy and Sweder van Wijnbergen, 'Transition Problems in Economic Reform: Agriculture in the North American Free Trade Agreement', *American Economic Review* (Sept. 1995) 85: 738–54.

forties, 830,000 in their fifties, and 760,000 in their sixties (10 per cent population growth per decade implies a doubling of population in slightly over seventy years). Suppose every new worker moves into new enterprises, which enjoy productivity gains of 10, 20, or 30 per cent per decade while old enterprises have stagnant productivity.

From this simple model it follows that economic productivity during a transition towards new directions (either of organizational form or of sectors of production) enjoys a tremendous multiplier effect from growth in the workforce, as shown in Table 6.1. Productivity growth in new enterprises of 20 per cent per decade produces *44 per cent growth in total production* in two decades with 10 per cent growth in the workforce. Against this, there would be only *18 per cent production growth* with no growth in the workforce.

TABLE 6.1: *Increase in production after two decades*

Productivity growth (percentage per decade)	Workforce growth 0 per decade (absolute and per capita) (per cent)	Workforce growth 10 per decade	
		absolute (per cent)	per capita (per cent)
0	0	20	20
10	8	32	26
20	18	44	37
30	28	58	48

When there is no growth of the workforce, absolute growth of production is identical to per capita growth. When the workforce is expanding, absolute growth exceeds per capita growth, which, however, still *exceeds* production growth without workforce growth. Hence, demographic growth contributes to economic transition and transformation in several ways. First, it produces a per capita surplus that can be taxed to provide greater public benefits. Secondly, it helps the new forms come to quicker dominance over old forms and raises the optimism of expectations, hence stimulating further contributions to the transformation. It should therefore come as no surprise that rapid economic growth often fades with declining demographic growth. Declining birth rates may be caused, as is often argued, by the economic prosperity, but they also contribute to slower economic growth. These reciprocal motors make growth rates partially self-limiting.

In the model, the effects of production growth follow from two kinds of source: first, productivity growth in new enterprises and, secondly, the multiplier on this effect from workforce growth. The first of these kinds of source takes at least two distinctively different forms. First, there are the standard transitions from old to new sectors of economic activity, among which the largest historical example is the transition from agriculture to manufacturing and other productive activities. Secondly, there is the apparent gain in productivity that could come from the transformation of a centrally controlled economy to a market economy. Here, there need be no transition from one sector to another, but there may be many transitions from old and inefficient enterprises to new entrepreneurial enterprises.

Consider the high rate of productivity growth of the South Korean economic expansion from about 1960 to the present day. Much of the productivity increase in South Korea came from the transition of its economy from agricultural and rural to industrial and urban production. China is now enjoying the overall production growth that follows from such a transition. Most of that transition has already happened in Russia, although part of the possible gains were forgone in the stifling control of the economy.[46] That previously forgone part of the gains is now much of what is available to the Russian people for growth over the next couple of decades of predictable workforce stability. The rest of what is available is transition out of heavy industry and inefficient farming into more productive sectors, which is merely the ongoing transition of the developed economies. Hence, even with successful policies, Russia is unlikely to achieve South Korean or Chinese rates of growth. And, if it proceeds year by year through low rates of growth, it will depress expectations, thereby depressing investment in growth. It is the misfortune of the liberalizing Russian regime that the prior Soviet regime took most of the benefits from economic transition

[46] It is commonly asserted that the Soviet regime coerced peasants off the land and into factories. In actual fact, the rates of movement from the land to cities in the Soviet Union were comparable to those during periods of comparable development in the United States and many other Western nations. Apart from its murderous treatment of kulaks, the Stalin regime was quite possibly not so much brutal as inefficient in its rate of encouraging movement off the land. Since it had the economy under central control, perhaps it should have encouraged faster movement off the land.

from agriculture to industry and from demographic growth, and now the new Russian regime must survive popular scrutiny while gaining little benefit from the general sectoral transition or from demographic growth, which has virtually stopped.

Finally, captured in the model are implications for the welfare of those who are not part of the intergenerational shift. The per capita gains from their production alone are 0 per cent in all decades in all conditions. They are relative losers in the changes if their productivity does not rise to match the gains of the new enterprises. If they are relative losers, they are likely also to be absolute losers in so far as many of the things which they currently consume and want may become, relative to their wages, more expensive as patterns of demand change. But they could also benefit from the changes through rising government investment in public works, welfare programmes, and education and retraining for displaced workers.

If the transition is not merely intergenerational but is conducted via closure or reduction of older firms, many people may be absolutely worse off as a direct result even while the economy in the aggregate booms. These people are potential Luddites in further political moves. Taken together across many kinds of industry and enterprise, from agriculture to manufacturing to bureaucratic organizations, they may constitute a blocking group for economic reform. If the next and future generations had votes, reform would win hands down. But it is the present generation that votes, and the interests of many in the present generation, especially those who are older, are not well served by reform. Demographic growth may therefore be more important for a democratic regime undergoing economic transition than for a non-democratic regime. With demographic growth, the number of those who benefit from the transition rises faster to become a majority of the working population.

In some of the former republics of the Soviet Union, economic transition through restructuring by hiring new workers into new firms rather than by closing old firms would be facilitated by demographic growth. But some of these areas are now side-tracked into destructive ethnic groupism, into fighting over shares of the current resources and over control of political office. They may therefore miss the opportune moment for restructuring their economies, the moment when restructuring could come more quickly through intergenerational shifts. If they do miss that moment, and demographic growth continues to reduce its rate, they may later face a harsher, more conflictive prospect of transition without the benefits of the multiplier of demographic growth. And they may face it from a condition of greater relative poverty than they suffer today.

One reason for the slow success of the industrial revolution in France is that France had a virtually stable population with little or no demographic growth during the nineteenth and early twentieth centuries. The German population grew relatively rapidly during the same period. Hence, that long period, which started with France as the dominant power of Europe, ended with Germany as the dominant power. Germany's dominance came not only from the greater numbers available for military service but also from its quicker move during the latter half of the period into modern industries that generated national wealth and contributed to national power. The United States and Australia both benefited from rapid demographic growth that enabled relatively free development of varied economic enterprises. The American reputation for innovativeness may owe much to the demographics of immigration, which allow for relatively easy shifting of workers into new areas. People do not have to leave old jobs to work on building the railways or programming computers; they can leave old countries.

Demographic change might work as well in centrally planned as in market economies. But, in general, its largest effects work through the growth of new industries and firms that gradually replace or substitute for old, established industries and firms. Aluminium and plastics displace steel. The microchip displaces wires, tubes, and other electronic components, and electronic equipment replaces mechanical equipment. The steel industry does not have to reorganize itself to help us through a beneficial transition. If it fails to change, it need merely fail to mobilize government to protect it against the future. *In moments of such transitions, a government that cannot easily be mobilized by dying firms or industries is of great benefit.*

Rapid demographic growth can create problems for constitutional order, as it perhaps does in Kenya and Bangladesh today. But it can dramatically ease the way for economic transitions that involve shifting the proportions of the workforce in various occupations and industries. In general such transitions happen intergenerationally. The young move into new enterprises, leaving declining and outmoded enterprises to the older generations, who may suffer economic decline. The computer world offers a conspicuous if rarefied example of dominance by the next generation. That world is peopled by probably the largest number of wealthy young entrepreneurs the world has ever seen. That world is also more open than perhaps any other in the United States to people from new immigrant groups and their children. It is sometimes supposed that Asian Americans have greater natural abilities in that world, and they may have. But it may be more important for them that opportunities are inherently best in an expanding world and the expanding world of the moment is electronics.

American and Eastern Comparisons

The broad US constitutional experience generalizes only to nations with diverse economies, or potentially diverse economies. A nation whose best returns in the international market are from a single or few specialties would get little advantage from a commerce clause or near equivalent. But there is a more general lesson to be drawn. The actual import of the Commerce Clause was to reduce the power of the states over economic development and not to empower the national government. To put it perversely, perhaps the greatest strength of the US Constitution in managing economic relations is its weakness. It does not empower government to do very much in economic life. In particular, it does not empower government to do much more than plead with business.[47] Much of the seemingly strong power it has in facing business is the kind of power business would want it to use, just as citizens must almost all welcome the imposition of power to make traffic flow well. The extraordinary strength of the Constitution or the government or the society is in government's *inability* to override the weaknesses of its empowerment from the flimsy constitution.

In the face of uncontrollable and poorly understood economic transitions, among the most important provisions of a constitution, especially as it affects business and the economy, must be those that eventually restrain government, not those that enable it. This is not

[47] Many economists hold that the federal corporate tax is a major distorter of economic activity in the United States. Ironically, that tax initially assumed its importance because of the supposed interest states had in controlling taxes levied on individuals. Yet again, it was politics and not economics that failed. And yet again, the problem that needed to be resolved was ending state-level control of part of the economy.

an a priori claim, but merely a generalization from the experience of many societies, a generalization sitting uncomfortably on too few cases, all, of course, from the past. The original Commerce Clause and the larger Constitution that was opportunistically wrapped around it was written not to weaken the authority of national government in the United States. Rather, it was written to weaken the authority of the individual states, an authority that had enabled them collectively to bring themselves to the edge of economic ruin. If its purpose was to be achieved, the Commerce Clause had to be vested in a moderately capable central government, and therefore an adequate government was designed for it. The Commerce Clause virtually secured the national government for commercial interests. Lindblom's thesis, cited above—that business is substantially in control of government without having to exert control because government needs its cooperation in governing the society—is already faintly written into the Constitution.

Although government in the United States has grown enormously more powerful over its two centuries, central politics in the United States has continued to be too weak to strike very hard at business even when unsympathetic interests have controlled the government. Central politics in Russia is dramatically different; it still has much of the character of earlier Soviet politics. Russian leaders can ignore constitutional constraints with relative impunity, as Boris Yeltsin did in disbanding the national parliament. Moreover, the contemporary threat to commerce in Russia is not the threat of localities to impose tariffs; therefore, a mere commerce clause would be inadequate to protect entrepreneurial efforts. The central threat is the possibility of national, not local, intervention. Hence, constitutional constraint to protect economic institutions in their investment in their futures cannot readily look effective enough to stimulate long-term positive expectations unless that threat is blocked.

The United States in the 1780s needed a constitution that would break the power of *the states* over commercial relations. *The Commerce Clause made federalism safe for trade and business.* Russia needs a constitution that will break the power of *the national state* over production and distribution. The Soviet past requires strong Russian action to establish new expectations. The Russians have a much harder task than the Americans had. As Madison observed earlier of the easier problem, 'From the trials of which I have been a witness I augur that great difficulties will be encountered

in every attempt to prevail on the Legislature to part with power'.[48]
Tell it to Yeltsin.

A final benefit of shock therapy is the possibility that speedy dismantling of the state apparatus of commercial control would make
intervention thereafter much harder by weakening the government.
Lacking a government that can willy-nilly intervene in business dealings helps to stabilize expectations. If a government has fewer
instruments available for such intervention, it is likely to intervene
less. This tendency might not be enough to justify severely weakened
government, because one might still suppose there are moments
when it would be better if the state could intervene. Hence, one must
balance the potential costs and benefits of greater and lesser state
power. It seems overwhelmingly likely that the nations of the former
Soviet Union would benefit from substantially weaker central government. Strong central government failed to make the Soviet economy prosper not merely because it was socialist in particular but
because it was controlling in general, often stupidly so.

Perhaps, as Madison feared, it is implausible that politicians will
write a constitution that weakens the possibilities of political control. But, with its embedded culture of wilful intervention, Russia
has special need of a government that cannot intervene easily. A simple constitution investing government with very limited powers is,
for the short run of a generation and plausibly for the longer run of
many generations, the only sensible response to the current style of
strong control, a style that Yeltsin has followed even in the name
of stopping government. But a weak constitution *per se* is inadequate
to demobilize authoritarian government. Such a constitution could
be given force by dismantling most of the remaining system of
directing the economy. Giving it such force would dramatically
enhance expectations for economic rebuilding, not least because it
would mean that changing from, say, Yeltsin to Zhirinovsky would
not easily wreck the economic trends. The alternative, so long as
those institutions are available, is likely to continue to be central control without central planning, which is essentially what early mercantilism was—seat-of-the-pants control, without much reliance on
intellect or theory.

There may be one other general lesson to draw from comparative
constitutional experiences. Guaranteeing the market in the early

[48] James Madison, Letter of 7 Aug. 1785 to James Monroe, in Kurland and Lerner,
The Founders' Constitution, ii. 481–2, at p. 482.

United States may well have helped secure democracy, and perhaps this lesson can be followed up in newly democratizing nations. But guaranteeing the market in general may undermine the prospects for greater domestic equality. Equality evidently requires government power in industrial societies. Indeed, equality is almost by definition a centralized concept. If economic productivity requires government weakness, productivity and equality are in conflict. This conclusion is at a more general level than that commonly discussed in economics under the rubric of the conflict between equality and efficiency (as discussed in Chapter 5). It is not merely a conflict between a particular policy to achieve greater productivity or equality. *It is a conflict between the kind of government that lacks the power to block great productivity in general and the kind that has the power deliberately to manage equality.*

John Roemer comments that the Soviet commitment to central control of the economy and suppression of the market was only their second biggest mistake. The biggest was to suppress opposition from which the society might have learned.[49] These two, while not logically bound together, may all too naturally fit together. The power to suppress something in particular is essentially the power to suppress in general. Even if we could overcome the incentive effects that put efficiency into conflict with equality, we might still reasonably forgo having the kind of government that could secure equality.

The growth of the modern US government has been driven by military and welfare concerns, and eventually it may acquire the power to trade productivity for equality on a grand scale. Soviet governments failed to achieve either efficiency or equality—although they may sometimes have done better than the United States and many other nations at the latter. Perhaps the only societies systematically successful at achieving equality have been primitive, extremely unproductive societies. In the face of this vast and distressing failure, however, many Russians might still seek to create an order that promises greater equality rather than one that promises greater productivity. If they ally with the various Poujadists clinging to past economic structures, they can probably be led to support strong government, which might be democratically unstoppable. As supporters of the quasi-fascist Zhirinovksy and those of Yeltsin agreed

[49] John E. Roemer, 'The Possibility of Market Socialism', in David Copp, Jean Hampton, and John E. Roemer, eds., *The Idea of Democracy* (Cambridge: Cambridge University Press, 1993): 347–67, at p. 365.

in voting for a constitution with strong presidential powers in the constitutional referendum in Russia in late 1993, so these disparate groups may produce a government none of them would want if it were controlled by any group other than itself. Since a generation of hegemony such as the Jeffersonians enjoyed may be out of the question in a democratic Russia, the adopted constitution may be a disaster if it lasts.

During the constitutional debates, Washington insisted that the Articles of Confederation be overhauled quickly. 'Otherwise', he wrote, 'like a house on fire, whilst the most regular mode of extinguishing it is contended for, the building is reduced to ashes'.[50] What was needed, Washington thought, was any solid national government. Madison, who entered the Philadelphia Convention in 1787 with clear ideas on what would be best, soon enough focused on what would be workable. The Russians may finally suffer from not having a Madison focused only on achieving a workable national government.

In the debate over shock versus incremental therapy the incrementalists (not the theorists, but the practitioners) may suppose there is a best path to follow through incremental changes. But, because the policy-makers will be changing, they may constantly reconsider what is the best path. Hence, 'the best' may be an empty category. As Washington urged, it is more important to settle on a rule and let the economy get on with it than to try to design a perfect government or, we may add, in the absence of perfect theory, to design one that could manage the economy perfectly from day to day. Dozens of rules might be good if they were applied consistently. Of these, plausibly the only one that could be applied consistently is the one that reduces government control. Then the government could focus on welfare policies that would *directly* ease the lives of individuals who lose in the transition rather than on policies that *indirectly* ease their lives by interfering with the transition. The transition might be stopped, but probably only by stopping the Russian people.

If the model of Table 6.1 is roughly correct, then demographic growth at the right time can contribute to the growth of positive expectations under the new order. *More generally, economic boom-time is especially propitious for establishing a new constitution.* To

---

[50] George Washington, Letter to Henry Knox, 3 Feb. 1787, in Kurland and Lerner, *The Founders' Constitution*, i. 188.

create a new order to face immediate economic failure invites negative expectations and enhances the prospects for the failure of the order, as in the United States under the US Articles of Confederation, in Weimar Germany, and possibly today in Russia, Romania, Serbia, and several other nations. The accidental association of negative economic expectations with a new regime may affect expectations for the regime itself. Many revolutionary regimes and juntas were able to come to power because the old regimes faced devastating crises. The new regimes have often then understandably failed to manage the crises and have been tarred with low expectations of their capacities.

The reverse may also be true—propitious conditions can help a regime become established. The creation of the US version of the modern welfare state with large, permanent government, which came into being in the 1930s under Franklin Roosevelt, is often called a second American revolution. That government may have gained its acceptance in part merely from the fact that it was there at the time of completion of a successful, popular war and at the time of resurgent economic prosperity. The lore of that government is that it became legitimate in the eyes of the people because it worked to rescue the economy. A contrary view is that the *de facto* Keynesian policies of wartime mobilization rescued the economy from the Depression. Against this view, Robert Higgs argues that the real effect was the change in expectations of the possibilities of the supposedly broken economy.[51] If either of the latter views is roughly right, the American welfare state may have become legitimate because of its accidental association with positive trends. The new regimes in Russia and other democratizing nations would benefit from similar associations. Some of them are more likely to suffer from association with economic decline.

Concluding Remarks

In the face of our generally poor economic understanding of the future, we should read Holmes's comment that a constitution 'is not intended to embody a particular economic theory' as rather a pre-

---

[51] Robert Higgs, 'Wartime Prosperity? A Reassessment of the U.S. Economy in the 1940s', *Journal of Economic History*, 52 (March 1992): 41–60.

scription than a theoretical or descriptive claim. There may be contexts in which the short-term requirements for a constitution to be successfully adopted run against the long-term requirement that it be economically enabling rather than commanding. In those contexts, we can plausibly expect eventual failure of the constitutional order. For example, there have been many revolutionary contexts in which an acceptable constitution would have had to require relatively egalitarian results, a specific theocratic social and economic order, or other particular social dispensation such as an anti-democratic or ethnic hierarchy. Such a constitution could not long be the effective guide of a successful polity in a hard-driving, competitive economic world. If, however, it did successfully regulate government structure and policy through dramatic economic transitions, it could do so only at substantial social and economic cost, such as the Communist political orders suffered.

There may be other complications that confound the prospects of a stable constitutional regime. For example, in the early 1990s the Eastern Europeans faced two changes at once: to democracy and to the market. The change to democracy is a public move towards participatory politics and citizen government. The change to market economics is a privatizing move. The two moves may be at war with each other. But relative consensus on both moves might finally trump the apparent conflict between them, especially if the move to the market succeeds quickly enough in producing economic growth and personal benefits.

7

Democracy on the Margin

> The advantages of possessing the control of the powers of the
> government, and thereby of its honors and emoluments, are, of
> themselves, exclusive of all other considerations, ample to
> divide . . . a community into two great hostile parties.
> John C. Calhoun, *A Disquisition on Government*

Divided Society

The division of our decisions into constitutional moments and post-
constitutional moments, with broad coordination on vague general
issues in the former and often substantially more conflict over lesser
issues in the latter, fits successful constitutional regimes. But in
moments of crisis in a previously stable society or in a society in
which the initial coordination is contrived or false, there may be
acute moments under the constitution that have the character of constitutional moments. Inability to coordinate then on broad general
principles of order can mean the failure of constitutionalism and of
democracy.

Because it faces severe limits on its workability, democracy is not
a panacea for politics. It works only on the margins of great issues.
The few big issues democracy can handle are those on which there is
broad consensus—such as the consensuses in the United Kingdom
and the United States on fighting World War II. Most forms of government could handle such issues about as well. Indeed, the government of the United Kingdom handled World War II by ceasing to be
democratically accountable for the duration of the war. For conflictive issues democracy can work only against a background of rough
coordination on order. Without that essentially prior coordination,

democracy is trammelled or irrelevant. And even with the relevant coordination on order, if precise theoretical claims are at issue, democracy works only in the sense that it reaches a result—but not in the sense that it gets the right result. Often, indeed, a democrat would want decisions not made democratically.

As Robert Dahl says, 'In a sense, what we ordinarily describe as democratic "politics" is merely the chaff. It is the surface manifestation, representing superficial conflicts. [These] disputes over policy alternatives are nearly always disputes over a set of alternatives that have already been winnowed down to those within the broad area of basic agreement'.[1] This is roughly Tocqueville's view as well: 'When a community actually has a mixed government—that is to say, when it is equally divided between adverse principles—it must either experience a revolution or fall into anarchy'.[2] We should qualify Dahl's claim with the note that 'the broad area of basic agreement' need only be an area in which the politically effective groups are in agreement.

Democracy is essentially a member of the mutual-benefit class of theories. If political divisions cut very much deeper than the marginal issues on which we can democratically compromise, democracy may no longer seem to produce mutual benefits. It then produces major—not marginal—winners and losers. Big disagreements bring us down. For example, democracy could not handle the conflict over slavery in the United States or the conflict over Algeria in France, and it could not even get off the ground in independent Burundi with its first democratic election that was rightly pilloried as merely an ethnic census.

Democracy as Group Census

When democratic outcomes merely mirror a simple census—of ethnicity or other group membership—they begin to be too conflictive for compromise and too disruptive for continued order. Electing a government by group census need not be a disaster. The government might turn out to be reasonable and relatively equitable. Or it might

[1] Robert A. Dahl, *A Preface to Democratic Theory* (Chicago: University of Chicago Press, 1956), 132–3.
[2] Alexis de Tocqueville, *Democracy in America*, 2 vols. (New York: Knopf, 1945; 1st edns. 1835, 1840), i. 260.

be that no census group is in a position to dominate the government. For example, an election that turned into a group or ethnic census in the former Yugoslavia might not have been a problem, because no group could have won overwhelmingly—Serbs at about a third of the total population were the largest group.

Commonly, however, election by group census is disastrous. Ethnic censuses in Croatia, Serbia, Kosovo, and Macedonia, would have produced huge majorities for one group over others—as they have done in both Croatia and Serbia under the lethal leadership of, respectively, Franjo Tudjman and Slobodan Milosevic. The 1993 election in Burundi that democratically brought the first Hutu president to office by a nearly two-to-one margin was reviled by Tutsis as *de facto* an ethnic census. The Hutu victory set off a bloody civil war that brought Tutsis back to autocratic power. (That civil war may have played a signalling role in the far greater violence of the ensuing civil war in Rwanda that brought the minority Tutsis to power there.) Recent elections in Sri Lanka have been ethnic censuses that have deepened conflict. India threatens to slide into ethnic census to replace its shaky democracy. Canada and Belgium might eventually be taken apart by ethnic census. Lani Guinier and others have proposed a territorially contrived ethnic census to allow the election of more blacks in the United States. The actual creation of substantially black districts had the perverse effect of benefiting the Republican Party in southern states in the congressional elections of 1994.[3]

There are at least two conspicuous conceptual problems with group census voting. First, such a system may run aground on the *changing structures of the relevant groups*. For example, ethnic censuses in Yugoslavia and other nations miss the large fraction of the population who are the product of intermarriage. And the fixing of shares of representation economically is entirely misguided if there is economic change. Luddites and related groups might often win restrictions that would cripple generally beneficial economic change. Allotting fixed numbers or percentages of seats in a representative body to a particular group—something that might initially be grounded in claims of democratic representativeness—can lead to severely unrepresentative results if the relative size of the group

---

[3] Government has often been based on group membership censuses of other kinds, such as corporatist government by guilds, estates, or other corporate groups, including worker and industry groups.

changes. Because of the massive shift out of agriculture, congressional districts that once made sense in the United States shifted to give a heavy bias to agricultural and rural interests against urban interests. The largest urban district in Texas had fifty times the population of the smallest rural district.

Differential demographic trends have changed balances in Belgium and rendered the earlier fixed allotment of seats to Maoris in the New Zealand parliament increasingly unfair. Beginning with the elections of 1994, the solution in New Zealand has been the creation of two overlapping electoral maps of the nation, one for Maori and Maori descendants only and the other for the general electorate. Maoris decide before each election in which district they will vote, and this determines the number of Maori districts. Oddly, if the government must periodically or eventually reconsider the weight of seats assigned to a declining group, the reconsideration can lead to direct conflict with the group. Under its new constitutional arrangements, the split into Maori and general election districts is adjusted automatically every five years by the Maoris themselves, so that the re-weighting is not conflictive.[4]

Secondly, a group census makes sense at all only to the extent that the issues at stake in government decisions are *issues on which position systematically correlates very strongly with group membership*. Typically, this will be true only for certain classes of matters. In particular, group membership and policy position correlate when government is in a position to allocate resources to various groups and might do so on the basis of the groups' support. But for such issues, government does not provide for the mutual advantage of all unless it is blind to group membership in its allocations or is carefully neutral in allocating according to percentage of total population or workforce. Then, a group census might be necessary for determining allocation percentages, but not for electing a government.

One might argue that group membership and policy position could correlate strongly on certain other policies, such as those concerning religious beliefs. For example, in the United States there is a relatively strong correlation between being Catholic and opposing the legality of abortion. Here, it is implausible to suppose that government serves mutual advantage unless the divisive issue is considered *less important* than the value of generalized order with

---

[4] For a brief account, see Jack Nagel, 'New Zealand's Novel Solution to the Problem of Minority Representation', *The Good Society*, 5 (Spring 1995): 25–7.

democratic decision-making. In general, this is a likely view, although Hobbes, Locke, and many others struggled through eras in which religion was seemingly the most important issue and was deeply divisive. Today religious visions have destroyed the prospects of democracy for the foreseeable future in Iran and threaten to do so as well in Algeria and Egypt. Even in the most stable democratic nation, there may be a fanatical religious minority who would risk the destruction of democracy to promulgate their views. It would be astonishing, however, if religious opposition to abortion, homosexuality, science, and other issues were deep-seated enough to destroy democratic governments in the North Atlantic community.

Interests and Democracy

Following Aristotle, Durkheim, and many others, Talcott Parsons insisted that it is the coincidence of values that makes a society cohere.[5] He supposed that nothing else could possibly bring about this result and he considered it a sociological fact that shared norms are a necessary part of the explanation of social order. But consider the possibility that mere interests could produce coherence. The way to secure the bulk of my interests is the way simultaneously to secure yours. A set of laws that covers all of us in the same way is what we both want. We might quibble a bit about particular laws, but we agree in general on the set of them. Similarly, on many major policy issues, we share interests to some extent, often to a great extent. Of course, I might like to have specially contrived laws that exempt just me from some burdens or hindrances—but only monarchs and senators can expect to get such treatment. Next best for me is a fairly extensive set of laws that cover me as well as everyone else. On this, I and virtually everyone else have interest in coordinating.

The first problem of government is to achieve order, so that we may individually be safe in our daily efforts to live with others and to work for our own benefit. If this interest is great enough and common enough, its protection is the background necessary for the marginal workings of democracy—as it is for any constructive form of government. Hobbes's theory, as outlined in Chapter 1, is essentially

[5] Talcott Parsons, *The Structure of Social Action* (New York: Free Press, 1968, 2nd edn.; 1st edn. 1937), 247–9 and *passim*.

a mutual-advantage theory of government.[6] In the conditions of his time in England, he supposed it true that virtually everyone would be a loser from any effort at revolution to create a different or a different kind of government. Therefore, he concluded that it was best to be loyal to the current government, almost independently of what that government happened to be. This conclusion obviously requires major empirical claims. But the claims seem superficially plausible, at least for most of the current forms of government, although they might not seem plausible for rule by the medieval Taliban in Afghanistan or by military troglodytes in Myanmar.

If democracy depends on a generalized background coordination on order, what can elicit coordination from all of us? Democracy works especially well when there is a large capital stock that is at risk if order breaks down, especially if the capital stock is spread fairly broadly through the society, as it is in contemporary industrial states. In such a case, if rebuilding the capital stock would take enormous time and effort, then all those who share sufficiently in it have an interest in maintaining order.[7] The distressing scenes of people weeping in the ruins or returning to their destroyed homes and lost belongings in the wars of Yugoslavia and even of impoverished Rwanda and Burundi exemplify the enormity of the interest these people had in order.[8]

It is an old thesis in the politics of the working class that class politics will be denatured by *embourgeoisement*—the growing wealth of workers as they gain stakes in homes and other things. John Goldthorpe *et al.* argue that English working-class attitudes towards politics do not show evidence of *embourgeoisement*.[9] But there may well have been a dramatic and important effect of *embourgeoisement* that their surveys did not capture. Workers might have been rallied for violent revolutionary activity a century ago or even in the 1930s. Without dramatic economic setbacks, it is hard to believe they could be mobilized for revolution today. Workers in successful industrial

[6] Russell Hardin, 'Hobbesian Political Order', *Political Theory*, 19 (May 1991): 156–80.
[7] Hobbes supposed we must all suffer net losses over our own lifetimes from any revolution—only a subsequent generation might benefit from our effort to change governments.
[8] For the lingering pain in Yugoslavia, see *New York Times*, 14 Sept. 1997: 1.1.
[9] John H. Goldthorpe, David Lockwood, Frank Bechhofer, and Jennifer Platt, *The Affluent Worker in the Class Structure* (Cambridge: Cambridge University Press, 1969). Adam Przeworski argues to the contrary in 'Material Interests, Class Compromise, and the Transition to Socialism', *Politics and Society,* 10 (1980) 125–53.

states today could not wage revolution without great personal losses to themselves and, most probably, their children. Revolutionary class action is likely to be a thing of the past in these nations unless there is prior economic failure that destroys what revolution might have destroyed.[10]

Revolutions are usually made by those who have relatively little to lose, for whom starting over is not radically inferior to continuing as things are. Of course, among those for whom starting over is often not a great burden are the young, who have yet to start much of anything. A spate of warfare might be entertaining to many of them and it might be a form of procrastination on deciding on a life. Among those who are older, the wealthy might instigate coups, but they do not often make revolutions. There is a somewhat odd exception to this claim, which is that colonial revolutions against foreign rulers are commonly made by the wealthy. For example, George Washington, Thomas Jefferson, *et al.*, were the élite of the colonies that became the United States. Perhaps in part for this reason, many students of revolution do not count such colonial secessions as that of the United States, Kenya, or the then Northern Rhodesia among the great revolutions that interest them.

Perhaps Hobbes's insight that even the instigators of rebellion are apt to lose from it requires profound understanding. But it seems more likely that many ordinary people would share that insight and would fear that there could be huge losses before there could be any gains from revolution. They might even expect their losses to outweigh their gains in the long term. Still, ordinary people seem willing to join in revolutionary and civil war conflicts, as in contemporary Yugoslavia and in Rwanda and Burundi. For most of the individuals, the explanation may simply be that, once the mayhem begins, they are involved whether they wanted to be or not. Then norms of exclusion begin to be invoked against anyone who does not go along with his or her group.[11]

What could have made Yugoslavs, Burundians, and Rwandans go to self-destructive civil war? Some of them perhaps did not think they shared in the material and other gains from order, so that they did not have much to lose—but this cannot have been the case for

[10] See further, Russell Hardin, 'Acting Together, Contributing Together', *Rationality and Society*, 3 (July 1991): 365–80.

[11] Russell Hardin, *One for All: The Logic of Group Conflict* (Princeton: Princeton University Press, 1995), ch. 4.

many people. Some of them perhaps did not expect their own material belongings and status to be at risk in attacks on other groups.
This, for example, may have been especially true of Serbs in Bosnia,
who were mostly rural while their war against Croats and Muslims
was fought in towns and cities, where the more prosperous others
lived. And some of them stood to gain from leadership of violent
attacks. Finally, and perhaps most importantly, in cases in which
order had already broken down or seemed very shaky, although violence would mean losses, these losses could be kept smaller for any
group that pre-emptively attacked.[12] In so far as this is true, no group
in such a position can be trusted unless it somehow convincingly
pre-commits to being democratic or there are institutional barriers to
stymie the recourse to pre-emptive attack. But, for groups, even
more than for nations, meaningful pre-commitment is exceedingly
difficult.

   Consider the Tutsi-dominated Rwandan rebels, who began their
civil war against the Hutu-dominated government in about 1990.
Three decades earlier, most Tutsis and many Hutus hostile to the
autocratic Hutu government were expelled from Rwanda and lived
in refugee camps just outside Rwanda. Their children were the main-
stay of the later rebel force that entered Rwanda and overthrew the
government and stopped Hutu carnage against Tutsis. No matter
what happened, they should have wanted to start over, because the
life they had in refugee camps was dismal. Indeed, they should perhaps have wanted to start over even if the cost of doing so was wag-
ing and winning a bloody civil war in Rwanda. The victorious Hutus
of 1959–61 won too much for their own good, and they and especially their children have since had to pay for it.

Constitutional Pre-commitment

Democracy can typically work well only where it serves the mutual
advantage of diverse interests to have democratic government. There
could be many contexts in which some group—usually a small
minority interest in conflict with a large interest—might be supposed
to have an interest in blocking or disrupting democratic government.

---

[12] Hardin, *One for All*, ch. 6

If that is so, then democracy is not mutually advantageous—it serves a majority group well but possibly not a minority group. Even in such cases, there might be, at least in principle, possibilities for compromise because failure to compromise leads to losses that could be avoided. Unfortunately, the in-principle possibilities may not be actual possibilities because neither the larger nor the smaller group may be able convincingly to pre-commit to abiding by the compromise. This is especially true if the terms of the compromise must necessarily be left somewhat open-ended because, as is often likely to be the case, future conflicts cannot be fully anticipated.

A standard device for securing pre-commitment to various arrangements under an acceptable compromise is to fix those arrangements in a constitution. Unfortunately, pre-commitment in these contexts succeeds only to the extent that it would be renewed at every subsequent stage for the good reason that it would still be in the interest of relevant parties. If interests or parties change, the initial pre-commitment is put at risk, perhaps grave risk. If it breaks, democracy might then enable one of the current groups to gain ascendancy contrary to the terms of the constitution. A constitutional agreement might therefore have the perverse result that, *by empowering government, it eventually empowers a nascent majority to dominate other groups.*

Even absolute constitutional barriers to change in the terms of a compromise do not work. Multi-lingual, multi-cultural, multi-ethnic, and multi-religious nations such as Belgium may attempt to fix the terms of representation in government to prevent turning an election into an ethnic census. In the longer run, such constitutional barriers may merely undercut the credibility of a constitution, especially if the population shifts in favour of one group over another.

For a particularly strenuous case of constitutional engineering, consider Tito's Yugoslavia. Under Tito, Yugoslavia was carved into quasi-ethnic regions that had constitutional standing to protect certain of their supposed interests—although it would be wrong to claim that the groups had substantial interests in conflict beyond the mere conflict over which group got what share of resources and power. At the same time, in practice, Tito was a nationalist—indeed he was multi-ethnic from Croatian, Montenegrin, and Serbian forebears—without primary attachment to one of these regions. These two stances fit badly together. A genuine nationalist should more plausibly have carved up the regions less tendentiously, without the seeming confusion of different ethnic 'nations' with geographically specific territories. Yugoslavia generally could not be mapped ethnically onto territories. For example, in its biggest cities and many of its smaller towns people of many ethnic backgrounds mingled. Perversely, however, Tito's system created, almost as though it were a matter of nature, leaders of each of the geographical territories who were themselves ethnically *and* territorially identified. As Yugoslavia neared its demise, the personal careers of certain of these regional leaders depended on their success in mobilizing ethnic support against the Titoist system. Only in Bosnia, which was too nearly evenly split between Croats, Muslims, and Serbs, did Tito's system seem to have natural support—until, of course, Tito's system collapsed nationally with the secessions of Slovenia and Croatia.[13]

Virtually all that has happened in the Yugoslav débâcle has been in violation of the constitutional pre-commitments to a strongly federal system. Milosevic altered the status of Kosovo and Vojvodina in order to gain two more votes in the national council of republics and autonomous regions. With Serbia's and Montenegro's votes already behind him, the addition of the two no-longer autonomous regions gave him half the total vote. The secessions of Slovenia and Croatia then gave him solid control. The secessions *de facto* made the rump Yugoslavia a Serbian empire, putting the majorities of the populations of Bosnia, Kosovo, and Macedonia at risk.

Pre-commitments are splendid—if they are followed by continued commitments to the same arrangements. If commitments waver, pre-commitments totter. In essence, they are worth nothing except as a signal about what the present commitments are, unless they are given force with institutional or other obstacles put in the way of reneging on them.

American Extremes

The American experience with democracy under the Constitution is historically fascinating in that it represents the two extremes of the coordination-theory account of constitutional democracy. The US Constitution worked remarkably well to coordinate the nation

---

[13] See further, Hardin, *One for All*, ch. 6.

during its first half century in what was, after all, a novel and unsure experiment. And it worked very well in the decades between 1876 and the 1930s. Between these two periods it failed almost as disastrously as the exceedingly brief experiment in democracy in Burundi in 1993.

Democracy has run into great risk in the United States on several occasions. Two of these stand out: the period of contest over slavery and the period of contest over economic policy during the Great Depression. In each of these times, a very important issue seemed to require a decision one way or the contrary way, with little room for mutual-advantage compromise; and there were large fractions of the population who lined up on each of the two sides. In both of these periods, significant numbers of the population seemed to think the divisive issue was the most important issue of the day, so important as to be worth wrecking the government to get the right outcome.

The contest over slavery actually split the nation. The Great Depression might also have split the nation if war and eventual economic prosperity had not saved the day. There have been other major crises, including the period of transition to party rule and then the change of parties after the election of 1800, the Missouri Compromise (on slavery in new states) of 1820, and, most recently, the period of contest over the Vietnam war. In these cases, compromise was relatively easy because leaders on both sides of the relevant contests preferred to make the transition without harming the constitutional arrangements. For example, Hamilton himself helped to engineer the transfer of power to Jefferson in 1801, as discussed in Chapter 3. The contest over the Vietnam War was similar to the Great Depression in that it was finally overcome by changing views of what was possible—in this instance, realization of the seeming impossibility of winning the war itself and the overwhelming costs of continuing to try to win it.

One can see the form of the special difficulty of democracy in the apparent compromises, from the constitutional era onward, over slavery. At the Constitutional Convention, northern opponents of slavery let it be, because they wanted southern states to join the new nation. And southerners accepted, as their compromise, the end of the slave trade by 1808 (natural increase had already nearly displaced the importation of new slaves). *De facto*, this issue was of concern only to South Carolina and Georgia, the only states that had not independently ended the slave trade. But representatives of these two states at the Constitutional Convention insisted that their states would not ratify the Constitution if it ended the slave trade. (In the event, the Georgia ratifying convention voted unanimously for the Constitution.) Northerners noted that to include a formal protection of the trade for any length of time in the new constitution went beyond what the Articles of Confederation guaranteed. This was a trivially rhetorical point in that the Articles permitted a single state to veto any action, which meant that the Continental Congress could not have legislated against the slave trade unless all states were willing. Hence, settling on a definite date for the end of the trade was a genuine bargain that could be made on the back of the fact that all eleven fully participating states in the Philadelphia debates wanted all thirteen states to be members of the new nation first and were willing to bargain on this issue.

Also at the convention, southerners wanted to count slaves fully in determining their states' populations for the purposes of determining the number of their representatives in the House of Representatives. But northerners wanted to count them not at all because they were property, not citizens. The two groups settled on counting a slave as three-fifths of a person for both representation and per capita taxation. This was a matter for possible compromise because the white men who wrote the Constitution had more interest in the economic prosperity to be attained from strong economic union than in the details of continued slavery in the South. In keeping with the general defeat of communitarian interests, however, the convention did not yield to bargaining over the form of ratification, which was by special convention or referendums in each of the states rather than by approval of state legislatures as Anti-Federalists such as Roger Sherman and Luther Martin wanted.

The legislative Missouri Compromise of 1820 protected the slave states' future interests in blocking national action to end slavery by balancing new states between free and slave states, beginning with free Maine and slave Missouri. On William Riker's account, John Knox Polk (president from 1845–9), believed that the renewal of politics over slavery in the 1840s and 1850s was almost entirely opportunistic.[14] He supposed that potential leaders on both sides took stands beyond their own beliefs in order to gain advantage in their

[14] William H. Riker, *Liberalism against Populism: A Confrontation between the Theory of Democracy and the Theory of Public Choice* (Prospect Heights, Il.: Waveland Press, 1988; 1st pub. 1982), ch. 9.

political careers. But it was also true that large numbers of voters voted stalwartly on the issue and that some leaders were genuinely abolitionist or were implacably committed to maintaining slavery. The potential destruction of the Democratic Party (the renamed Republican Party of Jefferson) that so worried Polk was, if not guaranteed, at least greatly facilitated by that party's national base that gave it hope for holding the presidency and the Congress only if it could continue to coordinate southern and northern voters on a joint programme.

What was not foreseen at the time of the constitutional debates was that slavery would become far more important economically to the deep South and that the growth of the nation into the western territories would tip the balance against the slave states. Cotton production rose from about five million pounds per year in 1791–5 to 1,749 million pounds per year in 1856–60.[15] This 350-fold increase radically altered the value of slavery. As noted above, the great flow of new immigrants went almost entirely to the northern and western states. The original economic census (for and against slavery) was therefore undercut both by changes in the commitments of the relevant groups and by substantial changes in their memberships. The Supreme Court, faced with difficult fugitive slave cases, held to or even exceeded the compromise on behalf of the southern states. But the national electorate of 1860, voting democratically with full manhood suffrage for whites, ignored the compromise and elected the anti-slavery Abraham Lincoln president, giving him enough support in Congress to shake the compromise. Pre-commitment in the form of various institutional structures to block or impede changes in the original compromise was then inadequate to satisfy southern leaders. The compromise was shattered, the South seceded and was crushed in the Civil War, and slaves were made citizens under northern hegemony.

In the Depression-era crisis over economic policy, democracy may have played a strong role in enabling President Roosevelt and

---

[15] C. Gordon Post, 'Introduction', to John C. Calhoun, *A Disquisition on Government and Selections from the Discourse* (Indianapolis: Bobbs-Merrill, 1953), p. x. Cotton exports increased 800-fold in that period. Therefore, the cotton states were firmly anti-tariff. South Carolina proposed nullification of the tariffs of 1828 and 1832. Under that doctrine, any state could declare federal legislation void within its own borders. That would have required revocation of the Commerce Clause. This was perhaps the first serious revival of Anti-Federalist politics since final ratification of the Constitution.

the Congress to alter constitutional arrangements beyond recognition. They dramatically expanded the quasi-legislative, quasi-executive, quasi-judicial regulatory state, contrary to the basic principles of Montesquieu, Madison, and the Constitution. Irrespective of whether their institutional redesign was well conceived, it may have dampened politics from the left at the time and thereby helped enable the nation to move on from the grim Depression. But the end result—massive administrative government with very limited oversight from the legislative, executive, and judicial branches—*de facto* replaced much of the prior constitutional scheme of government, in which there had originally been no quasi-autonomous fourth branch.[16] All of the restructuring was possible only because the president and the Congress were in rough agreement on shunting responsibility onto the new agencies and because the Supreme Court could soon be bullied into letting the changes stand as though they were exempt from constitutional review.

These two episodes produced drastic changes outside the Constitution. The Civil War conflict was handled extra-constitutionally and then it was patched over extra-constitutionally by the victorious northern states. The 1930s problems of economic failure were handled more nearly harmoniously but still extra-constitutionally. It is often said that the United Kingdom is virtually unique in having an unwritten constitution. In actual fact, the United States now has an unwritten alteration of its constitution in the creation of the fourth, enormously important branch of government. Why did the new system work? As in the adoption of the original Constitution by the thirteen states, the new system was a coordination resolution that built on broad consensus. However, the 1930s coordination was not on the Constitution *per se* but on doing something about the economic malaise of the Depression. Many critics of the time thought the malaise was itself the product of governmental, constitutional failure, and that its resolution required *de facto* constitutional revision.

We may loosely characterize the whole sweep of American experience with liberalism, constitutionalism, and democracy. From 1789 until about 1850, there was a regime of political and economic liberalism, constitutionalism, and democracy. From about 1850 to 1876 there was a massive breakdown of coordination and a failure of

[16] There are many accounts. See Cass R. Sunstein, *The Partial Constitution* (Cambridge, Mass.: Harvard University Press, 1993), ch. 2.

both constitutionalism and democracy. This era began with a long transitional period of political malaise. (As though to affirm Mill's and Tocqueville's disparaging remarks about American leaders, American schoolchildren who can name almost all the presidents typically cannot name those from 1849 to 1861—they did not matter in this period of radical failure.) This period was torn, of course, by extra-constitutional civil war and it was ended by an extra-constitutional bargain on who was 'elected' president in 1876. From 1861 to 1877, the Constitution was travestied. The corrupt resolution of 1877 that returned local power to the southern states and made Rutherford B. Hayes, Republican (not Jefferson's Party), president then did what Madison had striven so hard to block. It gave great power to the immediately arbitrary governments of the southern states and set up the reign of Jim Crow. Nevertheless, the prior dozen years of northern hegemony over the South after the Civil War was enough to make the end of formal slavery irreversible.

The period from 1877 to 1937 saw a restoration of constitutionalism and of democracy that was increasingly hamstrung for blacks in the south. The period since 1937 has seen the end of much of constitutionalism in large-scale economic matters, and the efflorescence of the administrative state, along with greater democracy for blacks. Throughout the two centuries, democracy has at best been limited in the ways that it must be in practice in any real society and it has often been virtually irrelevant.

TABLE 7.1. *Liberalism, constitutionalism, and democracy in the United States of America*

1789–c. 1850	Political and economic liberalism, constitutionalism, democracy
c. 1850–77	Breakdown of coordination on constitutionalism and democracy
1877–1937	Political and economic liberalism, constitutionalism, partial democracy
1937–	Political and economic liberalism, partial constitutionalism, democracy

Democracy and Economic Development

Most modern democratic nations grew relatively slowly into democracy. The suffrage expanded very slowly in England and France, with some retrenchment in France. It spread at first quickly but then quite slowly in the United States, with black men brought in only after the Civil War and all women only in 1920. (There was female suffrage in some states before the Nineteenth Amendment. Jeanette Rankin of Wyoming was elected to Congress in 1916. New Jersey had female suffrage in the first decade or so of the new nation.) In many colonial nations democracy was introduced full-blown overnight at independence, as it was in much of Eastern Europe in 1989 or immediately afterwards.

It is plausible that, in earlier times, mutual-advantage claims would have failed in, say, England for the entire adult populace but that they were valid for the smaller set of those eligible to vote. Clearly, mutual-advantage claims would have seemed like nonsense to politically sophisticated slaves in the United States until about the time of the Civil War. It was precisely because the majority was turning too heavily against slavery that the southern states pre-emptively seceded from the Union before they would have lost the slavery issue to democratic decision.

Or consider France after the Revolution. Napoleon created a vast class of small-holding peasants, who were essentially subsistence farmers. Suppose full-scale democracy had been introduced then with suffrage for all adults. Peasant agricultural interests would numerically have overwhelmed all other interests combined. It is hard to imagine that government organized around the interests of subsistence agriculture could have brought France to prosperity—perhaps ever, but surely not in the next century or two. Progress depended, rather, on moving people off such subsistence farms, which, as Marx recognized, were the central reason for the deplorable conditions of the peasant class. When they did vote, as in 1848, they voted stupidly with capitalism against their own interests (in socialism, Marx supposed) because they conservatively defended their way of life and supposed their problems were somehow caused by bad state policy rather than by the economic impossibility of organizing production their way and thereby being prosperous.[17]

[17] Karl Marx, *The Eighteenth Brumaire of Louis Bonaparte* (New York: International Publishers, 1963; 1st pub. 1852), esp. 118–35.

On Marx's account, they might have been much better off not en-titled to vote.

In agrarian nations in our time, land reform may be virtually nec-essary merely to stop the politics of land reform. It might actually harm almost everyone, but a very large number expect benefits from it and are willing to engage in substantial political activity to bring it about. One might think this an implausible, because irrational result. But it is only partly irrational. At the margin, I might be better off if I get my share of land. But if the way I get it is through a system that gives most farm families their own shares of land, then I might not be better off. The tendency to think of the marginal change is perhaps a mistake, but it is one which many people in many contexts make, for understandable reasons of their lack of special competence in more general economic or strategic reasoning.

Apart from farm workers, current plantation or *latifundia* owners, who are a very small number of people, expect losses from land reform unless they are compensated beyond the capacity of most governments. Naturally, they too are willing to engage in politics, by violent means if necessary. If land reform carries the day, then ordin-ary economic trends might drive most of the supposed beneficiaries and their children off the land. As people leave the land, there is typ-ically no loss of productivity, but there may often be grievous initial loss of well-being. The next generation might tend to be much better off than they would have been on the farm, but the current genera-tion might be losers for the remainder of their lives.

Both the reform of ownership patterns involved in land reform and the economic changes that impoverish small farmers and drive them from the land might be called structural changes. But the for-mer comes from an identifiable political action, whereas the latter seems to happen in a decentralized, uncontrolled way. There is, of course, some centralized control, although in many industrial nations the control is exercised with various subsidies and protec-tions perversely designed to help farmers stay on the land and to keep their children there, as in France, Japan, and the United States. The decline of farming as an occupation might once have occasioned strong reactions as something to be far more forcefully controlled to keep farmers or peasants on the land. But that posi-tion lacks credibility after two centuries of the radical move out of an agricultural economy that is essentially a subsistence industry for the bulk of the population into an economy that is diverse and that has only a very small, but highly productive, agricultural sector.

In the traditional cases of the move to greater democracy, piecemeal democratization may have been enormously functional in the long run. In these cases, an attempt at instant democracy with universal suffrage might have been much less successful even at bringing about a working, full-suffrage democracy. Why could instant liberal democracy suddenly work after 1989 in much of Eastern Europe? There had, of course, been a veneer of democracy under Communism, but there was not competitive democracy or genuinely open choice. Rather, there were elections, with strong incentives to vote even when there was no choice available. Hence, the peoples of Eastern Europe had the experience and the habit of voting but not the experience of democracy.

So why could they make it work? Perhaps because that was a unique time when *there was relatively wide consensus on how to organize the economy* and when general order of more basic kinds had been successfully achieved and was not at issue. The prior economic order was widely questioned, even reviled. A major reason for the consensus was the broad evidence of comparative economics and politics. For example, Czech and East German regions, which had once rivalled the wealth of regions of West Germany and France and exceeded that of Italy, had fallen far behind, especially at the level of individual prosperity. And their peoples had far greater restrictions on various freedoms. Many East Europeans knew people or even had relatives who had gone West to thrive personally, professionally, and financially. Many East Europeans did not wish to emigrate in order to thrive. Rather, they wanted to bring the West home.

While there were, and still are, proponents of central direction of the economy in all of these nations, the governments that have been elected have virtually all chosen to follow some path to market organization. Poland, the Czech Republic, Hungary, Slovakia, and Bulgaria, and the two renegade states from Yugoslavia, Slovenia and Croatia, have taken such a path with alacrity, and East Germany voted itself instantly into the West German market. Former Communists who have been elected to succeed previously elected non-Communists in Poland and Hungary, apparently on the strength of their protests that liberalization was being pursued too quickly and harshly, have nevertheless continued the basic policies.[18]

[18] István Deák, 'Post-Post-Communist Hungary', *New York Review of Books* (11 August 1994): 33–8.

This was a time when consensus was perhaps sufficiently broad that any kind of government might have been expected to make relevant policy, although experience in Belarus belies this claim.

Of course, it is too early to tell whether the conditions for democracy are adequate in any of these cases, and there is good reason to doubt that Russia and some of the Former Soviet Republics are ready for democracy. Beneath the current consensus on the need for economic reform, there may be other conflicts too deep and wide to be bridged by routine democratic compromise. In some of these nations, indeed, there are ethnic conflicts that cut very deeply in economic decisions on allocation of resources and jobs. And in others there may still be too great disagreement about fundamental economic policy, with continuing strong support from some quarters for central control of the economy. There are some clear losers from the move from central command to market economy and, coincidentally, there are sure to be losers from changes in economic demand as agriculture continues to be displaced by industry and as basic heavy industry is displaced by new electronic, communication, and other high-tech industries, as well as by service industries that were missing in the old system but that now spring up to meet the ready demand. Both these types of losing group pose potential opposition to market reforms (as discussed in Chapter 6, in the section on 'Economic Transition in a Constitutional Democracy').

Communal Good

A group-level version of Talcott Parsons's collective good, mentioned in Chapter 1, was behind some of the Anti-Federalist objections to the Philadelphia Constitution. Gordon Wood has argued that the Anti-Federalists were democrats striving against the Federalist aristocrats.[19] This seems fundamentally wrong in at least three important respects. First, Madison, the greatest of the Federalists, was a theorist of democracy of a kind that a harsh critic

[19] Gordon S. Wood, *The Creation of the American Republic, 1776–1787* (Chapel Hill, NC: North Carolina University Press, 1969); see also Wood, 'Interests and Disinteredness in the Making of the Constitution', in Richard Beeman, Stephen Botein, and Edward C. Carter II, eds., *Beyond Confederation: Origins of the Constitution and American National Identity* (Chapel Hill, NC: University of North Carolina Press, 1987), 69–109.

might call democratic aristocracy, as one might read from the sympathetic accounts of Samuel Beer and Jack Rakove.[20] What Madison opposed was small-scale democracy that would tend to produce narrow and narrow-minded majorities that would promulgate their own interests at the direct expense of local minorities. In many writings, but most famously in *Federalist*, 10, he supposed that national-level democracy would, by virtue of its large scale, produce representatives more nearly attuned to larger interests and less driven by local prejudices, which would be cancelled out in the national-level debates.

Secondly, the Anti-Federalists were primarily hostile to the national vision of the Federalists. The only aristocrats they opposed were the urbane men of money. Many of them, especially those not in attendance at Philadelphia, where, as noted in Chapter 3, only those who could afford to pay their own way and to absent themselves from their ordinary affairs were able to spend a long hot summer, were democrats only to a very limited extent. The eventual Anti-Federalists in attendance in Philadelphia were themselves relatively aristocratic. What they most shared with the Anti-Federalists not in attendance was principal loyalty to their localities. What they wanted was local government control of as much as possible. They wanted to be oligarchs in their small worlds rather than more nearly equal citizens in a larger world. The New York Anti-Federalists in control of the New York legislature extended the suffrage to include all adult males for the purpose of electing delegates to the state's ratifying convention, presumably in order to swamp the downstate Federalist vote. Such democracy was no part of their normal politics for electing the state government, which was dominated by relatively wealthy men. They were so democratic for the ratifying convention presumably because they expected the additional voters to add to the opposition to the Constitution.

Thirdly, and perhaps most obviously, many of the Anti-Federalists were primarily opposed to the loss of state sovereignty as represented in the representation of states, not persons, under the Articles of Confederation. While it was not impossible to suppose that one could have democracy through representation of states, it

---

[20] Samuel H. Beer, *To Make a Nation: The Rediscovery of American Federalism* (Cambridge, Mass.: Harvard University Press, 1993), ch. 8; Jack N. Rakove, 'The Structure of Politics at the Accession of George Washington', in Beeman *et al.*, *Beyond Confederation*, 261–94.

was a confusing and seemingly specious supposition. The apparent core of democratic thinking is that each person somehow counts equally. In the national government of states, as opposed to persons, fifty citizens of one state might count for no more than one citizen of another state. It was Madison and other Federalists who most objected to the mismatch of states under the government of the Articles of Confederation—Madison wanted representation by population, not by state. The putatively democratic Anti-Federalists generally preferred the government of the Articles to that implied by the new Constitution.

If it was not democracy *per se* to which the Anti-Federalists were committed, what was their driving value? In their writings, many of the Anti-Federalists were ideologically communitarians, including among their strongest advocates the communitarians of the Hudson River, western Pennsylvania, Rhode Island outside Providence, and many other local communities. In so far as these men believed in democracy, they did so because they believed there would be a harmonious local vision of what ought to be done by government. Hence, democracy would yield not an arbitration of conflicts but a simple expression of virtually unanimously held views.

Such democrats were not the wave of the future that Wood extols, the people who 'spoke for the emerging world of egalitarian democracy and the private pursuit of happiness'.[21] The latter are the descendants of Madison, not of the Anti-Federalists. The Anti-Federalists were not future-oriented democrats. They were oriented to the past even more than the Federalist quasi-aristocrats. Indeed, they were oriented to a past that was doomed. They were social Luddites.

Charles Beard supposed most of the Philadelphia conventioneers had little theory of government or politics.[22] It is surprising, then, how much theory was expounded during the ratification debates. Anti-Federalist theorists, such as Brutus, Cato, and Federal Farmer, put forth communitarian arguments, owing, no doubt, largely to Montesquieu. Here is Brutus: 'In a republic, the manners, sentiments, and interests of the people should be similar. If this be not the case, there will be a continually striving against those of the other. This will retard the operations of the government, and prevent such

---

[21] Wood, 'Interests and Disinteredness in the Making of the Constitution', 109.

[22] Charles A. Beard, *An Economic Interpretation of the Constitution of the United States* (New York: Macmillan, 1935; 1st pub. 1913).

conclusions as will promote the public good.'[23] This may sound profound but it is only profoundly silly. The objection that Brutus raised against the Constitution of 1787 was the fundamental objection of the Anti-Federalists: a large nation (about three million at that time) could not genuinely be represented by a small body of legislators. The society must be too diverse for a small number of people to know it well enough even to think of representing the populace.

The problem that Brutus identifies is, of course, real. But the idea that even a small society could have similar sentiments and interests was an idealization of the possibilities in any moderately commercial society, and, except for subsistence farming (which involved the large bulk of the population), virtually all of the United States was commercial in 1787. Commerce works through a division of labour, through specialization. If there were no specialization, there would be no point in commerce. Direct democracy in small communities would, hence, produce results little more in harmony with the interests of all than would a representative government over a larger populace. Diversity is the nature of the beast. The Hudson River Anti-Federalists opposed the Constitution in part because it would cut into the advantages they drew from trade regulated at the state level against the interests of neighbouring states, especially New Jersey. In their own economic lives, they depended on the division of labour.

A subjective assessment suggests that claims for communitarianism arise only from those who do not find themselves in the conditions of community and, one might suspect, who would deplore being trapped in community. This is clearly true of the leading Anti-Federalists. Brutus, for example, is generally thought to have been Robert Yates of Albany, a prosperous lawyer. Cato was George Clinton, lawyer and nearly lifetime politician—for eighteen-years governor of New York and eventual vice-president. True to his Anti-Federalist principles, as vice-president presiding over the Senate, he cast the deciding vote against renewal of the charter of the Bank of the United States. The identity of Federal Farmer is disputed; he is most often thought to be Richard Henry Lee, yet another very prosperous lifetime politician who, to his honour as a Virginian, struggled for the abolition of slavery in his state. If anyone could reasonably be called an aristocrat in the United States, Lee was

---

[23] Brutus, no. 1, 18 Oct. 1787, in Herbert J. Storing, ed., *The Complete Anti-Federalist*, 7 vols. (Chicago: University of Chicago Press, 1981), ii. 363–72, at p. 369.

an aristocrat. He was a descendant of a Cavalier who was a member of the privy council of Charles I and who, happily for his progeny, emigrated to Virginia before Charles's regime fell into disaster.

These men were communitarian theorists, perhaps, albeit not especially astute theorists. Federal Farmer is commonly held to be one of the best of the Anti-Federalist writers.[24] But he is far below the level of Madison, Hamilton, and even Jay, possibly because he had the harder case to make. Brutus gave the best answer to the *Federalist*, but not a compelling answer. But, whatever their political positions, none of these men lived the life of community—unless it was a particularly élite community that depended on a division of labour to define other groups lower down to support their elevated life. They are not plausible candidates to be actual communitarians. If there can be a professional disqualification from being a communitarian, surely practising lawyers are disqualified—after all, their existence is defined by Brutus's 'continually striving against' the interests of others. Unfortunately, therefore, it is hard to take the quasi-communitarian visions that they shared with Montesquieu seriously—because they did not take them seriously themselves in their own lives. (In this, they were like most of the academic communitarians of our time.)

The Anti-Federalist writers may have had other good reasons to oppose the shift from state-level to national-level authority. The central part of their case that fitted their lives was their commitment to their places in the smaller ponds of their states, places in which they were the local élite. Lee and Yates did not long survive the adoption of the Constitution, but Clinton went on to a major career in the larger federal government.[25] As did many of the Anti-Federalists who lived long enough, he prospered nationally after the rise of Jefferson, who shared some of their split intellectual personality with his own beliefs in a kind of social organization that was inherently élitist despite his ideological leanings to democracy.

Before the rise of Andrew Jackson, Jefferson's ostensibly agrarian party did not speak for or to most farmers. Indeed, that party carried on with the Hamiltonian policies it had reviled while Hamilton was secretary of the treasury, even continuing a national bank. It is a further peculiarity that American farmers became politically serious

[24] Storing, *The Complete Anti-Federalist*, ii. 214.
[25] Lee died in 1794; Yates died in 1801 (according to Beard, he died poor (*An Economic Interpretation of the Constitution*, 149)).

only when their day was virtually past. When they might have seized the government, they were generally irrelevant. When at last they tried, they supposed their economic woes were a matter of monetary policy rather than economic transition and they nominated an unctuous candidate, William Jennings Bryan, whose main claim was rhetorical flourish in his speech about the 'cross of gold' on which farmers were being crucified.[26] He was trounced three times and arguably brought more harm than good to those whose cause he espoused.

A second reason that farmers had so little impact on the adoption of the Constitution is perhaps that they could see little in the new programme of government that really affected them. Their communities were not after all in control of the state governments any more than they would be of the national government. And they were not heavily involved in commerce in the way that later farmers would be after the rise of the midwestern grain producers and cheap transportation to allow massive exports. Farmers would generally have benefited from low tariffs on manufactured goods, while manufacturers wanted protective tariffs (and they immediately applied to the new government for manifold protections). But farmers had little influence on state tariffs either. It is true that they were virtually unrepresented at the Philadelphia Convention and had no impact on the design of the new government.[27] But they had had no impact on the design of the government that would be superseded by the constitution.

A less charitable explanation for the absence of farming interests from the first decades of American politics after the Revolution

[26] Attribution of their woes to monetary policy has been a terminal illness of agrarian interests. A major focus of some of the Anti-Federalists was the Constitution's provision to redeem debts incurred by the nation at reasonably full value and its promise of a stable currency anchored in specie rather than an inflation-prone paper currency. The Anti-Federalists took the short-term view that it would be cheaper for debtors to let them pay in inflated paper money. In the long run, an unstable currency would generally depress economic activity. As discussed in Chapter 2 (in the discussion of Hobbes), stable expectations were an important part of the drive for the new constitution because a stable currency would mean greater economic prosperity. In the not-so-very long run, unstable currency would entail mutual *dis*advantage for all, including those, such as farmers, who tended to rely on debt and who therefore wanted instability in the short run.

[27] On Beard's account, not one member of the convention directly represented farming, although several had farmer fathers (*An Economic Interpretation of the Constitution*, 149, 88, 90), and Rossiter describes Jacob Broom of Delaware as a modestly successful farmer (Clinton Rossiter, *1787: The Grand Convention* (New York: Macmillan, 1966), 112).

would be Marx's: that the hardship and loneliness of subsistence farming, with its lack of mutually reinforcing class consciousness, was stupefying, so much so that when farmers did vote they might as often have voted for one party as for the other.[28] Indeed, the farm vote in the United States has historically been a swing vote rather than clearly aligned with one party. At the time of ratification, Rossiter said, 'Where men farmed largely for subsistence, where the printed word penetrated laboriously, where life was hard and horizons limited, there, in a land in which few of the better sort had settled and even fewer had risen to prosper, one found apathy, lethargy, and suspicion'.[29]

In any case, the absence of farm interests from the debates and the decision on the new government are striking evidence of how pervasively government depends not so much on support as on lack of active opposition. It requires merely that most people should not mutiny. By default, what was plausibly a majority of the electorate let Madison and his nationalist associates carry the day and the nation against local community.

Group Justice and Democracy

The main impulse for procedural protections of individuals in justice as order, as discussed in Chapter 4, has been universalist. Dyadic issues to be decided yes-no or guilty-not guilty are easily subject to quick coordination, as in mob actions, that can willy-nilly vary in principle from one apparently similar case to another. This would violate the universalist principle that like cases should be treated the same. The point of most contemporary theory in favour of protecting groups, on the contrary, is anti-universalist. A central claim of communitarians is that group visions of the right for their members cannot be judged universalistically. (Indeed, the seeming claim of much communitarian writing is that nothing about values can be judged universalistically.)[30] Hence, groups must be allowed autonomy to determine the right for themselves.

---

[28] Marx, *The Eighteenth Brumaire of Louis Bonaparte*, 123–8.
[29] Rossiter, *1787*, 296.
[30] For further discussion see Hardin, *One for All*, 186–8, 208–14.

Communitarians often implicitly take for granted that the kind of group with which they are concerned has consensual views on what is the right for its members.[31] If this assumption could be taken as true, we could say that the urge of communitarian theory is to guarantee something like democracy at levels below the state by prohibiting more or less universal democratic impositions from the state. On this view, democracy is internally inconsistent or is conflictive across levels of society and it is at the lower level that we should let it determine much of social order.

Principles of group justice might be conceived as analogous to principles of justice as order; they are merely applied not to individuals but to groups. At first sight, this might appear to be a simple analogy that could be worked out in detail to yield protection of group as opposed to individual liberties. Unfortunately, there are both difficult conceptual and empirical problems in carrying out the project of explicating group justice as order.

Conceptually, there is the problem of a multiplicity of groups in a given society, each group with rather different concerns and different accounts of the group good. How are different groups in a pluralist society to regulate their lives differently according to their own principles? Suppose in our society there are several groups, with varied principles for their own order, plus some number of people not in any of these groups. If there are conflicts between the groups, or between the groups and the non-member individuals, these must be regulated by some authority that stands over the groups and individuals. Whose principles determine these overarching rules?

Also conceptually, there is the related problem of how membership in a group is determined. Is it decided by, say, the group's leaders or governing bodies, by the spontaneous choices of members, or by the individual potential member? By the Ayatollah Khomeini, by neighbours, or by the Salman Rushdies of the world?

In addition to these conceptual problems, there is likely to be a major empirical difficulty in any claim for group principles. Few groups are apt to have genuinely consensual views on any rich array of governing principles. Typically, we are in need of governing principles in part because some people must be brought into order against their own wishes. But all of us might need some oversight to guarantee our adherence to common purposes or standards of

---

[31] I will not take up the epistemological issues at the core of this debate. I have discussed them fully in *One for All*, ch. 7.

behaviour. This is merely an instance of the two-stage analysis
above. I want a strong system of legal order that coerces everyone to
be orderly in various ways. I might nevertheless also wish to be able
to violate that system for my own personal advantage, for example,
by stealing from you. If I am sociologically astute, however, it is not
likely that I would want there not to be any general legal order,
because if there is none, there will be nothing I could steal from you.
Without order, we are all worse off, both those who would be obedient to the order we might have and those who would try to violate
it.[32] This anti-solipsist logic of democratic constraints works for
individual liberties and the system of individual justice as order, but
it may not work for group justice as order. Our group or our group
plus allies of other groups might readily vote the equivalent of a bill
of attainder against anyone who, say, blasphemes the god of the
Koran.

This is, of course, the core point of consensus that motivates liberal constitutionalism. It should also motivate constitutionalism
even in a society that elevates groups over individuals. The apparent
view of communitarian thinkers, both philosophical communitarians and practising communitarians, is that the account of Chapter
3 is too pessimistic for communities. Rather than the limited and relatively vague overarching principles on which we might coordinate
in liberal societies, in communities there is an even larger body of
norms on which there is sufficient consensus to motivate political
decisions, including *ex ante* constitutional decisions. Practising communitarians may often think their consensual norms are tantamount
to natural laws, so that they do not need specific constitutional constraints to prevent decisions taken *in medias res*. In actual experience,
however, this conclusion is apt to be either factually stupid, incoherent, or tyrannical in the sense that it frees leadership from constraint.

Empirically, the differences of view among members of any group
are apt to include differences about what general principles we
should have over us. If we resolve this problem democratically
within our group, those of us who lose in that determination might
then have recourse to the larger society and its government to block
our group's rules. Salman Rushdie disapproved of some of the religious strictures that Khomeini wished to enforce. Rushdie was not,

[32] This is essentially the argument of Hobbes, *Leviathan* (London: Penguin, 1968),
chs. 13–15. See Hardin, 'Hobbesian Political Order', *Political Theory* 19 (May 1991),
164–8.

of course, under the direct laws of Iran, but he has potentially been within the reach of Khomeini's fatwa or curse of death. In 1998, long after Khomeini's death, when the Iranian leadership wanted diplomatic recognition from the United Kingdom restored, the Iranian government publicly repudiated the fatwa. Soon afterwards, two Islamic fundamentalist organizations reinstated it and raised the bounty by more than half a million dollars, to over $3 million in total.[33]

In general, group consensus beyond a few commitments is likely to be a chimera. The history of orthodoxies is the history of splintering. The communitarian idyll of consensus on norms is romantic and phony. This is an empirical, not a normative claim. But, oddly, the communitarian normative idyll definitionally *requires an empirical consensus* so that there is no fallacy of composition in speaking of the popular sovereignty of the group. Hence, merely discovering that the facts do not fit it vitiates the normative vision.

One might suppose that to empower groups is to let them make specific decisions from group norms. But the split between *ex ante* and *in medias res* devices will be as cogent for group norms as for individual protections. Even members of a group must want *ex ante* to have institutions to block *in medias res* choice. For example, community standards on pornography should be brought to bear in setting the law, not in enforcing it. A law that leaves it entirely up to a jury to decide what is to count as pornography is hardly a law at all. Even a communitarian should want a jury to decide the facts of its case rather than to stipulate the content of the law.

Group constitutionalism will be like universalistic constitutionalism in that it will not be individualized as to persons. But it will typically be group specific rather than universal. It will include and exclude according to group norms. Communitarians argue that universalistic constitutionalism is *de facto* also group constitutionalism because the norms that underlie it are the norms of a particular mentality. For example, constitutional norms in the United States are those of bourgeois liberals. Indeed, although it may seem odd to call Hobbes a liberal, they are driven by the Hobbesian concerns of survival and welfare.

Against the communitarian criticism, one might note that the logic of the argument for individual liberty is very different from the

[33] *New Yorker*, 26 Oct. 1998: 56–7.

argument for group conformity in that it enables rather than restricts, as noted in Chapter 2 in the comparison of protections of liberty with religious restrictions. But much of the force of the communitarian urge in actual practice is to enable groups to have their own lifestyle and to protect their own norms. If it is true that giving licence to individuals to violate those norms for themselves undermines them for all, then the communitarian position might be defended with something like Mill's harm principle. The liberty of some harms others. Is this plausible? Yes. For example, there are likely to be many norms that must be either widely honoured or relatively weak. Marital fidelity, fair dealing, and honesty are all likely to be bolstered in individual cases by their wider practice and undermined by general licence. Religious beliefs similarly must depend heavily on group reinforcement, which is likely to be undermined by broad scepticism.

The weakness of an appeal to the harm principle, however, is that communitarian enforcement of norms is likely not only to enable but also to harm many, as it clearly does in such closed communities as the Amish and in the repressed communities dear to Tennessee Williams. The harm principle itself has a liberal ring and seems epistemologically ill-fitted to communitarianism.

It would be almost tautologous to say that we could do better with the core Hobbesian values if we could keep other, more divisive values out of politics, as Hobbes proposed that we do. It is also true that procedural fairness must largely be protected against intrusions of other values if it is to work well. When divisive, contrary groups' values intrude into justice as order, those who do not hold to the groups' norms are at risk from *de facto* mob rule with its popular variant of bills of attainder. It might be possible to work out relevant principles of procedural fairness in a system of group justice, but the absence there of a universalistic vision seems likely to undermine concern with such fairness.

James Crawford, writing about rights of peoples in international jurisprudence, notes that if minority rights are genuinely collective, rather than merely the aggregate of individual rights, 'then it presumably follows that dissenting members of minority groups can be compelled to comply with the wishes of the majority of the group'. This, he says, is merely the analogue of United Nations policy on plebiscites on self-determination. Dissenting 'members of "peoples" with a right to self-determination can be compelled to accept a form of self government which the majority of that "people" have elected or accepted'.[34] These may be analytically analogous, but one might suppose on the contrary that they are not analogous problems in practice. There is virtually no practical way not to have government, perhaps even territorial government.[35] Accepting government by majority decision commonly makes sense even on an individual account.[36] *There is no such practical necessity for having group norms enforced on dissentients*—there is merely a potentially deep conflict of values between some people and others.

Communitarianism poses a vision of sovereignty that is relatively new to articulate political theory. As a normative doctrine, communitarianism shares some of the rhetorical force of popular sovereignty. How could anyone not think groups should choose their own existence? No matter that Hobbes, John Adams, and others would think the proposition incoherent and hollow at its core in practice. Unfortunately, the actual problems of group democracy, especially its illiberal repression and its stultification of larger, cosmopolitan opportunities, can disrupt any democracy. Indeed, they are among the most destructive problems that democracies face, especially in the crude politics of race, religion, and ethnicity. Communitarian writers have yet to work out these difficulties or to give us even the rudiments of an answer to them.

Unequal Coordination

If liberalism, constitutionalism, and democracy are essentially mutual-advantage theories and if they therefore depend for their enforcement on the incentives citizens and governors have to coordinate on them, how do they work if some group or groups are left

[34] James Crawford, 'The Rights of Peoples: "Peoples" or "Governments"?' in Crawford, ed., *The Rights of Peoples* (Oxford: Oxford University Press, 1988), 55–68, at p. 60.
[35] There is precedent for the practice of non-territorial law in the Middle Ages. See Marc Bloch, *Feudal Society*, 2 vols. (Chicago: University of Chicago Press, 1961, trans. L. A. Manyon), i. 111.
[36] The issue is not always simple. When there is a permanent minority, then majority rule may not make sense for individuals in that minority. See contributions by Douglas Rae, Philip D. Straffin, Jr., and Brian Barry, and the editors' comments on them in Brian Barry and Russell Hardin, eds., *Rational Man and Irrational Society?* (Beverly Hills, Calif.: Sage, 1982), 305–40.

out of the generally beneficial regime? This is a difficult issue in virtually all liberal societies, as it was in the early United States, where the Anti-Federalists lost in the initial coordination on big national government. (It is still a difficult issue in the United States today for the communitarian intellectual descendants of the Anti-Federalists, who plump for a return to community without noting the hopelessness of their vision if the nation continues to be large.) Because of their presence, that coordination brought a change that was not mutually advantageous to all, but only to an apparent majority.

Suppose we have a successful coordination on a constitutional regime that does not seem to give equal standing to some group. That group's members may nevertheless find their interest is to acquiesce in the coordination, as the Anti-Federalists acquiesced to the constitution that created an unwanted national government. The price of mutiny may be too high for any benefits it might bring—even assuming away any problems of the logic of collective action that makes it not in the interest of an individual to act even when it is in the joint interest of the group to act. The group might simply have no substantial alternative regime it could hope to put in place. And the members might only be worse off if they engaged in overt opposition or if they tried to withdraw from the order. It might therefore not require coercion to keep them in order any more than it does for the groups that seem to benefit more generously from the order.

H. L. A. Hart argued that the success of government depends on the fact that enough people just do feel obligated to obey it that it can marshal the forces to compel others to obey.[37] A strong reason for many to feel obligated, or at least to feel it in their interest to acquiesce even without direct coercion, is that they genuinely can see it as to their advantage that the extant government continue. They are obligated merely in Hobbes's sense of being obliged.

The sociological question we must then answer is, when might people not see an extant government as to their advantage? To answer this question, consider first the perhaps common case of two groups that share in the mutual advantage of a constitutional order but share unequally. Theirs is an *unequal coordination*, as represented in Figure 3.3 in Chapter 3. The best of all worlds for the row group would be coordination on constitution (II, II); the best of all

---

[37] H. L. A. Hart, *The Concept of Law* (Oxford: Oxford University Press, 1961), 88. Also see Russell Hardin, 'Sanction and Obligation', *The Monist* 68 (July 1985): 403–18.

worlds for the Column group would be coordination on constitution (I, I). Second best for each group would be coordination on the other constitution. Neither group would prefer failure of coordination, with its attendant disorder and even violence, to its second-best constitutional order.

Examples of unequal coordination include the coordination between anglophone and francophone Canadians, French and Flemish-speaking Belgians, English speakers and non-English speakers throughout the world, especially in the world of technology, and Tutsis and Hutus in both Burundi and Rwanda, perhaps in fact even though possibly not as they sometimes perceive their cases.

Consider one of these cases. Under the present Canadian constitutional arrangements, it is widely believed by francophone Canadians that they are at a relative disadvantage because the English language has a privileged status in Canadian government and business. For francophone Canadians, a better order would be a Canadian constitution under which French and English languages were genuinely equal or in which there were offsetting privileges for francophone Canadians. Such a constitution is probably not politically feasible. Even if it were, it would not be self-enforcing because most anglophone Canadians would have no interest in learning French well enough to make it work. Many francophones evidently accept being unequal under the present constitution. If francophone Canadians were even worse off under the constitution, they might not prefer continued unequal status over the losses that might follow from independence. At that point, the joint coordination of anglophone and francophone Canadians on their unequal constitutional arrangement would no longer be a matter of mutual advantage.

One might suppose in such cases that spontaneous popular opposition might force a regime to change. Against this hope, anarchy with a constable might require few or no more constables when some large fraction of the society is in desperate shape than when all are prosperous from the order that the constables enforce. The refrain we hear from critics who say the United States is flirting with disaster or will reap the whirlwind from its urban ghettos that may someday engulf the society in class war is a false refrain. The problem of the ghetto poor is that they lack resources, including the organizational skills, even to lead decent lives and to find opportunities. But this means they lack the resources to wage open or guerrilla warfare. Ghetto dwellers might export some of their violent crime to nearby areas. But a police force no more hindered by concerns for civil liberties than virtually any European police force or the Japanese police force would stop and frisk enough relevant people to eliminate the weapons for easy crime.[38]

The smaller ethnic enclaves in many liberalizing nations can as easily be excluded from the general coordination on a better life as blacks have been from much of the American success. For example, Romania might go a long way towards liberalizing politically and economically without making the ethnic Hungarians in Romania great beneficiaries of the changes. That would be ironic because the ethnic Hungarians played the major signalling role in bringing down Ceauşescu in 1989. Hungarians in Timisoara demonstrated in such numbers that the regime was unable to suppress them without great violence.

The fact that such large numbers were hostile to the regime and could openly flout it without disastrous retribution probably informed the subsequent unruliness of a crowd in the capital of Bucharest that gave the clear message to everyone, including Ceauşescu, that he was massively unpopular. Hence, the Hungarians started the mass coordination that demolished the regime in an astonishingly mild revolution—more violent than those in Czechoslovakia, East Germany, and Poland, but still relatively gentle by traditional revolutionary standards.[39] They could not similarly expect to coordinate Romanians behind a programme of equal opportunity or autonomy for Hungarians. Hence, under a popular Romanian regime, the Hungarians could not coordinate widespread opposition to the regime to achieve a better status for Hungarians.

It might be a sociological law of government that, the more broadly based it is, the less it requires coercion to maintain order.

---

[38] The New York City police and perhaps others have recently begun to act as though traditional civil liberties were not in their way. Perhaps for that reason violent crime in New York and some other cities has fallen dramatically since the quiet, unheralded introduction of the new policy (*New York Times*, 23 July 1995, sect. 4). There is debate over the reasons for the decline. The then police commissioner of New York, William Bratton, attributed the success to better police organization and morale, but any European or Japanese must have strong suspicions that the fairly pervasive imposition of force and general harassment are more likely to have effect.

[39] Pavel Carpeanu, 'The Revolt of the Romanians', *New York Review of Books* (1 Feb. 1990): 30–1; Robert Cullen, 'Report from Romania: Down with the Tyrant', *New Yorker* (2 Apr. 1990): 94–112. Retrospectively, some think the events of 1989 were really a coup in which some elements of the government took advantage of disorder to dump Ceauşescu (*New York Times*, 25 Dec. 1994: 1.3; also see *New York Times*, 18 June 1995: 1.15).

There are, however, two difficulties with this claim: one sociological and one conceptual. Sociologically it is plausible that the response to coercion is dramatically curvilinear, so that the credible threat of coercion is all that is needed, although it might take occasional demonstrations of actual coercion to give credibility to the threat. Hence, the level of actual instances of coercion might be lower in a more autocratic than in a less autocratic state.

Conceptually, however, this is not the whole story on the appeal of a regime. Coercion lurks in the background for everyone. Large numbers may not be openly coerced or threatened with coercion but may merely acquiesce, as Caesar noted (in the epigraph to Chapter 4). Indeed, virtually all of us merely acquiesce on many things our government does or does not do. It is a peculiarity of democratic politics in real societies that almost everyone loses on almost every vote in the sense that almost all fail to get precisely or even approximately what they want. Most of us share the fate of the Anti-Federalists. We acquiesce in the face of a reality that offers us no better option. This is more or less the reason why no mutual-advantage theory can yield a normative justification on its own: each of us could be better off under some other possible regime. As one class of mutual-advantage theories, contractarian theories can only pretend to be genuinely normative. Rousseau, Kant, Scanlon, Barry, and others appeal to rationalist or reasonable-agreement claims that cannot convince anyone other than, seemingly, a philosopher. It is not only a mythical skinhead on a British Rail train to Oxford who cannot take such appeals seriously.[40]

Concluding Remarks

Democracy is inherently a device for regulating marginal political conflicts. That it works when it does is evidence of lack of deeply divisive conflicts that trump the value of general order. It does not work well if it is grounded in group census and, indeed, the claim for group census is implicitly a claim that conflicts are too grievous and broad for democracy. Democracy is in Hobbes's family of mutual-advantage devices. An extant government that takes the form of a

[40] See further, Russell Hardin, 'Political Obligation', in Alan Hamlin and Philip Pettit, eds., *The Good Polity* (Oxford: Basil Blackwell, 1989), 103–19. See p. 151.

mutual-advantage device merits our coordination on it to the extent that it serves our interests better than moving to an alternative would. Other strong claims for the normative value of democracy are not compelling—except, perhaps, causal claims that democracy achieves some good better than other forms of government could do, as in Millian defences of liberal democracy. If mutual advantage is the normative ground for democracy, individuals or groups whose mutual advantage is not served have little normative reason for adhering to democratic principles unless, for causal reasons, their adherence would help to effect some good, such as the general welfare.

Finally, democratic choice cannot easily be kept coherent if democracy is applied to the determination of membership in the choosing body. This last conclusion may well imply that some sharply divided societies cannot easily sustain coherent democratic choice of any kind. Membership, by whatever rule it is decided, must be irrevocable or subject to very strong protections against democratic reconsideration. Retrospective democratic reconsideration of whether someone or some group has full citizenship is analogous to a bill of attainder and can be deeply divisive.

Afterword: Whether Agreed to or Not

Justifying the Whole

The preceding chapters raise several normative issues. First, obviously, is the question of how we could morally justify a liberal, democratic, constitutional regime and its actions. Sociologically, as explanatory theories, liberalism, constitutionalism, and democracy may yield compelling accounts of the political order of many societies. This follows if they answer to the mutual advantage of the politically most important groups in modern societies. But they typically do not serve the mutual advantage of *everyone* in any particular society.[1] As Washington wrote to Madison before the Philadelphia Convention, his wish was 'that the Convention may adopt no temporizing expedient, but probe the defects of the Constitution to the bottom, and provide radical cures; *whether they are agreed to or not*'.[2]

I wish here to address the difficult problem of the constraints of possibility on what ought to be done when there is opportunity, for example, during constitutional moments or during liberalization, to make changes in the social order. From the preceding chapters, two points should be clear. First, liberal constitutional democracy is workable when it is because it is sociologically to the mutual advantage of the politically efficacious groups in the society. Hence, it is a system that Hobbes could have supported if his sociology had been less pessimistic about the possibilities of human interaction. Secondly, the fact that it works does not prima facie give a moral justification for it, although its workability is a fact that is morally

---

[1] Unless the comparison is that of Hobbes. Compared to Hobbes's miserable state of nature, almost any political order would be better for all.

[2] George Washington, Letter of 31 Mar. 1787 to James Madison, in Philip B. Kurland and Ralph Lerner, eds., *The Founders' Constitution*, 5 vols. (Chicago: University of Chicago Press, 1987), i. 189, emphasis added.

relevant. In particular, if ought implies can—that is, if we cannot morally argue that people ought to do what cannot be done—workability is a necessary part of the morally right order for society. It is merely not sufficient for morality.

One might be able to give a normative justification or criticism of the US Constitution and its political order or of other constitutions from the perspectives of various moral theories. For example, a modern utilitarian, Aristotelian, or Kantian might suppose we can do no better than to order society with liberalism, constitutionalism, and democracy when these work, as they seem to do in very many nations. That is not, however, an exercise that anyone seems to have attempted, except perhaps, to a very limited extent, from the perspective of something like consent theory, on which normative justifications of democracy are often based.

Liberalism has been justified in utilitarian terms and in deontological terms. It would be very difficult to imagine how a deontological account of the rightness of a particular political order in any modern liberal society would even be feasible. In his deontological libertarian theory, Robert Nozick argues that a social order is just if all entitlements in it were justly acquired, either through just consensual exchange or through just initial appropriation.[3] Initial appropriation must meet the Lockean proviso, which says that, if I mix my labour with it, I can simply take any unowned property *so long as there is as much and as good left for others*. Unfortunately, if we do run foul of the Lockean proviso, for whatever reason, or if prior exchanges were otherwise unjust, we are now at a loss to assess the justice of current entitlements. In a footnote, Nozick says that when there were historical violations of liberty and we now struggle to restore everyone to a position of right, we may have to resort to other moral theories, such as utilitarianism or distributive justice, to ground a new status quo, from which we may then proceed on our libertarian way.[4] For any society of interest today, we can be quite sure that justice has often been violated in the past and we now must find a theory with which to begin our assessment of it.

A quasi-utilitarian justification might be possible, but it would require a clear sense of how to trade off benefits and losses to some with benefits and losses to others, and this is not an exercise that

[3] Robert Nozick, *Anarchy, State, and Utopia* (New York: Basic Books, 1974), 174–82.
[4] Nozick, *Anarchy, State, and Utopia*, 153 n.

anyone has evidently even pretended to master on such a scale as would be required to judge a whole social order. A utilitarian account might seem to work if we could suppose some proxy inter-personal measure of welfare applies. One might suppose in principle that John Rawls's theory of justice has been designed specifically to assess whole social orders, but, again, evidently no one has gone so far as to apply it in that way. Utilitarian and Rawlsian assessments of a whole social order are likely to require similar proxy measures of welfare. Even with these, however, they may then founder on con-ceptual measurement issues. The utilitarian account will require some scale that allows rough addition or at least comparison of all welfares. And the Rawlsian account will require ways to determine both the levels of welfare of people and the cut-off points for saying that people up to some level are in, say, the worst-off class. The util-itarian problem was once thought to be easy. Probably no serious utilitarian today thinks it is easy. The Rawlsian problem is a persis-tent embarrassment to a theory that otherwise seems like a serious contender for assessing states in the real world.

Ideally, we would canvass how far we can go in bringing to bear moral theories that might seem to fit with the explanatory theories of acquiescence and mutual advantage. Acquiescence is a minimal ver-sion of consent. And mutual advantage is roughly an ordinal version of utilitarianism. But in its sociological or explanatory variant, mutual advantage seems unlikely to be clearly utilitarian, because it need not be the case that the welfare losses of those who are left out of the calculus of mutual advantage are balanced by the gains of those who are included in it. It might, however, approximate to a utilitar-ian assessment.

One cannot sensibly give such a justification from the supposed agreement of people to such a constitutional order, however, with-out grossly simplifying away the problems of coordination and col-lective action that make for acquiescence that cannot meaningfully be called agreement. This fact does not make a constitution bad but neither would agreement make it good. For most people in the United States most of the time, the order that the US Constitution brings about is a part of the necessity of the world in which they live. Indeed, as though by a miraculous instance of the false dictum that is implies ought, that constitution has come to be revered by almost everyone, even by those who seemingly would want massive revi-sions if there were opportunity for them to revise it. Already within a decade, the generation of the constitution-makers themselves had come, opponents and supporters alike, to hold it better than they seemed to think it when they were debating over its content and over whether to put its government in place. In some sense they were right to have raised their estimation of its quality. It had become better by then because it had successfully coordinated the nation.

Collective and Individual Values

There are at least three broad competing visions of society in the liberal and liberalizing nations of the world today. One of these is the hallowed medieval vision of Aquinas and many others: the vision of a collective purpose that we all share. This was not one of the visions in play in the US constitutional era, or ever for the United States as a whole. The second is what might be characterized as a multi-cultural variant of this, the vision of a shared but bounded, small community and the kind of virtue that it inspires in its citizens. This was the vision of the communitarian Anti-Federalists, who were, perhaps unwittingly for many of them, under the sway of Montesquieu. And the third is the liberal vision of Locke, Smith, Madison, and Mill that builds not on group or universal collective values but on diverse individual values. This vision has been the main focus of this book, because it was the central focus of the American constitutional era and of American political debate since, and it is the focus of the movement for liberalization in many nations today, from the Eastern nations of the former Soviet Bloc to many Third World nations.

The first of these visions has often turned dreadful and illiberal. If Talcott Parsons, as quoted below, is right that something like this vision must be shared for us to achieve social order, we must worry about the variance we will suffer in that order. Apart from nations ruled by petty tyrants, the largest group resisting liberalization in the world today is in the world of Islam, which includes a vision of a universal collective purpose. The second of these visions is a plausible view that was expressed by many of the most articulate of the Anti-Federalist writers. But it has often been false in the sense that its advocates, including many of its academic advocates today, would not choose to live it. At least the leaders of many secessionist groups in the world today would evidently choose to live it. In practice it does not commonly have the ideal features its exponents claim for it. In particular, it is typically élitist, oligarchic, and coercive rather than egalitarian and free. It is, in anything like the ideal claims for it, essentially unworkable in the complex modern world of liberal constitutional democracies, almost all of which are multi-cultural. The third of these visions has, like all of these visions, ancient roots both in practice and in theory, and its advocates have been heard throughout the preceding chapters, so I need not articulate it further here.

Parsons proclaimed the view—which he called a theorem—of the existence of 'an end *of* a society' that 'is an end common to the members of the society'. Furthermore, 'one of the central facts underlying the theorem is the existence of a *common end* (or *system* of ends) which disappears when individual actions are considered in isolation'.[5] Parsons cited as an unusual, because nearly pure, case 'the Calvinists of Geneva in Calvin's own time who might be said to be pursuing the common end of establishing the Kingdom of God on Earth'.[6] In our time, the movement of fundamentalist Islam proclaims such a common end as a universal end. According to a quip, everyone is born a Muslim; it is only their parents and their corrupt societies that make them Christians, Jews, or whatever. Medieval, proselytizing Christianity might have been the only other such collective value historically that was supposed to be genuinely universal. A contemporary variant of this view is Michel Rosenfeld's claim that constitution-making is about forming a 'predominant identity' in 'a fruitful interplay between the reinforcement of identity and the preservation of diversity'.[7] Nationalist movements commonly focus on a supposedly shared identity of some kind, but few contemporary liberal democracies can be characterized in this way unless the shared identity is relatively vacuous.

On a coordination account of the order of society, the ends of relevant groups may be in some sense the same but not in Parsons's sense. For example, we may collectively want government to provide liberal institutions that enable us to prosper individually. Hence, we want prosperity, which is a common but not a collective end. I can survive and have welfare when you do not; I can even have welfare at

---

[5] Talcott Parsons, *The Structure of Social Action* (New York: Free Press, 1968; 1st pub. 1937), 247–8. Parsons, who put the view forward as his own as well, saw it as clearly articulated by Vilfredo Pareto and Émile Durkheim.

[6] Parsons, *The Structure of Social Action*, 248.

[7] Michel Rosenfeld, ed., *Constitutionalism, Identity, Difference, and Legitimacy: Theoretical Perspectives* (Durham, NC: Duke University Press, 1994), 4.

your expense. But I may be more likely to have welfare under institutions that are generally, rather than prejudicially, welfare enhancing. This, however, is a Hobbesian value that Parsons thought conflictive, so that it could not be the value that unifies us to make society cohere.

Acquiescence and Mutual Advantage

The two criteria for workability that distinguish the successful workings of liberalism, constitutionalism, and democracy are the acquiescence of most people most of the time in the political order established by these and the mutual advantage of the politically effective groups in the society. Acquiescence is, in fact, much more generally required for political order of any kind, whether good or reprehensible. As Hobbes noted, even conquerors can obtain acquiescence. Mutual advantage is required only for relatively open political orders that depend on an even stronger kind of acquiescence by those with the political power to affect the order. In particular, it is required for any system that is procedurally democratic, with contested, open elections, and with a real prospect of defeat and loss of office for any person or party.

I have argued, especially in Chapter 4, that consent theory of many varieties does not work and, in the context of a complex society, is even incoherent. This conclusion should be qualified in a way that, however, cannot please consent theorists. Workability does not require consent. It requires only acquiescence. This is a minimalist— perhaps insultingly minimalist—version of consent. People can acquiesce for reasons that sound woefully like Hobbes's view of political obligation or Locke's view of promise-keeping: We acquiesce because if we do not we will be demolished or otherwise harmed.

Slaves have historically acquiesced in their servitude. Apologists in the American South said that their slaves did so because it was in their interest to be under their masters. Unfortunately, in a world of strategic interaction, 'in their interest' does not have a simple meaning. In such a world, our world, my action does not simply determine my outcome, which is determined rather by the combination of my own actions and the actions of all relevant others in interaction with me. What I choose to do may therefore guarantee that I do not get the best of my range of outcomes, but I may nevertheless do it because that action seems likely to get me a better outcome than I would get if I acted in a way that could bring about my best outcome only if everybody else acts in exactly the right way.

Consider a trivial example of this strategic fact. My best outcome when faced with a horrendous southbound traffic jam might require me to drive south in the northbound lanes, against oncoming traffic. That would in fact produce a good outcome only if virtually no one chose to drive in the right direction in the northbound lanes. Generally, I might not expect such good fortune and I would therefore choose to suffer in the traffic jam.

Similarly, the best outcome for a slave might require escaping from the slave holder. But actual success in escaping would depend on how good the enforcement system is, and in many historical contexts, such as the American South, attempting to escape might generally have been foolish. Even if it was not in slaves' interest individually to rebel, however, that does not mean it was 'in their interest' to be slaves. It was not in their interest in comparison to various other ways in which the world could have been organized. But even Bill Gates could make an analogous claim. He could say that the present world in which he has collected, as personal profit, roughly a thousand dollars per personal computer user is not as good for him as the world in which he could have collected two thousand dollars from each of them. (There may be a day when we could ask him which world is better, because he will have experienced both.)

The theorists whose names have come up most frequently in this book are Hobbes and Madison. That is in large part because they were pre-eminently concerned with workability. Acquiescence was Hobbes's central principle for citizens, because general acquiescence is necessary for government to work. Madison evidently agreed. After all, he suggested in *Federalist*, 63 that the people should leave the governing to the government under the constitution, which provided for '*the total exclusion of the people in their collective capacity from any share*' in the government.[8] They both supposed, and almost every theorist who is not an anarchist agrees, that having government and order are generally necessary if we are to live well. In a perhaps limited sense, we are all Hobbesians in our daily lives of

---

[8] See further discussion in Chapter 3, section on 'Institutions and Choice'.

acquiescence in what our governments are doing, most of which we will never even know. Most of us might not require quite such draconian enforcement as Hobbes might have thought necessary, but then most of us have not just come out of a viciously internecine civil war. Nevertheless, some of us are subjected to such enforcement as Hobbes's sovereign might impose.

Hobbes, Smith, Madison, and Tocqueville were sociologists before the era of sociology in a time when sociology, normative philosophy, and public discourse were commonly united in single works, such as in many of theirs. Indeed, they were surprisingly good sociologists.[9] Unfortunately, when the social sciences were detached from philosophy, social philosophy became unmoored. Even before the split, Mill, a relatively sensible philosopher, tended to drift into abstract reasoning, as in much of his writing on liberty. Philosophers less given to common sense, such as Kant and Hegel, did not even need to drift—they were evidently born directly into an abstract world. Contemporary moral, political, and legal philosophers are typically far more concerned with abstract, quasi-ideal theory than with workability.

Yet, even a theorist whose concern is with moral issues of governance must take problems of workability into consideration. This follows from Kant's dictum that ought implies can. Kant presumably meant his 'can' to have a very generous scope. One might prescribe as the solution to the world's problems of poverty that everyone rise early every day, work very hard for long hours, voluntarily hand over their pay-cheques to the central authorities, and let the authorities distribute resources according to need. Then there would be no poverty. Alas, you might object, we cannot expect people to behave in that way. Or, you might even want to say, people cannot do that. On a strenuous reading of Kant, people *can* do that; they merely do not do it. Hence, it might be plausible for a Kantian to say we ought to organize the world in this way to eliminate poverty.

---

[9] Raymond Aron thought Tocqueville was grievously underrated by French sociologists. In fairness, although his *Democracy in America* (New York: Knopf, 1945) is widely read and even more widely praised in the United States, Tocqueville's sociology is also underrated there. American sociologists would seldom include Tocqueville in the pantheon with Weber, Marx, Durkheim, and—I hesitate to mention the name in this company—Parsons. Tocqueville and Smith have not only the brilliance but also the breadth of these figures and, I think, greater clarity of intellect.

Concluding Remarks

The moral defence of liberalism, constitutionalism, and democracy cannot be that they meet some ideal standard of the good or the right but that, according to some criterion or criteria, they are better than any workable alternative. For some criteria, such as enhancement of autonomy, their value must be assessed systemically. We cannot say that a typical person's role in politics is autonomy-enhancing because for the typical person that role must be negligible and must contribute negligibly to the person's autonomy. Rather, we would have to be able to say (if it is true) that liberal constitutional democracy produces a society in which autonomy is enhanced. To show that this is true is, however, a social-scientific, not a philosophical enterprise, and it cannot be shown by argument. Indeed, it cannot easily be shown at all.

Unfortunately, while normative criteria such as autonomy have been of major concern to philosophers, especially those in the traditions of Kant and Mill, they have been of almost no concern to social scientists. Hence, there are almost no efforts to construct empirical measures of autonomy or to establish causal relations between it and other matters. The only standard moral concern on which there is a substantial body of social science research is welfare. This wealth of research has two somewhat contrary implications for welfarists. First, utilitarians can say much more about the fit of their theory with the world than can other moral theorists. Secondly, their critics can offer much sharper criticism than can critics of other moral theories. The latter fact indicates, however, something positive about the power and relevance of utilitarian argument. Recall Wolfgang Pauli's quip, cited in the Preface, that some explanation was 'not even wrong'. As least some claims about welfarism might be wrong.

Liberalism, constitutionalism, and democracy are sociologically mutual-advantage and, hence, coordination theories. Mutual advantage and coordination explain much of the way government and all significant institutions work,[10] but they do not morally justify a government or other institution or the results of the working of government or other institutions. If we wish to achieve outcomes that are

---

[10] See further, Russell Hardin, 'Institutional Commitment: Values or Incentives?' in Avner Ben Ner and Louis Putterman, eds., *Economics, Values, and Organization* (Cambridge: Cambridge University Press, 1998), 419–33.

moral on some principle, we must fit mutual-advantage institutions to such outcomes. Evidently there are institutions that can achieve reasonably high levels of justice as order—meaning criminal and civil justice, not distributive justice. And there are institutions that can produce substantial protection of individual political and economic liberties. These two can even be combined into institutions that achieve justice as order with protection of individual liberties while fostering high levels of economic prosperity. This is already a remarkable achievement.

Such achievements are plausible, however, only in societies in which there is already a high degree of coordination on some individual values and little coordination on exclusionary group values. How far might diversity go? It can clearly go so far as to produce implacable enmity leading to violence on the scale of that suffered in Burundi after its short-lived effort to have democratic government in 1993 or on the even more grotesque scale of Rwanda immediately afterwards. But the difference between Burundi and any less violently torn society is merely a difference of degree, not of kind. It is a difference in workability.

In any real society, mutual advantage can at best explain what happens. It can explain the motivations of the critical actors, and if enough of these cohere, liberalism, constitutionalism, and democracy can work. But the argument from mutual advantage cannot morally justify the results without some strong additional consideration, a moral consideration. Unfortunately, there is none available. We might find some other argument that does happen to rank the results of a constitutional liberal democracy as good or right, but that argument will not depend on the explanation from mutual advantage.

In sum, liberalism, constitutionalism, and democracy do not *per se* make good societies, although they are arguably necessary parts of the structure of a good society. But it is also not true that merely having the psychology for or commitment to a good society will make one. In particular, the makings of a civil society are not the makings of good government under a constitutional regime. What is generally required for a constitutional regime to work is that it serve the relative interests of major political groups in the society, that is, groups that are politically efficacious. Hence, a successful constitutional order must, sociologically, be a mutual-advantage order. If the groups whose advantage is served by the order are classically liberal, then we might further expect the order to be generally benign and the society to have the capacity, depending on resources and lack of massive external conflict, to be a good society. In general, this is an improbable prospect in any society that is riven by deep conflicts between politically efficacious groups, especially conflicts over the distribution of fixed or limited resources, including social position and government jobs, or over intractable matters of language or religion.

Appendix: Other Liberalisms

Any label as appealing as liberalism is apt to be claimed by advocates of varied causes and positions. Hence, the story of liberalism is the story of a cacophony of labels, many of them confusing or, at best, unenlightening. Most of the labels have been merely descriptive in some way without any analytical bite. John Dewey characterized political and economic liberalism jointly as the 'old' liberalism and he pushed for a 'new' liberalism. Although it is descriptively accurate, the distinction 'new versus old' is especially annoying in its analytical vacuity. Indeed, it seems like a trick of persuasive definition, since new typically sounds better than old, at least in America. Dewey said that the label liberalism itself dates only from the early nineteenth century.[1] Nevertheless, the ideas of political and economic liberalism were already well debated by then in the writings of John Milton (1608–74), Algernon Sidney (1622–83), John Locke (1632–1704), Bernard Mandeville (1670?–1733), Montesquieu (1689–1755), David Hume (1711–76), Adam Smith (1723–90), and many others. And they were deliberately designed into the US Constitution at the Philadelphia Convention in 1787. They did not need our label to prevail either in fact or in argument.

A striking fact about many of the new labels for ostensibly variant liberalisms is that those labels and their categories have been around for a long while—most of, or more than, a century—but that the liberalisms they represent have yet to have much effect. The original liberalisms reversed this history: elements of them were long in effect before they were well understood, although there was arguably more invention in the case of political liberalism. Economic liberalism had been working piecemeal for centuries before Mandeville, Hume, Smith, and others began to recognize it. One might say with less conviction that political liberalism also had a past history that eased the task of Hobbes and Locke in coming to formulate its theory.

This different history is indicative of an important strategic difference between the original liberalisms and some of the later ones. The original liberalisms were and are self-enforcing because they are mutually advantageous

---

[1] John Dewey, *Liberalism and Social Action*, in *The Later Works of Dewey, 1925–1953*, xi (Carbondale, Ill.: Southern Illinois University Press, 1987; 1st pub. 1935), 1–65, at p. 6.

to important, politically efficacious, large groups in the societies they influence. Because they were self-enforcing, they had survival power and they could take root and grow over time without their being yet understood. This is not true of the variant liberalisms of modern times that are discussed below. For example, contemporary welfare liberalism is still in want of an intellectual grounding, of a theory of how it can be made to work. We can be confident that merely constraining government cannot be a major part of any programme of welfare liberalism, as it was for economic and political liberalism. In welfare liberalism, government is not the source of the problem but it must, rather, be a major part of the solution. And welfare liberalism requires redistribution, which is inherently conflictive and not likely to be a matter of mutual advantage.

Out of the welter of categories of liberalism that have filled twentieth-century debate, three are fairly widely mentioned and are clearly relevant to fundamentally important aspects of liberal societies, and a fourth is widely asserted and at least arguably important. These are the following. First is what we can call social liberalism, which is liberation from the deadening weight of burdensome social conventions. Second is the liberalism that Dewey wanted and that we may call institutional liberalism, which is liberation from the snares of large private organizations on analogy with the liberation from the snares of government under political and economic liberalism. Third is what is commonly called welfare liberalism, which is primarily liberation from poverty and its concomitants. Fourth is group liberalism, which focuses not on liberty for individuals but for groups. All of these sound close to the welfarist vision of traditional political and economic liberalism, whose point is to make life better, but they require very different strategic devices that go beyond constraining government.

Social Liberalism

Social liberalism has had a long history, with articulate concern for it in Mill's *On Liberty* and other classical liberal works. It has perhaps left some trace in the US Constitution in the prohibition of a state religion. Its greatest impact on any political programme, however, has probably been in French revolutionary moves against the Catholic Church, Communist efforts to break the hold of religion and various customary constraints, the turn-of-the-century Chinese move to break the coercive custom of women's foot-binding, and other efforts, some of them worse than the ills they were intended to cure, as in Pol Pot's destruction of everything he could destroy in Cambodian culture, whether good or bad, at the cost of upwards of a million lives and the radical impoverishment of virtually the entire population. Most of these effects required government action, although the foot-binding in China was broken by creating an opposite norm from the ground up in one of the most remarkable social changes on record.[2]

Social liberalism is typically contrary to notions of group autonomy. Breaking the hold of a social norm may mean loosening the hold of a particular community on its members. For example, undermining destructive religious norms is likely to undermine ties to a religious community and even to create conflict within such a community, in either case causing a decline in group cohesion. Social liberalism therefore should be anathema to communitarians. Strangely, however, many of the Anti-Federalist opponents of the US Constitution favoured the introduction of a bill of rights that would specifically protect individuals. Such rights might indirectly protect communities through the protection of individuals who have communal values. The Supreme Court recently protected the Amish as a group, however, by ruling that individual Amish children could have their apparent right (in the state of Wisconsin) to at least a tenth grade education reduced in order, somewhat forcibly, to keep them loyal to their community.[3] Immanuel Kant argued that for one generation to stifle the intellectual and moral development of a later generation in this way is to commit a crime against human nature.[4] In this instance, the Court abused future generations in order to satisfy the demands of the current generation of adult Amish. One might have expected the Anti-Federalist communitarians to favour such group rights.

Institutional Liberalism

Institutional liberalism was a response to crude aspects of economic life in the brightest moments of capitalism from, say, 1840 to 1929 in the United States and roughly the same period in England. The triumph of capitalism did not end grotesque poverty and inequality but, in the view of many, exacerbated them. Or, at the very least, one can say that economic liberalism and the market have benefited some far more than others, that they are not neutral in their impact. Dewey's most articulate statement of the need for institutional liberalism was delivered in 1935 during the darkest days of capitalism when, oddly, it was arguably beside the point for the problems that were most urgent then. These problems were still poverty and inequality, especially as aggravated by unemployment. But their solution was not,

[2] See Gerald Mackie, 'Ending Footbinding and Infibulation: A Convention Account', *American Sociological Review*, 61 (Dec. 1996): 999–1017.

[3] *Wisconsin v. Yoder, et al.*, 406 U.S., pp. 205–49. See further, Russell Hardin, *One for All: The Logic of Group Conflict* (Princeton: Princeton University Press, 1995), 201–3.

[4] Immanuel Kant, 'An Answer to the Question: What Is Enlightenment?' In Kant, *Perpetual Peace and Other Essays on Politics, History, and Morals*, trans. Ted Humphrey (Indianapolis: Hackett, 1983; 1st edn. 1784).

as in institutional liberalism, in liberation from the intrusions of large private organizations. The unemployed of the 1930s did not need to be liberated from such institutions. They would, rather, have benefited from the greater success of these institutions.

How can we fit Dewey's institutional liberalism with the earlier liberalisms? It was, of course, motivated by a concern for welfare, and in this it is similar to all liberalisms. The conceptual analogy with political and economic liberalisms is that it liberates. The earlier liberalisms liberated from arbitrary government intrusions into people's lives and from government control of the economy. The arbitrary intrusions that provoked political liberalism were star chambers, bills of attainder, arrests without warrant, billeting of troops without permission or recompense, seizure of presses, political imprisonment, and virtually anything else an uncontrolled government might choose to do or demand. The intrusions that were against economic liberalism were the panoply of practices of government economic control in the heavy-handed system of mercantilism, in which friends and relatives of the crown were given economic privileges and in which workers and producers were harassed by destructive regulations on what they could do and where they could do it. These regulations restricted mobility, closed off cities from independent artisans and traders, required long apprenticeships to qualify for work, gave strict monopolies to some, and blocked trade with foreign enterprises. Dewey's institutional liberalism was intended to overcome the similarly grim intrusions of large institutions other than government. It aimed to liberate from the control of large private organizations.

Welfare Liberalism

Institutional liberalism made sense in the heyday of rampant capitalism in the latter nineteenth and early twentieth centuries, when trusts seemed rapacious and destructive in the lives of many people. It made less sense in the 1930s and arguably even less today, when the problems of grim, inherited poverty and lack of opportunity are not the result of suppression by private institutions. There is no clearly defined set of institutions from whose control or intrusions people must be liberated in order to overcome their poverty. Indeed, the solution to poverty, as with the solution to unemployment in the Depression years, is most likely to come from large institutions, from the deliberate intrusions of large institutions. What these problems need might be social welfare liberalism by government to empower people economically and politically, as has been argued by a long line of critics beginning at latest from Thomas Hill Green more than a century ago when the poverty of many seemed to fit uneasily with the claims for liberty as an emancipator. Green and others have since argued for action by government to improve the lot of many.[5] Green's version of this liberty was grounded in a vague conception of the common good, so that it is not clearly in the tradition of liberalism as individually focused.

The best understanding of welfare liberalism that we can derive from the experience of post-war welfare programmes in many nations is that it is not plausibly seen as a matter of mutual advantage. A genuine programme of greater welfare for the worst off in our societies depends, as a matter of political fact, on the sufferance of other major groups. Such a programme would involve substantial conflict of interest between these groups and the worst off. Hence, achieving or maintaining such a programme is not merely a coordination problem. It would therefore not be self-enforcing but would require constant commitments to keep it going and it would be vulnerable at any moment to attack from those who would expect to gain from curtailing welfare programmes. Even in its harshest days, such as the years of McCarthyite anti-Communism, political liberalism in the United States has not been so vulnerable to attack as welfare liberalism has—although in other nations political liberalism has succumbed. And economic liberalism survived even the most threatening years of the Great Depression in the United States.

Group Liberalism

In recent decades, there have been many demands for attention to group 'rights' or group protections of various kinds. Virtually any other liberalism could be called group liberalism, but I will reserve the term for protections of specifically identifiable groups. For example, protection of an immigrant group's use of its native language in its dealings with government and in the education of its children would be an instance of group liberalism. All the other liberalisms canvassed work by protecting individuals. Group liberalism is very odd in that it somehow elevates the relevant group above its members by protecting the group, plausibly *against its own members*.

We could characterize demands for group protections in two ways. First, it might be an extension of some of the earlier demands for institutional liberalism to protect workers or consumers against private institutions. For example, workers are a group who can claim that they need general enforcement of a rule to enable them to mobilize against corporations.[6] Similarly, government may determine limits on the terms of contracts covering either

---

[5] Thomas Hill Green, 'Liberal Legislation and Freedom of Contract', in *The Works of Thomas Hill Green*, ed. R. L. Nettleship (London: Longmans, Green, 1888; 1st pub. 1880) iii. 370–6.

[6] Mill argued, as an example, that workers might require legal backing to enforce their unanimous preference for a reduction from a ten-hour to a nine-hour day, because without legal enforcement, individual workers would have an incentive to

relations between unequal parties or relations that have significant external effects on those not party to the contract. This facilitates what groups can do or protects them against harm of various kinds. For such protections, a liberal government might adopt something akin to Mill's harm principle. But, unless group liberalism is to conflict with economic liberalism, government should not avoid harms by manipulating specific aspects of the economy. For example, government might protect workers as a group against the harm brought about by economic change. But it should do this with worker-specific programmes rather than by artificially keeping a failing firm or an obsolescent industry in business.

Secondly, demands for group protections might be an extension of the descriptive theory of interest-group liberalism, which characterizes American politics in the quasi-Madisonian system of a plurality of interests engaged in trying to influence national policy. But in the pluralism of interests, the groups are typically contending for favour directly from the government. In the newer group liberalism, groups are demanding protections against government and private agencies. For example, they demand protection against government requirements on how to educate their children and against the freedom of speech of film makers and television programming. Strategically, such liberalism is a hodgepodge.

One of the demands of groups in our time is for the official protection of minority languages. In the United States such protection probably makes the first-generation speakers of Spanish, Korean, or Vietnamese better off. But it might partially cripple the next generation because, typically, it means making sure that the next generation is educated in the minority language and perhaps thereby made less able to assume a full role in the larger community. Hence, protecting the supposed group interest requires action against the interest and incentives of some group members. At the very least, this makes group liberalism a very complex version of liberalism. It can hardly be defended either on standard welfarist or autonomy grounds. And it conflicts with social liberalism and possibly with institutional liberalism.

Finally, advocates of group liberalism in its stronger variants demand impositions on the larger society and even their own members, and they often want government to manage these impositions. Hence, group liberalism is often profoundly illiberal in any sensible prior reading of that notion. Many who are not members of groups that want group autonomy defend group protections despite the illiberal implications. Their positive argument for group rights is, roughly, that giving groups status, even with some

free-ride on the abstinence of others and to work an extra hour for bonus wages, thus destroying the nine-hour day. John Stuart Mill, *Principles of Political Economy*, ed. John M. Robson (Toronto: University of Toronto Press, 1965; 1st pub. 1848), book 5, ch. 11, sect. 12: 958. See also Russell Hardin, *Morality within the Limits of Reason* (Chicago: University of Chicago Press, 1988), 92–4; L. T. Hobhouse, *Liberalism* (Oxford: Oxford University Press, 1948; 1st pub. 1911), pp. 32–3, 37–9.

controls over individual group members, allows the group members to enjoy benefits that would otherwise be at risk from the corrosive effects of the larger society. Hence, government protection of a group is merely a means to protecting its members.

The Civil Rights Movement

It is instructive to see how these various liberalisms come into play in an actual case. The Civil Rights Movement in the United States captures the whole range of concerns of the various liberalisms. That movement in the 1950s and 1960s was primarily a movement to extend political liberalism to cover a previously excluded group, and in this it was first directed at government: at Jim Crow laws and at courts that refused to enforce liberal laws that would give blacks easier access to politics and the market economy. Substantial success in this movement was inadequate to overcome the deeper problems of racism and, therefore, the movement also pushed for laws to force private institutions to end discrimination of many varieties. In this, its programme was that of Dewey's institutional liberalism. Even this programme, however, would prove inadequate to overcome the inequalities of blacks in American society. Two further projects would be needed: ending the pervasive, non-institutional racism of social conventions and ending poverty. And some in the black community would go further and demand group rights, although they typically would want autonomy as a way of escaping racism and white institutional controls rather than as a way of protecting religious or other group-level values.

By far the more important of these last two projects in the short run is ending poverty, which is not the result of current racism or suppression by private or public institutions. The most stalwart economic liberals might insist that the best cure for poverty is the market. But even if this cure might eventually work, it is clearly taking so long that millions of people now living will not benefit from it. And their children will commonly be so badly educated as to be nearly disqualified from work in the market should it finally bring opportunities to their world. This project is that of what is commonly called welfare liberalism—or what was, in milder uses of that term, socialism.

As Gary Becker and others argue, employers would hire efficiently with no regard to race if there were no laws constraining them or no social convention of racism that would damage their business if they did hire minority workers.[7] The firms that were slowest in interracial hiring were those

---

[7] Gary S. Becker, *The Economics of Discrimination* (Chicago: University of Chicago Press, 1971, 2nd edn.; 1st pub. 1957).

whose employees dealt with the public, firms such as Sears, rather than those whose employees worked inside factories, such as the auto makers. Merchandisers feared racist reaction against the presence of blacks on their sales staffs.

Similarly, John Howard Griffin concluded in his study of racism in the South that even the norms of racial discrimination were backed by the failure of those who were not racist to express and act upon their views.[8] They failed in part perhaps because they did not know how many they were and in part because the convention of racism was a coordination norm that could easily be enforced against violators unless these were mobilized, as they finally were by the early successes of the Civil Rights Movement and by the changing laws. This aspect of the civil rights effort is a case of social liberalism that mixed both state action and spontaneous action to create or support an alternative convention. It would be too optimistic to say that it has fully succeeded or will do so soon. Effective law against discrimination is actually in the interest of most large business firms and similar laws are in the interest of many other competitive institutions, such as universities. Even a racist chairman of the board of a large manufacturing firm has an incentive to pay attention only to costs and productivity of workers in the factory. Hence, such law is an instance of both economic liberalism against state laws that harmed commerce and of social liberalism to change social norms.

Although poverty is the more important of these two problems, breaking illiberal social conventions of racism will be exceedingly difficult just because they are typically coordination norms that are self-enforcing. Simply contriving a new coordination will not displace them. In his long and acute discussion of slavery in America, Tocqueville noted that 'The greatest difficulty [with slavery] in antiquity was that of altering the law; among the moderns it is that of altering the customs, and as far as we are concerned, the real obstacles begin where those of the ancients left off'.[9] He argued that once southern slavery was past, racial prejudice would long remain. Slavery required legal enforcement and could be ended by changing the law. Racism is conventional and cannot easily be reached by law.

Strategic Differences

Consider the strategic natures of these further liberalisms in comparison to political and economic liberalism. There are two issues. First there is the role

[8] John Howard Griffin, *Black Like Me* (New York: New American Library, 1976; 1st edn. 1961), 153.
[9] Alexis de Tocqueville, *Democracy in America*, 2 vols. (New York: Knopf, 1945; 1st edns. 1835 and 1840; trans. Henry Reeve and rev. by Francis Bowen), i. 367.

of government, whether it is to be constrained or put to use. Secondly, there is the game-theoretic structure of the larger interactions at stake. All of the liberalisms discussed in this Appendix differ from the earlier political and economic liberalisms in that they virtually require government action in their support. On the other issue, however, they differ. Liberalism, constitutionalism, and democracy, when they work, are coordinations on mutual-advantage regimes. Because they are coordinations, they are self-enforcing. The regime of institutional liberalism, at least as it affects large institutions, might readily be mutually advantageous and self-enforcing in a democratic society. Social liberalism, which involves the breaking of destructive social conventions, would also be self-enforcing if once achieved. Unfortunately, welfare and group liberalisms are not strategically analogous to political and economic liberalism. The resolution of poverty and the maintenance of group autonomy for selected groups are not likely to be mutually advantageous for the most politically important groups in liberal societies. They do not serve the interests of the middle class and the politically influential, wealthy entrepreneurial class. Nor are resolutions of these problems likely to be self-enforcing in the way the old liberalisms, once in place, are self-enforcing or as a workable constitution is self-enforcing.

F. A. Hayek attributes welfare liberalism to the constructivist continental philosophy inspired by Descartes.[10] He supposes the view that we should master our world intellectually is the background of this liberalism and its cousin, socialism. Hence, political and economic liberalisms descend to us from ancient times after passing through the Scottish Enlightenment and the English Whigs. Welfare liberalism is in a quite different tradition that descends through the French Enlightenment and Voltaire and Rousseau. Hence, they are quite different visions with, to use my terminology and not Hayek's, different strategic assumptions. The assumptions of political and economic liberalism are those of spontaneous individual creation and therefore liberation from the control of others; the assumptions of welfare liberalism are those of intellectual and theoretical mastery for the liberation from the constraints of nature. Independently of the validity of his historical and intellectual claims, Hayek's strategic implications are arguably right. Political and economic liberalism were directed *at government intrusions*, which were to be stopped; welfare liberalism is directed *at government to intrude* in order to overcome problems of social and economic failure, independently of the causes of the failure.

With Dewey, one could speak of stages of liberalism: liberation from despotic and oligarchic political control, liberation from government economic decisions over who is to work or produce or trade, liberation from

[10] F. A. Hayek, 'Liberalism', in Hayek, *New Studies in Philosophy, Politics, Economics, and the History of Ideas* (Chicago: University of Chicago Press, 1978), 119–51; 'The Principles of a Liberal Social Order', in Hayek, *Studies in Philosophy, Politics and Economics* (Chicago: University of Chicago Press, 1967), 160–77.

the depredations of institutionalized private power, liberation from the dead hand of many social conventions, and perhaps other liberations. Dewey would put the first three of these in this historical order, although I think it is misleading to put economic liberalism in the order in which it was first articulated as opposed to the order in which it began to work its way on to the scene (see further, Chapter 2). To date, we have genuinely articulate accounts of only the first two of these and a still emerging account of the third.

When political and economic liberalisms were joined in the same governments, especially beginning with that created by the US Constitution, they were joined without subordinating one to the other or curtailing the application of one on behalf of the other. Dewey's vague prescription—substantial government control of the economy—for a new liberalism in the 1930s would have been likely to have curtailed economic liberty and perhaps, therefore, political liberty on behalf of a nascent welfare liberty. The welfare state that has grown up mostly after World War II in the West can, as the best experiences suggest, similarly be built alongside, instead of on the partial ruins of, the old political and economic liberalisms. Apart from making education and culture relatively available, no one has seriously proposed any general scheme for breaking the hold of perverse social conventions. I will also not propose such a scheme. As far as the Western liberal constitutional democracies are concerned, my account is retrospective. As far as many, many other nations are concerned, it is still, surprisingly, prospective.

If Dewey were alive to comment on this book, he might characterize it as the 'old liberalism, constitutionalism, and democracy'. It is old because it does not address what he thought was the central problem in the established liberal democracies of our—or his—time, which is the liberation of people from the impositions of large *private* organizations on individual liberty and welfare. He supposed that this was the new problem of liberalism. He also supposed that the problem must be handled by government action. We had long been liberated from governments that imposed aristocratic control of society and mercantilist control of the economy, and now we needed to be liberated from private power that had arisen under the regime of old liberalism. He wrote that, 'after early liberalism had done its work, society faced a new problem, that of social organization'.[11] Because he was writing in the depths of the Depression, it is plausible that most of what Dewey thought we needed was what could be handled by social welfare programmes that do not infringe old economic liberalism beyond the standard infringement of taxation, with which advocates of the old liberalism were always content.

---

[11] Dewey, *Liberalism and Social Action*, 39. See also, C. E. Lindblom, *Politics and Markets: The World's Political-Economic Systems* (New York, Basic Books, 1977), 45–51; Grant McConnell, *Private Power and American Democracy* (New York: Knopf, 1966).

I agree that most societies would benefit from more than merely the liberating features of the 'old' liberalism—although I speak of it in this book as
simply liberalism because I think the 'more' that most societies need is probably not a grand change in the terms or regime of liberalism. But, in any case,
my purpose here is limited to analysing liberalism, constitutionalism, and
democracy in their roles in dramatically altering the lot of citizens in the
modern constitutional democracies. Understanding that role is, at this
moment, not merely a matter of historical curiosity or of the articulation of
the history of thought. It is, rather, a matter of urgent concern in large parts
of the world in which the achievement of liberal, constitutional democracy
is currently, and rightly, the central political urge, the first and virtually only
item on the political agenda for the current generation.

References

Adams, John. 1987. 'Defence of the Constitution of Government of the United States', in Philip B. Kurland and Ralph Lerner, eds., *The Founder's Constitution*. Chicago: University of Chicago Press, 1987.

Almond, Gabriel A., and Verba, Sidney. 1963. *The Civic Culture: Political Attitudes and Democracy in Five Nations*. Princeton: Princeton University Press.

Anderson, Thornton. 1994. *Creating the Constitution: The Convention of 1787 and the First Congress*. University Park, Pa.: Penn State Press.

Apolte, Thomas. 1995. 'Democracy, Dictatorship, and Transformation: A Proposal for a Constitution-Guided Systematic Change in Formerly Soviet Republics'. *Constitutional Political Economy*. 6: 5–20.

Aristotle. 1998. *Politics*. Indianapolis: Hackett, trans. C. D. C. Reeve.

Aslund, Anders. 1995. *How Russia Became a Market Economy*. Washington: Brookings Institution.

Austin, John. 1954. *The Providence of Jurisprudence Determined*. New York: Noonday; 1st pub. 1832.

Ayer, A. J. 1990. *Thomas Paine*. New York: Atheneum, 1988; reprinted by University of Chicago Press.

Barry, Brian. 1995. *Justice as Impartiality*. Oxford: Oxford University Press.

—— and Hardin, Russell. eds. 1982. *Rational Man and Irrational Society?* Beverly Hills, Calif.: Sage.

Bates, Robert H. 1981. *Markets and States in Tropical Africa: The Political Basis of Agricultural Policies*. Berkeley: University of California Press.

Beard, Charles A. 1935. *An Economic Interpretation of the Constitution of the United States*. New York: Macmillan; 1st pub. 1913.

—— and Beard, Mary R. 1930. *The Rise of American Civilization*, 2 vols. New York: Macmillan; 1st pub. 1927.

Becker, Gary S. 1971. *The Economics of Discrimination*. Chicago: University of Chicago Press, 2nd edn.; 1st pub. 1957.

Beer, Samuel H. 1993. *To Make a Nation: The Rediscovery of American Federalism*. Cambridge, Mass.: Harvard University Press.

—— 1994. 'Constitutionalism, Medieval and Modern'. Presented at a conference on constitutionalism at the Murphy Institute, Tulane University, 18–20 February.

Beitz, Charles R. 1989. *Political Equality*. Princeton: Princeton University Press.

Bell, Daniel. 1976. *The Cultural Contradictions of Capitalism*. London: Heinemann.

Bellow, Saul. 1977. *Mr Sammler's Planet*. Harmondsworth: Penguin; 1st pub. 1970.

Benn, Stanley I., and Peters, Richard S. 1959. *Social Principles and the Democratic State*. London: George Allen and Unwin; reprinted as *The Principles of Political Thought: Social Foundations of the Democratic State*. New York: Free Press, 1965.

Bermeo, Nancy. 1994. 'Democracy in Europe'. *Daedalus* (Spring): 159–77.

Berry, Wendell. 1993. *Sex, Economy, Freedom, and Community: Eight Essays*. New York: Pantheon.

Bloch, Marc. 1961. *Feudal Society*, 2 vols. Chicago: University of Chicago Press, 1961, trans. L. A. Manyon.

Bloom, Allen. 1988. *The Closing of the American Mind*. New York: Basic Books.

Boettke, Peter J. 1995. 'Credibility, Commitment, and Soviet Economic Reform', in Edward Lazear, ed., *Realities of Reform*. Stanford, Calif.: Hoover Institution Press, 247–75.

Bonn, Moritz J. 1932. *The Crisis of Capitalism in America*. New York: John Day.

Braybrooke, David. 1987. *Meeting Needs: Studies in Moral, Political, and Legal Philosophy*. Princeton: Princeton University Press.

Brennan, Geoffrey, and Buchanan, James M. 1985. *The Reason of Rules: Constitutional Political Economy*. Cambridge: Cambridge University Press.

Brooks, Karen, Guasch, J. Louis, Braverman, Avishay, and Csaki, Csaba. 1991. 'Agriculture and the Transition to the Market'. *Journal of Economic Perspectives*. 5 (Fall): 149–61.

Brühlmeier, Daniel. 1992. 'Demokratische Revolutionen', in Karen Gloy, ed. *Demokratie-Theorie: Ein West-Ost-Dialog*. Tübingen: Francke Verlag, 64–83.

Buchanan, James M., and Gordon Tullock. 1962. *The Calculus of Consent: Logical Foundations of Constitutional Government*. Ann Arbor: University of Michigan Press.

Buruma, Ian. 1990. 'There's No Place Like Heimat', *New York Review of Books* (20 Dec.): 34–43.

Caballero, Ricardo J., and Hammour, Mohamad L. 1994. 'The Cleansing Effect of Recessions', *American Economic Review*. 84 (Dec.): 1350–68.

Calhoun, John C. 1953. *Discourse on the American Constitution*, excerpted in *A Disquisition on Government and Selections from the Discourse*. Indianapolis: Bobbs-Merrill, with an introduction by C. Gordon Post; 1st pub. 1853.

Carpeanu, Pavel. 1990. 'The Revolt of the Romanians'. *New York Review of Books* (1 Feb.): 30–1.

Carter, April. 1973. *Direct Action and Liberal Democracy*. New York: Harper and Row.

Christiano, Thomas. 1996. *The Rule of the Many: Fundamental Issues in Democratic Theory*. Boulder, Colo.: Westview Press.

Cohen, G. A. 1995. 'The Pareto Argument for Inequality'. *Social Philosophy and Policy*. 12 (Winter): 160–85.

Condorcet, Jean Antoine. 1999. 'Essay on the Application of Mathematics to the Theory of Decision-Making', in *Selected Writings*. Indianapolis: Hackett; 1st pub. 1795.

Constant, Benjamin. 1988. *Principles of Politics Applicable to All Representative Governments*, in Constant. *Political Writings*, ed. Biancamaria Fontana. Cambridge: Cambridge University Press, 171–305; 1st pub. 1815.

Crawford, James. 1988. 'The Rights of Peoples: "Peoples" or "Governments"?' in Crawford, ed., *The Rights of Peoples*. Oxford: Oxford University Press, 55–68.

Cullen, Robert. 1990. 'Report from Romania: Down with the Tyrant'. *New Yorker* (2 Apr.): 94–112.

Dahl, Robert A. 1956. *A Preface to Democratic Theory*. Chicago: University of Chicago Press.

Dahrendorf, Ralf. 1968. 'In Praise of Thrasymachus', in Dahrendorf, *Essays in the Theory of Society*. Stanford: Stanford University Press, 129–50.

Deak, István. 1994. 'Post-Post-Communist Hungary'. *New York Review of Books* (11 Aug.): 33–8.

Desai, Padma. 1995. 'Beyond Shock Therapy'. *Journal of Democracy*. 6 (Apr.): 102–12.

Dewey, John. 1978. *Ethics*, vol. v of *The Middle Works, 1899–1924, of John Dewey*. Carbondale, Ill.: Southern Illinois University Press; 1st pub. 1908.

—— 1987. *Liberalism and Social Action*, in *The Later Works of Dewey, 1925–1953*, xi. Carbondale, Ill.: Southern Illinois University Press, 1–65; 1st pub. 1935.

Dostoevsky, Fyodor. 1958. *The Brothers Karamazov*. Harmondsworth: Penguin; 1st pub. 1880.

Downs, Anthony. 1957. *An Economic Theory of Democracy*. New York: Harper and Row.

Durkheim, Emile. 1933. *The Division of Labor in Society*. New York: Macmillan; 1st pub. 1893.

Dymski, Gary A., and Elliot, John E. 1988. 'Capitalism and the Democratic Economy'. *Social Philosophy and Policy*. 6 (Autumn): 140–64.

Eavey, Cheryl L., and Miller, Gary J. 1989. 'Constitutional Conflict in State and Nation', in Bernard Grofman and Donald Wittman, eds., *The Federalist Papers and the New Institutionalism*. New York: Agathon, 205–19.

Ellman, Michael. 1994. 'The Increase in Death and Disease under "Katastroika" '. *Cambridge Journal of Economics* (Aug.): 329–55.

Elster, Jon. 1990. 'When Communism Dissolves'. *London Review of Books* (25 Jan.): 3–6.

Eskridge, William, and Ferejohn, John. 1994. 'The Elastic Commerce Clause: A Political Theory of American Federalism'. *Vanderbilt Law Review*. 47 (Oct.): 1355–1400.

Farber, Daniel A., Eskridge, William N., and Frickey, Philip P. 1993. *Cases and Materials on Constitutional Law: Themes for the Constitution's Third Century*. St Paul, Minn.: West Publishing Co.

Farrand, Max. ed. 1937. *The Records of the Federal Convention of 1787*, 4 vols. New Haven: Yale University Press, rev. edn.; 1st pub. 1911.

Ferguson, Adam. 1980. *An Essay on the History of Civil Society*. New Brunswick: Transaction; 1st pub. 1767.

Fink, Evelyn C., and Riker, William H. 1989. 'The Strategy of Ratification', in Bernard Grofman and Donald Wittman, eds., *The Federalist Papers and the New Institutionalism*. New York: Agathon, 220–55.

Fried, Charles. 1981. *Contract As Promise*. Cambridge, Mass.: Harvard University Press.

Friedman, Milton. 1962. *Capitalism and Freedom*. Chicago: University of Chicago Press.

Fuller, Lon L. 1969. *The Morality of Law*. New Haven: Yale University Press, revd.; 1st pub. 1964.

Galbraith, John Kenneth. 1990. 'The Rush to Capitalism'. *New York Review of Books* (25 Oct.): 51–2.

Gargan, Edward A. 1992. 'A Revolution Transforms India: Socialism's Out, Free Market In'. *New York Times* (29 Mar.): section 1.

Gauthier, David. 1986. *Morals by Agreement*. Oxford: Oxford University Press.

Gewirth, Alan. 1978. *Reason and Morality*. Chicago: University of Chicago Press.

Giesey, Ralph A. 1968. *If Not, Not: The Oath of the Aragonese and the Legendary Laws of Sobrarbe*. Princeton: Princeton University Press.

Gilmore, Grant. 1974. *The Death of Contract*. Columbus, Oh.: Ohio State University Press.

Goldthorpe, John H., Lockwood, David, Bechhofer, Frank, and Platt, Jennifer. 1969. *The Affluent Worker in the Class Structure*. Cambridge: Cambridge University Press.

Goodin, Robert E. 1985. *Protecting the Vulnerable: A Reanalysis of Our Social Responsibilities*. Chicago: University of Chicago Press.

Green, Philip, ed. 1993. *Democracy*. Atlantic Highlands: Humanities Press.

Green, Thomas Hill. 1888. 'Liberal Legislation and Freedom of Contract', in *The Works of Thomas Hill Green*, vol. 3, ed. R. L. Nettleship. London: Longmans, Green, 370–6; 1st pub. 1880.

Greenawalt, Kent. 1988. *Religious Convictions and Political Choice*. New York: Oxford University Press.

Griffin, John Howard. 1976. *Black Like Me*. New York: New American Library; 1st pub. 1961.

Griffin, Stephen M. 1998. 'The Problem of Constitutional Change in the United States', in John Ferejohn, Jack Rakove, and Jonathan Riley, eds., 'Constitutional Culture and Democratic Rule', book manuscript, Tulane University (presented at the conference 'Constitutions and Constitutionalism', Murphy Institute, Tulane University, New Orleans, 11–12 Mar. 1995).

Grofman, Bernard, and Wittman, Donald. eds.1989. *The Federalist Papers and the New Institutionalism*. New York: Agathon Press.

Guizot, François. 1828. *Cours d'histoire moderne: Histoire générale de la civilisation en Europe, depuis la chute de l'empire romain jusqu'à la révolution française*. Paris: Pichon and Didier.

Gunther, Gerald. 1991. *Constitutional Law*. Westbury, NY: Foundation Press, 12th edn.

Habermas, Jürgen. 1984. *The Theory of Communicative Action*, i: *Reason and the Rationalization of Society*. Boston: Beacon, trans. Thomas McCarthy.

—— 1989. 'Towards a Communication-Concept of Rational Collective Will-Formation: A Thought Experiment'. *Ratio Juris* (July) 2: 144–54.

Hamilton, Alexander, Jay, John, and Madison, James. 1961. *The Federalist Papers*. New York: New American Library; 1st pub. 1787.

Hampton, Jean. 1986. *Hobbes and the Social Contract Tradition*. Cambridge: Cambridge University Press.

Hardin, Russell. 1971. 'Emigration, Occupational Mobility, and Institutionalization: The German Democratic Republic'. Cambridge, Mass.: MIT dissertation.

—— 1982. *Collective Action*. Baltimore: Johns Hopkins University Press for Resources for the Future.

—— 1982. 'Exchange Theory on Strategic Bases'. *Social Science Information*. 2: 251–72.

—— 1985. 'Sanction and Obligation'. *The Monist* 68 (July): 403–18.

—— 1987. 'Does Might Make Right?' in J. Roland Pennock and John W. Chapman, eds., *NOMOS*. 29: *Authority Revisited*. New York: New York University Press, 201–17.

—— 1988. *Morality within the Limits of Reason*. Chicago: University of Chicago Press.

—— 1988. 'Bargaining for Justice'. *Social Philosophy and Policy*. 5 (Spring): 65–74.

—— 1989. 'Why a Constitution?' in Grofman and Wittman (1989: 100–20).

—— 1989. 'Political Obligation', in Alan Hamlin and Philip Pettit, eds., *The Good Polity*. Oxford: Basil Blackwell, 103–19.

Hardin, Russell. 1990. 'Contractarianism: Wistful Thinking'. *Constitutional Political Economy.* 1: 35–52.

—— 1990. 'Public Choice vs. Democracy', in John W. Chapman, ed., *NOMOS.* 32: *Majorities and Minorities.* New York: New York University Press, 184–203.

—— 1991. 'Acting Together, Contributing Together'. *Rationality and Society.* 3 (July): 365–80.

—— 1991. 'Hobbesian Political Order'. *Political Theory.* 19 (May): 156–80.

—— 1991. 'To Rule in No Matters, To Obey in None'. Contemporary Philosophy, 13/12 (Nov.–Dec.): 6–12.

—— 1992. 'Efficiency vs. Equality and the Demise of Socialism'. *Canadian Journal of Philosophy.* 22: 149–61.

—— 1992. 'The Morality of Law and Economics'. *Law and Philosophy.* 11 (Nov.): 331–84.

—— 1993. 'Altruism and Mutual Advantage'. *Social Service Review.* 67: 358–73.

—— 1993. 'Efficiency', in Robert E. Goodin and Philip Pettit, eds., *Companion to Contemporary Political Philosophy.* Oxford: Basil Blackwell, 462–70.

—— 1993. 'Liberalism: Political and Economic'. *Social Philosophy and Policy.* 10 (June): 121–44.

—— 1995. 'Contested Community'. *Society.* 32 (July/Aug.): 23–9.

—— 1995. *One for All: The Logic of Group Conflict.* Princeton: Princeton University Press.

—— 1995. 'Institutional Morality', in Geoffrey Brennan and Robert E. Goodin, eds., *The Theory of Institutional Design.* Cambridge: Cambridge University Press, 126–53.

—— 1995. 'International Deontology'. *Ethics and International Affairs.* 9: 133–45.

—— 1996. 'Magic on the Frontier: The Norm of Efficiency'. *University of Pennsylvania Law Review.* 144 (May): 1987–2020.

—— 1998. 'Institutional Commitment: Values or Incentives?' in Avner Ben Ner and Louis Putterman, eds., *Economics, Values, and Organization.* Cambridge: Cambridge University Press, 419–33.

—— 1998. 'Trust in Government', in Valerie Braithwaite and Margaret Levi, eds., *Trust and Governance.* New York: Russell Sage Foundation, 9–27.

—— 1998. 'Reasonable Agreement: Political Not Normative', 137–53 in Paul J. Kelly, ed., *Impartiality, Neutrality and Justice: Re-reading Brian Barry's Justice as Impartiality.* Edinburgh: Edinburgh University Press.

—— Forthcoming. 'Democratic Epistemology and Accountability', *Social Policy and Philosophy.* 17.

Harrington, James. 1924. *The Commonwealth of Oceana*, ed. S. B. Liljegren. Heidelberg; 1st pub. 1656.

Hart, H. L. A. 1961. *The Concept of Law*. Oxford: Oxford University Press.

—— 1983. 'Between Utility and Rights', in Hart, *Essays in Jurisprudence and Philosophy*. Oxford: Oxford University Press, 198–222; 1st pub. 1979.

Hayek, Friedrich A. 1948. *Individualism and Economic Order*. Chicago: University of Chicago Press; reprinted by Gateway, n.d.

—— 1967. 'The Principles of a Liberal Social Order', in Hayek. *Studies in Philosophy, Politics and Economics*. Chicago: University of Chicago Press, 160–77.

—— 1978. 'Liberalism', in Hayek. *New Studies in Philosophy, Politics, Economics, and the History of Ideas*. Chicago: University of Chicago Press, 119–51.

—— 1989. *The Fatal Conceit: The Errors of Socialism*. Chicago: University of Chicago Press; 1st pub. 1988.

Heller, Hermann. 1933. 'Power, Political', in Edwin R. A. Seligman and Alvin Johnson, eds., *Encyclopaedia of the Social Sciences*, xii 300–5. New York: Macmillan.

Higgs, Robert. 1992. 'Wartime Prosperity? A Reassessment of the U. S. Economy in the 1940s'. *Journal of Economic History*. 52 (Mar.): 41–60.

Hill, Christopher. 1975. *The World Turned Upside Down: Radical Ideas during the English Revolution*. Harmondsworth, Middlesex: Penguin.

Hirschman, Albert O. 1982. *Shifting Involvements: Private Interest and Public Action*. Princeton: Princeton University Press.

—— 1990. 'Good News Is Not Bad News'. *New York Review of Books* (11 Oct.): 20–2.

Hobbes, Thomas. [1651] 1968. *Leviathan*. London: Penguin, ed. C. B. Macpherson. Originally published, London: Andrew Cooke, 1651.

—— 1983. *De Cive*, ed. Howard Warrender. Oxford: Oxford University Press; 1st pub. in Latin 1642; in English 1651.

Hobhouse, L. T. 1948. *Liberalism*. Oxford: Oxford University Press; 1st pub. 1911.

—— 1994. 'Government by the People', in Hobhouse, *Liberalism and Other Writings*, ed. James Meadowcroft. Cambridge: Cambridge University Press, 123–35; essay 1st pub. 1910.

Hume, David. 1742. 'Of The Rise and Progress of the Arts and Sciences', in Hume, *Essays Moral Political and Literary*, ed. Eugene Miller. Indianapolis: Liberty Press, 111–37.

—— 1975. *An Enquiry Concerning the Principles of Morals*, in Hume, *Enquiries concerning Human Understanding and concerning the Principles of Morals*. ed. L. A. Selby-Bigge and P. H. Nidditch. Oxford: Oxford University Press; 1st pub. 1751.

—— 1978. *A Treatise of Human Nature*, ed. L. A. Selby-Bigge and P. H. Nidditch. Oxford: Oxford University Press, 2nd edn.; 1st pub. 1739–40.

Hume, David. 1985. *Essays Moral, Political, and Literary*, ed. Eugene F. Miller. Indianapolis: Liberty Press.

—— 1985. 'Idea of a Perfect Commonwealth' in Hume, *Essays Moral, Political, and Literary*, ed. Eugene F. Miller. Indianapolis: Liberty Press, 512–29; 1st pub. 1752.

—— 1985. 'Of the Original Contract', in Hume, *Essays Moral, Political, and Literary*, ed. Eugene Miller. Indianapolis: Liberty Press, 465–87; 1st pub. 1748.

Hunter, Brian, ed. 1991. *The Statesman's Year-Book 1991–92*. New York: St Martin's.

Inouye, Kyoko. 1991. *MacArthur's Japanese Constitution*. Chicago: University of Chicago Press.

Ishiguro, Kazuo. 1990. *The Remains of the Day*. New York: Vintage; 1st pub. 1989.

Jefferson, Thomas. 1984. Letter to John Holmes of 22 April 1820, in Jefferson, *Writings*. New York: Library of America, 1433–5.

—— 1987. Letter to James Madison of 6 September 1789, in Philip Kurland and Ralph Lerner, *The Founders' Constitution*. Chicago: University of Chicago Press, i. 68–70.

Jouvenel, Bertrand de. 1952. *The Ethics of Redistribution*. Cambridge: Cambridge University Press; reprinted by Liberty Press, 1990.

—— 1957. *Sovereignty: An Inquiry into the Political Good*. Chicago: University of Chicago Press, trans. J. F. Huntington.

Kammen, Michael. 1986. *The Origins of the American Constitution: A Documentary History*. New York: Penguin.

Kandell, Jonathan. 1991. 'Prosperity Born of Pain'. *New York Times Magazine* (7 July): 14 ff.

Kant, Immanuel. 1983. 'An Answer to the Question: What Is Enlightenment?' in Kant, *Perpetual Peace and Other Essays on Politics, History, and Morals*, trans. Ted Humphrey. Indianapolis: Hackett; 1st pub. 1784.

—— 1983. 'On the Proverb: That May Be True in Theory, but Is of No Practical Use', in Kant, *Perpetual Peace and Other Essays*, 77, trans. Ted Humphrey. Indianapolis: Hackett (viii. 297 in the Prussian Academy of Sciences edn. of Kant's works); 1st pub. 1793.

Karl, Terry Lynn. 1995. 'The Hybrid Regimes of Central America'. *Journal of Democracy* (July) 6: 72–86.

Kateb, George. 1969. 'The Majority Principle: Calhoun and His Antecedents'. *Political Science Quarterly*. 84 Dec.: 595–617.

Kavka, Gregory S. 1986. *Hobbesian Moral and Political Theory*. Princeton: Princeton University Press.

Komarek, Valtr. 1992. 'Shock Therapy and Its Victims'. *New York Times* (5 Jan.): 4, OpEd.

Krueger, Anne. 1993. *Political Economy of Reform in Developing Countries*. Cambridge, Mass.: MIT Press.

Kurland, Philip, and Lerner, Ralph.eds. 1987. *The Founders' Constitution*, 5 vols. Chicago: University of Chicago Press.

Lange, Oskar. 1938. *On the Economic Theory of Socialism*. Minneapolis: University of Minnesota Press.

Lefort, Claude. 1988. 'From Equality to Freedom: Fragments of an Interpretation of Democracy in America', in Lefort, *Democracy and Political Theory*, 183–209. Minneapolis: University of Minnesota Press; trans. David Macey.

Leichter, Howard M. 1991. *Free to Be Foolish: Politics and Health Promotion in the United States and Great Britain*. Princeton: Princeton University Press.

Levi, Margaret. 1988. *Of Rule and Revenue*. Berkeley: University of California Press.

Levy, Santiago, and van Wijnbergen, Sweder. 1995. 'Transition Problems in Economic Reform: Agriculture in the North American Free Trade Agreement'. *American Economic Review*. 85 (Sept.): 738–54.

Lian, Peng, and Wei, Shang-Jin. 1998. 'To Shock or Not to Shock? Economics and Political Economy of Large-Scale Reforms'. *Economics and Politics* 10 (July): 161–83.

Lindblom, C. E. 1977. *Politics and Markets: The World's Political-Economic Systems*. New York: Basic Books.

Lipset, Seymour Martin. 1995. 'Malaise and Resiliency in America'. *Journal of Democracy* (July) 6: 4–18.

Litwack, John M. 1991. 'Legality and Market Reform in Soviet-Type Economies'. *Journal of Economic Perspectives*. 5: 77–89.

Lochner v. New York, 198 US (Oct. term, 1904): 45.

Locke, John. 1950. *A Letter Concerning Toleration*. Indianapolis: Bobbs-Merrill; 1st pub. 1689.

—— 1988. *Two Treatises of Government*. Cambridge: Cambridge University Press; 1st pub. 1690.

McConnell, Grant. 1966. *Private Power and American Democracy*. New York: Knopf.

McDonald, Forrest. 1958. *We the People: The Economic Origins of the Constitution*. Chicago: University of Chicago Press.

McGuire, Robert A., and Ohsfeldt, Robert L. 1989. 'Public Choice Analysis and the Ratification of the Constitution', in Bernard Grofman and Donald Wittman, eds., *The Federalist Papers and the New Institutionalism*. New York: Agathon, 175–204.

Mackie, Gerald. 1966. 'Ending Footbinding and Infibulation: A Convention Account'. *American Sociological Review*. 61 (Dec.): 999–1017.

MacNeil, Ian. 1980. *The New Social Contract*. New Haven: Yale University Press.

Main, Jackson Turner. 1974. *The Antifederalists: Critics of the Constitution, 1781–1788*. New York: Norton; 1st pub. 1961.

Maine, Henry Sumner. 1906. *Ancient Law: Its Connection with the Early History of Society and its Relation to Modern Ideas*. London: John Morrow, 10th edn.

Mandeville, Bernard. 1924. *The Fable of the Bees: Private Vices, Publick Benefits*, ed. F. B. Kaye. Oxford: Oxford University Press; 1st pub. 1714; reprinted by Liberty Press, 1988.

Manin, Bernard. 1995. *Principes du gouvernement représentatif*. Paris: Calmann-Lévy.

Maravall, José María. 1994. 'The Myth of the Authoritarian Advantage'. *Journal of Democracy*. 5 (Oct.): 17–31.

Marshall, Geoffrey. 1984. *Constitutional Conventions: The Rules and Forms of Political Accountability*. Oxford: Oxford University Press.

Marshall, T. H. 1950. *Citizenship and Social Class*. Cambridge: Cambridge University Press.

Marx, Karl. 1963. *The Eighteenth Brumaire of Louis Bonaparte*. New York: International Publishers; 1st pub. 1852.

—— 1977. 'On the Jewish Question', Part I, in David McLellan, ed., *Karl Marx: Selected Writings*. Oxford: Oxford University Press.

Meyers, Marvin. 1981. *The Mind of the Founder: Sources of the Political Thought of James Madison*. Hanover, NH: University Press of New England, rev. edn.

Michels, Robert. 1966. *Political Parties: A Sociological Study of the Oligarchical Tendencies of Modern Democracy*, ed. S. M. Lipset. New York: Free Press; 1st pub. 1911.

Michnik, Adam. 1990. 'The Two Faces of Europe'. *New York Review of Books* (19 July): 7.

Mill, John Stuart. 1965. *Principles of Political Economy*, ed. John M. Robson. Toronto: University of Toronto Press; 1st pub. 1848.

—— 1977. 'De Tocqueville on Democracy in America, II', in Mill, *Essays on Politics and Society*, ed. J. M. Robson, *Collected Works of John Stuart Mill*, xviii. 153–204. Toronto: University of Toronto Press.

—— 1977. 'Civilization', in Mill, *Essays on Politics and Society*, ed. J. M. Robson, *Collected Works of John Stuart Mill*, xviii. 117–47. Toronto: University of Toronto Press.

—— 1977. *On Liberty*, in Mill, *Essays on Politics and Society*, ed. J. M. Robson, *Collected Works of John Stuart Mill*, xviii. 209–310. Toronto: University of Toronto Press.

—— 1977. *Considerations on Representative Government*, in Mill, *Essays on Politics and Society*, ed. J. M. Robson, *Collected Works*, xix. 371–577. Toronto: University of Toronto Press; 1st pub. 1861.

—— 1984. 'Statement on Marriage', in John M. Robson, ed., *Essays on Equality, Law, and Education*, xxi. 99 of *Collected Works of John Stuart Mill*. Toronto: University of Toronto Press.

Montesquieu, Charles le Secondat, baron de. 1989. *The Spirit of the Laws*. Cambridge: Cambridge University Press; 1st pub. 1748.

Morgan, Edmund S. 1988. *Inventing the People: The Rise of Popular Sovereignty in England and America*. New York: Norton.

—— 1994. 'Pioneers of Paranoia'. *New York Review of Books* (6 Oct.): 11–13.

Mueller, John. Forthcoming. *Democracy, Capitalism, and Ralph's Pretty Good Grocery*. Princeton: Princeton University Press.

Musil, Robert. 1988. *Der Mann ohne Eigenschafren* (The Man Without Qualities). Reinbek bei Hamburg: Rowohlt; 1st pub. 1930, 1932, 1936.

Nagel, Jack. 1995. 'New Zealand's Novel Solution to the Problem of Minority Representation'. *The Good Society*. 5 (Spring): 25–7.

Nedelsky, Jennifer. 1990. *Private Property and the Limits of American Constitutionalism: The Madisonian Framework and Its Legacy*. Chicago: University of Chicago Press.

Norton, Anne. 1986. *Alternative Americas: A Reading of Antebellum Political Culture*. Chicago: University of Chicago Press.

Nozick, Robert. 1974. *Anarchy, State, and Utopia*. New York: Basic Books.

Okun, Arthur M. 1975. *Equality and Efficiency: The Big Tradeoff*. Washington: Brookings.

Olson, Mancur, Jr. 1982. *The Rise and Decline of Nations*. New Haven: Yale University Press.

O'Neill, William L. 1993. *A Democracy at War: America's Fight at Home and Abroad in World War II*. New York: Free Press.

Pareto, Vilfredo. 1971. *Manual of Political Economy*, trans. Ann S. Schwier. New York: Augustus M. Kelley; 1st pub. 1927.

Parsons, Talcott. 1968. *The Structure of Social Action*. New York: Free Press; 1st pub. 1937.

Pateman, Carole. 1970. *Participation and Democratic Theory*. Cambridge: Cambridge University Press.

Peattie, Lisa. 1969. 'Cuban Notes'. *Massachusetts Review*. (Autumn): 673–74.

Perlez, Jane. 1995. 'The Fist in the Velvet Glove'. *New York Times Magazine* (16 July): 17–19.

Pharr, Susan J., and Putnam, Robert D. eds. 1998. 'What's Troubling the Trilateral Democracies'. Book manuscript, Harvard University.

Polanyi, Michael. 1980. *The Logic of Liberty: Reflections and Rejoinders*. Chicago: University of Chicago Press; 1st pub. 1951.

Polinsky, A. Mitchell. 1989. *An Introduction to Law and Economics*. Boston: Little, Brown, 2nd edn.

Popkin, Samuel L. 1979. *The Rational Peasant: The Political Economy of Rural Society in Vietnam*. Berkeley: University of California Press.

Przeworski, Adam. 1980. 'Material Interests, Class Compromise, and the Transition to Socialism'. *Politics and Society*. 10: 125–53.

Przeworski, Adam. 1991. *Democracy and the Market: Political and Economic Reforms in Eastern Europe and Latin America.* Cambridge: Cambridge University Press.

—— and Limongi, Fernando. 1993. 'Political Regimes and Economic Growth'. *Journal of Economic Perspectives* (Summer) 7: 51–69.

Putnam, Robert D. 1995. 'Bowling Alone: America's Declining Social Capital'. *Journal of Democracy* (Jan.) 6: 65–78.

Rakove, Jack N. 1987. 'The Structure of Politics at the Accession of George Washington', in Richard Beeman, Stephen Betein, and Edward C. Carter, II, eds., *Beyond Confederation: Origins of the Constitution and American National Identity.* Chapel Hill, NC: University of North Carolina Press, 261–94.

—— 1991. 'Parchment Barriers and the Politics of Rights', in Michael J. Lacey and Knud Haakonssen, eds., *A Culture of Rights: The Bill of Rights in Philosophy, Politics, and Law, 1791 and 1991.* Cambridge: Cambridge University Press, 98–143.

—— Forthcoming. 'The Madisonian Solution'. Manuscript presented at the conference 'Constitutions and Constitutionalism', Murphy Institute, Tulane University, New Orleans, 11–12 Mar. 1995.

Rawls, John. 1971. *A Theory of Justice.* Cambridge, Mass.: Harvard University Press.

—— 1985. 'Justice As Fairness: Political not Metaphysical'. *Philosophy and Public Affairs* (Summer) 14: 223–51.

Reid, John Phillip. 1989. *The Concept of Representation in the Age of the American Revolution.* Chicago: University of Chicago Press.

Riker, William H. 1988. *Liberalism against Populism: A Confrontation between the Theory of Democracy and the Theory of Public Choice.* Prospect Heights, Ill.: Waveland Press; 1st pub. 1982.

Robert, Henry M. 1951. *Robert's Rules of Order Revised.* Chicago: Scott, Foresman.

Roemer, John E. 1993. 'The Possibility of Market Socialism' in David Copp, Jean Hampton, and John E. Roemer, eds., *The Idea of Democracy.* Cambridge: Cambridge University Press, 347–67.

Rosenfeld, Michel. ed. 1994. *Constitutionalism, Identity, Difference, and Legitimacy: Theoretical Perspectives.* Durham, NC: Duke University Press.

Rossiter, Clinton. 1966. *1787: The Grand Convention.* New York: Macmillan.

Rousseau, Jean-Jacques. 1983. *On the Social Contract*, trans. Donald A. Cress. Indianapolis: Hackett; 1st pub. 1762.

Sachs, Jeffrey. 1993. *Poland's Jump to the Market.* Cambridge, Mass.: MIT Press.

Saguir, Julio. 1991. 'In Search of Institutional Design: A Comparison between the Constitutional Processes of Argentina and the United States'. Ph.D. thesis, University of Chicago.

Scanlon, Thomas M. 1982. 'Contractualism and Utilitarianism', in Amartya Sen and Bernard Williams, eds., *Utilitarianism and Beyond*. Cambridge: Cambridge University Press, 103–28.

Schaffer, Frederic C. 1998. *Democracy in Transition: Understanding Politics in an Unfamiliar Culture*. Ithaca, NY: Cornell University Press.

Schelling, Thomas C. 1960. *The Strategy of Conflict*. Cambridge, Mass.: Harvard University Press.

Schine, Cathleen. 1993. *Rameau's Niece*. New York: Penguin.

Schmemann, Serge. 1998. 'How Do You Succeed in a Cashless Society'. *New York Times Magazine* (27 Dec.): 36–9.

Schneewind, J. B. 1990. 'The Misfortunes of Virtue'. *Ethics*. 101: 42–63.

Schumpeter, Joseph A. 1950. *Capitalism, Socialism and Democracy*. New York: Harper, 3rd edn; 1st pub. 1942.

Schusterman, Richard. 1994. 'Pragmatism and Liberalism between Dewey and Rorty'. *Political Theory*. (Aug.): 391–413.

Scott, James C. 1976. *The Moral Economy of the Peasant: Rebellion and Subsistence in Southeast Asia*. New Haven: Yale University Press.

Sen, Amartya. 1970. 'The Impossibility of a Paretian Liberal'. *Journal of Political Economy*. 78: 152–7.

—— 1982. 'Liberty as Control: An Appraisal', in *Social and Political Philosophy*, vol. vii of *Midwest Studies in Philosophy*, eds. Peter A. French, Theodore E. Uehling, Jr., and Howard K. Wettstein. Minneapolis: University of Minnesota Press.

Sidgwick, Henry. 1907. *The Methods of Ethics*. London: Macmillan, 7th edn.

Skinner, Quentin. 1978. *The Foundations of Modern Political Thought*, 2 vols. Cambridge: Cambridge University Press.

Smith, Adam. 1976. *An Inquiry into the Nature and Causes of the Wealth of Nations*, ed. R. H. Campbell, A. S. Skinner, and W. B. Todd. Oxford: Oxford University Press; reprinted by Liberty Press, 1979; 1st pub. 1776.

Smith, Albert Henry. ed. 1907. *The Writings of Benjamin Franklin*. New York: Macmillan.

Spencer, Herbert. 1884. *The Principles of Sociology*. New York: Appleton, 2 vols.

Stein, Herbert. 1989. 'The Triumph of the Adaptive Society'. Frank E. Seidman Lecture in Political Economy (Memphis: Rhodes College, 14 Sept.).

Stinchcombe, Arthur L. 1980. 'Is the Prisoner's Dilemma All of Sociology?' *Inquiry*. 23: 187–92

Stone, Geoffrey. 1991. *Constitutional Law*. Boston: Little, Brown, 2nd edn.

Storing, Herbert J. ed. 1981. *The Complete Anti-Federalist*, 7 vols. Chicago: University of Chicago Press.

Sunstein, Cass R. 1993. *The Partial Constitution*. Cambridge, Mass.: Harvard University Press.

Swift, Elaine K. 1993. 'The Making of an American House of Lords: The U. S. Senate in the Constitutional Convention of 1787'. *Studies in American Political Development*. 7: 177–224.

—— 1996. *The Making of an American Senate: Reconstitutive Change in Congress 1787–1841*. Ann Arbor: University of Michigan Press.

Taylor, A. J. P. 1965. *English History 1914–1945*. Oxford: Oxford University Press.

Tocqueville, Alexis de. 1945. *Democracy in America*, 2 vols. New York: Knopf; trans. Henry Reeve and rev. by Francis Bowen; reprinted Vintage, 1990; 1st pub. 1835 and 1840.

—— 1966. *Democracy in America*. New York: Harper and Row; trans. George Lawrence; 1st pub. 1835 and 1840.

Tolstoy, Leo. 1939. *Anna Karenina*, 2 vols. London: Oxford University Press, trans. Louise and Aylmer Maude; 1st pub. 1875–7.

Tyler, Tom R. 1990. *Why People Obey the Law*. New Haven: Yale University Press.

Ullmann-Margalit, Edna. 1977. *The Emergence of Norms*. Oxford: Oxford University Press.

von Humboldt, Wilhelm. 1969. *The Limits of State Action*. Cambridge: Cambridge University Press (written 1791–2); 1st pub. 1854.

von Mises, Ludwig. 1981. *Socialism: An Economic and Sociological Analysis*. Indianapolis: Liberty Press; 1st pub. 1922.

Vorhies F., and Glahe, F. 1988. 'Political Liberty and Social Development: An Empirical Investigation'. *Public Choice*. 58: 45–71.

Walzer, Michael. 'Editor's Page.' 1990. *Dissent* (Spring).

White, Leslie A. 1959. *The Evolution of Culture: The Development of Civilisation to the Fall of Rome*. New York: McGraw-Hill.

Will, George F. 1983. *Statecraft as Soulcraft*. New York: Simon and Schuster.

Wilson, James. 1987. 'Lectures on Law', in Robert Green McCloskey, ed,. *The Works of James Wilson*, 2 vols. Cambridge, Mass.: Harvard University Press, 1967; essay 1st pub. 1791; excerpted in Philip B. Kurland and Ralph Lerner, eds., *The Founders' Constitution*. Chicago: University of Chicago Press, 1987. i. 73.

Winstanley, Gerarrd. 1941. *The Law of Freedom in a Platform or, True Magistracy Restored*, ed. Robert W. Kenny. New York: Shocken; 1st pub. 1652.

Wisconsin v. Yoder, et al., 406 U.S., 205–49.

Wood, Gordon S. 1969. *The Creation of the American Republic, 1776–1787*. Chapel Hill, NC: North Carolina University Press; reprinted Norton, 1972.

—— 1987. 'Interests and Disinteredness in the Making of the Constitution', in Richard Beeman, Stephen Botein, and Edward C. Carter II, eds.,

Beyond Confederation: Origins of the Constitution and American National Identity. Chapel Hill, NC: University of North Carolina Press, 69–109.

Wright, Benjamin F. 1958. *Consensus and Continuity, 1776–1787*. Boston: Boston University Press.

Wrong, Dennis. 1994. *The Problem of Order: What Unites and Divides Society*. New York: Free Press.

Index

Baker v. Carr 101
Balfour, Arthur 29
Baltic states 221
Bangladesh 268
Bank of the United States 297
bankruptcy 209
bargains:
  and ethnic conflict 194
  in contract, social contract 39
  in Philadelphia 87, 96–9, 119–20,
    127, 128
  in social contract 87
  in some constitutions 98
  no, over ratification 287
  over slavery 120, 287
  under a constitution 96, 139
Barry, Brian 38, 39, 145, 309
Baryshnikov, Mikhail 76
Beard, Charles:
  economic interests and the US
    Constitution 106
  on farm interests at the convention
    299
  on Hamilton 226
  on Philadelphia conventioneers 296
  on ratification vote 125
Becker, Gary 328
Beer, Samuel 246, 295
Beitz, Charles 150, 159
Belarus 294
Belgium 22, 61, 279, 284
Bell, Daniel 46
Bellow, Saul 169, 177
beneficence, in utilitarianism 19
Bentham, Jeremy 5, 62, 214
Berlin Wall, the 207, 211
Bermeo, Nancy 216, 258
Besitzstandswahrung (status preservation) 195, 202, 209, 261
bill of attainder 302
bills of attainder 158, 325
black markets 207
blacks:
  and Jim Crow 328
  and poverty in US 328
  and US democracy 290
  exclusion of, from US success 308
  male suffrage of in US 291
  mob action against 159
  see also racism; slavery; Civil

Rights Movement
Bloom, Allen 176, 177
Bonn, Moritz J. 208–9
Bosnia 22, 285
Braniff Airlines 71
Bratton, William 308
Braybrooke, David 77
Brazil 79, 131
Brennan, Geoffrey 25, 109, 111
Broom, Jacob 299
Brutus, an Anti-Federalist:
  answer to *Federalist Papers* 298
  as Robert Yates 297
  on lawyers 298
  on republicanism 100, 296
  on size of House of
    Representatives 297
  on vagueness of US Constitution,
    132–3
Bryan, William Jennings 299
Buchanan, James M. 25, 109, 111,
  138, 145, 158
Bulgaria 293
Buren, President Martin Van 120, 239
Burma, *see* Myanmar
Burr, Aaron 137, 251
Buruma, Ian 213
Burundi:
  attempt at democracy in 37, 84,
    166, 277, 278, 286
  civil war in 278, 281–2
  election of 1993 as ethnic census in
    278
  ethnic conflict in 22, 221, 320
  unequal coordination in 307
Bush, President George 157
business:
  allied with workers against farmers
    254
  and Commerce Clause 254–5
  and mercantilism 238
  as serving interests of government
    264, 270
  freedom from politics of 241
  power of 162
  rise of 254

Caesar, a Federalist:
  on acquiescence 35, 82, 114, 141,
    144, 171, 309

prisoner's dilemma (*cont.*):
  and contract vision 97, 140
  as exchange 86–8, 91
  as not the constitutional problem
    93–4, 96, 113
  coordination element of 92
  game matrix of 91
  in state of nature 146
  iterated 117, 146
property and exchange 56
property, private 70, 210
Przeworski, Adam 185, 238
publicity, principle of 164
Publius (Hamilton, Jay, and Madison)
  86, 89, 127, 133–4
Puritans 4, 37

Quebec 122

racism:
  and coordination 15, 328–9
  coordination against 329
  Griffin on 328
  norm of 15, 23, 28, 192, 328
Radical utilitarians 214
Rakove, Jack 295
Randolph, Edmund 103, 111
Rankin, Jeanette 291
ratification 125
  and Anti-Federalists 17, 127
  and Caesar on popular acquies-
    cence 35
  and farmers 300
  and *Federalist Papers* 4
  by Connecticut 125
  by Delaware 108
  by Georgia 108
  by New Hampshire 111, 125
  by New Jersey 108
  by New York 108, 125
  by North Carolina 103, 108, 125,
    252
  by Pennsylvania 108, 125
  by Rhode Island 103, 108, 111,
    125, 252
  by special convention or referen-
    dum 287
  by Virginia 111
  debates on 101; and large vs. small
    states 247; Anti-Federalist com-

    munitarianism in 125, 236;
    Federalist vs. Anti-Federalist
    conflict in 251; Madison on
    Anti-Federalist position in 127;
    Montesquieu's views in 61; size
    of House of Representatives in,
    100; theory in, 296
  farmer votes on 126
  Federalists' strategy on 106
  of US Constitution 94, 108–9,
    120–1, 125, 135, 252
  political contrivance in 103
  rural vs. urban votes on 29
Rawls, John:
  contractarianism of 39, 145, 150
  fairness theory of 33
  on inequality 204
  on obligation 19
  theory of justice of 33–4, 313
  two-stage theory of 159
reasonable agreement:
  and claim of universal appeal 38
  and social contract 10
  as consent 149
  as not rationalist 150–1
  as variant of contractarianism 39,
    143
  implausibility of 152, 309
  in Barry 309
  in Beitz 150, 159
  in Scanlon 10, 150
recessions 262
recoordination as obstacle to change
  16, 90
redistribution 8, 323
Reid, John Phillip 179–80
religion:
  and political liberalism 1, 41–2, 63
  and scepticism 48
  and social division 42, 280, 305,
    321
  and social liberalism 323
  freedom of 74–5
  Hobbes on 4
  in Geneva 149
  in US Constitution 74, 323
  Locke on 28, 44, 48, 58, 64, 187,
    188
representation:
  and ethnic census 278, 284